TWENTY
K.R. NARAYANAN
ORATIONS

ESSAYS BY EMINENT PERSONS
ON THE RAPIDLY TRANSFORMING
INDIAN ECONOMY

TWENTY
K.R. NARAYANAN
ORATIONS

ESSAYS BY EMINENT PERSONS
ON THE RAPIDLY TRANSFORMING
INDIAN ECONOMY

EDITED BY
RAGHBENDRA JHA

Australian
National
University

PRESS

To the memory of Dr K.R. Narayanan

ANU PRESS

Published by ANU Press
The Australian National University
Acton ACT 2601, Australia
Email: anupress@anu.edu.au

Available to download for free at press.anu.edu.au

ISBN (print): 9781760464349
ISBN (online): 9781760464356

WorldCat (print): 1247155802
WorldCat (online): 1248765159

DOI: 10.22459/TKRNO.2021

Cover design and layout by ANU Press

Contents

An Introduction to the Volume

Raghbendra Jha

The Australia South Asia Research Centre (ASARC) was established in 1994 in one of the premier universities of the world — The Australian National University (ANU). ASARC was inaugurated in April 1994 by Professor R.D. Terrell, AO, Vice-Chancellor of ANU; Professor Gareth Evans, AC, QC, Minister for Foreign Affairs and Trade, Australian Government; and His Excellency Dr K.R. Narayanan, Vice-President (later president) of India. ASARC was given the broad mandate of pursuing research into the economics and politics of the South Asia region, taking into account Australia's national interests and the dynamics of economic cooperation and interaction in the Asia-Pacific and Indian Ocean regions.

Whereas such research would be pursued by the centre's faculty and graduate students, ASARC also needed a public forum with a global reach to involve the best minds working on economic development in India as well as to honour its founder, Dr K.R. Narayanan. The K.R. Narayanan Oration series was conceived in response to these twin needs.

The first oration was held in 1994 and the 20th in 2018. After the 10th oration (in 2006), ASARC collected the texts of these 10 lectures into a commemorative volume — *The First Ten K.R. Narayanan Orations: Essays by Eminent Persons on the Rapidly Transforming Indian Economy* — as a mark of its contribution to debate on the nascent process of economic reform in India. This volume was published by ANU E Press in 2006 and was launched by His Excellency Major General Michael Jeffery, Governor-General of the Commonwealth of Australia, at ANU. A copy was also presented to His Excellency (late) Dr A.P.J. Abdul Kalam, President of India.

In the 15 years since the first edition was published, the Indian economy has gone through several and substantial changes. For instance, data from the World Development Indicators of the World Bank show that gross national income purchasing power parity (PPP) in 2011 prices more than doubled from $3.94*10^{12}$ in 2006 to $7.96*10^{12}$ in 2016.[1] Several years ago, India attained the milestone of becoming the third-largest economy in the world in PPP terms behind China and the US. In 2019–20, real GDP growth was 4.2 per cent per annum and population growth was at 1 per cent per annum, giving per capita GDP growth of 3.2 per cent. Real GDP growth was expected to strengthen, but the ongoing COVID-19 pandemic reduced India's growth quite sharply in the fiscal year 2020–21. The International Monetary Fund (IMF) and the Reserve Bank of India have estimated that Indian real GDP growth will be negative during the fiscal year 2020–21. However, good performance in the agricultural sector and a good rebound in industrial growth during the second quarter have led some commentators to believe that growth may yet be positive during 2020–21, but barely so. Most commentators expect a sharp rebound in the range of 8 per cent economic growth by 2022–23.

Currently, India is going through an unprecedented demographic transition with the median age at 27 years in 2018.[2] This means that more than half a billion people are below the age of 27 in India. Given rapidly improving health indicators, these young workers can look forward to having long life spans of work and saving. The burden of supporting the very young and the old will commensurately diminish over time. This unprecedented expansion of GDP and the proportion of the young has coincided with a substantial opening up of the Indian economy in the areas of international trade and investment as well as increasing opportunities for the large Indian diaspora living outside the county.

At the same time, many challenges have confronted India during this period. The most immediate challenges are the ongoing health and economic crises thrown up by the COVID-19 pandemic. Addressing these challenges will involve sustained effort over a long period of time. Robust policy measures will be needed involving inter alia repairing damaged supply chains, ensuring high rates of expansion in the manufacturing

---

1   This data is drawn from 'India', The World Bank, accessed 15 May 2018, data.worldbank.org/country/india?view=chart.

2   See 'India Population', Worldometer, accessed 15 May 2018, www.worldometers.info/world-population/india-population/.

sector to ensure job opportunities for India's large and rapidly growing labour force, sustaining short-term demand expansion, augmenting the country's public health capacity, and ensuring that India's public debt remains sustainable and the banking system remains strong. Because the last Narayanan Oration was held two years before the pandemic struck, this volume does not deal with these challenges. However, it does deal with other key ongoing challenges, particularly environmental degradation including carbon and other greenhouse gas emissions, sharp hikes in food and commodity prices and the global financial crisis (GFC). There is the additional issue of continuing with economic reforms in a democratic and very diverse country. It can well be argued that the financial sector reforms initiated when P.V. Narasimha Rao was prime minister need to be followed through with many structural and governance reforms before India can safely be considered ready for a long period of high GDP growth. Such GDP growth is needed to remove, once and for all, the mass poverty that has prevailed in the country for decades and rapidly improve living standards. The present volume can also be seen as an account of how India has been dealing with these challenges.

The present volume builds on the previous one and collects all 20 orations along with this new introduction. The topics covered in the orations include broad perspectives on tax reforms; India's space program and its role in economic development; prospects for the Indian economy; democratisation of India's reforms; the transformation of India's monetary policy regime from one of excessive controls to one guided by market principles; food security and India's agricultural future; India's blue economy; financial inclusion; political economy issues, including meeting the challenges to the economy in the aftermath of the GFC; the acceleration in India's growth rate in the 21st century; and the role of science, technology and innovation in shaping India's future. As mentioned, the list of topics covered by this volume does not include the ongoing COVID-19 pandemic because the last oration in the series was held in 2018.

These topics cover a very wide canvas and the orators themselves are not just leading experts in their respective fields, but have contributed significantly to policymaking in India in general and the reforms in particular. They are also household names in India. This has led to widespread recognition of the Narayanan Oration series as one of the very best India oration series anywhere in the world. I now briefly summarise the contents of the orations.

Although the current phase of India's economic reforms program began in earnest in 1991 with Dr Manmohan Singh as finance minister strongly supported by Prime Minister (late) P.V. Narasimha Rao, background work for the reforms program had begun earlier, in particular during the period when (late) Rajiv Gandhi was India's prime minister. During that period, a significant amount of preparatory work for the reforms program was done. Four of the most significant contributors to this work, as well as outstanding articulators of the reforms program, have since delivered the Narayanan Oration. Thus Dr Raja Chelliah (deceased), one of the leading experts on public finance and chair of an important government committee constituted by Gandhi to institute tax reforms in India, delivered the first oration in 1994. Chelliah gave a lucid account of the tax reforms that had taken place in India and laid down a roadmap for subsequent reform. Various governments since then have broadly followed the Chelliah Committee's recommendations in respect of tax reforms. This has not only led to a degree of fiscal consolidation, but also a more harmonised tax structure and an improved revenue performance, among several other benefits.

In the 1995 oration, Professor U.R. Rao (deceased), one of India's foremost space scientists who was then a member of the Space Commission of India, gave an account of the role that space research had already played in India's economic development. Applications of space research had revolutionised many critical areas of infrastructure such as weather forecasting, satellite communication and imaging, food security, distance education and the like. Solutions to the ever growing and changing problems faced by Indians, indeed the entire humankind, could not be sought in resources available on Earth alone. In fact, it was more economical and efficient to address many of these problems by harnessing space research.

Professor Jagdish Bhagwati (Columbia University, US) had been a staunch advocate of pro-market reforms even in the 1960s when most economists in India were inclined to favour central planning. When Manmohan Singh's reforms were initiated in 1991, Bhagwati (along with T.N. Srinivasan) provided a robust intellectual backdrop and a roadmap for these reforms. In the 1996 oration, Bhagwati gave a succinct account of the reforms program India had embarked upon and the tasks that lay ahead. Although the reforms program had yielded some dividends, he argued that much remained to be done.

The 1999 oration was delivered by P. Chidambaram who, as a minister in Rajiv Gandhi's cabinet and in several subsequent cabinets, had a ringside view and an important direct role in the reforms program. Chidambaram made important contributions to India's tariff reforms program (as minister of commerce) as well as to tax and expenditure policies (as finance minister), and to administrative reforms (as minister of personnel affairs). In his oration, Chidambaram emphasised the need for the democratisation of the Indian reforms program since, in a democratic country such as India, political support is essential for the success of any reforms program.

Another major policy initiative during Prime Minister Rajiv Gandhi's tenure was the constitution of a committee to advise on the transition to a monetary policy regime characterised by market-based instruments with the Reserve Bank of India (India's central bank) progressively becoming more independent of the Ministry of Finance. Some of the most significant steps in this direction were begun when Dr C. Rangarajan was deputy governor and then governor of the Reserve Bank of India. Among his many lasting contributions to monetary policymaking in India are the breaking of the, till then, automatic link between central government deficits and changes in the money supply; the devising of several market-based instruments; and designing an appropriate monetary policy response to the balance of payments crisis in the early 1990s. In his 2001 Narayanan Oration, Rangarajan gave a lucid account of monetary policy reforms in India and the tasks that lay ahead.

In the 2002 Narayanan Oration, Lord Meghnad Desai (from the London School of Economics, UK) gave a vivid account of the political dimensions of economic reforms in India. The pro-reform political space in India is small and political parties in opposition have sometimes taken a populist or anti-reform stance whereas the same political parties may have been pro-reform when in power. Lord Desai pointed out the significance of timing in the reforms strategy and argued that political consensus in favour of reforms needed to be consolidated swiftly to ensure that rapid growth was sustained and that the fruits of the reforms percolated to the poor. He argued that only the formation of a German-style grand coalition between the Congress and the Bharatiya Janata Party could deliver this.

In his 2003 oration, Professor Pranab Bardhan (from the University of California Berkeley, US) argued that democracy in India had empowered many marginal groups and had made them assertive partners in the decision-making process. In this transition, however, several disjunctures had appeared. In particular, the state had, at the margin, been abdicating its responsibilities in relation to the provision of many basic services like quality education. Addressing these junctures should be a matter of the highest priority for Indian policymakers because, in the absence of such efforts, it would be difficult to sustain any program of economic reforms. Such efforts were necessary to ensure sustained reductions in poverty and/or inequality in democratic India.

The 2004 Narayanan Oration was delivered by Dr Vijay Kelkar who, as a distinguished economist and policymaker, has contributed much to sustaining the economic reforms program. For instance, he chaired an influential tax reforms committee and worked as minister of state in the Ministry of Finance until 2004. Kelkar's oration sought to underscore the strengths that the Indian economy had been amassing since the reforms program began as well as the supply-side dividends that are expected to last for at least a couple of decades. He emphasised that the role of deep reforms in a number of areas — including foreign trade, taxation, financial markets and policy, investment and budgetary consolidation along with important supply-side changes such as India's demographic dividend — had placed the economy on a path of sustainable higher growth that could well accelerate in the future.

The Narayanan Oration has featured high-quality speakers in two areas intimately linked to sustaining rapid economic growth — science and food security, and space research. In the 2005 oration, the distinguished agricultural scientist Dr M.S. Swaminathan, often known as the father of India's green revolution, presented an overview of the difficulties the country had overcome on the food security front. He outlined a number of emerging challenges in regard to food security and making agricultural growth sustainable with respect to, among other factors, its impact on the environment. Swaminathan discussed the contours of an evergreen revolution policy and sketched the implications of this for the Indian Government as well as global arrangements and agreements.

In the 2006 oration, Dr K. Kasturirangan, another of India's top space scientists, traced the growth of India's space program over the past 45 years and argued that this program had distinguished itself through its focus on societal applications of advanced technology; unbroken chains of innovation in the organisation of a multidisciplinary venture of high risk nature; and accomplishments of multidimensional character engaging industry, academia and international bodies. The program had overcome a myriad of challenges emanating from difficulties in the creation of a scientific organisational culture in a bureaucratic set-up: from forging linkages between creators and users of technologies to coping with geopolitical vicissitudes of technology denials; and from sustaining confidence of multi-party democratic political systems to maintaining a conscious drive for cost efficiency, autonomy and the ethic of social responsibility. Kasturirangan also outlined a conceptual model as to how India's space achievements could be shared with neighbouring countries.

The rapid growth of India's economy and developments in the world economy have combined to produce new challenges. One of the most pressing of these challenges — climate change — was addressed by Dr R.K. Pachauri (deceased), Director-General of The Energy and Resources Institute (India) and Chairman of the Intergovernmental Panel on Climate Change, in the 2007 Narayanan Oration. Pachauri argued that, although the concept of sustainable development had been espoused by the Brundtland Commission several years earlier, the recently discovered threat of irreversible climate change had started to spur the world into action. He reviewed the potential for the mitigation of climate change and argued that Australia was in an advantageous position to take a leadership role in this region. He also argued that coordinated action by Australia and India to address climate change would be superior to the two countries acting alone.

The 2008 oration was delivered by Sunita Narain, Director of the Centre for Science and Environment (India). She argued that we are living in an age of the environment in which environmental issues are interlinked and the world is coming to the realisation that the current consumption growth model cannot be sustained. Further, she maintained that while this realisation is leading to some action, there is a major difference between the environmental approaches of the rich and the poor. Rich countries have come to this realisation after long periods of wealth accumulation and high consumption whereas less well-off countries like India have to confront this issue against the backdrop of mass poverty and substantial inequality. The poor have always tackled environmental issues in their own way and equity is a prerequisite to managing scarce resources in a sustainable manner in a country like India. In this context, leapfrogging technologies and people's widespread participation become central to the task of ameliorating environmental degradation.

A trajectory of Indian science and technology from the 20th to the 21st century was the theme of the 2009 oration by the celebrated scientist Dr Roddam Narasimha (deceased), FRS, from the Jawaharlal Nehru Centre for Advanced Scientific Research (India). He provided a succinct and insightful account of the path of development that Indian science has taken from the 20th to the 21st century. The untapped technological capacity of the nation at the time of independence was roughly equivalent to what was available in the US about 200 years ago (i.e. there was immense scope for development of India's scientific and technological capacities). Drawing on his own experience as a space scientist, Narasimha provided an account of how rocket science had developed in India from the establishment of the National Committee on Space Research in 1962 to the present time in which India was regarded as being at the forefront of space technology. He examined the impact of the 1991 economic reforms program on the development of India's prowess in science and technology. Other areas of scientific development in India discussed by the author included parallel computing and supercomputers.

Montek Singh Ahluwalia, Deputy Chairman of the Planning Commission, delivered the 2010 oration on the topic 'India's Prospects in the Post-Crisis World'. 'Crisis' here refers to the 2008 GFC. This was also the time when India's Planning Commission had started work on the country's Twelfth Five-Year Plan (2012–17). Ahluwalia believed that the Indian economy's trend growth rate was rising. Indeed, it was above 9 per cent for the four years to 2008–09. After the slowdown in India's economic growth following the GFC, he expected the growth rate to recover to 8 per cent and above relatively quickly so that India would emerge as a major economic powerhouse, second only to China in Asia. A key question concerned whether this assumption was safe or whether the economy would again lose momentum. Ahluwalia reviewed the major reasons for India's recent growth acceleration. These included factors from both the supply- and the demand-sides. He also pointed out challenges for the economic reforms program to address, such as inclusivity of economic growth, adequate provision of basic services like health, water and electricity, and addressing the emerging challenges of rapid urbanisation of the Indian population.

Dr Duvvuri Subbarao, Governor of the Reserve Bank of India, delivered the 2011 oration. He provided an account of how the Indian economy in general, and the Reserve Bank of India in particular, had addressed the many challenges thrown up by the GFC since September 2008. He argued that the GFC was a crisis of unusual proportions since it engulfed more or less the whole world. The Indian economy, too, was affected and the growth rate of output and exports started to slip. The investment and credit climate worsened considerably and the outlook for the economy gradually became bleaker. He discussed why India was caught up in the crisis and how policymakers had addressed it. Finally, he recounted some key lessons that could be learnt for better economic management of any future crises, including the realisation that i) the decoupling of economies does not work in a globalised world economy, ii) global imbalances need to be addressed at the global level, iii) global coordination is central to attaining stability, iv) price stability and macroeconomic stability do not guarantee financial stability, v) microeconomic prudential regulations need to be supplemented by macro-prudential oversight, vi) capital controls may be unavoidable in certain circumstances, vii) economic policy cannot be guided by scientific principles alone, and viii) having a sense of history is critical to addressing macroeconomic crises.

Dr Kaushik Basu, Chief Economic Adviser, Ministry of Finance, Government of India, and Professor of Economics at Cornell University, delivered the 2012 oration. This oration dealt with the emergence of India as a major economy on the global stage and the challenges and risks this entailed. Basu began with a recount of the major economic policy reforms in India as well as a summary of the performance of the economy. He then concentrated on discussing the impact of the GFC on the Indian economy and how policy had responded to these challenges, including a slowdown of output growth and investment. He demonstrated that these downturns were short-term in nature and did not reflect any long-term downward trend in India's economic growth path. Both China and India started their modern phase of development in the late 1940s. In the intervening decades, China had managed to get its economic house in order and India had managed to get its political house in order, building a robust democracy with free speech and a free press, which Basu saw as the more important achievement. He also discussed some policy reforms that could easily be undertaken and would stand India in good stead for the future.

Dr Kiran Mazumdar-Shaw, Chairperson of Biocon, India, delivered the 2015 oration. A successful innovator and businessperson in the area of biotechnology, Mazumdar-Shaw began by observing that information technology, communication technology and biotechnology are rapidly and disruptively changing the way we communicate with each other, conduct research and approach issues related to health. A key challenge, therefore, is to ensure that we have the right business and financing models for the rapid development of innovations in these sectors to facilitate the ongoing technological revolution. She discussed ongoing cooperation between Australia and India in these areas and outlined many promising opportunities for the future.

The Hon. Arun Jaitley, Minister for Finance, Corporate Affairs and Information and Broadcasting, Government of India, delivered the 2016 K.R. Narayanan Oration. He recounted the major economic reform and welfare programs initiated by the government of Prime Minister Modi, which came to power in 2014. In particular, he focused on the key area of financial inclusion. If large sections of the population were outside the formal economy, these people would participate only tangentially in formal economic activity so that benefits of government programs would not adequately trickle down to them. With this in mind, the new government in India aggressively pursued what is now recognised as the world's largest program of financial inclusion. This policy worked through the so-called 'JAM trinity'. JAM is an acronym for Jana Dhana (J), Aadhar (A) and mobile (M). Jana Dhana accounts are bank accounts opened by ordinary people (even with zero balance), and Aadhar is a unique identifying card (using biometric technology) that has been introduced for India's population. A person's Jana Dhana (or other bank) account is linked to their Aadhar card and this account can be operated through mobile phones. This policy has led to a massive expansion of bank accounts and other associated benefits such as insurance, direct benefit transfers in respect of government subsidies and other support programs. As is evidenced by further developments, the JAM program has facilitated the implementation of many new policy measures in India.

The 2017 oration was delivered by Admiral R.K. Dhowan, PVSM, AVSM, YSM, immediate past chief of the Indian Navy and current chairman of the National Maritime Foundation. He spoke of India's engagement with the oceans in general and the country's blue economy in particular. It is evident that the Indian Ocean has emerged as the world's centre of gravity in the maritime domain. India sits astride busy sea lines of communication that transit across the Indian Ocean. It has a long coastline of 7,516 km, over 1,300 islands and islets, and an exclusive economic zone of over 2 million sq. km, as well as 12 major ports and over 200 minor and intermediate ports, and 90 per cent of the country's trade by volume transits by sea. India has a vibrant shipbuilding industry, a thriving fishing industry, offshore oil and gas interests, and deep-seabed mining areas in the central Indian Ocean. Thus, India has vast maritime interests. These comprise the enablers of the so-called 'blue economy'. This economy would need to be harnessed by the efficient utilisation of marine resources without hurting the environment. In these areas, Australia and India have much in common and can partner effectively in a broad range of blue economy and maritime activities.

The 2018 Narayanan Oration was delivered by Padma Vibhushan recipient Dr R.A. Mashelkar, FRS, Chairman of the National Innovation Foundation of India. He argued that rising inequality of economic outcomes and attendant social disharmony are matters of global concern, particularly because the reduction of such inequality would take an unacceptably long amount of time. However, he claimed that it was possible to reduce inequality of access through what he called 'ASSURED' innovation. ASSURED stands for affordable (A), scalable (S), sustainable (S), user-friendly (U), rapid (R), excellent (E) and distinctive (D). Mashelkar argued that a game-changing combination of policy, technological and non-technological innovations could achieve ASSURED innovation. He illustrated these possibilities with examples of exemplary innovation in India that had changed the lives of millions in a broad range of areas including health care and communications. A concerted program of government procurement and support could help accelerate and disseminate innovation in these and other areas. Thus, ASSURED innovation could be a 'single word' indicating a national innovation strategy for any nation that wished to achieve accelerated inclusive growth. He showed how ASSURED innovation could enable corporates to shift to a new high-impact paradigm of 'doing well *by* doing good', rather than the old paradigm of 'doing well *and* doing good'.

This collection of the Narayanan Orations is thus at once both an expert account of key aspects of the economic development process in India and a peek into India's potential in the future. As such, the publication of these essays marks a watershed in the intellectual debate on India's economic reforms program and should be welcomed by all those interested in the economic development of the country.

Apart from the orators themselves, a number of individuals have contributed to the success of the Narayanan Oration series. Dr K.R. Narayanan sent messages of introduction for the 1994, 1995, 1996, 1999 and 2001 orations and remained a supporter of the oration series almost until his tragic demise in November 2005. Dr Narayanan was vice-president of India during the 1994, 1995 and 1996 orations and president during the 1999 and 2001 orations. His successor, His Excellency President Dr A.P.J Abdul Kalam, sent messages for the 2002, 2004, 2005 and 2006 orations. Her Excellency President Pratibha Patil sent messages for the 2007, 2008, 2009, 2010, 2011 and 2012 orations. Subsequently, His Excellency President Pranab Mukherjee sent messages for the 2016 and 2017 orations, and His Excellency President Ram Nath Kovind for the 2018 oration. These messages are printed along with the respective accompanying orations. ASARC is honoured to have the high office of the president of India continue to be associated with the oration.

We are much obliged to the Australia–India Council (AIC) for its consistent and unflinching financial support for this oration. In addition, several members of the AIC have participated generously and enthusiastically in the planning of the oration series.

We are also grateful to our other funding agencies over the years: the Australian Bureau of Statistics (2001); the Network Economics Consulting Group (2001–03); The Australian National University's National Institute for Asia and the Pacific (2004), National Institute of Economics and Business (2003–05), and Research School of Pacific and Asian Studies (2004 and 2006); and the Australian Centre for International Agricultural Research (2005). The 2018 oration was co-hosted by the Research School of Physics and Engineering at ANU, which provided generous financial and logistical support.

In Canberra, the office of the High Commissioner of India has been very helpful in organising the oration. The high commissioner read out Dr Narayanan's messages. Since 2002, the high commissioner has read out the messages sent by the incumbent president of India. We are grateful to their excellencies A.M. Khaleeli (1994), G.S. Parthasarathy (1995–96), Jordana Pavel (acting 1999), R.S. Rathore (2001–03), P.P. Shukla (2004–06), Deputy High Commissioner Vinod Kumar (2009), Sujatha Singh (2009–10), Biren Nanda (2011–12), Navdeep Suri (2016) and Dr A.M. Gondane (2017–18) for reading out the messages.

The first four Narayanan Orations were organised by (the now deceased) Dr Ric Shand, first executive director of ASARC, to whom we remain deeply grateful. I have organised the remaining 16 orations. Over the years, a number of professional staff members of ASARC and the Arndt-Corden Department of Economics have organised the details of the oration and helped to ensure that each oration was a success. Carolyn Sweeney managed the 1994–96 and 1999 orations, and Hilda Heidemanns, Loan Dao-Czezowski and Bonny Allen were associated with the 2001 oration. ASARC is grateful to all of them for their contributions. Stephanie Hancock worked tirelessly and efficiently in organising the minutest detail of many of the past orations. Sandra Zec and Heeok Kyung have also helped with several of the orations. Several PhD students at the Arndt-Corden Department of Economics helped out at various times. ASARC expresses its sincere gratitude to all of them.

At ANU E Press (now ANU Press), Vic Elliott and Lorena Kanellopoulos were supportive throughout and saw the first edition of this book through from conception to final product with efficiency and good humour. My thanks to them and other staff involved in the production, storage and distribution of this book. Emily Tinker has been very supportive throughout the process of production of this updated edition.

In producing this second edition, I received very helpful editorial comments from my colleague, Andrew Kennedy. I am grateful to him for these and also for his encouragement. However, all opinions expressed in this introductory essay are mine.

Canberra
March 2021

About the Australia–India Council

The Australia–India Council (AIC) was established on 21 May 1992 in response to a recommendation by the Senate Standing Committee on Foreign Affairs, Defence and Trade, following an inquiry into Australia's relations with India.

The AIC's purpose is to broaden the relationship between Australia and India by encouraging and supporting contacts and increasing levels of knowledge and understanding between the peoples and institutions of the two countries. The council initiates or supports a range of activities designed to promote a greater awareness of Australia in India and a greater awareness of India in Australia, including visits and exchanges between the two countries, development of institutional links and support of studies in each country of the other. The council offers support, in the form of funding, for projects likely to contribute to the development of the relationship, within the context of AIC objectives and guidelines.

By initiating and supporting a range of activities that have put it on the map, the council has played a recognised and respected role in promoting the relationship between Australia and India. It has informed and educated Australians about India, and it has informed persons interested in the bilateral relationship about the way it is developing. It has furthered the Australian Government's foreign policy and trade objectives and added value to Australia–India relations.

Australian Government | Australia-India Council

Oration 1:
1994 K.R. Narayanan Oration

Message from the Vice-President
of the Republic of India

I am honoured to learn that the Australia South Asia Research Centre (ASARC) of The Australian National University (ANU) has instituted a K.R. Narayanan Oration and that the inaugural Oration is being given by Dr Raja J. Chelliah, Minister of State and Fiscal Adviser, Ministry of Finance, Government of India.

I have very pleasant memory of inaugurating the Australia South Asia Research Centre (ASARC) of The Australian National University in April 1994. I believe that it was one of the significant events that took place during my official visit to Australia. That a centre for the study of the economic development of South Asia as a whole has been established at a reputed university like ANU is important in itself. South Asia is a subcontinent constituting nearly one-sixth of the world population. Endowed with rich natural and human resources it occupies a strategic position on the world map. From ancient times to our own it has been open to influences from and has influenced the rest of the world particularly Africa, West Africa, South-East Asia, East Asia and the Asia-Pacific. Today South Asia is going through a new phase of economic development and far-reaching liberalisation. It has created an objectively favourable environment for promoting regional cooperation among South Asia nations and for expanding cooperation with Australia and the wider circle of the Asia-Pacific. In this context I am happy that the Australia South Asia Research Centre has taken the initiative to hold a conference on Economic Liberalisation in South Asia. I congratulate ASARC for this very constructive initiative and wish it every success.

I am particularly glad that on this occasion Dr Raja Chelliah is delivering the K.R. Narayanan Oration on the subject of 'Reforming India's Tax Base for Economic Development'. Dr Chelliah is a distinguished friend and an eminent economist who is part of the fundamental intellectual brain-work behind India's liberalisation policy. I am sure that his oration and his participation in the conference will throw light on the new economic policy that is transforming India into a dynamic economy and an active player in the evolving Asian and the global economic system.

K.R. Narayanan
New Delhi
1994

Reforming India's Tax Base for Economic Development

Raja J. Chelliah

Introduction

I deem it a great honour and privilege to be invited to deliver the first K.R. Narayanan Oration under the auspices of the Australia South Asia Research Centre of the prestigious Australian National University. It is an honour to be invited by such a prestigious educational centre and a privilege to deliver a lecture named after a national leader of my country, Mr K.R. Narayanan, who is now the Vice-President of India. Both as an academician and as a political leader, he is held in great respect in India. I am happy that this oration has been named after him and will be delivered every year.

Great challenges are taking place in India. The wide-ranging economic reform program encompasses every major sector of the economy. One of the important sectors of reform is the tax system. Since I have been associated with the work of reforms in this area, I have chosen to speak on the subject of 'Reforming the Tax Base for Economic Development'.

Tax reform has been an integral part of the economic reforms of most countries that have undertaken structural adjustment programs. Even in the developed countries, tax reforms have been a prominent feature during the 1980s. One of the important reasons impelling governments of the developing countries embarking on economic reform programs to undertake tax reform has been the need to cut the fiscal deficit through higher growth of revenues. That is perhaps also the reason why multilateral agencies supporting structural adjustment programs have usually insisted on tax reform. But in most developing countries including India thoroughgoing tax reform was needed in order to improve the efficiency of resource allocation, to remove obstacles to the smooth flow of business activities, to minimise costs and to improve the equity of the system. Improvement in equity was needed not merely for its own sake, but also for encouraging tax compliance.

The need for reforms and the nature of reforms in other important areas such as industrial policy, the financial sector, trade policy and foreign exchange regime, as a prerequisite for improving efficiency and accelerating growth has been widely discussed and understood. The need for tax reform exactly for the same reasons has not been fully appreciated or understood by the general public and by policymakers. Even economists in general in India have only stressed the need for higher tax revenues and better enforcement to ensure vertical equity. The economic aspects of taxation were neglected in India by economists themselves, which is one of the reasons why we ended up by having a complicated and irrational tax system.

Taxation was thus an area of darkness. It was, therefore, especially difficult to make people understand the serious shortcomings of the system and the nature of the reforms needed. However, the task had to be undertaken because the tax system was one of the major contributory factors to the inefficient functioning of the economy and the distortions in resource allocation.

The Pre-Reform Structure

A brief description of the pre-reform structure of direct and indirect taxes in India may be given as a prelude to a discussion of tax reform.

Direct Taxes

Although direct taxes formed less than 3 per cent of GDP on the eve of reform (about 20 per cent of total tax revenues), they exerted a profound influence on economic decisions, the generation and availability of savings for the private sector and the pattern of investment. The impact of the direct taxes on the economy was disproportionate to their relatively small share in total tax revenues.

The system of direct taxes was unnecessarily complicated, deficient in terms of horizontal equity and destructive of incentives because of high combined marginal rates of personal income and wealth taxation as well as high rates of taxation of corporate profits. Erosion of horizontal equity arose through unjustified concessions, provision of tax shelters in the form of untaxed perquisites and weak enforcement which made it possible for a large section of the tax payable population to get away with no or little payment of tax. The top marginal rate of income tax including surcharge was 56 per cent and the top marginal rate of wealth tax was 2 per cent. Thus with a marginal rate of return of 10 per cent on wealth, the combined marginal rate of income and wealth taxes on capital income worked out to 76 per cent. As there was no automatic indexation of inflation and as the average rate of inflation was around 8 per cent during the '80s, the real rate of return after tax was negative if the nominal rate of return before tax was 10 per cent. This was so even if no wealth tax was payable.

The rate of corporate profit tax for widely held companies was 45 per cent whereas for closely held companies the rate was 50 per cent. On this there was a surcharge of 15 per cent (the rate of profits tax for foreign companies was 65 per cent). Such high rates of corporate profits tax combined with a tax on dividend as part of regular income in the hands of the shareholders led naturally to a low rate of return to equity holders, besides leaving very little in the hands of companies, which are the main engine of industrial growth, for investment.

Such high rates could continue only because of large-scale evasion and because of the provision of adequate tax shelters for those who advocated and introduced the high rates of tax. Members of parliament and Central government ministers receive relatively low salaries but then they are granted a sitting allowance which is exempt from tax. A proportion of government servants as well as ministers and members of parliament were and are provided with living accommodation for which they are charged very nominal rates while the market rent for the accommodation would be several times higher. If the fortunate occupant of government accommodation paid 10 per cent of his salary as rent, no perquisite value is deemed to arise. Similarly, senior civil servants and top personnel in the organised private sector receive perquisites, which are not subject to tax fully; for example, use of telephones provided by the employer, leave travel concession, use of passenger cars given by the employer for private purposes on payment of relatively low charges. In a similar fashion very liberal rules for the valuation of house property for wealth tax purposes

5

made possible for some groups of people to pay very little wealth tax. The tax law was unnecessarily complicated partly because of the provision of several concessions and deductions, but also because the tax department wanted to provide safeguards against every possible attempt at tax avoidance and tax evasion. The result was the generation of a plethora of disputes, growing litigation, with the Tribunals and High Courts coming to have such a large volume of pending cases that one could not hope to get a decision on an income tax case from the High Court within a period of 10 years. Most of the disputes related to minor points of interpretation involving insignificant amounts of money were taking up enormous time and effort, which was totally meaningless in view of the large-scale evasion of direct taxes.

Indirect Taxes

We had built up a totally irrational structure of indirect taxes. The Constitution provides for the imposition of a number of indirect taxes. But the major ones are customs and excise duties leviable by the Central government and the sales tax other than inter-State sales tax leviable by the State governments (the inter-State sales tax is levied under Central legislation). The irrationality in the indirect tax structure arose partly because of the nature of the Constitutional provisions but mainly because, in developing the indirect tax structure after independence, no attention was paid to the economic consequences of different ways of levying indirect taxes.

Prior to 1986, the indirect taxes levied by the Centre — customs, Union excise and Central sales tax — taken by themselves or the Central indirect taxes and the major indirect taxes levied by the States and the local authorities — taxes on intra-State sales, the passengers and goods tax, the electricity duty and the octroi[1] taken together did not constitute an integrated and rational system. There were levies that have been developed independently with no coordination, and acted and reacted on one another with little government intervention. They were all cascading type taxes, except for the limited operation of a rule under the Central excise which provided credit for tax paid on inputs and the similarly limited concessional treatment granted to inputs in the sales tax laws in some States. The taxes were levied at widely different rates and the total impact

---

1   Defined as a tax on the entry of goods into a local area for consumption or use therein.

on relative prices or on the pattern of expenditure of households could not be easily known; nor did the government bother about such matters although they swore by the commitment to progression and equity in the distribution of tax burden. To quote the Tax Reforms Committee:

> It was a truly irrational system from the economic as well as equity point of view; and the misallocation of resources and the loss of welfare caused by the high and desperate import duties and the multi-rated cascading type excise and sales taxes was palpable. While the unduly large number of rates resulted in classification disputes, the high rates spawned evasion abetted by corruption (Ministry of Finance, Government of India 1991, p. 98).

In 1986 a system called MODVAT was introduced in the Central excise under which excise paid on many important inputs became eligible for credit against tax payable on output. This represented a major step in the reform of the Central indirect tax system. However, under the MODVAT system only tax paid on inputs that physically get incorporated in output or those that get consumed in the process of production qualified for set-off. Capital goods were not covered by MODVAT. Also three important sectors, namely, petroleum products, tobacco products and textile products were kept outside this system. After the changes introduced in 1986, there was hardly any progress towards a full-fledged value-added tax.

While there had been some sincere attempt to reform the Central excise, there was no attempt to reform the import duty structure. In fact, in pursuit of the revenue objective, duty rates were considerably raised in the late '80s. At the beginning of the '90s, the Indian import duty structure

> presented a bewildering picture of combination of 'basic' and 'auxiliary' duties with combined rates on different goods varying widely and often consisting of double application of *ad valorem* and specific duties. (Ministry of Finance, Government of India 1991, p. 38)

The duty rates ranged from over 400 per cent *ad valorem* to 0 per cent. With the bulk of the imports falling in the range of 50 to 150 per cent, the average effective rate worked out to 85 per cent excluding exempted items (around 50 per cent if they are included). Furthermore, the statute gave only the maximum rates. The actual rates applied to different products or their varieties were fixed through numerous executive notifications.

The notifications gave exemptions or concessional treatment to particular classes of users or sub-categories of goods, introducing further rate differentiation.

The special treatment given to the small-scale sector under the excise taxation system represented and still represents another distortion. The concessional tax system extended to this sector has been a source of substantial tax evasion. The exemption of a substantial part of the industrial sector from excise taxation represents an obstacle to the introduction of a full-fledged value-added tax.

As can be easily imagined, the application of many rates of excises led to numerous classification disputes. Much time, effort and money was expended by the department and the assessees in relation to disputes regarding classification. Of course, if the tax is limited to the manufacturing stage, there is always a temptation for the producers to under-estimate the values of the products. Apart from this, there have been problems arising from the difficulty in unambiguously defining the manufacturer's price.

On the irrational and complicated structure of central indirect taxes represented by import and excise duties, was imposed the State sales taxes. The State sales taxes are levied on industrial as well as agricultural products; however, numerous exemptions are granted. The sales tax is imposed on prices inclusive of excise. Various types of sales taxes were experimented with by the different States, but most of them have shifted, in the main, to a first-stage, single-point tax, although in some States this is supplemented by a low rate turnover tax or an additional tax payable by the larger dealers.[2]

The sales taxes in the different States are also levied at many rates and the rates of tax on particular commodities vary between States. As already noted, in general the sales taxes levied by the States are of the cascading type. To quote a recent report by the National Institute of Public Finance and Policy (1994), *Reform of Domestic Trade Taxes in India*:

> Neither the structures nor the procedures are, however, simple in any State. Also, with the shift in the point of levy to the first point, the problems in excise taxation associated with the definition of manufacturing, under valuation and commodity classification,

---

2   Most interestingly, the additional sales tax is not to be passed on to the buyers according to law which has been upheld by the courts. Of course, nothing can prevent the dealers from altering the price if they can.

are revisited when one looks at the sales tax system. In sheer complexity and irrationality, the sales tax systems, as they are structured and implemented at present, surpass the excise even at their worst (p. 12).

This is not all. In 1956 the Central government enacted the Central Sales Tax Act authorising the States to impose a tax on inter-State sales emanating from within their respective territories. The tax was imposed on the recommendation of the Taxation Enquiry Commission, 1953–54, which argued that the producing State (i.e. state of origin) should get a small part of the total sales tax burden that could be imposed on a commodity. That Commission recommended that the rate of the inter-State sales tax (or Central sales tax) should be fixed by the Central government and suggested a 1 per cent rate of tax, presumably believing that such a low rate of tax would not be a serious barrier to inter-State trade nor lead to any significant cascading. In course of time, the rate of Central sales tax was raised by the Central government in stages to 4 per cent which taken together with the unremitted sales tax on inputs not only became an effective barrier to inter-State trade but also added significantly to the total cascading effect. Incidentally, the 4 per cent inter-State sales tax combined with the unremitted sales tax on inputs made possible substantial tax exportation by the industrially more advanced States. It is obvious that the rate of Central sales tax was raised with connivance of the Central planners in the mistaken belief that such increases would enable the States as a whole to raise more resources, whereas in fact the taxable capacity of the States to which there was net exportation of inter-State sales tax was reduced.

The Logic of Tax Reform

The complicated structure and deficiencies of the Indian tax system and the way in which the taxes were administered were mind boggling. But the shortcomings were so prominent that it was easy to lay down the basic lines of reform and suggest the ultimate structure that the government should aim to bring into existence. The problem was to initiate the first steps and then recommend other measures in proper sequence so as to reach the final goal. In practice, the tax reform process encounters much opposition because of ignorance and inertia. Also, there are always losers and gainers when changes are to be effected and long-term gains are often overlooked because of fear of short-term losses. But the job had to be done because, as was pointed out earlier, the irrational and totally antiquated tax structure in the country was a stumbling block to accelerating the growth of the economy. It is to be said to the credit of the Central government of India that within a period of three years they have brought about very substantial reform of the structure of the Central taxes, although even in the Central sphere much remains to be done in the field of administration. Tax reform has barely started in the realm of the State governments.

The principles that have guided tax reform in India may be briefly stated as follows:

a. economic rationality which involves (i) removal or avoidance of distortions in economic decision making as well as of unnecessary cost escalation, and (ii) ensuring that economic incentives will not be affected to any significant extent by the tax structure and tax rates.

b. horizontal equity is as important as vertical equity. Hence a satisfactory definition of income (if that is chosen as the index of ability) and a tax system that would enable one to move close to the fulfilment of horizontal equity were called for.

c. broad bases with limited concessions. This would mean simplicity of structure and make possible the reduction in rates.

d. Reduction of the high rates prevailing particularly marginal rates, both to preserve incentives and to encourage compliance.

e. Ensuring that the well-to-do sections will pay proportionately more taxes. This should be ensured not through high marginal rates of income and wealth taxes but through a proper combination of taxes on income and wealth and taxes on expenditure. A steep degree of progression was undesirable and was in any case unenforceable.

f. Considerable improvement in tax administration and enforcement.

The above-mentioned principles or criteria laid down by the Tax Reform Committee were broadly accepted by the government. These principles have been generally applied in the reform of tax systems in many other countries. In the context of globalisation of Indian economy which the government wanted to promote, it was necessary to align the Indian tax system in important respects with those of our trading partners; and if India wanted to attract foreign investment, the rate of corporate profits tax could not be far out of line with those in countries competing for the same capital flows. Thus a regime of moderate rates had to be brought into existence for several important reasons. However, it must be pointed out that if the reforms suggested were fully implemented, there would not only be greater horizontal equity — which should be a great gain — but also a sufficient degree of vertical equity. In fact, if enforcement was strengthened, the actual degree of progression would perhaps be greater than under the previous regime. This assumes much more effective tax enforcement which would become possible due to the reform.

Reform Carried Out To-Date

Import Duties

The import duty structure has been simplified by the amalgamation of the basic and auxiliary duties. On the eve of reform the combined duty rates ranged from 250 per cent to 0 per cent and the number of statutory rates, which were many, were effectively multiplied by special or concessional rates brought about through notifications. By now the peak rate has been reduced to 65 per cent and the total number of statutory rates has come down to 14. With the reduction of the peak rate, there has been general reduction in the level of rates and with such reduction a large number of notifications have been abolished. The import duty structure has become much simpler and less irrational, although several anomalies exist and the rates on raw materials such as metals and certain intermediate products particularly chemicals still remain high. The Tax Reforms Committee suggested that by 1997–78 (at the latest) the rates of import duty should range between 30 and 10 per cent (There should be no zero duty items). The only exception was to be consumer goods whose imports are now banned. When they are allowed in, the Committee suggested that the rate of duty initially should be 50 per cent to give time for the domestic industry to adjust itself. It is clear that we still have a long way to go to arrive at the structure recommended by the Tax Reforms Committee which itself has been criticised for not going far enough.

Union Excise Duty

Here again there has been progress in terms of reform towards a full-fledged value-added tax. A major reform has been to make capital goods eligible for MODVAT credit. Additionally, the rates of duty have been unified and the number of rates has been brought down to 10 apart from the rate of tax on tobacco products. Another major change is the switch over from specific duties to *ad valorem* duties which would facilitate the introduction of the value-added tax and also would make revenue more responsive to increases in nominal income. With the reduction in import duties, almost all imports have been made subject to countervailing duty and the countervailing duty in turn has been made eligible for MODVAT credit like the excise duty. There have also been several procedural improvements and subject to certain limitations the invoice has been made the basis of tax assessment. Some attempt has also been made to broaden the base through the removal of exemptions, although here the fear of political opposition and the strong pressures exerted by the affected groups have prevented the inclusion of many commodities within the tax net whose exemptions are clearly unjustified (for example, umbrellas and bicycles). But there is no denying the fact that the excise tax system is a much more rational and simpler system today than it was in 1991.

Direct Taxes

The direct tax structure has been greatly simplified. There is now only one rate of corporate profits tax for all domestic companies at 40 per cent. The personal income tax is levied at three rates: 20, 30 and 40 per cent and the surcharge on personal income tax has been removed, while the surcharge on the corporate profits tax (retained for revenue reasons) is expected to be abolished shortly. The rate of tax on branches of foreign companies has been brought down from 65 to 55 per cent.

Government has not found it possible to bring under tax all perquisites wholly or partially and thus remove tax shelters. Also, many tax concessions for industry continue such as partial tax holiday for a specified period of time for new industries or those located in backward States. Since the several perquisites of government employees, public sector employees and ministers have not been brought under tax, it is difficult to justify strict taxation of all perquisites in the private sector. The real solution is, of course, to raise the salaries of senior government officials and ministers and subject all their incomes in money and kind to tax. But this would demand a major change in the salary structure and is not likely to take place soon. Meanwhile, some broadening of the income tax base has been accomplished. For example, the property incomes of minor children is now included in the income of the parents. Again, all capital gains are now subject to tax provided taxable income including capital gains rises beyond the exemption level. Long-term capital gains which are worked out after proper indexation are taxable at a separate lower rate. Now there is no possibility of avoiding the tax on long-term capital gains by investing the proceeds in approved securities as could be done in the past. An attempt has also been made to broaden the base through the introduction of a presumptive tax in the form of a fixed sum payment by small businesses, and for certain classes of businesses an estimated income scheme has been introduced according to which the net taxable income is simply taken to be a given percentage of gross receipts, so that the assessee is freed of the necessity to produce detailed accounts and claim deductions and allowances. Lastly, efforts are under way to introduce comprehensive computerisation of the operations of the income tax department, which in the course of time would lead to the broadening of the base. However, it must be pointed out that the existence of several untaxed perquisites constitutes a violation of the principles of horizontal equity. This problem remains on the agenda of further tax reform.

The wealth tax on all assets other than what are termed as unproductive assets has been abolished. Unproductive assets which include jewellery, bullion, real estate (excluding one house where the assessee resides), passenger automobiles, yachts, aeroplanes, and urban land are subject to a flat 1 per cent tax on the excess of their value over Rs 1.5 million. This tax together with the marginal rate of income tax at 40 per cent represents in our view a sufficient degree of progression. In fact, with buoyancy in revenues it should be possible to reduce the marginal rate of personal income tax as well as the rate of corporate profits tax to 30 per cent which in the Indian context would lead to substantial improvement in tax compliance.

As noted earlier, one of the major shortcomings of the indirect tax system in India was the absence of any tax on the service sector — i.e. the value added by the service sector has been left untouched. It is clear that if a comprehensive value-added tax is to be introduced, the tax on services must become an integral part of the system. A beginning has been made in this respect. Recently, tax at 5 per cent has been introduced on telephone services, on the services of stock brokers, and on premia for insurance of jewellery, real estate and passenger automobiles. There is also a so-called expenditure tax which is a tax to be paid on hotel bills whether for food or accommodation (cheaper hotels are exempt). The idea is that more and more services will be brought under tax and after a sufficient number of services are included, the services tax will be merged with the

Union excise, in terms of eligibility for obtaining set-off for taxes paid on services by the manufacturers of goods and for getting set-off for taxes paid on goods by the producers of services. The regime of indirect taxes levied by the State governments still remains basically unreformed and quite unsatisfactory. The State indirect taxes, of which the sales tax forms the major component, are a source of distortion and cause hindrance to the smooth flow of trade and economic activity. The main sources of distortion are the sales tax and the octroi.

The major shortcomings of the existing system of State and local indirect taxes may be summarised briefly:

a. The sales tax is levied on the price inclusive of excise at every stage of manufacture.

b. In most States, there is no complete set off for the sales tax paid on inputs; however, the cascading is to some extent mitigated by the lower rate of tax for inputs bought by manufacturers. The administration of the special rate creates problems.

c. The inter-State sales tax (or the Central sales tax) levied by most State governments at the maximum rate of 4 per cent (except where reduced for reasons of competition) acts as a hindrance to inter-State trade and also adds to the total cascading effect.

d. The octroi levied by local authorities in several States not only leads to physical obstacles to the smooth flow of trade but acts as an additional trade barrier in the economic sense. By the same token it adds to the cascading effect.

e. The sales tax in general is levied at multiple rates creating compliance problems and leading to classification disputes. There is unnecessary interference with consumer preferences.

f. Most State governments rely on the so called first-point tax, that is, they levy the tax on the first sale in the State effected by the manufacturers and importers. As the first-point tax does not cover the value added at subsequent stages, the rates have to be higher than otherwise and there is temptation and attempt to undervalue commodities at the stage of taxation.

g. In their quest for revenue some States have levied a low rate, multi-point tax or turnover tax in addition to the first-point tax, thus further complicating the structure and adding to cascading.

h. States indulge in intense tax competition: the rates of tax on particular commodities are reduced from time to time in order to divert trade and industry from other States. This competition has sometimes led to the bizarre situation in which taxes on motor vehicles become lower than those on foodgrains.

i. The States also offer tax incentives under the sales tax to attract industries. Such offers by several States tend to become a zero-sum game which leads to the erosion of the tax base and artificial diversion of trade.

j. The administration of State taxes leaves much to be desired. The whole system needs to be modernised and computerised. As things stand now, assessments are kept pending too long and there is much prolonged litigation.

The State governments have become aware that their tax systems should be rationalised and tax administration modernised. They are now making efforts to bring about greater uniformity in their sales tax systems. A committee of State Finance Ministers has been appointed by the Finance Minister of India. Under the auspices of this committee, work is being done to fix floor rates for particular groups of commodities (to prevent tax competition) to rationalise the systems of incentives and to evolve uniform procedures. With only three or four rates besides zero, it should be possible for the State governments to adopt a State value-added tax. This would essentially involve two steps:

The first is to give full credit for tax paid on inputs by manufacturers against the tax payable by them; and the second is to convert the single point tax into a multi-point tax with a set-off for tax paid at the earlier stage. Before these steps are taken, there would have to be a fairly widespread educational program and training of the officers. The Government of India is expected to provide assistance in respect of these matters.

Conclusion

Several critics of the tax reform program in India have tended to judge the success or failure of the program in terms of increases in revenue that the reform has brought about. Adequacy of increase is measured in terms of revenue to GDP ratio. To be sure, one of the objectives of tax reform is to improve revenue elasticity and the tax ratio. However, it should be remembered that the impact of the reform on revenue increase will not be immediate; tax compliance will increase with reduction in rates only gradually. Similarly, improvements in tax enforcement will take time. It has been emphasised in the Report of the Tax Reforms Committee that mere reduction in rates would not lead to an increase in compliance and that stricter enforcement, which becomes easier with rate reduction, is a necessary complementary step. Secondly, the growth in revenue is not to be measured only by the tax ratio. A major objective of the tax reform is to facilitate and promote faster growth of the economy. What is needed is not an immediate increase in the tax ratio but a faster growth in revenue arising from a higher growth rate of the economy. With an elasticity greater than one, in course of time, the tax ratio will rise. It could be said with some confidence that the tax system has been reformed in India significantly enough to facilitate a higher rate of growth.

It must be admitted, however, that the structural reform is far from complete, although quite a bit of ground has been covered in a short period of three years. Again, there has been only slow progress in the reform of the tax administration. Tax policymakers and tax administrators will have their hands full in the coming years.

References

Ministry of Finance, Government of India (1991), *Tax Reforms Committee, Interim Report*, New Delhi, India: Ministry of Finance, Government of India.

National Institute of Public Finance and Policy (1994), 'Reform of Domestic Trade Taxes in India: Issues and Options', New Delhi, www.nipfp.org.in/media/pdf/books/BK_39/Reform%20Of%20Domestic%20Trade%20Taxes%20In%20India%20Issues%20And%20Options.pdf

Oration 2:
1995 K.R. Narayanan Oration

Message from the Vice-President
of the Republic of India

In April 1994 I had the pleasure of inaugurating the Australia South Asia Research Centre at The Australian National University. I have vivid memories of the occasion. A distinguished audience was present along with the Foreign Minister of Australia, Senator Gareth Evans and the former Prime Minister of Australia Mr Gough Whitlam and representatives of the South Asian Missions in Canberra.

The establishment of an annual lecture to commemorate that occasion was a significant step. The first lecture in the series was given by Dr Raja J. Chelliah. I am glad that the second oration this year will be given by Professor U.R. Rao on 'Space Technology for Sustainable Development in Asia'. Professor Rao is one of the pioneers of India's space program to the present stage. He is taking it to the threshold of self-reliance in designing and building satellites and in achieving launch capability.

Space explorations and the practical applications for space technology have opened up exciting vistas for human knowledge and the progress of mankind. It has already conferred great benefits on humanity through the development of telecommunications, television broadcasting, meteorology, disaster warning and natural resources survey and management. India has developed these capabilities in the mainstream of international cooperation. The significance of space science and technology for sustainable development in Asia is self-evident. Large parts of this ancient continent are still afflicted by poverty, illiteracy and general underdevelopment, and therefore cooperation in this field among the countries of the Asian region is of great importance. I am sure that Professor Rao and his wide experience of expertise will throw light on the prospects of such cooperation in Asia.

K.R. Narayanan
New Delhi
1995

Space Technology for Sustainable Development in Asia

U.R. Rao

I am indeed honoured at being invited to deliver the prestigious second K.R. Narayanan Oration of the Australia South Asia Research Centre at The Australian National University, Canberra. My pleasure is all the more since I have intimately known and closely worked with Dr Narayanan, Vice President of India, who is an unique combination of an outstanding journalist, successful diplomat, honest politician and above all a self-effacing, humble and exemplary human being. He firmly believed that the welfare of the world depends on creating a new world order guided by the spirit of sharing and cooperation at the international level involving politics, economics, social engineering and all the resources of science and technology. Quoting his own words, 'The development of the awesome power of the science and technology has to be animated by the spirit of humanism for the good of mankind and not for purposes of exploitation or destruction'. In tune with his philosophy, I have chosen the topic 'Space Technology for Sustainable Development' for this lecture.

The spectacular achievements in the last three decades have firmly established the capability of space technology for bringing out a socioeconomic revolution in the world because of its immense potential to transform even stagnant societies in a most cost effective and timely manner. While the ability to view in entire electromagnetic spectrum enabled space exploration to unveil the magnificent panorama of the vast cosmos, satellites from their vantage point in space have been able to provide a synoptic, repetitive and instantaneous access to any point on our planet, virtually shrinking time and distance. The vast and unlimited potential benefits of space technology have already extended to communication, meteorology, TV broadcast, education, agriculture, industrial growth, resource management, environmental pollution, disaster mitigation, flood and drought management, health and entertainment, virtually touching every facet of human endeavour (Rao 1995a).

In spite of these spectacular advances, as Smt. Indira Gandhi stated at the UNISPACE '82 conference:

> It is pertinent to ask if such spectacular advances, which in some way have brought the world together have also contributed to reducing the glaring disparities which divide people, the rich and the poor, the haves and the have-nots. The promise of gains from advanced technologies elude the majority of peoples, whose aspirations for a better and richer life remain unfulfilled.

Developing countries, in particular, which account for over 75 per cent of the world population, suffering from serious shortage of resources and capital, lack of trained man power, large-scale illiteracy, low agricultural productivity, industrial backwardness and exploding population, have become the target of the pollution of rampant poverty. In spite of the food grain production increasing at an average rate of about 3 per cent per year, the food productivity in the developing countries continues to remain very low varying between 0.5 to 2.5 t/ha as against the world average of 2.6 t/ha leave alone the productivity of over 4.5 t/ha in the developed nations (Figure 1). With the steadily increasing population in these countries more than offsetting the increased food production, over 65 countries are today facing serious food deficit and acute famine conditions (Rao 1991). The Asia-Pacific region alone accounts for a staggering 65 per cent of world's extremely poor population, sustaining on less than 2,000 calories/day. The gap between the total food grain production in the world and the demand is expected to reach 140 million tons by 2000 and with the projected increase in population from the present 5.7 billion to 8.5 billion by the year 2025 and 11 billion by 2100, the situation is bound to become explosive.

The term sustainable development coined several years ago has now become a common currency. The World Commission on Environment in its report *Our Common Future* (1987) defined sustainable development as:

> development that meets the needs of the present without compromising the ability of the future generations to meet their own needs. It is not a fixed state of harmony, but rather a process

of change in which the exploitation of resources, the direction of investments, the orientation of technological development and institutional changes are made consistent with future as well as present needs.

Unless sustainable development to overcome poverty alleviation concurrently addresses food, economic and health security for achieving substantial improvement in the quality of life across the world, we will surely fail in our attempt to reverse the prevalent state of scarcity and social structure of inequity in our society.

Serious concern for the well-being of humanity has led to the definition of more appropriate indices, such as sustainable livelihood security index (SLSI), for providing a realistic and accurate representation of the quality of life. Fundamentally, assessment of quality of life must encompass four basic components namely food sufficiency, ecological integrity, economic security and social equity. While ecological security covers environmental degradation over land, forest and water, economic efficiency deals with input/output ratio of productivity in monetary terms. The social equity factor essentially deals with human aspects in a given region in terms of their statistics below the poverty line, literacy rate, nutritional status, health care aspects and employment opportunities. It is only through the adoption of a holistic approach involving sustainable development strategies that we can ensure a reasonable quality of life to meet the basic requirements of the present as well as future generations. Considering that each 1 per cent growth in population would require at least 2.5 per cent growth in GNP as demographic investment, providing food, economic and health security to all the people in the world becomes our greatest challenge.

Social Dimensions of the Pollution of Poverty

The rampant pollution of poverty in the developing nations is further being severely stretched on an elastic scale due to the explosive growth in population. Even with the assumption of reaching the replacement fertility rate of 21 per thousand by 2025 based on an optimistic extrapolation of reduction in crude birth rate during the last two decades, the present level of population of 4.3 billion in the developing countries will cross 7.2 billion by 2025 and reach 9.4 billion in 2100 as compared to the total population of the affluent societies, expected to stabilise below 2 billion (UN 1994). Asian regions, which accounted for 3.1 billion or 59 per cent of the global population of 5.4 billion in 1990, will cross 5.9 billion by 2100 (Figure 2) of which the share of India alone is likely to be around 1.8 billion. It is clear that the only choice we have is to appeal to science and technology for rapidly building up the necessary carrying capacity to meet the basic demands of the population projected by the realistic scenario. The impressive economic breakthrough achieved by the East Asian Tiger countries is a good example of the impact of rapid industrial development and massive literacy program in substantially improving their GNP.

An immediate consequence of the population growth is the decrease in the available per capita arable land from 0.17 ha to just about 0.1 ha (Rao 1991; World Resources Institute 1992), which will inevitably force large-scale migration of rural people into urban areas in search of gainful employment. Globally the urban population has increased from 1.4 billion in 1970 to 2.6 billion in 1992 and is expected to cross 3.5 billion by 2000, which means almost 55 per cent of the global population will reside in cities by the turn of this century. The developing countries in Asia, Africa and Latin America are witnessing exactly the same phenomena of urbanisation which occurred in the developed west 50 years ago. Urban population in Asia which has already crossed 1 billion is increasing at the phenomenal rate of almost 4 per cent per year as compared to less than 1.2 per cent in America and Europe (World Bank 1994). In India, the urban population has dramatically increased from a mere 30 million in 1900 to over 260 million and is expected to cross 400 million by 2000. Inadequate public transportation, scarcity of safe drinking water and poor sanitation have turned all our major cities into sources of concentrated hazard instead of engines of growth. The solid waste generated each day by the megacities in Asia is over 80 to 100 tons per million, almost twice that in the western cities, turning them into breeding grounds of all communicable diseases. The city of Calcutta alone produces over half a million ton of solid waste every year, half of which is not even collected, let alone recycled.

Despite of the exponential growth in communication capabilities all across the world in the last 50 years, the glaring differences in the development of communication infrastructure between developed and developing nations is very striking. Communication infrastructure like many other social parameters such as energy consumption and literacy, is traditionally considered as an indicator of the level of economic development. Even with the impact of satellite communication revolution, the availability of telephones in the metropolitan cities of the developing countries is less than one for every 100 persons as against one for every two persons in the developed societies. The picture in the rural developing areas is even more dismal with over 2,000 persons having to compete for access to a single telephone (Rao 1993). While practically all the developing countries have taken some advantage of satellite communication, only just about 20 out of the 170 geostationary satellites in orbit today, belong to the developing nations and at the present rate of growth, the share of the developing countries either in leased transponders or in terms of dedicated satellites is unlikely to exceed 15 per cent of the global usage even by the year 2000.

The close organic linkage between development and education is abundantly clear from the existence of the powerful functional relationship between the literacy index of a country and its gross national product. Analysis indicates that least developed countries with 70–80 per cent illiteracy have only a per capita income of about $200 per year whereas middle-income group of nations with illiteracy rates of 35–50 per cent have an annual per capita income of about $600 as against over $10,000 annual per capita income enjoyed by the citizens of developed nations having less than 5 per cent illiterates (Gao and Rao 1992) (Figure 3). According to UNESCO 1985 statistics, almost 30 per cent of the global population were illiterates, 98 per cent of whom belonged to the developing countries. The geographical distribution of illiterate population indicates that Asia alone accounted for 75 per cent of the total illiterates, in the world, Africa coming a close second with 18 per cent and the rest 7 per cent being distributed in Latin America and other parts of the world (Rao 1995a; World Bank 1994), most of them being in dispersed and remote rural areas. Unless eradication of illiteracy is tackled on a war footing and not by mere slogan adoption, over 2.5 billion or about 30 per cent out of an estimated 7.2 billion population in the developing countries will continue to remain illiterate even by the year 2025 (Rao 1988).

In spite of the wide recognition that the existing socioeconomic imbalance between developed and developing nations is directly attributable to the significant difference in their levels of educational advancement, lack of adequate resources continues to prevent the developing countries from overcoming their fundamental disadvantage. In 1986 alone, out of a total investment of about $800 billion on education, 40 developed nations accounted for 80 per cent of this expenditure while the total share of the 161 developing nations (Rao 1995b; Gao and Rao 1992) was just 14 per cent. The annual per capita investment in all forms of education including higher education in the third world countries is hardly $25 per year compared to over $500 per year in the developed world. Many of the rural areas of the third-world countries do not even possess an elementary education facility and where schools exist, they seldom have more than a single qualified teacher and are often run without even a blackboard. Typical is the example of China, where most of the teachers employed in the primary schools, are those who graduated from the same schools under poorly qualified teachers, resulting in massive inbreeding which has perpetuated the vicious circle. It is estimated that over 3 million poorly qualified teachers in China comprising of 40 per cent of teacher population in primary schools and 72 per cent in junior schools are continuing to cater to the educational growth of that country (Liu 1994). Statistics clearly indicate that the birth rate as well as infant mortality of children drastically gets reduced with the increase in female literacy level. Considering that education of women is most crucial for achieving social equilibrium, through population control and health care (Figure 4), the task of eradicating illiteracy among women who constitute over 60 per cent of the total illiterates in a developing society, becomes the single most important goal for promoting cultural growth and socioeconomic prosperity of any rural society. The answer clearly lies in the wide spread utilisation of distance education involving satellite-based TV and radio broadcasting media, which are most ideally suited to provide basic education as well as continuing education to the vast, inaccessible and sparsely distributed population of the world.

State of Agriculture and Environment

A dramatic increase in the global food grain production since the 1960s occurred with the initiation of the green revolution, which was primarily based on the high technology package involving large-scale use of chemical fertilisers, pesticides, high response better seeds and extensive irrigation. The increase in India's annual foodgrain production from just about 55 million tons in 1947 to about 180 million tons in the 1990s is clearly a result of the emphasis given to large-scale irrigation which has risen from less than 20 per cent to over 35 per cent of total arable land of 160 million ha during this period. Ironically however, the negative repercussions of the very practice of irrigation due to water logging, inadequate drainage and indiscriminate use of chemical fertilisers have resulted in making the soil in the irrigated areas highly saline and unproductive. It is estimated that over one-third of the approximately 200 million ha of irrigated cultivable land in the world is already salt affected (Swaminathan 1980). Almost 40 per cent of the highly fertile Indo-gangetic plain in India, which was once the cradle of civilisation, suffers from intense salinity making it unfavourable for crop growth. Almost 25 per cent of the arable land area in every continent has become problem land with another 25 per cent having very low productivity.

The extreme pressure of population and industrialisation particularly in the developing countries has resulted in the annual rate of deforestation of 17 million ha including almost 4 million ha in Asia (Figure 5). An imperative consequence of deforestation is increased run-off of rain water and severe soil erosion resulting in the deterioration of the top soil, degradation of land and sedimentation of water bases. The high rate of soil erosion in deforested areas in India, China and elsewhere ranges from 10 t/ha in the plains to almost 30 t/ha in the north-eastern hilly regions, as against just 1 t/ha in the forested area. Worldwide soil erosion has reached the limit of 100 million tons per year as against 45 million tons in 1860 and less than 16 million tons 300 years ago. Extensive deforestation has resulted in increased carbon dioxide in the atmosphere, increased rain precipitation run off from 20 per cent to almost 50 per cent, frequent flooding and a gradual extinction of biodiversity (Khoshoo 1990; Brown 1992). Overgrazing, deforestation, encroachment by agricultural crops and general mismanagement of land and water resources have resulted in increasing desertification in Asia, Africa and Latin America. About 3,000 million ha, a quarter earth's land surface has now turned out as desert or damaged by factors that contribute to desertification. On a global scale the desertification is increasing almost by 1 million ha per year. The changes in climatic and rain patterns gradually setting in because of deforestation are yet to be fully understood due to our inadequate understanding of the phenomena, particularly the energy exchange between the surface aerodynamic roughness over the forest and the atmosphere above it.

Management of water resources particularly in the developing countries, has been even more pathetic. Optimal management of water becomes crucial in the dry land tracts of tropical countries where most of the precipitation occurs in less than 100 days as compared to mid- and high-latitude countries where snow and rain precipitation continue to keep the soil moisture intact for almost eight months in a year. With the added problems of higher temperature regimes and higher evapo-transpiration rates, need for optimal harvesting of run off and recharging of underground aquifers in tropical countries assumes paramount importance. Although major irrigation projects and big dams have contributed to improved agricultural production in the last few decades, the problem of water-logging, salinisation and loss of valuable bio-resources have led to gradual degradation of land in many areas in the developing world. Intensive use of chemical fertilisers and pesticides combined with poor management of water-sheds and highly fragmented land holdings have resulted in severe water stress, pesticide contamination not only in the water but also in the agricultural crops, resulting in the severe degradation of over 1.2 billion ha across the world, in the last 45 years alone (Figure 6). The material delivery from rivers to the oceans which was just 9.3 billion tons 50 years ago has now increased to 25 billion tons a year, with the largest discharge of over 15 billion tons per year coming from Asia alone.

Superimposed on these seemingly insurmountable difficulties is the real prospect of the widely accepted global warming scenario due to the unprecedented anthropogenic intervention causing a rapid increase in the green house gases, upsetting the delicate greenhouse equilibrium which could lead to irreversible climatic changes (Ramanathan 1985). Particularly since the beginning of the industrial revolution, CO_2 concentration in the atmosphere has steadily increased from 280 ppmv to 350 ppmv and at the present rate of increase is expected to reach 450 ppmv by 2050. Concentration of methane in the atmosphere has also been increasing steadily at the rate of about 0.9 per cent per year and has now already reached 1.7 ppmv. Detailed rigorous analysis of surface temperature over the last century indicates an average increase in global temperature of about 0.5°C. While the primary cause of the global temperature increase in the past has been the increasing atmospheric concentration of CO_2 due to industrialisation, fossil fuel burning and extensive deforestation, the rapid increase of CFCs in the last decade which has large residence time of over 100 years in the atmosphere has further added to the global environmental problem. In spite of the universal adoption of the Montreal Protocol the spectre of global warming, which can cause depletion of ozone, rise in sea level, inundation of highly populated coastal areas and severe modification of climatic and rain pattern, continues to pose a real threat unless all countries, both developed and developing, make appropriate structural adjustments in their lifestyle and consumption pattern.

Communication Revolution

The remarkable developments in space communication in just three decades since the successful relay of TV signals across the Atlantic in 1962 using TELSTAR, have brought us to the threshold of achieving the capability of establishing human connectivity anywhere in the world, on land, air or sea. The superior quality and reliability of satellite links in combination with their high percentage of availability, distance insensitivity, high degree of flexibility for rapid reconfiguration and their ability to aggregate small requirements to provide cost effective specialised services across vast territories have made satellite communication the most vital link for establishing human connectivity promoting a new perspective of our planet, that of a global village. The evolutionary nature of satellite communication is reflected in their capacity increase, from just 240 voice channels in 1965 to the present day satellites which on an average can easily carry over 20,000 voice circuits, in addition to several TV channels (Pant 1994). Practically all the developing nations in the world today including Asian countries have taken advantage of satellite communication by either leasing transponders from international systems like INTELSAT, INMARSAT and INTER SPUTNIK or by establishing regional systems like Arabsat.

Recognising the paramount need of the governments, societies and institutions to quickly respond to fast changing situations in a demassified society where niche markets, customised services and rapid transactions are essential to successfully compete in the liberalised global market place, a few Asian countries like India (INSAT), Indonesia (PALAPA), China (CHINASAT), Japan (JCSAT) and Australia (AUSSAT) have already established their own satellite communication systems. Other Asian countries like Korea (KOREASAT), Thailand (THAICOM) and Malaysia (MEASAT) are in the process of establishing their own communication systems to meet their growing requirements of telecommunication and TV distribution services.

Unlike most of the countries, India decided to build its own indigenous technology base and use space technology for solving its national problems on a self-reliant basis. Establishing the feasibility of using satellite medium for imparting education in health, hygiene, family planning and better agricultural practices to over 2,400 remote rural villages through the year long Satellite Instructional Television Experiment (SITE) conducted using NASA's ATS satellite during 1975, India successfully launched and operated its own three axis stabilised experimental satellite APPLE in 1981 followed by the introduction of the unique, multipurpose INSAT series of communication satellites to provide operational services on a continuing basis. INSAT system, with over 5,000 two-way speech circuits covering 140 routes amounting to 150,000 route km initiated a communication revolution in the country (Figure 7) connecting for the first time, even remote rural areas and off-shore islands with the main stream of the nation using Low Cost Terminals (LCTs). The nationwide geographic reach of INSAT satellite has been advantageously used for a variety of applications such as administrative, business and computer communications through a number of captive networks using small terminals. New specialised services such as rural telegraphy to remote areas, news service, facsimile transmission and emergency communication for post disaster relief operations have been commissioned. The National Information Center's Network (NICNET) using VSATs and spread-spectrum techniques with over 700 micro-terminals provides reliable data communication links interconnecting district headquarters, state capitals, and central government departments. The Remote Area Business and Message Network (RABMN), to provide data communication between city-based industries and construction projects located in remote areas is already operational with over 450 micro-terminals and with a registered demand for more than 2,000 terminals (Rao 1995b).

Similar expansion of telecommunication to provide low cost VSAT services in addition to point to point communication has been achieved in China, Australia, Indonesia and other countries in Asia either through satellites procured from abroad or through leased transponders. Increasingly all over the world the future trends in communication is towards establishing personalised communication services to meet the needs of the people at individual and group levels. Remarkable developments in digital compression techniques, use of advanced modulation systems for optimal utilisation of space segment and innovative use of low-cost VSATs to provide several value-added services have initiated the new age of information super-highway making it possible to have information on demand. The merging of large computation and communication capabilities through technological innovations are paving the way for the establishment of seamless networks to provide personalised communication and multimedia services including audio, video and data transmission, thus creating a world where communication, information, entertainment and motivation are literally at the will of one's fingertips. The imminent introduction of mobile communication services in the next three years will surely make the dream of every communication engineer of establishing human connectivity anywhere in the world, on land, air or sea come true.

Space Technology for Universal Education

The phenomenal success of the Satellite Instructional Television Experiment (SITE) conducted in India followed by similar experiments conducted elsewhere in the Appalachian Region, Rocky Mountains, Alaska, Canada, China and Latin America in the mid-'70s and early '80s, clearly established the tremendous potential of using satellite TV for educational purposes (Rao 1987). It is very satisfying to note that operational beginning of satellite-based distance education facility is already making a significant impact in Indonesia, providing an effective educational system to the sparsely distributed population in 14,000 individual islands stretching across a distance of over 5,000 km, many of which are inaccessible mountainous or jungle terrain. Successful use of PALAPA satellite in Indonesia, INSAT in India and AUSSAT in Australia have prompted other developing countries like Brazil, China and Mexico also to develop their own satellite-based educational system. Extensive use of satellite medium in China provides 31 hour adult educational programs every day to 30 million people annually through 6,300 TVRO earth stations and more than 50,000 learning centres.

Most dramatic impact of INSAT has been in the rapid expansion of TV dissemination in the country through installation of more than 600 TV transmitters and use of a large number of direct reception community sets in sparsely populated areas, for providing access to over 80 per cent of India's population, through national and regional transmissions. INSAT is being extensively used for Educational TV broadcasting with about 100 hours of programming per month to over 4,000 schools and colleges. An effective educational system requires not just a one-way system of instruction but a two-way interactive communication system enabling the target audience to ask questions and obtain clarifications from experts, in real time. Special inexpensive talk back facilities have been developed within ISRO to promote this activity in the country and a number of selected large-scale experiments aimed at improving the level of understanding of rural people, providing refresher courses to industrial workers in cities and specialised education to schools and colleges were conducted to demonstrate the effectiveness of the satellite media for imparting interactive education (Rao 1995b). Recognising the acute need for eradication of illiteracy, particularly in the rural areas, ISRO has conceived of dedicated GRAMSAT satellites (Rao 1993) (Figure 8), carrying six to eight high-powered C-band and Ku-band transponders which together with video compression techniques can disseminate region and culture specific audio visual programs of relevance in each of the regional languages through rebroadcast mode on to an ordinary TV set.

Vast improvements in technology have made it possible to reach millions of homes with antenna dish sizes as small as 90 to 45 cm in Ku-band. The recent upsurge in video compression technology now enables several TV channels to be carried on a single transponder. Availability of about 150 channels from a single satellite location can entirely change the complexion of home entertainment through direct to home television broadcast. Video-on-demand which includes specific group interest programs in addition to general entertainment programs, allows individuals to choose and even manipulate programs of their choice. What was cost prohibitive yesterday has suddenly become affordable today with the availability of TV using only a small space segment resource in an economic way which can have a dramatic impact on educational and developmental services.

Management of Natural Disasters

The enormous havoc and dislocation caused by natural and man-made disasters have become a great burden particularly on the highly populated and poverty stricken developing countries causing perpetual misery to thousands of lives and livestock. Over the past 20 years alone, these extreme natural disasters have resulted in the loss of life of more than 3 million people and have affected over 800 million people all over the world, causing damage to property to the tune of $50–100 billion, 50 per cent of which is due to floods and cyclones. Over 60 per cent of all the major disasters have occurred in the developing countries, two-thirds of which have been in the developing Asian regions (Rao 1995a; World Resources Institute 1992). Even though extreme natural events such as floods, drought, cyclones and earthquakes are not totally under human control, prediction of occurrence of some of these events with a good degree of certainty is possible, thanks to the developments in space technology. Instead of collectively taking up the challenge of preventing or at least mitigating the effects of such disasters, providing aids after the events which are both inadequate and untimely has only resulted in perpetuating the misery of the worst affected, silently suffering victims of disasters.

An effective disaster management system consists of four main components — disaster prediction, disaster warning, disaster management and disaster relief. Disaster warning is a basic prerequisite for ensuring disaster preparedness and in some cases to help in the prevention of disaster itself. Clearly the most important application of satellites is in detecting, predicting and delivering early warning of impending disasters such as flood, drought, cyclone and even forest fires (Rao et al. 1987; Heath 1994). Continuous monitoring by both geostationary and low earth orbiting weather satellites like GOES, INSAT, METEOSAT and NOAA is capable of providing early warning on cyclones and floods. Forest fires, environmental hazards, volcanic eruptions and even propagation of desert locust phenomena can be detected well in time by remote-sensing satellites like, LANDSAT, SPOT and IRS. Sustainable development strategy must address this important issue in order to provide stability and reasonable security to the vulnerable rural population in these countries. Remote-sensing information are now operationally used to regularly monitor flood conditions, volume of water flow and damage assessment. From such a database collected over years, it is possible to identify different risk zones in the flood prone area based on the severity index for flood proneness of each zone. Optimal treatment of each zone on a long-term basis, depending on the severity, can then be attempted to achieve reduction in flood damage without impairing environmental integrity (Rao 1993) (Figure 9).

Data relay and communication satellites have the ability not only to deliver early warnings on various disasters but also in disseminating requisite information on hazard awareness and educating the local people in preparing themselves to face such hazards. Locale specific unattended Disaster Warning Systems (DWS) installed by India along the vulnerable eastern coast of the country, using communication and meteorological capability of INSAT multipurpose satellites, have proven their immense value in providing timely warning on cyclone and flood disasters over the last 10 years. Most dramatic use of DWS, consisting of over 150 disaster warning receivers was during the cyclone that hit the eastern coast of India in May 1990, enabling the civic authorities to evacuate over 170,000 people from the cyclone affected area, which saved thousands of lives and livestock. But for the operation of DWS, analysis of cyclone events which occurred in the pre INSAT era indicates that the total human death toll would have been at least 20,000 during this event, as against only 800 deaths recorded (Rao 1995a; 1995b).

Drought is a complex phenomena, the causes for which are many involving both natural and induced factors such as atmospheric perturbation, climatic variability, sea surface temperature changes and human intervention, ranging from deforestation and poor land management to destabilisation of greenhouse effect. While it is difficult to identify the exact onset and the end of drought because of its slow creeping nature, remote-sensing derived Vegetation Index (VI) has been very effective in monitoring drought conditions on a real time basis, often helping the decision makers to initiate appropriate strategies for recovery by changing crop patterns and practices. The use of meteorological satellite data to assess spatial and temporal inadequacies of rainfall at critical crop stages and subsequent assessment of the crop condition status based on VI analysis provide an excellent drought monitoring mechanism. Comparison of the temporal changes in the bi-weekly VI indices with the corresponding figures in a normal year can easily provide advance information on the onset of drought conditions in any given region (Figure 10). Under the National Agricultural Drought Assessment and Monitoring System (NADAMS), bi-weekly drought bulletins are issued, almost on real time, to all the drought prone districts in India to enable decision makers to assess the severity of drought and take appropriate remedial measures (Rao 1995c).

Food Security

The solution for providing food security to the world without affecting ecological balance lies in the adoption of new scientific tools available, particularly the use of vital inputs from space remote-sensing and biotechnological advances. While India and China have built an impressive capability in space technology by developing their own launch vehicles, communication and remote-sensing satellites and application programs, other countries in Asia have also successfully used space imageries available from international satellites for monitoring and management of their natural resources through cooperative arrangements. India for example, has effectively used its own IRS series of remote-sensing satellites to establish and continuously monitor its national forest inventory and to prevent further encroachment of its forest wealth. Extensive use of satellite imageries for mapping soil characteristics, land-use in terms of single crop, double crop, fallow and residual land areas, meteorological parameters and water resources have led to the identification of agro-climatically coherent regions having homogeneous characteristics such as slope, soil depth, texture and water holding capacity, which are vital for developing locale-specific and agro-climatically suitable cropping patterns. The ability to identify saline/alkaline soils at micro-levels using space imageries have enabled the application of suitable measures to reduce soil salinity and adoption of alternate crops or cropping patterns to restore the fertility of the land to the original level. Country-wide mapping of wasteland at micro-level has been able to identify 54 million ha of wasteland (Figure 11), about half of which can be reclaimed for productive agricultural usage with appropriate corrective actions (Rao 1995a; 1995c).

Repetitive coverage provided by satellites has been widely used for mapping the temporal changes in water bodies and reservoirs in addition to providing a reliable estimate of water storage in the reservoirs thereby facilitating optimal scheduling of irrigation. A classic example is the country-wide hydrogeomorphological mapping from space showing ground water prospect areas which has improved the rate of success of finding underground water to 92 per cent compared to 45 per cent achieved using purely conventional methods. Models based on the area extent of seasonal snow fall have been developed to predict snow-melt runoff into the reservoirs. Identification of waterlogged pockets in the command areas of irrigation projects and inventory of crop lands and cropping patterns have facilitated efficient water use, thereby increasing the cropping intensity. Remote-sensing data are being extensively used to predict the acreage and yield of all major crops and also to identify degraded watersheds for initiating appropriate conservation measures for soil and water (Rao 1995c). Space imageries have fully established their ability for substantially improving the marine fish catch by identifying areas of rich fish shoals based on ocean temperatures and phytoplankton density measurements.

Doubling or in some cases tripling of food grain productivity is required to meet the basic minimal requirements of the projected population growth in many of the developing countries in Asia, Africa and Latin America. Even though the global cultivable land area can in principle be increased from the present 1,500 million ha to about 2,150 million ha through reclamation of culturable wasteland, the prospect of such increase is limited to less than 10 per cent, or about 60 million ha over the presently cultivated crop land of 820 million ha in Asian continent. Historically, it is recognised that increase in the area of cultivation in the recent past has in fact only contributed to less than 10 per cent increase in the food grain output. Even with the possible reclamation of about 25 million ha of wasteland and exploitation of the full irrigation potential by doubling the presently irrigated area of 40 million ha, the annual food grain output in India can at best be increased to 250 million tons as against the requirement of 450 million tons by 2050. Analysis by the world bank and FAO have clearly pointed out that countries like India and China cannot support beyond 1.5 times their present population (FAO 1988; Murai et al. 1990) using the present agricultural technology.

The challenge of providing adequate food security to the growing population can only be solved by achieving substantially higher yields through initiation of sustainable integrated development strategies. Significant advances in biotechnology have resulted in a variety of new genetic breeds, early maturing dwarf varieties of crops, pest-resistant hybrid varieties and suitable cultivation strategies. Combined with integrated pest management strategy, use of bio-pesticides and conservation of top soil and water resources, these biotechnological advances have led to a substantial increase in the genetic potential up to 8–10 t/ha under controlled conditions, which implies that achieving an average yield of 4–5 t/ha even in field conditions is well within our technological capability. Practical realisation on nationwide scales, however, must take into account the boundary conditions imposed by ecological, environmental, social and cultural factors in each country to ensure long-term sustainability. This requires a clear understanding of land capability, continuous monitoring and optimal management of natural resources, and use appropriate agricultural practices.

Sustainable development of natural resources is obviously dependent on maintaining the fragile balance between productivity functions and conservation practices through monitoring and identification of problem areas requiring application of energy intensive agricultural practices, crop rotation, bio-fertilisers and reclamation of underutilised lands. It calls for the integration of various renewable and non-renewable resources, characterisation of coherent zones of agricultural identities and identification of physical constraints as well as ecological problems at the micro-level of each watershed. Combining space derived vital inputs on soil characteristics, agricultural practices, underground and surface water resources, forest cover, environmental status and meteorological information with collateral data on socioeconomic factors it is possible to subdivide each watershed into 400–500 micro-level homogeneous units for identifying suitable conservation measures and appropriate biotechnological practices to significantly enhance the production on a sustainable basis (Figure 12). In the few selected watersheds where sustainable integrated development strategy has been implemented, as in the cases of drought prone districts of Anantapur and Ahmednagar in India, two healthy crops are now grown and the water table has gone up by almost 3–5 metres in the last three years as against non-availability of even drinking water in summer months (Rao 1995a; Rao, Chandrasekhar and Jayaraman 1995).

International Cooperation and Policy Issues

While the spectacular advances in science and technology and space technology in particular, can provide appropriate solutions to meet the basic requirements of all the nations, the success of meeting the global challenges of the next century clearly depends on the ability of both North and South in making wise choices concerning the future path of progress. Despite of the fact that space exploration, for the first time, has given us a new perspective of our own beautiful planet, true appreciation of this global view is yet to percolate into the conflicting minds concerned solely with immediate national interests and artificial geographical boundaries. The concept of oneness of humankind has been an integral part of the Indian heritage which was enunciated in our great epic Mahabharata:

> This is mine that is another's
> Such reckonings are for the narrow minded
> For the noble hearted
> The whole world is one family.

The last few decades of inadequate efforts to bridge the inequities between the developed and the developing societies have been primarily through aids and soft loans, largely due to moral dictates of guilt complex. It is essential that we clearly realise that the prevalent extensive deforestation, illiteracy, lack of basic resources such as food and water, non-availability of technological know-how will drive the developing world through the same suicidal pathway followed earlier by the developed world, in their anxiety to achieve rapid development. While the developed countries which have contributed maximally to the deterioration of the global environment in the past will discover alternate environment friendly technological solutions, rapid deterioration of the ecological state cannot be stopped unless such technologies are made available to the 75 per cent of the world's population. In other words, the betterment of human society as a whole has to be viewed as an implicit requirement for the very survival of this planet.

The emerging independent nations of the South, on the other hand, have to create a new social order which starts recognising that not only the quantitative transformation but the very survival of their society depends on the optimal utilisation of science and technology. The sociopolitical system in most of the developing countries, which is self-serving, near sighted and devoid of scientific temper, still regards science and technology only as an embroidery and not the main social fabric of their culture. There is an urgent need for the developing countries to replace the widespread political opportunism with a healthy scientific attitude and seriously tackle the problem of rapid rural development, eradication of illiteracy, establishment of basic communication infrastructure and industrialisation not through vote-catching, populist schemes but by purposeful, action-oriented approach. Accomplishment of these tasks needs the total involvement of highly skilled and fully committed scientists, massive education at the grassroot levels and widespread dissemination of scientific culture — in other words, the 'greening' of the human mind.

Despite of the creation of a conducive atmosphere for promotion of international cooperation with the end of the cold war, agreements reached during the Rio summit, general acceptance of Montreal Protocol for the preservation of the environment and signing of the GATT agreement, the technological gap between the developed and the developing nations is continuing to grow. While GATT has introduced a few concessions to the developing nations for a limited period of time to enable them to compete in the global market place on equal footing, the possibility of invoking highly subjective criteria to apply trade sanctions and restrictions on newly industrialised countries continues to pose a threat to the third world nations. Even the so called free market trade in reality has been adroitly used for commercial exploitation. Exploitation of global market by fixing prices based on opportunity cost and not on production economics, till the competition builds up has been followed throughout history while at the same time propagating ethical approaches to market demand. Instead of providing preferential access to developing countries for selling their products and services in the global market, attempts are made to restrict the competition in the name of fair geographical returns policy, application of quota system and equally dubious arguments based on level playing field and human rights (Rao 1995a).

Security concerns as perceived by developed nations have greatly influenced the level and nature of international cooperation. One of the major regimes impinging on the transfer of components, equipment, information and technologies particularly related to space programs is the Missile Technology Control Regime (MTCR). Although at the beginning, MTCR had the laudable objective of restricting the proliferation of only missile related technologies and not peaceful space programs, slowly over the years, high technology components and equipment required even for peaceful programs have been denied as a part of the implementation strategy. The release of the same components for sale immediately after such components are either indigenously developed or become available from alternate sources has left a strong impression that such technology regimes have been turned into a strong weapon in the armour of the developed countries for commercial and political gains. Philosophical statements, such as 'if we are to lead the world towards a hopeful future, we must understand that technology is part of the planetary environment, to be shared like air and water with the rest of the mankind', are pronounced in every conceivable international forum. The reality, however, is that science and technology has become the most powerful currency of power, monopolised and zealously guarded by a minority of few advanced nations, who have employed technological hegemonism — as a means of influencing and controlling the developing world.

The key to the development of a proper strategy for survival clearly depends on achieving integrated sustainable development through both national and international cooperation. It calls for the initiation of a new sustainable green revolution, taking into account the lessons learnt from past experience, to meet the basic needs of the present and future generations through adoption of environment friendly scientific and technological approach aimed at achieving rapid progress without sacrificing the 'owl'. As beautifully summarised at the 1992 Rio Summit (UN 1992):

> Humanity stands at a defining moment in history. We are confronted with a perpetuation of disparities between and within nations, a worsening of poverty, hunger, ill health and illiteracy, and the continuing deterioration of the eco-systems on which we depend for our wellbeing. However, integration of environment and development concerns and greater attention to them will lead to the fulfillment of basic needs, improved living standard for all, better protected and managed eco-systems and a safe, more prosperous future. No nation can achieve this on its own; but together we can in a global partnership for sustainable development.

Conclusion

Interconnectivity of both natural and anthropogenic phenomena occurring anywhere on the earth, through weather, climate, geosphere and biosphere have inextricably linked the fate of each country with that of the world as a whole. The fact that the increase in green house gases, deforestation and depletion of ozone result in global warming affecting the entire global climate, disturbances in El Niño and ENSO off the coast of Peru can result in severe drought across Asia, Australia and Africa, or volcanic eruptions and industrial activity can change pattern of rain precipitation across the world clearly emphasise the necessity to take a global view for the survival of humankind, as a whole.

The fundamental aspect of long-term sustainable development strategy is based on the paradigm of technological innovations, economic determinism and physical constraints arising out of the need to strike a judicious balance between ultimate exploitability and regenerative capacity. This essentially means that all nations must think globally and act locally, because the survival of the planet as a whole depends on the restoration of equity and assurance of minimal needs to all the people in the world. With his remarkable insight, President Kennedy stated over 30 years ago that:

> Never before has man had such capacity to control his own environment, to end thirst and hunger, to conquer poverty and disease, to banish illiteracy and massive human misery. We have the power to make this the best generation of mankind or to make it the last.

We hope that the human kind will have the wisdom to choose the former and strive ceaselessly towards achieving sustainable integrated development of our planet as a whole to enable all peoples of the world, both in the developed and the developing countries, to live a reasonably good quality of life. It is only then we can make Isiah's prophecy come true that

> The desert shall rejoice
> and blossom as the rose…
> The parched ground shall become a pool
> and the thirsty land springs of water.

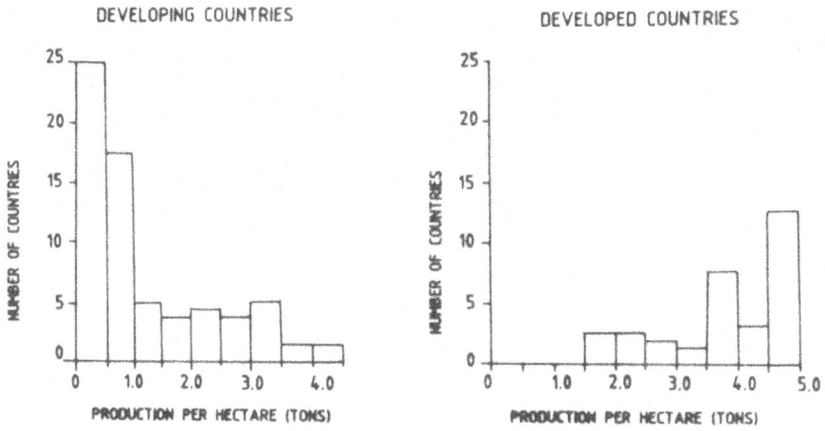

Figure 1: Foodgrain productivity in developed and developing countries

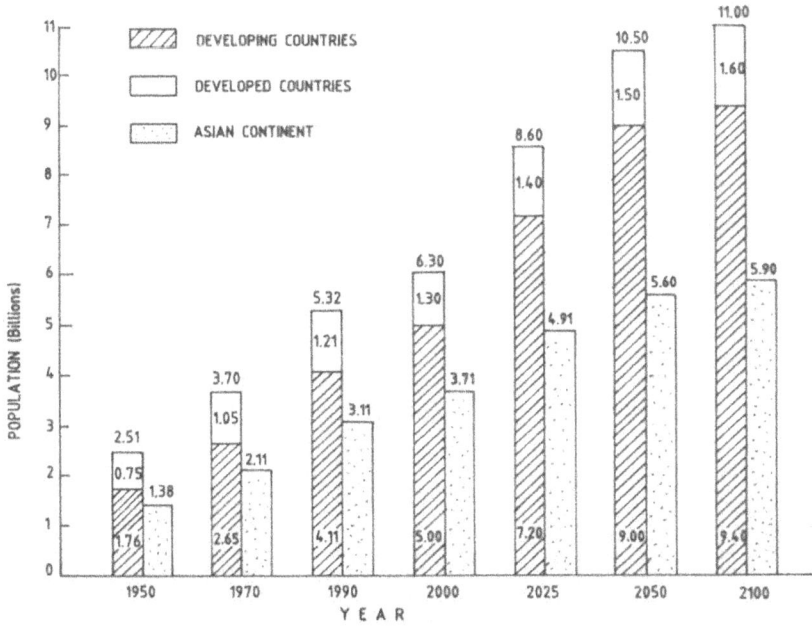

Figure 2: Growth of population in the developed and developing countries of the world

39

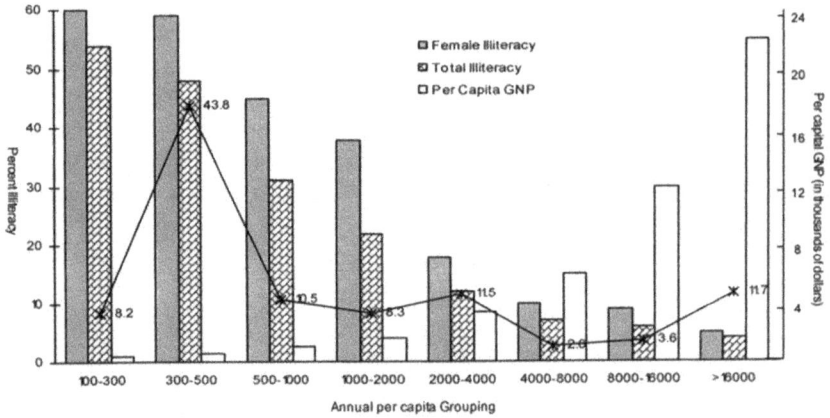

Figure 3: Literacy and per capital GNP (the numbers in the diagram indicate the per cent global population under each grouping)

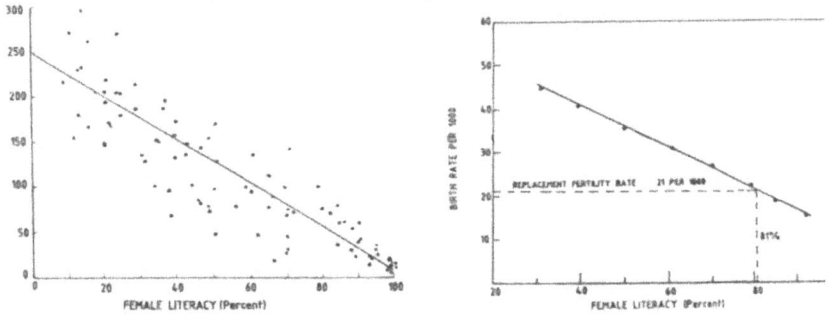

Figure 4: Relation between female literacy and fertility rate and mortality rate

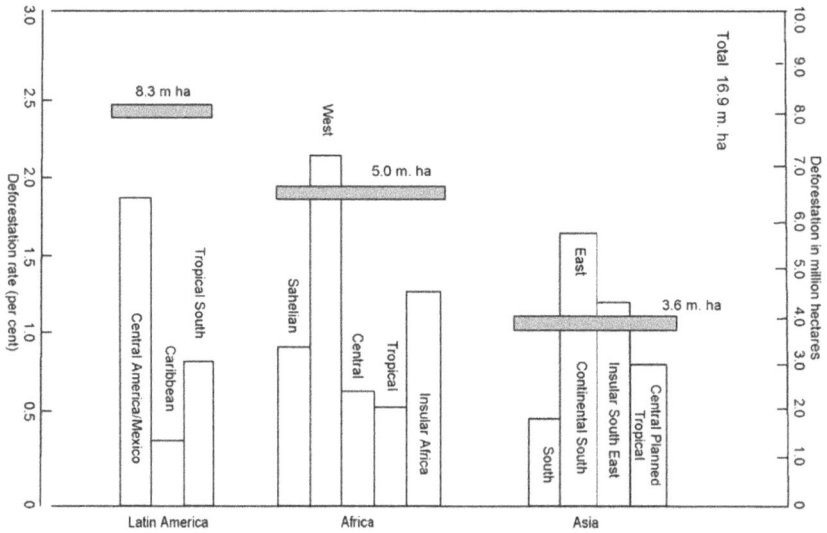

Figure 5: Annual deforestation in the tropical region (1981–90)

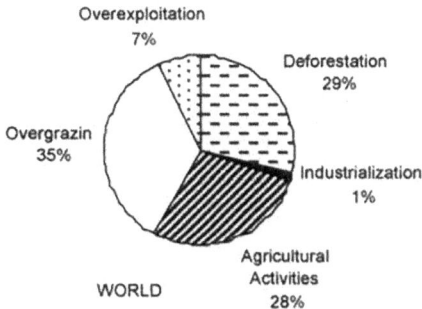

(total degraded land: 1.2 billion hectares)

Causes of land degradation	Per cent of total degraded land						
	Asia	Africa	North America	South America	Central America	Europe	Oceania
Deforestation	40	14	0	41	22	38	12
Industrialisation	1	0	0	0	0	9	0
Agricultural activities	27	24	66	26	45	29	8
Overgrazing	26	49	30	28	15	23	80
Overexploitation	6	13	4	5	18	0	0

Figure 6: Causes of land degradation in past 45 years

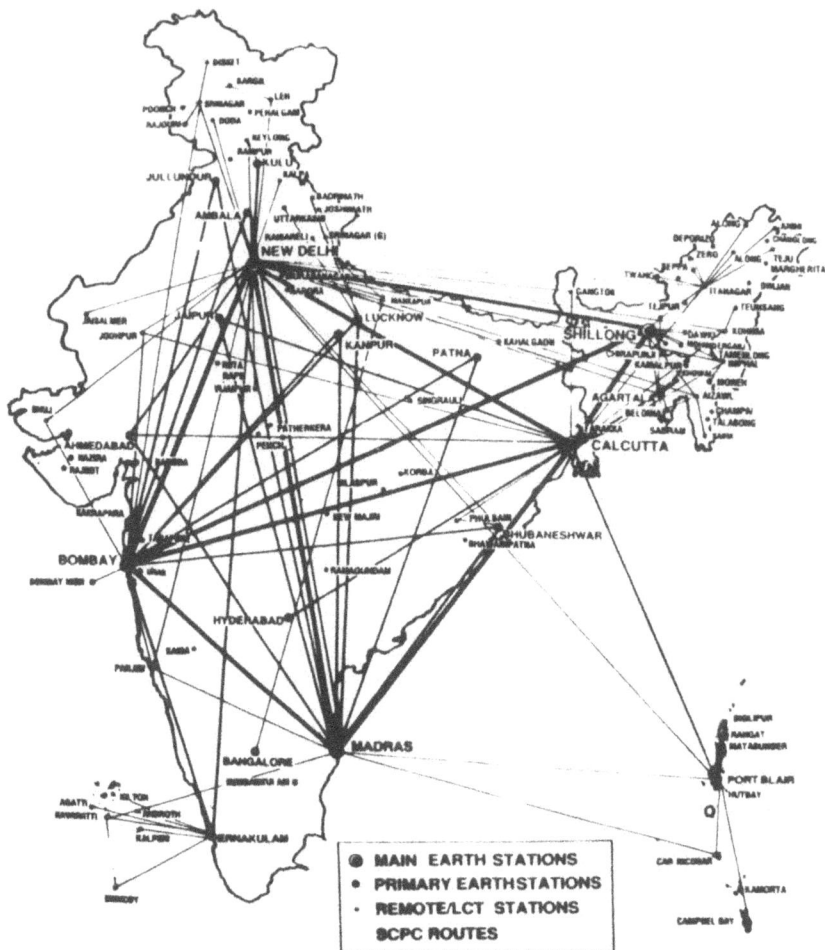

Figure 7: Satellite telecommunications in India

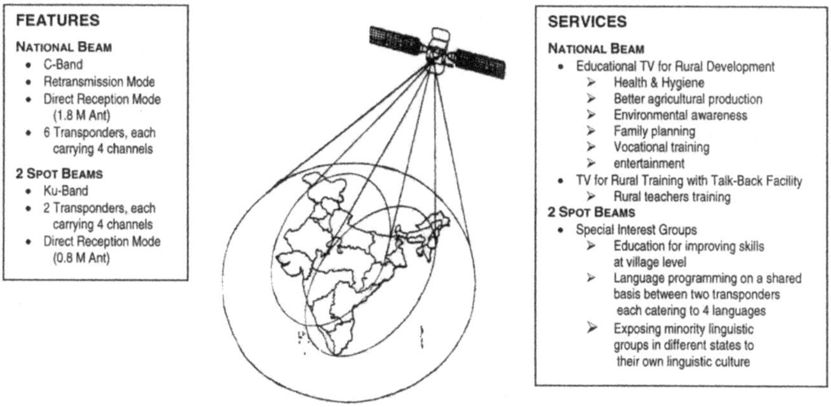
FEATURES
NATIONAL BEAM
• C-Band
• Retransmission Mode
• Direct Reception Mode (1.8 M Ant)
• 6 Transponders, each carrying 4 channels
2 SPOT BEAMS
• Ku-Band
• 2 Transponders, each carrying 4 channels
• Direct Reception Mode (0.8 M Ant)
SERVICES
NATIONAL BEAM
• Educational TV for Rural Development
➢ Health & Hygiene
➢ Better agricultural production
➢ Environmental awareness
➢ Family planning
➢ Vocational training
➢ entertainment
• TV for Rural Training with Talk-Back Facility
➢ Rural teachers training
2 SPOT BEAMS
• Special Interest Groups
➢ Education for improving skills at village level
➢ Language programming on a shared basis between two transponders each catering to 4 languages
➢ Exposing minority linguistic groups in different states to their own linguistic culture

Figure 8: Gramsat (concept)

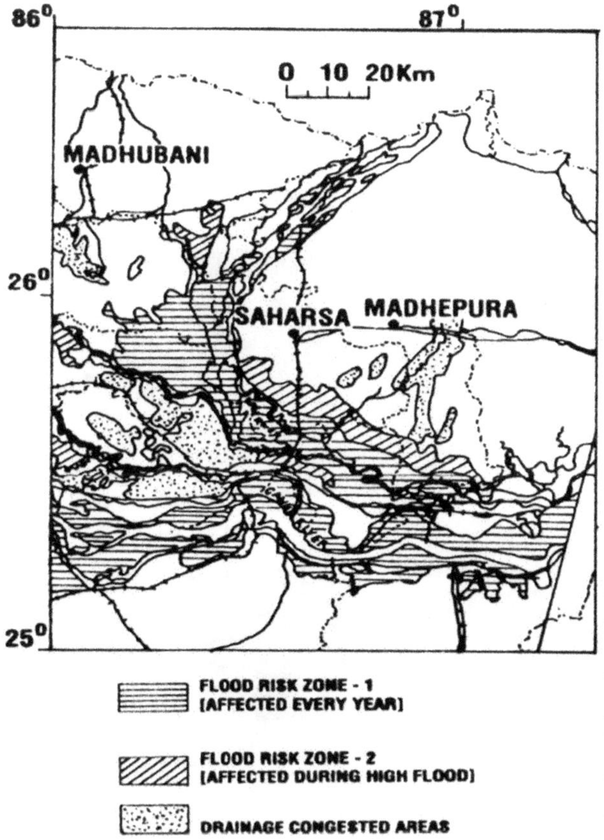
86°
87°
0 10 20Km
MADHUBANI
26°
SAHARSA
MADHEPURA
25°
FLOOD RISK ZONE - 1
(AFFECTED EVERY YEAR)
FLOOD RISK ZONE - 2
(AFFECTED DURING HIGH FLOOD)
DRAINAGE CONGESTED AREAS

Figure 9: Flood risk zone map of part of Ganga basin

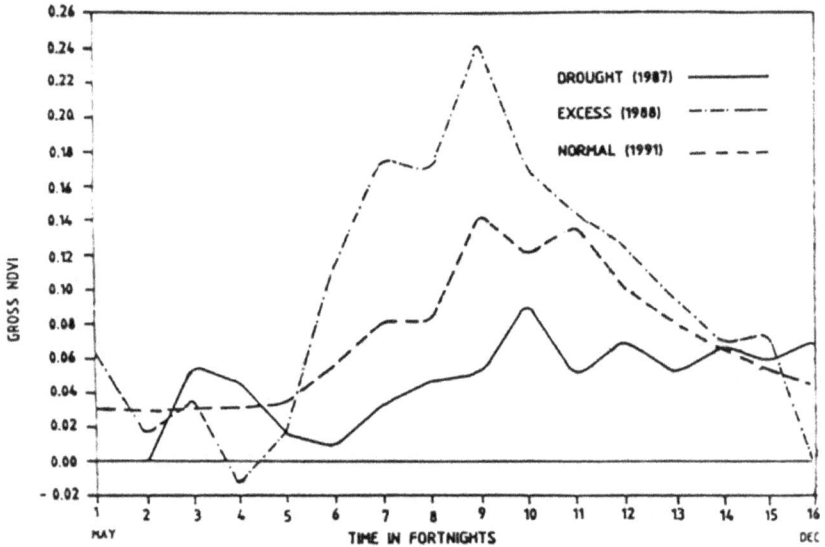

Figure 10: NDVI indicating seasonal vegetation conditions (Bhiwani district, India)

GENERAL LAND USE

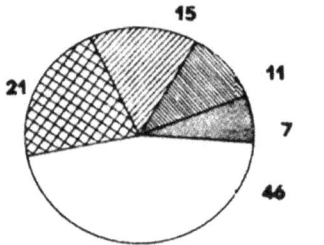

330 Mha

☐ NET SOWN AREA
▨ FOREST
▨ NON-AGRICULTURE
▨ UNCULTIVATED
▨ FALLOW LAND

WASTELAND CATEGORIES

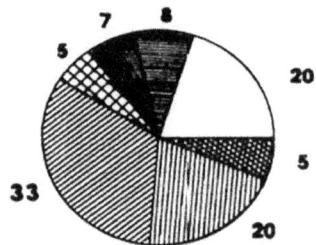

53.3 Mha

RECLAIMABLE
☐ UPLAND
■ GULLIED
■ SALINE
▨ JHUM
NON-RECLAIMABLE
▨ SNOW
▦ SANDY
■ BARREN/ROCKY

Figure 11: Typical land-use pattern in a developing country — India

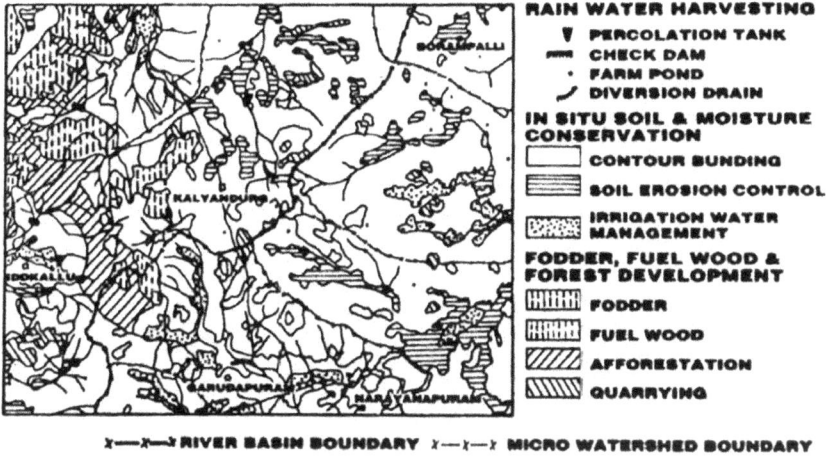

Figure 12a: Resources management at micro-level of sustainable development — Drought-prone area

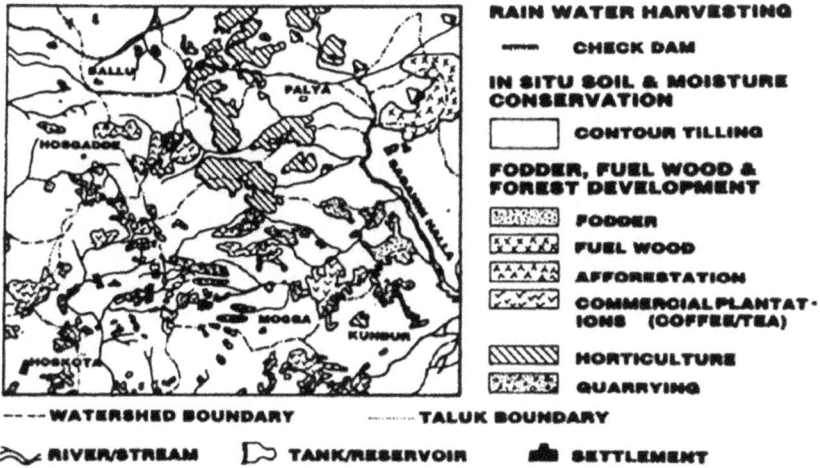

Figure 12b: Resources management at micro-level of sustainable development — Hill area

References

Brown, L. (ed.) (1992), *State of the World*, W.W. Norton & Co., New York.

FAO (Food and Agricultural Organization) (1988), *World Agriculture, Towards 2000*, FAP Report, Rome.

Gao, F. and Rao, U.R. (eds) (1992), *Space and Education in Developing Countries*, Proceedings of 43rd IAF Congress, Washington DC.

Heath, G. (ed.) (1994), *Space Safety and Rescue,* Science and Technology Series, Vol. 84, American Astronautical Society, Washington.

Khoshoo T.N. (1990), *Indian Geosphere-Biosphere*, in T.N. Khoshoo and M. Sharma (eds), Proceedings of National Academy of Sciences, 178.

Liu, D. (ed.) (1994), *Satellite Communication for Mass Education*, Proceedings of 45th IAF Congress, Jerusalem.

Murai, S., et al. (1990), 'What Population Can the Earth Feed', Report, Mitsubishi Research Institute, Japan.

Pant, N. (1994), 'Satellite Communication Technology and Application, 1995–2010', *Journal of Spacecraft Technology*, 4(1).

Ramanathan V., et al. (1985), 'Trace Gas Trends and Their Potential in Climate Change', *Journal of Geophysical Research*, 90, 5547.

Rao, U.R. (1987), *Perspectives in Communication*, Vol. 2, World Scientific Publishing Company, Singapore, 1422.

Rao, U.R. (ed.) (1988), *Space and Humanity*, Proceedings of 39th IAF Congress, Bangalore, India.

Rao, U.R. (1991), 'Remote Sensing for Sustainable Development', Vikram Sarabhai Memorial Lecture, Anna University Madras, India.

Rao, U.R. (1993), 'Space Technology for Achieving Socio-Economic Revolution', 29th Sri Ram Memorial Lecture, Sri Ram Institute for Industrial Research, New Delhi.

Rao, U.R. (1995a), *Space Technology for Sustainable Development*, Tata McGraw Hill, New Delhi.

Rao, U.R. (1995b), *Satellite Communication in India — Past, Present and Future*, Proceedings of SATCOM ASIA 1995 Conference, Hong Kong.

Rao, U.R. (1995c), 'Space Technology for Enhancing Sustainable Carrying Capacity', Zaheer Hussain Memorial Lecture, Zaher Hussein Foundation, New Delhi.

Rao, U.R., et al. (1987), *Earth Safety and Disaster Response Employing Space Borne Systems*, Proceedings of 38th IAF Congress, Brighton, UK.

Rao, U.R., Chandrasekhar, M.G. and Jayaraman, V. (1995), *Space and Agenda 21 — Caring for the Planet Earth*, Prism Books, Bangalore, India.

Swaminathan, M.S. (1980), *Perspectives in World Agriculture*, CAB.

United Nations (UN) (1992), *Proceedings of UN Conference on Environment and Development*, Rio De Janerio, Brazil.

United Nations (UN) (1994), *World Population Projections*, United Nations, New York.

World Bank (1993), *The East Asian Miracle*, World Bank Policy Research Report, Oxford University Press, New York.

World Bank (1994), *World Development Report 1994*, Oxford University Press, New York.

World Commission on Environment (1987), *Our Common Future*, Report of World Commission on Environment and Development, Oxford University Press, New York.

World Resources Institute (1992), *Report of World Resources Institute*, Oxford University Press, New York.

Oration 3:
1996 K.R. Narayanan Oration

Message from the Vice-President
of the Republic of India

I am happy to see that the Australia South Asia Research Centre inaugurated during my official visit to Australia in 1994 has maintained lively and meaningful contacts with the region and continued the intellectual exploration of its developmental problems. The K.R. Narayanan Oration has become an annual event eagerly looked forward to by the academic community.

I am glad to learn that the third lecture in the series is being given by the reputed economist Professor Jagdish Bhagwati. Professor Bhagwati is an economist who has made distinctly original contributions to the study and understanding of contemporary Indian and international economic problems. It is of special importance that he is delivering the lecture in the context of the annual Australian Conference of Economists and as a prelude to the *Australia India — New Horizons* event sponsored by the Government of Australia and scheduled to take place in India later this year. The subject-matter of his lecture: 'India: Retrospect and Prospect' is particularly relevant today when India is entering the fiftieth anniversary of its independence.

Compared to the immense needs of the country and the kind of progress made by the Asian Tigers, India's achievements during the last 50 years might look unspectacular. But the progress made has been steady and all-round, making it possible for the country to move forward rapidly into the future on foundations that are firm and maintaining stability and balance for a vast pluralist society marked by uneven development and baffling social problems.

The most remarkable fact that stands out prominently is that India has developed a democratic system of government that has faced several social, economic, political and security crises during the last five decades, and emerged successful and stronger out of them. In the economic field an achievement of fundamental significance was what has been called the Green Revolution. The magnitude of it can be realised when one recalls the succession of famines that devastated the country before independence and the major famines some of the developing countries had gone through not very long ago. But it has to be recognised that poverty is still with us and that the number of people living below the poverty level is unacceptably high. So is the level of illiteracy in the country. In the world index of human development, India occupies a low position. However, the rise in the average expectation of life from 27 years in 1947 to 60 years today is striking and is the outcome of the slow but steady progress in economic conditions and human development factors. In my state of Kerala, which population-wise is equal to two Australias, the index of human development is more or less the same as that of several advanced developed countries with average expectation of life at 71, literacy level at 100 per cent, infantile mortality rate at 13 per thousand and population growth rate at 1.3 per cent. This is an indication that it might not be impossible for the rest of India also to achieve similar levels of success with proper policies and proper implementation of policies and programs.

The biggest event happening in India since 1991 has been the massive process of economic reforms with liberalisation and restructuring of the economy and its opening up to the rest of the world. Though in the circumstances of India some caution may have to be observed in regard to speed of liberalisation. It has already led to results that are sizeable and significant. In spite of the daunting nature of the tasks facing Indian development, I should venture to be optimistic about the prospects before India. I would personally look forward to Professor Jagdish Bhagwati's analysis and forecasts in regard to this important issue. I am sure that his Lecture would be a stimulating and rewarding intellectual experience.

K.R. Narayanan
New Delhi 1996

India: Retrospect and Prospect

Jagdish Bhagwati

At the outset, I must thank you for the great honour that you have extended to me by inviting me to give the K.R. Narayanan Oration. The honour is twofold.

Vice President Narayanan, whom I have the privilege of knowing well, is a man of great courtesy, charm, acuteness of intellect, and accomplishment. I believe that men and women matter. They defy the tenets of historical determinism, shaping instead of bending to history. They lead themselves, and their nations, to what Prime Minister Jawaharlal Nehru, a great and moving orator, called their 'tryst with destiny'. Dr Narayanan is one of them. But, let me assure the economists assembled here, he is also a man of impeccable taste: he studied economics and even enjoys the dismal science!

And that brings me to the other reason why I am flattered by your invitation today. Australia is in the memories of every Indian of my generation, of course. Many were the days when we ran truant from our school to watch the Indian cricketers locked in combat with the visiting Australians, fascinated in particular by the incredible speed of Lindwall and Miller as they terrified our batsmen: those were the days of exhilarating five-day Test Matches between Cricket *Teams*, not the fast-track deviants now played between *Squads*! And Don Bradman was to us, as to you, a legend.

But as I grew older, and my tastes turned to Economics, and within that to International Economics, I also realised that Australia had produced many of the best international economists in the world: Murray Kemp, Max Corden, Trevor Swan, Ross Garnaut and Heinz Arndt among them.

For me to come to Australia finally is to come therefore, not just to the country of the irresistible koala, of the exotic kangaroo, of genius in cricket and tennis, of *Breaker Morant* and a wonderful cinema, and of a literature crowned by the Nobel Prize, but also to a great scholarly tradition in the subject closest to my heart. But that is not all. Mr Vice-Chancellor, I must add that your world-renowned university has housed many of the splendid economists that Australia has produced: there could then be no better place for me to be giving this Oration than right here!

Indeed, Mr Vice-Chancellor, I would be remiss if, on an occasion that celebrates the growing friendship between our two countries, I did not also recall the fact that I first met Trevor Swan of your university, a venerated figure among Australian and indeed all economists, in India in 1958, I believe. He had come as part of an advisory team of eminent economists that included Ian Little of Oxford and was led by Paul Rosenstein-Rodan of MIT, a great development economist. Swan had come with enthusiasm, eager to put his expert Australian shoulder to the wheel in India's developmental efforts.

Mr Vice-Chancellor, I must entertain you by recalling the contrasting story of the *reluctant* economic adviser that the Nobel laureate, Princeton economist Arthur Lewis regaled his friends with. Once he found himself invited to a fundraising luncheon by the Princeton University President for the Iranian Ambassador in Washington, a man known only to those who read the Style sections of the newspapers because he used the sudden oil wealth of his nation to entertain flamboyantly the likes of Elizabeth Taylor. So, Lewis was minding his manners and quietly getting through the lunch when he was suddenly startled to hear the President promising the Ambassador: 'We would be happy to send Professor Lewis to Iran to help you with planning your development'. As he walked back morose from the luncheon, Lewis ran into the sociologist Marion Levy, a man of some wit, who asked him what the matter was. When Lewis told him, Levy said: 'Arthur, you should have told the President that Professors can be bought, but not sold.'

As it happens, Trevor Swan's early visit to India provides me with the main theme of the Oration today: the reasons why India's monumental developmental efforts went astray and why, for the very same reasons, the current reforms hold great promise. Swan came to India at a time, in the early 1960s, when India's developmental efforts were attracting attention worldwide. And the attention and interest were equally from economists.

To understand this, and also to put the subsequent disenchantment into perspective, let me explain why what we were doing in India through the 1950s was sensible *and* worthy of the huge interest everywhere.

India in the 1950s: On Track, Phase I

At her independence in 1947, India already had a fair degree of industrialisation under her belt. Textiles and steel were among the many industries that had come up exclusively from market forces and with domestic investment, under a colonial government that certainly had not seen itself as a developmental agency and had therefore virtually abstained from 'infant industry' protection or promotion. India also enjoyed the presence of an active entrepreneurial class and a modest but definite integration into the world economy. The country was also endowed with a first-rate civil service and administrative structure, world-class leaders and a democratic form of government.

But the poverty was huge, with corresponding standards of living appalling for many, the literacy levels were abysmal even as the higher levels of education were impressive, and the challenge to the new government was clearly immense.

The *key strategy* that defined the resulting developmental effort was the decision to target efforts at accelerating the growth rate. Given the immensity of the poverty, simple redistribution was considered to be both negligible in its immediate impact and of little sustained value. The central anti-poverty strategy had therefore to be the creation of increasing numbers of jobs that would draw ever more of the underemployed and unemployed into gainful employment that would yield them both greater incomes and higher standards of living. Accelerated growth was thus regarded as an instrumental variable, a policy outcome that would in turn reduce poverty, the latter being the true objective of our efforts.

I have often reminded the critics of Indian strategy, who attack it from the perspective of poverty which is juxtaposed against growth, that it is incorrect to think that the Indian planners got it wrong by going for growth rather than attacking poverty: they confuse means with ends. In fact, the phrase 'minimum income' and the aim of providing it to India's poor were very much part of the lexicon and at the heart of our thinking and analysis when I worked in the Indian Planning Commission in the early 1960s.

Equally, the populist notion that pushing growth to kill poverty is a passive and conservative 'trickle-down' strategy is wholly obtuse. In the Indian context, it was an active and radical, what I have called 'pull-up' strategy. Nor were we unmindful that added policy instruments were necessary to ensure that the growth process would indeed extend to all groups. For instance, just as the United States has a 'structural' inner-city problem, we have (among others) a 'tribal' problem: each underprivileged group fails to have equal and ready access to the mainstream economy. Nor were social expenditures relegated to oblivion. The first Five-Year Plan itself had addressed this matter, and the Planning Commission had at the time a distinguished social worker, Mrs Durgabai Deshmukh, as a member who formidably minded her portfolio on the social questions.

But substantial and expanding sums could not be spent on the social questions and on the improvement of the ability of the underprivileged to access the growing mainstream economy *unless* you had growth in the first place. Spending on education and on public health, chief among our concerns, could not be expanded or even sustained unless a growing economy produced the added revenues to finance these and other expenditures.

To those who use the cliche of 'development with a human face', I respond:

> Yes, indeed. But remember that the face cannot exist by itself, except as a mask in a museum, but must be joined to the body; and if the body is emaciated, the face must wither no matter how much we seek to humanise and pretty it up.

So, we return to growth as the centrepiece of the Indian strategy for assaulting poverty and providing minimum incomes to the poor. And we must remember that it was the government's task to accelerate economic growth. I believe that we could say, in a stylised way but with plausibility, that the central conception underlying India's growth-accelerating strategy was the devising of a planning framework that would produce the enhanced investment rates. Thus, the objective was to jolt the economy up into a higher-investment mode that would generate, say, a 5 per cent growth rate as against the conventional lower-investment equilibrium with a 2 to 2.5 per cent growth rate.

The planning framework then rested on two legs. First, it sought to make the escalated growth credible to private investors so that they would proceed to invest on an enhanced basis in a self-fulfilling prophecy. Second, it aimed at generating the added savings to finance the investments so induced.

The Five-Year Plan framework was an important aspect of this two-pronged policy. Simply by demonstrating that the government was committed to a higher growth rate, it assured potential investors that demand would grow at higher rates and that the risk of investment would be correspondingly reduced. Besides, at the core of the plan there was commitment to substantial governmental spending, mostly on infrastructure, that added yet greater credibility to the high-growth scenario in what was otherwise an 'indicative' plan in terms of its investment profile. Moreover, the commitment to use fiscal policy to raise public savings to levels necessary to finance the projected growth of investment was also a credibility-enhancing factor for bringing about the enhanced investment.

The bulk of the 1950s can then be called the favourable Phase I of Indian developmental effort; and it broadly coincides, in approach, to much of the East Asian experience where, however, the Five-Year Plan framework was not utilised. The governmental intervention, as described, led to an investment boom and hence to an enhanced growth. I may, in fact, recharacterise what happened, in more familiar technical terms, by reference to the Rosenstein-Rodan argument that has now been formalised by Vishny and Shleifer in their fine article in the *Journal of Political Economy* as a case of multiple equilibria.[1] In his classic 1943 *Economic Journal* article,[2] which is arguably the most beautiful piece of creative writing on development, Rosenstein-Rodan was basically arguing that, for developing countries stuck in a Nash equilibrium with low levels of investment, there existed a superior cooperative equilibrium with higher levels of investment and growth.

The Indian planners, in formulating the first Five-Year Plan (1951–56), were essentially exploiting this insight. This was an indicative plan, without the straitjacket of controls and targeted allocations that would presumably reflect the contours of the superior equilibrium. In fact, it is absurd to

---

1   Andrei Shleifer and Robert W. Vishny (1988), 'The Efficiency of Investment in the Presence of Aggregate Demand Spillovers', *Journal of Political Economy*, 96(6): 1221–31.
2   P.N. Rosenstein-Rodan (1943), 'Problems of Industrialisation of Eastern and Southern-Eastern Europe', *The Economic Journal*, 53(210–211): 202–211.

imagine that anyone, either in India or in East Asia, could have worked out such a Rosenstein-Rodan–Vishny–Shleifer equilibrium even if there had been complete information to do so! What did happen instead was that, as I already suggested, the large component of public spending on infrastructure which was built into these indicative programs made the government's commitment to kicking the system up into some bastardised version of the Rosenstein-Rodan–Vishny–Shleifer equilibrium quite credible to the private sector, triggering the self-fulfilling private sector investment response that lifted the economy into higher investment and growth rates.[3]

What Went Wrong: Derailing after the 1950s, Phase II

What went wrong with India, and was still not entirely manifest when Swan arrived in India, can be characterised by contrasting India with East Asia once we go beyond the 1950s. In fact, by understanding better why East Asia went ahead to build greater success post-1950s helps us to understand why India went ahead to decline instead in her economic performance: hence, I will focus on East Asia's success and its causes for now.

Let me begin by observing that, in my judgement, the critical difference was that India turned to the IS (import substitution) strategy and East Asia to the EP (export promotion) strategy. A central implication, which I have not drawn sharply in my earlier writings (which have focused, not on the inducement to invest, but rather on the social returns from investment) is that India, during this Phase II, handicapped the private inducement to invest, while East Asia wound up enhancing it.

---

3   Dani Rodrik seems to share broadly this view of how private investment rose but seems to err in two ways. He seems to suggest, presumably in sympathy with the Amsden–Wade thinking, that the bureaucrats could figure out the sectoral contours of the superior equilibrium, a presumption that I find ludicrous especially having seen the best bureaucrats in India confess to their inability to choose industrial favourites on any rational grounds. Moreover, he extends the argument well beyond the 1950s whereas, as I argue later in the text, this makes little sense. See Dani Rodrik (1995), 'Getting Interventions Right: How Over the Home Markets South Korea and Taiwan Grew Rich' *Economic Policy*, 10(20): 53–107.

India turned inwards, starting with a balance of payments crisis in 1956–57 which precipitated the imposition of exchange controls which then became endemic to the regime, reflecting the currency overvaluation that implies the effective pursuit of an IS strategy. Again, the explicit pursuit of an IS strategy was also desired, reflecting the economic logic of elasticity pessimism that characterised the thinking of India's planners.

The result was that the inducement to invest in the economy was constrained by the growth of demand from the agricultural sector, reflecting in turn the growth of that sector. But agriculture has grown almost nowhere by more than 4 per cent per annum over a sustained period of over a decade, so that the increment at the margin in India's private investment rate was badly constrained by the fact that it was cut off from the elastic world markets and forced to depend on inevitably sluggish domestic agricultural expansion. Thus, it became customary for Indian economists to talk about 'balanced growth' and about the problem of raising the investment rate which, by the mid-1980s, was still in the range of 19–20 per cent.

By contrast, the East Asian investment rate began its take-off to phenomenal levels because East Asia turned to the EP strategy. The elimination of the 'bias against exports', and indeed a net (if mild) excess of the effective exchange rate for exports over the effective exchange rate for imports (signifying the relative profitability of the foreign over the home market), ensured that the world markets were profitable to aim for, assuring in turn that the inducement to invest was no longer constrained by the growth of the domestic market as in the IS strategy. Private domestic savings were either raised to match the increased private investment by policy deliberately encouraging them or by the sheer prospect of higher returns.

This argumentation is not easy to defend once you face up to what my student Don Davis, now at Harvard, has called the 'tyranny of the Stolper-Samuelson': for, when this theorem holds, wages and rentals on capital are inversely related.[4] When exports are the labour-intensive, the EP strategy may be expected to raise the wage of labour but depress the return to capital, thus depressing, not raising, the inducement to invest. Clearly,

---

4   I am drawing here on the preliminary draft of Don Davis's paper, 'Miracles of Accumulation: Models of Trade and Growth in East Asia' (mimeo), Department of Economics, Harvard University, January 1996.

therefore, the force of Stolper-Samuelson argument must be broken: as indeed it can be by relaxing one or more of the assumptions underlying that theorem.

Thus, Davis suggests that the forces of comparative advantage may be argued to have been sufficiently strong as to make East Asia specialise in the production of the labour-intensive goods. This

> decouples factor returns from the factor price frontier for the capital intensive good, leaving wages and rentals dependent only on productivity in the labor intensive good and the price of that good. In moving from autarky to free trade, both factor prices can rise, inducing an accumulation 'miracle'.

Another way out would be to assume productivity differences across countries, as in Ricardian theory. In this case:

> if we assume that the relative productivity gap of East Asia relative to the rest of the world is largest in the capital intensive sectors, and that trade serves to close this gap, then it is again possible for both wages and rentals to rise.[5]

While therefore it is possible to formalise the argument I have made that the EP strategy increased the inducement to invest, I must also address Dani Rodrik's recent objection that exports were a relatively small part of the economy at the outset so that EP strategy could not have resulted in any significant impact, and therefore the source of the investment must be found in governmental subventions and interventions whereas the growth of trade is simply a *passive* result of the growth induced by these other factors. This argument is unpersuasive because East Asia would have run into precisely the problem of demand constraint that India was afflicted with if an IS strategy had been followed, with the efficacy of these other policies in generating investment seriously impaired. Moreover, the ultra-EP strategy, with its mild bias in favour of the export market and the policy-backed ethos of getting into world markets, meant that export incentives must have played a major role in influencing investment decisions, not just in the exporting industries, but also in the much larger

---

5   Ibid., p. 2. Davis proceeds to formalise these ideas in a dynamic framework, more appropriate to the accumulation problem at hand.

range of non-traded but tradeable industries.[6] In any event, the growth of exports from East Asia was so phenomenal that the share of initial exports in GNP quickly rose to levels that would lay Rodrik's objection to rest, even if it were conceptually correct.

The flip side of the process was, of course, the generation of substantial export earnings that enabled the growing investment to be implemented by *imports of equipment embodying new technical change.*

Now, if the social marginal product (SMP) of this equipment exceeded the cost of its importation, there would be a 'surplus' that would accrue as an income gain to East Asia and would also, as I argue below, boost the growth rate. For this argument to hold, however, the international cost of the newer-vintage equipment must not reflect fully its SMP for East Asia. In a competitive international market for equipment, therefore, I must assume that East Asia was a small player whose higher SMP did not pull up the world price to reflect the higher SMP — i.e. that East Asia could, even without 'piracy' and 'theft' of intellectual property (which was widespread in the region until the new WTO regime), get embodied technology at bargain prices. This seems a reasonable assumption to make, especially when one sees that the world prices of the last-but-one vintage equipment fall drastically due to rapid obsolescence in the presence of quick product innovation: just think of your PCs. (To understand fully the foregoing point, note that an economy in 1970 such as Soviet Russia's which was confined to using its own 1930s-vintage technology in equipment would *not* lose to East Asia which could use a heuristically 20 times more productive 1960s technology if East Asia had to pay a 20 times greater price for it. The surplus arises because East Asia pays, say, only a five times greater price in world markets for equipment that is 20 times more productive in East Asia.)

---

6   Rodrik (op. cit.) also seems to think it pertinent that the export incentive, in the shape of the real exchange rate, did not continue improving. However, it is not necessary for it to be improving continuously for the export incentives to operate. Thus, an excess of the effective exchange rate for exportables over that for importables (as distinct from continuous increase in this difference) will suffice to provide a continuing incentive for the export Martin Wolf has also critiqued Rodrik's anti-EP-strategy argumentation, as also the Krugman argumentation, in two excellent recent columns in the *Financial Times,* 'The Tyranny of Numbers' and 'A Lesson for the Chinese'.

This argument is illustrated in Figure 1 in a simple diagram, with the SMP curve for increasing imports of the vintage capital equipment for East Asia put against the international cost of importing it, the striped area then representing the surplus that accrues to East Asia.

But there may also be another reservation about this argument's effect on the growth rate, as distinct from its effect on income. It is fair to say that, thanks to the focus on the steady state in Solow-type models, it has now become fashionable to assert that the gains from trade, like any allocative efficiency gains, amount to one-time gains, not affecting the growth rate. This is, however, wrong-headed as a general assertion. Thus, consider the simple Harrod–Domar corn-producing-corn growth model with labour a slack variable. If allocative efficiency regarding land use (say, from one inefficient farm to another efficient farm) leads to a greater return to the total amount of ('invested') corn being put into the ground, the marginal capital-output ratio will fall, *ceteris paribus*, and will lead to a permanently higher growth rate. Similarly, it takes no sweat for a first-rate theorist to construct models where trade in capital goods leads to higher growth rates, without building in externalities, etc. and relying exclusively on the fact that they can be imported more cheaply than constructed under autarky.

Thus, T.N. Srinivasan has extended the Mahalanobis-type putty-clay model to include trade and demonstrated precisely this.[7] Thus, he assumes (in place of just one capital and one consumer good in the autarkic version) that there are two of each class of goods, with the marginal product of capital constant in each sector as in the Harrod–Domar model. The social utility function and the function that transforms the output of the two investment goods into aggregate investment are Cobb–Douglas. There is no inter-sectoral (i.e. between the consumer goods and the capital goods sectors), as against intra-sectoral (i.e. between the two goods in each sector), mobility of capital: this is the clay assumption.

---

7   See his comment on 'Two Strategies for Economic Development: Using Ideas and Producing Ideas', by Romer, *Proceedings of the World Bank Annual Conference on Development Economics 1992*, World Bank, Washington DC, 1993. Srinivasan also makes the valid point that the Mahalanobis–Feldman putty-clay models are among the earlier examples of 'endogenous' growth theory since the growth rate is determined by the discretionary policy choice of the share of investment goods being allocated to the capital goods sector. The neglect of the considerable literature on such models by the originators of the current endogenous growth theorists is to be attributed to the fact that these theorists have come to their models from the Solow model and have no acquaintance with the growth models that came up in the context of developmental problems in the 1960s. Of course, most of us are rediscovering great ideas all the time!

Assuming that all four goods are produced under autarky, that free trade is undertaken at fixed terms of trade, and that the share of investment going to augmenting capacity in each of the two sectors is fixed exogenously, Srinivasan then demonstrates plausibly that free trade in consumer goods (but with autarky continuing in investment goods) will raise welfare relative to autarky but not affect the growth rate of income or utility. On the other hand, freeing trade in investment goods will have a positive effect on transitional as well as on long-run (steady state) growth effect, and also a beneficial welfare effect relative to autarky. The vulgar belief that trade gains cannot affect the growth rate is thus easily disposed of.

However, how does one reconcile the 'surplus' argument with the findings that TFP growth has been a negligible factor in East Asia? So, is my story plausible but not borne out by the facts, as is often the case with our most interesting theories? I think not.

Thus, consider precisely the case where the imported equipment is 20 times more productive in Period 2 than in Period 1, but its price is only five times as high. If the valuation of this equipment is at domestic (producer) opportunity cost, as it should be, then it will indeed be priced 20 times higher than the older-vintage equipment of Period 1, so the measure of capital contribution at the level of the industry will rise commensurately and I presume that the estimated TFP growth in the industry will be zero: in that case, my thesis about the surplus is totally compatible with measured TFP emerging as negligible. But, of course, if the equipment is priced at its international cost, then I presume that TFP growth will pick up three-fourths of the gain that accrues from the 'surplus' of SMP over the international cost. My guess then is that, in East Asia, the former was the case. This might have been, not because the accountants were smart and valued Period 2 equipment at domestic opportunity cost, but because I guess that much of the imported equipment may have gone through importing trading firms which collected the three-fourths premium rather than the producing firms.

The role of literacy and education comes in precisely at the stage of the second step in my story above. For, the productivity or SMP of the imported equipment would be greater with a workforce that was literate and would be further enhanced if many had even secondary education. Thus, as shown in Figure 2, the SMP curve could shift to the right with literacy and education, leading to greater surplus for any given international cost of newer-vintage equipment.

Here I may cite Little,[8] using the pretext that a lecture justifies the informality of argumentation that a conference paper does not:

> It was largely from the experience of conducting this [1975, South Korean] survey, involving visits to the [28 randomly selected] firms ranging from 1.5 to 3.5 hours, that my own impressions of such matters as the acquisition of technology and skills on the part of the labour force ... were formed. I also visited a number of high exporting medium-size labour-intensive firms in Taiwan in 1976 ... Two points are mainly relevant in the present context. First the technology was simple, non-proprietary and easily acquired ... Secondly, both Korean and Taiwan workers were very quick to learn. Employees would usually reach the expected high level of productivity within a few weeks. This would probably not have been the case if the standards of primary education had not been high.

Of course, as these economies grew rapidly, the demand for secondary and higher education in turn would rise and a virtuous circle would follow: primary education would enhance the growth that the EP strategy brought whereas the enhanced growth would demand and lead to a more educated workforce. I see therefore primary education and literacy as playing an enhancing, rather than an initiating, role in the EP-strategy-led East Asian drama.

Thus, my story of East Asia's success, and by contrast that of India's failure, combines in its own way three major elements, in that order: (i) the enhanced inducement to invest due to the EP strategy; (ii) the benefit from the surplus of domestic SMP over international cost of imported newer-vintage capital equipment; and (iii) the raising of this SMP by the presence of a literate workforce. But if the main plot is this, the story has doubtless many sub-plots. I will touch on just one of them, especially as the analysis dates back to the early 1970s and to the NBER project, which I had the pleasure of codirecting with Professor Anne Krueger, yet another of Australia's gifts to Economics.

---

8   Ian Little (1994), 'Picking Winners: The East Asian Experience', *Social Market Foundation Occasional Paper*, London.

In my synthesis volume[9] for the NBER Project findings, I had noted that among the advantages of the EP strategy, which the project had found beneficial, one had to count the fact that trade barriers-jumping DFI in the IS countries was likely to be limited for these countries by the size of the domestic market by which it was motivated — there are shades here of the inducement-to-invest argument I have made today, but only in the faintest strokes. Secondly, such DFI as was attracted in the IS countries was also likely to be less productive because it would be going into economic regimes characterised by significant trade distortions that could even generate negative value added at socially relevant world prices — a possibility that was discussed by me (based on an extension to the DFI issue of the contribution by Harry Johnson to the theory of immiserising growth in tariff-distorted economies)[10] and then nailed down in well-known articles into a certainty under certain conditions by Hirofumi Uzawa[11] and by Richard Brecher and Carlos Diaz Alejandro[12] independently. I should mention that both these (thoroughly plausible in terms of their economic rationale) hypotheses have been examined, with some success, in cross-country regressions by another former student of mine, V.N. Balasubramanyam at Lancaster University and his co-authors.[13] So, this element may also be added to the explanation of East Asia's superior performance relative to that of IS-strategy-plagued countries such as India.[14]

---

9   Jagdish N. Bhagwati (1978), *Anatomy of Consequences of Exchange Control Regimes*, NBER, Ballinger, Cambridge, Mass.

10   See Jagdish Bhagwati (1973), 'The Theory of Immiserising Growth: Further Applications', in Michael Connolly and Alexander Swoboda (eds), *International Trade and Money*, Toronto University Press, Toronto.

11   Hirofumi Uzawa (1969), 'Shihon Jiyuka to Kokumin Keizai (Liberalisation of Foreign Investments and the National Economy)', *Economisuto*, 23(December): 105–22.

12   Richard Brecher and Carlos Diaz Alejandro (1977), 'Tariffs, Foreign Capital and Immiserising Growth', *Journal of International Economics*, (4): 317–22.

13   See, in particular, V.N. Balasubramanyam and M.A. Salisu (1991), 'EP, IS and Direct Foreign Investment in LDCs', in A. Koekkoek and L.B.M. Mennes (eds), *International Trade and Global Development: Essays in Honour of Jagdish Bhagwati*, Routledge, London, for the former hypothesis; and V.N. Balasubramanyam, M.A. Salisu and David Sapsford (1996), 'Foreign Direct Investment and Growth in EP and IS countries', *The Economic Journal*, 106(434): 92–105, for an indirect test of the latter hypothesis (explaining growth as the dependent variable).

14   Of course, as Magnus Blomstrom has reminded me, I should also note that there is considerable evidence at the micro-level of beneficial spillover effects from DFI, including from several studies he has undertaken in developing countries. However, reconciling this evidence with the contention that there is little evidence of TFP in the Lau–Young-type studies remains an unresolved issue.

Indeed, the inefficiency of the limited investment that did occur is the other side of India's miseries in the post-1950s Phase II. As India turned inward, the absence of competition and its salutary effects on efficiency were also lost. This loss was further compounded as the original, promotional apparatus established in the Ministry of Industry (the DGTD) turned swiftly into a restrictive agency instead. The government turned from indicative planning to a mechanism for masterminding, with the aid of a stifling licensing system, the production, investment and import decisions in the economy to a degree unimaginable to anyone outside the regime. I am reminded that, eventually when, in the early 1990s just prior to the beginning of the reforms in earnest in 1991 under what we might call Phase III, *The Economist* ran a long piece on India, describing and denouncing its policies, a visiting Russian economist, Maxim Boycko, who then went on to play a major part in the Russian privatisation program of Anatoly Chubais, told me: 'that article could well have been describing the Soviet Union'. We had clearly reproduced beautifully the disadvantages of communism without any of its benefits!

In addition, the early policy adopted in the 1950s itself, under which a growing share of the country's investments would occur in the public sector, spawned inefficient public sector enterprises whose losses would make a significant contribution to a macro-crisis in the 1980s and which, in addition, crippled the efficiency of the private sector as well since the public sector enterprises supplied, or rather failed to adequately and efficiently supply, infrastructure inputs such as electricity and transportation over which they were granted monopoly of production.

So, if I were to summarise briefly the period of three decades between the end of the 1950s and of the 1980s, I would reach the following sobering conclusion:

We had started out in the 1950s with:

- high growth rates
- openness to trade and investment
- a promotional state
- social expenditure awareness
- macrostability
- optimism; and hence
- admiration of the world.

But we ended the 1980s with:

- low growth rates[15]
- closure to trade and investment
- a licence-obsessed, restrictive state
- inability to sustain social expenditures
- macroinstability, indeed crisis
- pessimism; and therefore
- marginalisation of India in world affairs.

Why Did the Reforms Happen?
The Sources of Phase III

The full story of why the reforms finally began to happen in 1991, under the minority government of Prime Minister Rao, awaits research: we are still too close to it. But I have some candidates that have a bearing on my speculation as to the prospects of India not reversing the existing reforms and of her continuing to undertake further reforms.

First, 1991 saw India perilously close to declaring bankruptcy as the reserves shrank rapidly towards nothing. The macroeconomic crisis, developing steadily as the internal budget deficit got out of hand and reliance on external borrowing became unprecedented, was finally at hand. As many have observed for South America, a macroeconomic crisis, where you rush for the lifeline that the Bretton Woods institutions provides, clears your head as well as the prospect of a hanging. The notion that India, during what I have called Phase II here, had now come to a turning point where it was more readily manifest than ever that her economic policies could not be allowed to continue unchanged. And so the changes, attempted sporadically in the past, would finally begin in earnest.

But then add also the fact that no Bretton Woods support would have been forthcoming without a dose of conditionality pointing in the same direction. The spread of reforms worldwide, before India was getting to

---

15   The 1980s had higher than the 'Hindu growth rate' of 3 to 3.5 per cent during the preceding two decades but, as has been discussed by many, it was based on excessive internal spending and both internal and external borrowing, and hence was clearly unsustainable. It in fact led directly to the huge external crisis that forced the reforms of Phase III.

them, meant that the IMF–World Bank conditionality could no longer be dismissed as ideological; it had been legitimated as sensible prescription which only reflected what we had all learned in three decades of experience.

But I suspect that it also reflected a sense in the leadership of the Prime Minister and his chosen Finance Minister who would spearhead the reforms that they had here a chance to make history, putting the economy finally on to a path that was bound to work and bring them glory. An India which had played a major role in world affairs in the 1950s was now a marginal player on that very stage, a reflection of her having shot herself in the foot. The historical parallel was with Gorbachev contemplating the decline of the Soviet Union and seeking to seize the moment with *perestroika*: the English Sovietologist has recorded how Gorbachev and Scheverdnadze had discussed that things simply could not go on as they had in the Soviet Union, and that they had to seize the moment.

India's elite, including the bureaucracy, also came to realise that there was a growing dissonance between India's traditional claim to respect and attention and her shrinking ability to command them as her economic policies and failure became more widely known and a subject of derision. I suspect that the worst psychological state to be in is to have a superiority complex and an inferior status!

The Reforms to Date and Prospects

The reforms that have been initiated are many; and they continue to arrive in many little moves, almost continually. But much of importance remains to be done. Should we condemn the reformers for hastening only slowly?

Remember that, to some extent, changing India's uniquely damaging policy framework, nourished over three decades, is a task akin to cleaning up after a typhoon: the task is enormous and cannot be done all at once. It is also hard to double guess politicians beyond a point when, while they move in the right direction, they claim that they must be allowed to traverse the political minefields in a democracy as they, and not we technocrats, see fit as far as speed and strategy are concerned. The last time when technocratic full-speed-ahead advice to a reforming government backfired badly was when shock therapy was prescribed for Russia, with a backlash that gave Russia much political turmoil and little economic progress while returning Jeffrey Sachs unceremoniously to begin a life again at Harvard. I am reminded of his famous line: 'you cannot cross a chasm in two leaps', to which Padma Desai (I should confess my bias since she is my wife) replied: 'you cannot cross it in one leap either unless you are Indiana Jones; so you drop a bridge instead'.

Yet governments can indeed be too slow for their own, and their societies', good. My judgement is that the initial speed and scope of reforms in India were just about right. India took very definite and substantial steps towards freeing the economy: the industrial licensing system has been virtually dismantled, current account convertibility is virtually in place, and the astringent attitude to direct foreign investment (DFI) which had led to an incredibly low annual inflow of equity capital of just about US$100 million annually by 1990, has been reversed both in rhetoric and in policy actions.

This early harvest is not yet sumptuous, for these reforms are still to be deepened further. The current account convertibility still goes hand in hand with wholly muddled thinking that permits nearly all consumer goods to be still subjected to strict import controls on the silly ground that we 'do not need such imports'! The DFI policy, while better, is still far from what is necessary to attract substantial inflows: the Enron affair, and now the withdrawal on grounds of inordinate delays in clearance by Amoco from a $1 billion coal based methane gas project again in energy-starved India, just reported in the *Asian Wall Street Journal* (20–21 September 1996), suggest that much needs to be done, and fairly quickly, if India is to move effectively into its outward orientation mode nearly a quarter century after the East Asian NIE countries did and about a decade after the other ASEAN NECs have done. I am an optimist on this front since I believe that these dramatic instances will, given India's open democratic system, lead to enough pressure from below to weed out the remaining inefficiencies.

The greater difficulties lie, however, in the speed at which important residual reforms can be carried out, now that the Rao government has been replaced by a weak coalition government. The two areas where reforms are necessary and critical, if the outward orientation is to produce growth rates of 9–10 per cent rather than of 6 per cent, are the public sector which cries out to be privatised now and the ability of firms to extract greater efficiency from its labour force, including through changed laws that permit the laying off of workers as necessary, though with appropriate safeguards. In neither area can one expect this coalition government, which has two Communist cabinet members with trade union backgrounds, to bite the bullet. True, the communists in Bengal have shown flexibility in going out to get DFI and talked the talk of 'capitalist roaders'. But what you do when the rules are set by the centre which you have no part of, and you must compete for resources in the market place at the state level, is entirely different from what you would do if you are at the centre making the rules.

On the other hand, the new Prime Minister is pragmatic and his personal experience of the Global Age is from the Silicon Valley in Bangalore in his own state of Karnataka: and that gives him an optimistic view of the benefits to India from integrating rapidly into the world economy. And the new Finance Minister is as committed to reforms as the old one; in fact, the two had joined hands in the Rao government as the leading reformers of their time.

So, you can be an optimist or a pessimist as to whether we in India will change from second to third gear in our reforms or whether we will coast along in second gear. Only time will tell.

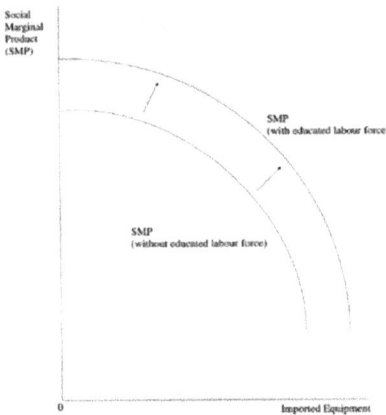

Figure 1

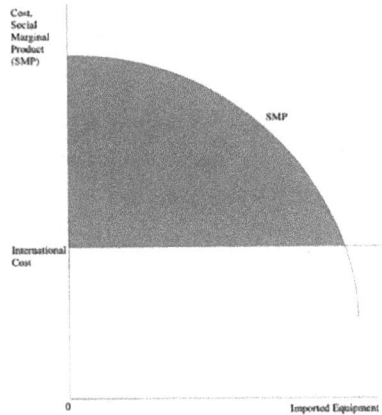

Figure 2

Oration 4:
1999 K.R. Narayanan Oration

Message from the President
of the Republic of India

I am glad that the annual lecture to commemorate the inauguration of the Australia South Asia Research Centre in April 1994 at The Australian National University has been taking place every year without interruption. These lectures delivered by distinguished economists have contributed meaningfully to the understanding of vital aspects of the South Asian economy in this period of change and reforms. I am glad to learn that this year the oration is given by Mr P. Chidambaram, a former Finance Minister of India who played a leading role in the liberalisation process of the Indian economy. Mr Chidambaram with his profound knowledge of economics and wide ranging experience in government and public life of India would, I am confident, make the lecture an illuminating exercise in the understanding of the complex process of economic transformation that is taking place in India in all its multiple dimensions.

It is refreshing that Mr Chidambaram will give special emphasis in his oration upon the third tier of government in India, that is, at the grassroots level. What invests the Indian experiment with depth and significance is that the reform process is not a superficial phenomenon affecting the upper crust of society, but involves the participation of millions of men and women at the village level. The Panchayati Raj institutions in India have made democratic decentralisation a reality. Three million elected representatives of the people at the grassroots level, 1 million of whom are women, are today participants in both decision-making and implementation of developmental programs at the grassroots level. The 474 District *panchayats*, 5,906 intermediate-level *panchayats* and over 227,000 village *panchayats* now constitute powerful self-propelled engines to promote the developments goals of the country. The success of this exercise of unprecedented scale in devolution of power has varied in different parts of the country depending on the extent of devolution of finances and responsibilities along with necessary training and capacity building. There is no doubt, however, of the potential for these evolving institutions to become vibrant vehicles of self-governance, transforming the quality of life in India's villages with democratic participation and paying heed to the demand for social justice by the generality of the people.

I am confident that Mr Chidambaram will more than do justice in his oration to this very import subject which has far reaching consequences for India's polity and development, and which would be of interest to all democratic countries.

K.R. Narayanan
New Delhi
1999

Stronger Branches, Deeper Roots: The Democratisation of India's Economic Reforms

P. Chidambaram

It is a privilege to be invited to The Australian National University. ANU has had a long association with India. Sir John Crawford, one of your former Chancellors, played a key role in the 1960s in making the Green Revolution possible in India, and we are grateful for that. Few institutions around the world have a centre dedicated to research on South Asia. This university has set an example by establishing the Australia South Asia Research Centre (ASARC). I have no doubt that the seed that was sown in 1994 will grow into a huge tree, providing opportunity to hundreds of scholars to study the unfolding South Asian drama.

There could have been no better occasion for me to visit here — which is also my first visit to your beautiful country — than to deliver the K.R. Narayanan Oration. It is my privilege to have known Mr Narayanan personally for many years. Mr Narayanan is a distinguished son of India and has impeccable intellectual and moral credentials. He has served his country with commitment and far-sightedness. His rise to the high office of President is a modern-day version of 'log cabin to the President's House', and throughout his life he had no assets other than hard work, integrity and humility. I hope I can measure up to the great honour attached to a lecture that bears his name.

The Development Challenge

India is a large and diverse country and its development has many dimensions. A population of nearly a billion people is just one aspect that sets it apart from most developing countries. True, China makes a good comparison. But China does not have the religious, ethnic, social or cultural variations and diversities that mark India. No other nation has such a large underclass — of backward castes and classes — that seeks empowerment. We cannot also forget that, unlike in many other developing countries, democracy has flourished in India for over five decades now and has struck deep roots. Its federal polity and the division of political power make the nature of State intervention in the economy somewhat different from other systems. Therefore, while comparisons with East Asia and China could certainly help in analysing India's economic trajectory and the success or failure of its policy responses, such an approach suffers from obvious limitations. India's development problem has to be probed on its own and solutions found that are specific to its needs. The theme that I have chosen for my lecture today rests on this premise. My endeavour would be to look at both the political and economic aspects of the development challenge in India.

Soon after India launched its reforms in 1991, its economy responded strongly to the bold initiatives taken by the government. The foreign exchange crisis of 1991 had brought down the GDP growth rate to a mere 0.8 per cent in 1991–92. The rebound thereafter was strong and, during the five years ending 1996–97, GDP growth rate averaged 6.9 per cent, the highest ever for a five-year period. This was accompanied by a turnaround in macroeconomic balances. The current account deficit improved from a high of 3.5 per cent in 1991 to 1.2 per cent in 1996–97 and the debt-service ratio declined from 32.4 per cent to 23 per cent. External debt as a percentage of GDP fell to 25 per cent in 1996–97 from a high of 37 per cent a few years earlier. Fiscal deficit of the Centre declined from 8.6 per cent in 1990–91 to 5.1 per cent in 1996–97. Foreign exchange reserves improved dramatically, rising from a mere $1 billion to over $27 billion now. And this has happened despite substantial liberalisation of the trade regime and reduction in tariffs.

While the improvement in the macro-economy has been remarkable, no less remarkable have been the changes that have taken place at the grassroots. Let me give you a flavour of the impact of economic reforms on the rural population of India who constitute the bulk of our poor, illiterate and deprived. Between the National Sample Survey 46th round (July 1990 – June 1991) and the 53rd round (January 1997 – December 1997), the total number of employed in rural India increased from 268 million to 294 million, a gain of 26 million in the space of six years. While no accurate estimates are yet available for changes in rural per capita income, an indication can be had from the changes in real wages of unskilled agricultural labour. After a sharp decline in 1991–92, the first year of reform, real wages increased at an average annual rate of 3.6 per cent in the next six years. Gross capital formation in agriculture, another useful indicator, shows a 50 per cent rise at constant prices in the six years between 1991–92 and 1996–97. What is more remarkable is that there is a clear shift in favour of private investment in agriculture, and the share of private investment has increased from 75 per cent to 83 per cent. These changes are also reflected in the social indicators for rural India. Infant mortality rate for rural areas has declined from 86 per thousand live births to less than 80 per thousand (the national average is 71). Literacy in rural areas has improved from 44.7 per cent to 56 per cent (the national average is 62 per cent). The birth rate for the whole country has declined from 29.5 per thousand to 27.2 and the death rate from 9.8 per thousand to 8.9. These tentative trends are consistent with the view that rapid economic growth has brought about an improvement in the living standards of the people in general.

During the last two years, however, while macroeconomic balances have not deteriorated, growth rate of GDP has tended to slow down to about 5 per cent. The IMF's forecast for the current year (1999–2000) is that the GDP growth would once again be only 5.1 per cent. The sector responsible for the slowdown is manufacturing, where growth has slipped from a peak of 15 per cent in 1995–96 to less than 4 per cent in 1998–99. What has also raised concern is that during the '90s, as a whole, trend growth rate in agriculture has been lower than it was in the '80s.

Recent researches have confirmed that economic growth has contributed much more to reduction of poverty in India than subsidies or the government's anti-poverty interventions targeted at the poor. The rate of decline in the poverty ratio in the late 1980s and early 1990s has been double the rate achieved in the 1970s. This happened because the average growth rate of GDP improved from 3.5 per cent in the 1970s to 5.3 per cent in the 1980s and even higher to 7 per cent during 1994–95, 1995–96 and 1996–97. Clearly, India needs to sustain GDP growth rates of 7 per cent plus to eliminate poverty over the next 15 to 20 years. What is also required is some sort of balanced growth across sectors because of the pivotal role of agricultural growth in poverty alleviation.

Three Constraints

Among the constraints to sustainability of high growth and poverty reduction in India, three are most apparent.

First, India's infrastructure is in urgent need of repair and expansion. Huge amounts need to be invested in ports, power generation and distribution, telecommunication, railways, roads and bridges, irrigation systems and water resources, infrastructure in urban and rural settlements, and afforestation and rehabilitation of degraded land.

Second, the quality of India's human resources is abysmally poor. India has the highest number of illiterate people among all countries. A third of India's children between the ages of six and 10 do not get to school. Of the children that do, a good number drop out well before they acquire the skills needed to earn a decent wage. India has also the world's largest share of children who remain malnourished. A large proportion of the Indian population does not have access to basic health care or basics like drinking water, shelter and toilets. Communicable diseases and prenatal and maternal mortality cause about 470 deaths per 100,000 persons in India — a rate four times that of China. In sum, a third of all Indians are poor, malnourished, illiterate and in bad health, and a robust growth rate of population only adds more to the bottom third of the Indian people. In a country like India, reduction in population growth becomes a crucial variable. Experience of some Indian States clearly suggests that a fall in population growth rate has strong linkages with social indicators like health and literacy, particularly of women.

Third, the government needs to redefine itself both in terms of what it should do and what it must spend on. While deregulation has already reduced the role of government in industry, infrastructure and services, and has expanded the space for the private sector, much more needs to be done. The process of privatisation remains tardy. But deregulation and privatisation alone will not help. This is because high fiscal deficits continue to threaten the sustainability of the growth process. Huge borrowings by the government hamper resource mobilisation by the private sector and keep interest rates high. It follows that redefinition of government is closely linked with fiscal reform, especially reduction of the deficit and re-orientation of expenditure.

Trends in Indian Polity

It is necessary to look at these constraints within the setting provided by the emerging trends in the Indian polity and society. The most visible feature of the polity is the emergence of regional political and social forces and their urge for autonomy and empowerment. Over the last decade or so these urges have found a vehicle in regional political parties and they have played a key role in coalition governments at the Centre. The coalition governments have responded to the growing clout of regional parties by devolving more powers of decision-making from the Centre to the States. This trend cannot now be reversed as its roots go deep. Indeed, State governments are also under pressure to further decentralise power and resources to local bodies. Indian society is witnessing a process of great churning. The old order is dead. Sections at the lowest rung of society, the *dalits*[1] and the backward castes, minorities and women are now seeking social equality and their rightful place in the power structure. Alongside, there has been a surge in the activities of thousands of non-governmental organisations seeking to find decentralised solutions to developmental, cultural and social problems faced by the people. This social change, as well as the people's urge to participate in the development agenda and seek localised solutions to their problems, is bringing to the fore the role of local bodies, called Gram (i.e. village) *panchayats*, Nagarpalikas and Zila *parishads*.

The initial phase of reforms under the Congress government (1991–96) was driven by compulsion, external pressure and a few committed individuals. By a quirk of fate, many parties that had long opposed structural reforms came to power in 1996 under the banner of the United Front government. The United Front government surprised its critics by not only reaffirming the reform process but vigorously pursuing reforms in new areas. For instance, it was the United Front government which reformed direct taxes, began dismantling the administered price mechanism for

---

1   The former untouchables who suffer the worst discrimination.

petroleum products, and won the approval of the Inter-State Council (a body comprising the Chief Ministers of all the States) to accept 29 recommendations on Centre-State financial relations.

That government also introduced a slew of draft legislations ranging from company law to income tax to foreign exchange to insurance. The BJP-led government which assumed office in March 1998 came in with a reputation of being a right-wing coalition, rooted, however, not in reform but in atavism. After farcical posturing with outdated ideas like Swadeshi (self-reliance, or, more accurately, autarchy) and outrageous suggestions like withdrawal from WTO, the government settled down to the business of governance and categorically reaffirmed both the content and direction of the economic reforms that had started in 1991. The positive fall out of this was a new policy on information technology and a major overhaul of excise duties. Thus, the 1990s has witnessed the forging of an unspoken consensus among all the parties which cover the entire political spectrum of India. The Congress and the BJP have emerged as the two poles. Regional parties which dominated the United Front have shown a tendency to gather around one or the other pole. Many observers discern a definite trend towards a two-party system. While there is some basis for this conclusion, I do not think political life in India would ever be so simple. As the two major parties move towards the centre, they are in danger of losing their USP, although, I must confess, in the case of the BJP it would be better off if it loses its Unwanted Selling Points more rapidly! I also believe that there is political space for the Communist parties; there is space for a Green party as well. The two-party system would eventually dominate India's system with a peculiar Indian variation: the Congress and the BJP will be the two dominant parties at the Centre, but at the State level it is possible that the two-party system may be dominated by two regional parties excluding either or both the Congress and the BJP.

Even if single-party governments replace coalitions at the Centre, they will have to accommodate regional and sub-regional aspirations and even nurture them. They will also have to provide representation to backward castes, the *dalits*, the minorities and women. Indeed, both the leading national political parties, the Congress and BJP, are now supporting demands by sub-regional forces for formation of new States. Both are wooing the *dalits*, backward castes and minorities and debating legislation to reserve seats for women in elected bodies. There is a realisation across the political spectrum that if the country were to be governed effectively, its diversity would have to be respected and nourished. The constraints to India's growth which I noted earlier would have to be addressed within this changing political matrix.

Indeed, this framework is no different from the one visualised by the architects of India's Constitution five decades ago. They clearly defined the division of responsibilities between the Centre and the States and enumerated them in the Union list, the States' list and the Concurrent list. These lists entrust the State governments with substantial responsibilities for development. Thus, States play a determining role in development of agriculture, water resources, land relations, environment and forests, rural roads and state highways, minor ports, electricity and rural and urban services. They are also responsible for human development through investments in key areas as health and education. To enable them to fulfil their responsibilities, the Constitution also empowers them with rights to raise taxes, get a share in funds available with the Centre, and levy user charges on various economic and social services provided to the people. The Constitution also provides for rights and responsibilities of local bodies like *panchayats* and municipal bodies. The Indian Constitution envisages that the States are as much, if not more, responsible for development as the Centre.

One may ask that if the framework was already provided for in the Constitution, then what went wrong? The framework worked, but only for a few years after independence. Thereafter, India suffered a phase when the Centre encroached upon the powers and autonomy of the States. The States in turn usurped the powers of local bodies. This was a logical fall-out of the centralised model of planned development India chose in the mid-'50s, which ensured that all economic decisions were directed by the Centre. The result was that the Centre sought to assume a larger responsibility for development than assigned to it in the Constitution. It floated centrally sponsored schemes and procrastinated on sharing all the tax revenues with State governments. States were required to seek clearances from the Centre for setting up projects for infrastructure and human development. Before the economic reforms of 1991, the States had little autonomy in attracting private domestic or foreign capital because investment, financial, industrial, sectoral and locational policies were controlled by the Centre. Local initiatives, especially initiatives that would have been possible through local bodies, perished under the

Centre-directed and Centre-controlled economic model of development. In turn, States neglected their local bodies: in many States local bodies ceased to exist as elections to such bodies were not held for 10–20 years.

The coincidence of economic reforms and the emergence of regional political forces in the '90s have acted as a catalyst to trigger devolution of power to the States. The United Front government (1996–98) offered to abolish or transfer to the States centrally sponsored schemes. It also liberalised policies to allow States to attract more private capital. The United Front government also accepted the recommendation of the Finance Commission that 29 per cent of all central tax revenues should be shared with the States. The change in the correlation of forces in favour of States is evident from the fact that the BJP-led coalition government that followed has continued with decentralising power to the States.

Is Empowerment of States Enough?

But empowerment of States is just one side of the coin. To deliver on the development front, the States will have to perform and not just rest content with acquiring more powers. The overall record thus far has been uninspiring. Most States' finances are in a mess and they often have to resort to overdrafts to pay salaries to their employees. The latest figures show that the States' combined fiscal deficit had increased to a high of 3.6 per cent of GDP. In 1985–86, this figure was 2.7 per cent.

Disturbingly, the States' fiscal deficit is rising not because they are spending more on development. The bulk of the States' expenditure is devoted to salaries and pensions, interest payments, and covering losses of public enterprises or losses incurred by electricity and irrigation boards. The interest burden on States has risen from 1.4 per cent of GDP in 1985–86 to 2.3 per cent now. Not surprisingly, their development effort is faltering: capital expenditure on social and economic services has fallen from 3.1 per cent of GDP in 1985–86 to around 2 per cent now. The States' expenditure on key social services like health and education is falling as a proportion of their total expenditure. Likewise, their commitment to developing critical infrastructure has weakened. They are unable to find resources even for maintenance of existing roads, public transportation systems and irrigation facilities. They cannot meet the growing energy needs of industry and agriculture because the state electricity boards have accumulated losses of over Rs 150 billion. The urban and rural settlements are in a state of decay. And even as their wasteful expenditures are going beyond control, their taxation systems have lost the ability to deliver the revenue growth needed to plug the widening resources gap.

It will be evident that the three constraints to growth and development I outlined earlier are in full play at the level of the States. Since the States are responsible for a substantial part of the development effort, it is plain that reforms at the Centre alone cannot resolve the issue. The answer clearly lies in reforms at the State level: reforming States hold the key to India's economic future.

Fortunately, some States have seen the writing on the wall and launched welcome initiatives. Orissa, Haryana, Andhra Pradesh and Uttar Pradesh have launched comprehensive power sector reforms to dissolve their electricity boards and establish separate companies for generation and distribution of power, and have drawn up plans for privatisation of both generation and distribution. They have set up regulatory agencies to eliminate government's interference in the power sector, and to set tariffs for various categories of consumers. Hopefully, the huge subsidies being doled out will now be phased out and the power sector in these States would become financially sustainable. The power reforms experiment in these four States has motivated other States like Karnataka to launch similar reforms. Incidentally, these five States are ruled by five different political parties.

Similar initiatives have been launched in other areas of infrastructure. Karnataka and Andhra Pradesh have created infrastructure funds to boost investments in large infrastructure projects. Andhra Pradesh and Gujarat are upgrading their State highways and are revamping their road departments to improve the quality of road construction and maintenance. Many States are seeking private investors to rebuild high-density corridors into toll-based highways or expressways. Almost all States along India's large coastline are inducing private investors to build new ports on a BOT basis.

Some States have also launched new programs in the social sector. States like Rajasthan, Uttar Pradesh and Madhya Pradesh have embarked on improving their primary school systems to universalise primary education. Andhra Pradesh and Karnataka are reforming their health systems to improve the quality and reach of health services. Some States have launched ambitious programs for reproductive health and women and child development. Kerala and Tamil Nadu have already reached the replacement level of fertility of 2.1.

Fiscal Reform: The Critical Variable

While all these are steps in the right direction they still fall far short of the truly enormous requirements of the large Indian population. Even as many States are deregulating to woo private investors, it is obvious that private capital cannot satisfy all the requirements. There are critical areas in social sector and infrastructure where only the government can provide the necessary money as well as drive. Many of the programs, especially in the social sector, are not backed by fiscal reform and realignment of public expenditure. In the absence of fiscal reform, the critical minimum effort in infrastructure and human development is sadly missing. Fiscal reform at the state level is the one crucial element for redirecting State governments' energies towards the social sector and infrastructure.

Furthermore, these programs would not be sustainable unless they are conceived, designed and owned by the people and communities themselves. Most Indian States have large populations: a good number have more than 60 million people and one is large enough to qualify as the sixth largest country in the world! Within each State there are substantial regional variations in social structures and ethnicity, resource endowments, land relations, agro-climatic conditions, cropping patterns and the like. Quite often programs and projects conceived in State capitals fail to account for such variations, and communities are not taken into confidence. Also, centralised implementation of projects prevents transparency and vested interests tend to gain at the expense of the people. A good example is the plethora of anti-poverty programs and subsidies targeted at the poor. Their achievements in terms of poverty reduction have been found to be questionable and far from commensurate with the huge amount of funds poured into them. If the States have to ensure that reforms deliver at the grassroots they have no option but to decentralise in favour of local elected bodies at the village and municipal levels.

Panchayats: The Third Tier

Over two-thirds of the 1 billion Indian population lives in over 500,000 small villages and the remainder in a few thousand urban and semi-urban settlements. As I said earlier, the setting for development may change from one set of villages to another. To ensure that these varying needs are addressed and programs are implemented in a decentralised manner, the Congress government under Rajiv Gandhi (1985–89) sought to strengthen the role of the 'third tier' in India's administrative structure comprising elected local bodies. Subsequently in 1992, the Indian Parliament enacted two critical changes in the Indian Constitution, called the 73rd and 74th amendments, that created a multi-level structure of 'Panchayati Raj' institutions at the district, intermediate and village levels. The aim was to put in place elected local bodies as institutions of self-government and enhance their role in development.

This Constitutional and legal initiative opened a new window of opportunity for State governments to deal with the constraints that thwart India's development. However, not many States have grabbed the opportunity and the establishments in State capitals continue to resist decentralisation of power and resources. Fortunately, some States are utilising the constitutional changes to empower their local bodies. A noteworthy example in this context is the manner in which Madhya Pradesh, a large Indian state, is implementing a program to universalise primary education through a program called the Education Guarantee Scheme (EGS). It has redefined the Indian State by including in it the village *panchayat* and the local community and excluding the civil service apparatus that allocates money and manages a large educational bureaucracy. Any community that has 25 children but does not have access to a primary school can demand a school. The demandeurs should select a locally available teacher and present a claim to the *gram panchayat*, which passes it on to the authorities at the district level. The district administration shall respond within 90 days of the demand. While the government lays down the curriculum and pays for textbooks, midday meals for children, and the salary and training of the teacher appointed by the village *panchayat*, the latter, along with the community, has to provide land for the school. This demand-driven system has been phenomenally successful: in 1998, over 40 primary schools have come up each day of the year. More has happened for primary education in Madhya Pradesh over the last two years than in the five decades prior to the launch of the EGS. The success of EGS belies the argument that tradition-bound communities are not alive to the value of education for their children. It also shows that they are willing to take charge of primary education for their children, and can do a better job than the bureaucracy.

Another bold initiative is underway in the state of Andhra Pradesh. In June 1997, the State legislature passed the *Andhra Pradesh Farmers Management of Irrigation Systems Act*. The Act provides for creation of

Water Users Associations all over the State which in turn elect their Managing Committees. The State government has empowered the WUAs and their committees to manage the irrigation systems at the level of the village — i.e. beyond the main feeder canal. They maintain records of water use, collect dues from member farmers, ensure proper distribution of water, and are also allowed to spend on repair and maintenance of the network. Over 10,000 such associations have been formed. Preliminary assessments show better maintenance of the irrigation system, increase in the area of cultivated land and improved collection of revenues. This needs to be set against the abysmal performance of irrigation departments in most States, which are bankrupt, and unable to maintain the existing channels, let alone create new ones.

The government of Andhra Pradesh has launched another new development initiative called 'Janmabhoomi'. The program is based on identification and prioritisation of needs by the communities themselves through the institution of the village *panchayat*. People share the cost of community works to which government also contributes, they execute the works through self-help groups, review and audit the expenditure and own the assets thus created. The projects executed through the program include roads, drains, buildings for schools and colleges, drinking water, health clinics, irrigation facilities, etc. Over the last two years a number of such projects have been completed and commissioned. Even allowing for some waste and leakages, assets worth billions of rupees have been added to the community, and there is a growing sense of community ownership and responsibility.

Many more such community-based programs are under implementation in the States. The common feature that marks all such success stories is participation by people's institutions like elected local bodies, self-help groups or cooperatives. True, in all these success stories there are other features like meticulous planning, social leadership, external technological and managerial inputs and availability of resources. However, there is little doubt that people's participation, and the resulting beneficiary orientation of such schemes, has been the critical input.

Another feature of successful development programs has been their holistic approach. It has been realised that the development of the poor cannot be achieved through any one single activity. Development has to be a multidimensional process that addresses problems of illiteracy, ill health and infrastructure. The range of activities being addressed in the Janmabhoomi program in Andhra Pradesh illustrates this point. Janmabhoomi also confirms the fundamental fact that only programs identified by the community deliver the maximum results. Development occurs when it is an interactive and democratic process, because then alone it addresses the numerous dimensions of backwardness.

As I said earlier, the potential for sustainable development revealed by the 73rd and 74th amendments is still not being tapped by most State governments, although some have begun to move in that direction. In most States, the power elite continues to resist decentralisation, and implementation of 'Panchayati Raj' has turned out be an exercise in bureaucratic expansion. The concept itself continues to be plagued by numerous problems. There are legal ambiguities that allow States to keep local bodies weak and ineffective, and some more constitutional changes may be necessary to plug the loopholes. Another problem is the lack of resources available to local bodies, as State governments and State Finance Commissions have yet to work out the terms of sharing of taxable resources. Local bodies have also not yet been fully empowered to levy and collect taxes, user charges and other revenues. Only in a few cases have municipalities been allowed to issue bonds. Another hurdle is the limited expertise at the village level considering the high levels of illiteracy among village communities and their relative isolation. And not to be overlooked is that the villages and communities have their own elite and inequitable power structures, patron–client relations, and caste equations, which resist and arrest any social or economic change. There are numerous such problems that I need not spell out here. Scholars at this Centre interested in pursuing the subject can easily dip into the vast body of literature available.

The Tree: With Branches and Roots

Friends, a discussion on economic reforms in India tends to look at what the Indian government in New Delhi is doing. Investors and even scholars often base their judgement on the pace and quality of reforms by assessing the actions of the Central government. There cannot be any doubt that the overall policy environment has to be created by the Centre. For instance, some of the constraints to growth in India lie in the policies concerning the financial sector, international trade, privatisation of public sector enterprises, legal systems, taxation, and fiscal issues like subsidies. The Central government has to continue reforms in all these areas to improve the environment for growth and development. None can underestimate the catalytic role played by the policy framework created by the Centre.

But the role of the Central government in the Indian reform process ought not to be exaggerated either. For example, fiscal reforms, easily the most important macroeconomic issue, cannot be assessed only in terms of measures outlined in the central budget. Fiscal deficits in the States are as substantial and as relevant. My endeavour today has been to draw your attention to the large and crucial space occupied by two other layers in the institutional framework for reform in India: the State governments and the third tier comprising local bodies or other elected community-based organisations. India cannot sustain high rates of growth and make its people prosper without activating these two layers as well. Indeed, all three have to move in tandem, with each one reinforcing and invigorating the other. If the policy framework at the Centre is the main trunk of the Indian tree of development, the States are like its branches and local bodies and people-based organisations are its roots. The tree can grow bigger and its trunk more sturdy only if the branches are stronger and wider and the roots go deeper into the earth. I can see democracy driving this process in India.

We have put behind us the years when moderate growth rates ensured small islands of prosperity in a sea of poverty. Today, every section of the Indian people aspires for a better life. For the very poor, better life will mean, in their lifetime, perhaps no more than better water, better housing, better schools, and better medical care. The road to that better life is in better governance, and the very poor have awakened to the fact that self-governance is indeed better governance. The 73rd and 74th Amendments to the Indian Constitution ensured the democratisation of India's polity. Out of 227,000 village *panchayats*, fully one-third are headed by women. The *dalits* control up to 22.5 per cent of the elected offices. The minorities and the backward castes have also discovered 'empowerment'. Driven by aspiration and fortified by empowerment, the people of India will reap the benefits of an open and competitive economy. More and more people will share the benefits of growth and development.

The democratisation of India's economy is underway. And therein lies the reason for our hopes and our dreams.

Oration 5:
2001 K.R. Narayanan Oration

Message from the President
of the Republic of India

I am glad that since the establishment of the K.R. Narayanan Oration in 1994 to commemorate the inauguration of the Australia South Asia Research Centre of The Australian National University, remarkable personalities from the academic, intellectual and public spheres have delivered orations on a variety of issues of contemporary significance. Beginning with Dr Raja Chelliah who delivered the first oration in 1994, other outstanding personalities such as Jagdish Bhagwati and Mr P. Chidambaram through their masterly orations have enriched our understanding of different subjects. It is particularly noteworthy that all these prominent figures have played major roles in fashioning India's agenda for development both at the academic and practical levels.

I am glad that this year's oration is being delivered by another renowned economist, Dr C. Rangarajan, who is presently serving as the Governor of Andra Pradesh. I am happy that the topic of Dr Rangarajan's lecture is 'Monetary Policy in a Developing Economy — The Indian Experience'.

Hailed as one of the chief architects of India's monetary policy for several years, Dr Rangarajan during his long and distinguished career, particularly during his association with the Reserve Bank of India as Deputy Governor and subsequently as Governor, devised a monetary policy which would facilitate growth and ensure price stability. Most of the measures such as simplification and deregulation of interest rate structure, policy formulations for improving lendable resources of the Reserve Bank of India, upgradations of the information technologies and introduction of competition in the financial system, have contributed to lay down the foundation of a monetary policy to further strengthen India's new economic environment.

While doing so Dr Rangarajan has proved that in developing countries growth of the economy and price stability can be appropriately blended. New economic policies must not only ensure prosperity and growth, these must also serve other defined goals for the society as a whole. As a moving force behind the liberalisation of our economy and as an active player and economic strategist for building up of a dynamic economy, Dr Rangarajan's contributions have become significant. I am sure that his oration will be an insightful exercise in understanding the economic transformation of India in all its ramifications. I am sure the range of ideas, the depth of understanding and the wide experience of Dr Rangarajan will be of importance for all developing countries grappling with the emerging realities of liberalisation and financial reforms.

K.R. Narayanan
New Delhi
2001

Monetary Policy in a Developing Economy — The Indian Experience

C. Rangarajan

It is a great honour to be asked to deliver the K.R. Narayanan Oration of this year. It is an honour in more ways than one. First, the invitation has come from the prestigious Australia South Asia Research Centre of The Australian National University which has done commendable work in studying the political and economic developments in South Asia and particularly India. The growing integration of the world economy has made the work of the Centre extremely valuable and relevant. Second, the oration is named after one of the most distinguished sons of India, who today occupies the exalted position of the President of India. Narayanan's contributions to India's public life are immense. With quiet diplomacy and skilful and strategic interventions, he has steered the country during difficult times, particularly in the last few years. Through his scholarship and statesmanship, he has endeared himself to one and all. It is truly a great privilege to deliver the lecture bearing his name.

Developments in Monetary Policy

I have chosen to speak to you today on the Indian experience with respect to monetary policy as an instrument of economic management. Developments in monetary policy closely mirror the changes in overall economic policy. The decade of 1990s has seen far reaching changes in India's economic policy. The content and approach to economic policy underwent a sea change. The country has become a more open economy. The roles of state and market are getting redefined. There is a common thread running through the various measures introduced since 1991 and that is to improve the productivity and efficiency of the system. This is sought to be achieved by imparting a greater element of competition in the system. It is in this context that monetary policy in India acquired a new role. Financial sector reforms which were an integral part of the economic reforms program created a new institutional environment in which monetary policy had to operate.

In industrially advanced countries, after decades of eclipse, monetary policy re-emerged as a potent instrument of economic policy, in the fight against inflation in the 1980s. Issues relating to the conduct of monetary policy came to the forefront of policy debates in the 1980s. The relative importance of growth and price stability as the objective of monetary policy as well as the appropriate intermediate target of monetary policy became the focus of attention. Over the years, a consensus has emerged among the industrially advanced countries that the dominant objective of monetary policy should be price stability. Differences, however, exist among central banks even in these countries as regards the appropriate intermediate target. While some central banks consider monetary aggregates and, therefore, monetary targeting as operationally meaningful, some others focus on the interest rate. There is also the more recent practice to ignore intermediate targets and focus on the final goal such as inflation targeting.

A similar trend regarding monetary policy is discernible in developing economies as well. Much of the early literature on development economics focused on real factors such as savings, investment and technology as mainsprings of growth. Very little attention was paid to the financial system as a contributory factor to economic growth even though attention was paid to develop financial institutions which provide short-term and long-term credit. In fact, many writers felt that inflation was endemic in the process of economic growth and it was accordingly treated more as a consequence of structural imbalance than as a monetary phenomenon. However, with the accumulated evidence, it became clear that any process of economic growth in which monetary expansion was disregarded led to inflationary pressures with a consequent impact on economic growth. Accordingly, the importance of price stability and, therefore, the need to use monetary policy for that purpose also assumed importance in developing economies. Nonetheless, the debate on the extent to which price stability should be deemed to be the overriding objective of monetary policy in such economies continues.

The Reserve Bank of India was set up in 1935. Like all central banks in developing countries, the Reserve Bank has been playing a developmental and a regulatory role. In its developmental role, the Reserve Bank focused attention on deepening and widening the financial system. It played a major part in building up appropriate financial institutions to promote savings and investment. In the realm of agricultural credit, term finance to industries and credit to export, the apex institutions that are now operating were essentially spun off from the Reserve Bank. Strengthening and establishing new institutions to meet the country's requirements is a continuing process. The promotional role had taken the Reserve Bank into the area of credit allocation as well. Pre-emption of credit for certain sectors and that too at concessional rates of interest became part of the overall policy. Commercial banks over time had been required to provide a certain percentage of their total credit to certain sectors which were regarded as 'priority sector'.

An active role by the Reserve Bank of India in terms of regulating the growth in money and credit became evident only after 1950s. During the 1950s the average annual increase in the wholesale price was only 1.8 per cent. However, during the 1960s, the average annual increase was 6.2 per cent and in the 1970s, it was around 10.3 per cent. In the early years of planning, there was considerable discussion on the role of deficit financing in fostering economic growth. The First Plan said: 'Judicious credit creation somewhat in anticipation of the increase in production and availability of genuine savings has also a part to play'. Thus, deficit financing, which in the Indian context meant Reserve Bank credit to the government, was assigned a place in the financing of the plan, though its quantum was to be limited to the extent it was non-inflationary. Monetary growth, particularly in the 1950s, was extremely moderate. However, as each successive plan came under a resource crunch, there was an increasing dependence on market borrowing and deficit financing. These became pronounced in the 1970s and thereafter. The single most important factor influencing the conduct of monetary policy after 1970 had been the phenomenal increase in reserve money contributed primarily by the Reserve Bank credit to the government.

To summarise, the system as it existed at the end of 1970s was characterised by the following features. The Reserve Bank of India as the central monetary authority prescribed all the interest rates on deposits and lending. The commercial banks were required to allocate a certain percentage of credit to what were designated as 'priority sector'. Credit to parties above a stipulated amount required prior authorisation from the central bank. After the nationalisation of major commercial banks in 1969, nearly 85 per cent of the total bank assets came under public sector. Apart from small private banks, foreign banks were allowed to operate with limited branches.

The increase in the scale of borrowing by the government resulted in: (a) the steady rise in statutory liquidity ratio requiring banks to invest higher and higher proportion of their deposits in government securities which carried less than 'market rates'; and (b) the Reserve Bank of India becoming a residual subscriber to securities and Treasury Bills leading to monetisation of the deficit. The Reserve Bank had, therefore, to address itself to the difficult task of neutralising to the extent possible the expansionary impact of deficits. The increasing liquidity of the banking sector resulting from rising levels of reserve money had to be continually mopped up. The instrument of open market operations was not available for this task since the interest rates on government securities were well below 'market rates'. The task of absorbing excess liquidity in the system had to be undertaken mainly through increasing the cash reserve ratio. In fact, in mid-1991, the cash reserve requirement was 25 per cent on incremental deposits. In addition, the statutory liquidity ratio was 38.5 per cent. Thus, nearly 63.5 per cent of incremental deposits was pre-empted in one form or another.

In 1983, the Reserve Bank of India appointed a committee under the Chairmanship of the distinguished economist Professor Sukhamoy Chakravarty to review the working of the Indian Monetary System. I was a member of the Committee. The Committee's Report covered a wide range. One of its major recommendations was to regulate money supply consistent with the expected growth rate in real income and a tolerable level of inflation. Recognising the fact that government borrowing from the Reserve Bank had been a major factor contributing to the increase in reserve money and therefore, money supply, the Committee wanted an agreement between the Central Government and the Reserve Bank on the level of monetary expansion and the extent of monetisation of the fiscal deficit. Without such a coordination, the Committee felt that Reserve Bank's efforts to contain monetary expansion within the limits set by expected increase in output could become impossible. While this recommendation of the Committee was accepted in principle, it could take a concrete shape only in the '90s.

In the wake of the economic crisis in 1991 triggered by a difficult balance of payments situation, the government introduced far reaching changes in India's economic policy. Monetary policy was used effectively to overcome the balance of payments crisis and promptly restore stability. An extremely tight monetary policy was put in place to reap the full benefits of the devaluation of the rupee that was announced. However, it did not stop with that. Financial sector reforms became an integral part of the new reform program. Reform of the banking sector and capital market was intended to help and accelerate the growth of the real sector. Banking sector reforms covered a wide gamut. The most important of the reforms was the prescription of prudential norms including capital-adequacy ratio. In addition, certain key changes were made with respect to monetary policy environment which gave to commercial banks greater autonomy in relation to the management of their liabilities and assets. First and foremost, the administered structure of interest rates was dismantled step by step. Banks in India today enjoy the complete freedom to prescribe the deposit rates and interest rates on loans except in the case of very small loans and export credit. Second, the government began borrowing at market rates of interest. The auction system was introduced both in relation to Treasury Bills and dated securities. Third, with the economic reforms emphasising a reduction in fiscal deficit, pre-emptions in the form of cash reserve ratio and statutory liquidity ratio were steadily brought down. Fourth, while the allocation of credit for the priority sector credit continued, the extent of cross subsidisation in terms of interest rates was considerably brought down because of the reform of the interest rate structure.

Monetary policy in the 1990s in India had to deal with several issues, some of which traditional but some totally new in the context of the increasingly open economy in which the country had to operate. In the first few years, monetary policy had to contend with the consequences of devaluation and the need to quickly restore price stability to obtain the full benefits of devaluation. While the fiscal deficit was being brought down, the question of monetisation of the deficit continued to remain an issue and a solution had to be found. This eventually led to a new agreement between government and RBI on financing deficit. The system of ad-hoc Treasury Bills under which the Government of India could replenish its cash balances by issuing Treasury Bills in favour of the Reserve Bank and which had the effect of monetising deficit was phased out. It was replaced by a system of Ways and Means Advances which had a fixed ceiling. The Reserve Bank of India continued to subscribe to the dated securities at its discretion. During 1993 and 1994, for the first time monetary policy had to deal with the monetary impact of capital inflows with the foreign exchange reserves increasing sharply from $9.2 billion in March 1992 to $25.1 billion in March 1995. In 1995–96, the change in perception with reference to exchange rate after a prolonged period of nominal exchange rate stability vis-a-vis the US dollar brought into play the use of monetary policy to stabilise the rupee — an entirely new experience for the central bank. Similar situations arose later on also at the time of the East Asian crisis. Monetary policy had begun to operate within a changed institutional framework brought about by the financial sector reforms. It is this change in the institutional framework that gave a new dimension to monetary policy. New transmission channels opened up. Indirect monetary controls gradually assumed importance. With the progressive dismantling of the administered interest rate structure and the evolution of a regime of market determined interest rate on government securities, open market operations including 'repo' and 'reverse repo' operations emerged for the first time as an instrument of monetary control. Bank Rate acquired a new role in the changed context. The '90s paved the way for the emergence of monetary policy as an independent instrument of economic policy.

Monetary policy in the 1990s had also to be conducted in the context of the financial sector reforms. The need to reduce non-performing assets and to conform to the new prudential norms put the banking industry under great strain. While introducing banking sector reforms, care had to be taken to ensure that there was no compromise with the basic objectives of monetary policy.

In the post-reform period, the Indian economy has done well. Since 1992–93 the average annual growth rate of the economy in real terms has been 6.3 per cent. The average inflation rate, as measured by the wholesale price index in the 1990s has been 7.2 per cent. However, the significant fact to note is that the average inflation rate since 1996–97 has been less than 5 per cent. Broad money grew at an average annual rate of 17 per cent per annum. The exchange rate of the rupee in terms of US dollar has declined by 24 per cent since July, 1997. This decline is smaller than what other countries in this region have experienced. The current account deficit has averaged since 1992–93 at 1 per cent of the GDP. The foreign exchange reserves in the country have risen from about $5 billion to $43 billion as of a recent date. These broad macroeconomic indicators show a substantial improvement in the Indian economy, even though several concerns such as slow reduction in poverty ratio and slow growth rate in agriculture persist.

Issues of Concern

Let me now focus on some of the issues which came to be debated extensively during 1990s. These issues are not specific to India or developing economies. They have been debated in the context of the developed countries also. Nevertheless, these issues which I want to highlight have a special significance for developing countries like India.

Objective

The first question that needs to be addressed relates to the objective or objectives of monetary policy. A recurring question is whether monetary policy should be concerned with all the goals of economic policy. The issue of 'objective' has become important because of the need to provide a clear guidance to monetary policymakers. Indeed, this aspect has assumed added significance in the context of the increasing stress on the autonomy of Central Banks. Autonomy goes with accountability and accountability in turn requires a clear enunciation of the goals.

Since the inception of development planning, the broad objectives of India's economic policy have been to achieve a faster rate of growth, ensure reasonable degree of price stability and promote distributive justice. Working of monetary policy in India over the past several decades would reveal that monetary policy has emphasised these broad objectives of our economic policy. In one of my earlier articles, I had said:

> In a broad sense the objectives of monetary policy can be no
> different from the over all objectives of economic policy. The broad
> objectives of monetary policy in India have been: (1) to maintain
> a reasonable degree of price stability and (2) to help accelerate
> the rate of economic growth. The emphasis as between the two
> objectives has changed from year to year, depending upon the
> conditions prevailing in that year and in the previous year.

The question of a dominant objective arises essentially because of the multiplicity of objectives and the inherent conflict among such objectives. Jan Tinbergen had argued decades ago that there should be as many instruments as there are objectives, if all objectives are to be fulfilled. Faced with multiple objectives that are equally relevant and desirable, there is always the problem of assigning to each instrument the most appropriate objective. This 'assignment rule' favours monetary policy as the most appropriate instrument to achieve the objective of price stability. It is this line of reasoning which has led to the single objective approach.

The crucial question that is being debated in India as elsewhere is whether the pursuit of the objective of price stability by monetary authorities undermines the ability of the economy to attain and sustain high growth. A considerable part of the relevant research effort has been devoted to the trade-off between economic growth and price stability. Empirical evidence on the relationship between growth and inflation in a cross country framework is somewhat inconclusive because such studies include countries with an inflation rate as low as one to two per cent to those with inflation rates going beyond 200 to 300 per cent. These studies, however, clearly establish that growth rates become increasingly negative at higher rates of inflation.

The case of price stability as the objective of monetary policy rests on the assumption that volatility in prices creates uncertainty in decision-making. Rising prices adversely affect savings while they make speculative investments more attractive. The most important contribution of the financial system to an economy is its ability to augment savings and allocate resources more efficiently. A regime of rising prices vitiates the atmosphere for promotion of savings and allocation of investment. Apart from all these, there is a social dimension particularly in developing countries. Inflation adversely affects those who have no hedges against it and that includes all the poorer sections of the community. The fiscal consolidation also becomes easier in an environment of reasonable degree of price stability. In a period of rising prices, the gap between revenues and expenditures widens. Expenditures tend to grow at a faster rate than revenues because many components of expenditures such as employees' compensation are closely linked to variations in prices.

The question that recurs very often in the minds of the policymakers is whether in the short run, there is a trade-off between inflation and growth which can be exploited. In the industrial countries, a solution is sought through the adoption of Taylor's rule which prescribes that the signal interest rate be fixed taking into account the deviations of inflation rate from the target and actual output from its potential. In this rule, the coefficient of inflation deviation term is fixed at a level higher than unity. While the rule is intuitively appealing, there are serious problems in determining the value of the coefficients. In this context, the critical question to raise is: At what level of inflation, do adverse consequences begin to set in? It is this inflation threshold which will provide some guidance to the policymakers. Below and around this threshold level of inflation, there is greater manoeuvrability for the policymakers to take into account other considerations. Interestingly, the Chakravarty Committee regarded the acceptable rise in prices as 4 per cent. This, according to the Committee, will reflect changes in relative prices necessary to attract resources to growth sectors. I have myself indicated that in the Indian context, inflation rate in the range of 5 to 6 per cent may be acceptable. There is some amount of judgement involved in this, as econometric models are not in a position to capture all the costs of inflation. This approach provides some guidance as to when policy has to become tight or to be loosened. It is also necessary for the policymakers to note that this order of inflation is higher than what the industrial countries are aiming at. This will have some implications for the exchange rate of the currency. While the open economy helps to overcome domestic supply shocks, it also imposes the burden to keep the inflation rate in alignment with other countries.

Intermediate Target

The second issue relates to the intermediate target. In India since the mid-'80s the target chosen has been broad money. The Chakaravarty Committee recommended a system of flexible monetary targeting. It is true that central banks in several countries in the industrial world have abandoned intermediate targets and have focussed on the final target such as inflation control. While this has the advantage of specifying the ultimate objective in clear and precise terms, it must be admitted that there is some uncertainty regarding the route through which this will be achieved. One of the reasons for the abandonment of intermediate targets in these countries has been the breakdown of the relationship between monetary aggregates and the inflation rate. The demand function for money has been found to be unstable. However, in India, studies show that the money demand function is a stable function of select variables and it can be used to reasonably predict inflation. Several statistical functions of the demand for money estimated by using the equilibrium and disequilibrium analysis provide overwhelming evidence on the long run stability of the money demand function. Perhaps some of the factors that have contributed to the instability of the demand function for money in the industrially advanced countries such as financial innovations and large movements of funds across the border are yet to have the same impact in India. In the demand function for money in India, income emerges as the most dominant variable. Such a function enables the authorities to estimate the appropriate growth in money supply, given the expected increase in real output and the acceptable level in price increase. With the freeing of the interest rate structure, interest rate may also emerge as an appropriate intermediate variable in the coming years. In fact, with the inflation rate coming down and remaining in a narrow range, it will be possible to focus on interest rate along with overall monetary aggregates. However, as of now, money supply seems to be an appropriate target. Such a target is relatively well understood by the public and provides unambiguously the stance of monetary policy.

The literature on monetary economics talks of four distinct monetary transmission channels. They are: (1) Quantum Channel, especially relating to money supply and credit; (2) Interest Rate Channel; (3) Exchange Rate Channel; and (4) Asset Prices Channel. While the emphasis in India so far has been on the quantum channel, with the development of financial markets and closer integration of such markets, the interest rate channel will assume importance. It must be noted that at the equilibrium both quantity and price are determined. Changes in interest rates cannot be ordained. The appropriate quantitative changes in money will have to be brought about even though the signal for change may be given by the price variable like interest rate.

Level of Interest Rate

Another question of importance that has arisen relates to the appropriate level of interest rate. The nominal interest rate comprises of three elements: (1) the real rate of interest; (2) inflation expectations; and (3) a discount factor for uncertainties. The effectiveness of monetary policy to bring down the nominal interest rate will depend on the impact that this policy will have on inflation expectations and on the perception of uncertainty in the economy. A monetary policy that is geared to maintain reasonable price stability, if it is successful, can help to bring down the interest rate in sympathy with the downward drift in inflation. Inflationary expectations can be broken, if the monetary authority enjoys high credibility. However, this leaves the real rate of interest to be determined. The real interest rate is not an observed variable. The real interest rate is influenced by several long-term factors such as saving and investment balance in the economy and the rate of return on capital. Theory tells us that on an economy-wide basis, this rate should not exceed the real rate of growth. In fast growing economies the real rate of interest will be higher. In South Korea during the years of very rapid economic growth the real rate of interest was around 6 to 7 per cent in several years. The real rate of interest is thus related to the rate of growth of the economy. In the early 1990s in India, the real rate of interest was low because the inflation rate was in the range of 8 to 10 per cent. However, with the break in the inflation rate beginning 1996–97, the real rate of interest has gone up. As mentioned earlier, the inflation rate on an average has remained at less than 5 per cent since 1996–97. However, it must be kept in mind that the real rate of interest will have to be relatively higher in developing economies which seek to maintain a high savings rate and which aim at growing at more than 6 to 7 per cent per annum. This is typically the situation in India. A situation of high real rate of interest accompanied by high growth rate must be distinguished from other situations when real rates of interest may remain high. In this context, it is worth noting that the high level of nominal interest rate in developing economies may also be due to high intermediation costs. Improved efficiency can reduce the spread between the deposit rate and lending rate and bring the lending rate in closer alignment with fundamental factors.

Exchange Rate Management

The role of monetary authority in exchange rate management came into focus in the 1990s. Since 1975, the exchange rate of the rupee was determined with reference to the daily exchange rate movements of a selected number of currencies of the countries which were India's major trading partners. The Reserve Bank of India was required to maintain the exchange rate within a band on either side of a base 'basket' value. This allowed the achievement of a medium-term real effective exchange rate (REER) objective through changes in the NEER. Such a regime could be maintained only with the support of extensive exchange controls and import controls. The reform measures introduced in 1991 included significant changes in the foreign trade regime and exchange rate management. The devaluation of the rupee in mid-1991 was followed by a system of dual exchange rate system in March 1992. A year later, the dual system was abolished and the country moved towards a unified market determined exchange rate system. The monetary authority does not intervene in the market process of rate determination as long as orderly conditions prevail in the exchange market and the exchange rate reflects macroeconomic fundamentals.

The approach to exchange rate by the monetary authorities in the developed world generally has been to let the market determine the rate. However, there have been several exceptions. There have been occasions when central banks in these countries have intervened, some times in a concerted way, when exchange markets became volatile. The Indian experience with market determined exchange rate system is that there have been several occasions when the RBI had to intervene strongly to prevent volatility. This happened in 1995 and 1996 and later in 1997 and 1998 at the time of the East Asian crisis. The impact of the East Asian crisis on the Indian market was minimal. This was partly due to the reason that while India subscribed to current account convertibility under Clause VIII of the IMF agreement, the capital account liberalisation was undertaken cautiously. Besides, India's current account deficit during this period was low. In fact, in 1991, a High-Level Committee on Balance of Payments had made specific recommendations regarding the level of current account deficit, the size and composition of capital flows, the management of external debt including short-term debt and the quantum of foreign exchange reserves. Implementation of these recommendations stood India in good stead at the time of the East Asian crisis.

In narrow, underdeveloped markets like in India, there is a tendency for the herd instinct which amplifies the fluctuations. This can cause volatile and destabilising movements in the exchange rate which may go beyond any correction, required by the fundamentals. Even in developed markets there is a tendency for the market to 'overshoot', when a critical mass in terms of the perception of overvaluation in the exchange rate is reached. With narrow markets, the danger is greater. On such occasions, the monetary authority has to step in to ensure orderly market conditions. The monetary authority must, however, recognise that integration of markets is inevitable and therefore action must be spread across the markets to achieve results.

In developing economies like India, trade flows both visible and invisible, dominate the balance of payments. That is why for the exchange rate regime in India, continuous monitoring of the real exchange rate with an appropriate base becomes important. It provides valuable information to the authorities on the behaviour of the current account to which it is intrinsically linked. A monetary policy geared to domestic price stability in this situation helps to avoid disruptive adjustments in the exchange rate. In that sense monetary policy and exchange rate management become intertwined.

Financial Stability

Increasingly macroeconomic stability as an objective of central banking is closely linked to financial stability. It is easy to see how the two are interlinked. Financial stability broadly implies the stability of the important institutions and markets forming part of the financial system. Financial stability requires that the key institutions in the financial system are stable, in that, there is a high degree of confidence about meeting contractual obligations without interruption or outside assistance. While the complementarity between the objectives of macrostability and financial stability is easily recognised, the one question that needs to be addressed is whether there can be a conflict between the two objectives. It is not inconceivable to have situations in which the price stability objective might call for a restrictive policy, while the financial market conditions may demand a somewhat liberal policy to provide relief. The Reserve Bank of India was extremely conscious of this dilemma. Banking sector reforms were in full swing in the 1990s which necessarily put the banking system under strain. While facilitating the smooth transition, RBI took care that there was no dilution of the basic objectives of monetary policy. However, viewed as part of overall economic stability, financial stability need not run at cross-purpose with other dimensions of macroeconomic stability. Normally, price stability should provide an environment favourable to financial stability. If on occasions dealing directly with financial stability becomes necessary, it must be done as in the case of intervention in the foreign exchange markets. Actions to maintain financial stability in those circumstances may be in the long run interest of economic stability.

Autonomy of Central Banks

Autonomy of central banks has become an article of faith in the industrial countries. It has been written into the constitution setting up the European Central Bank. The literature on this subject is growing. There is a general consensus to give instrument independence to central banks among countries that have decided that the single objective of monetary policy is inflation control. Autonomy implies discretion to central banks to decide on the timing and nature of monetary policy intervention. It also calls for transparency in relation to both objectives and strategies. The increased use of explicit targets by central banks is part of the broader move to build credibility through transparency. It is quite true that in India, monetary policy has been very much conditioned by the stance of fiscal policy. The system of the scheme of ad hoc Treasury Bills facilitated monetisation of the fiscal deficit without limit and without prior approval.

The 1990s saw the phasing out of the system and the introduction of the scheme of Ways and Means Advance. This was a major step towards the achievement of greater discretion. The Fiscal Responsibility Bill that is now before the Indian Parliament takes this to its logical conclusion. When enacted this would be a great step forward not only in fiscal but monetary management. Two associated comments may be made in this context.

First, an autonomous central bank does not mean lack of coordination with the government. Nor does it imply lack of harmony. In fact, harmony in the sense in which it is used in classical symphonic music will be achieved. In a symphony, different artistes play different notes simultaneously but in effect create a blend that produces the best of music. However, the stances of monetary policy and fiscal policy cannot run at cross-purposes. For example, a lax fiscal policy accompanied by a tight monetary policy can lead to a sharp increase in interest rate. On the other hand, an accommodative monetary policy in a period of lax fiscal policy can lead to explosive increase in prices. While monetary and fiscal coordination is desirable, it is important at the same time that the monetary authority which has its own specific agenda must have the institutional autonomy and should not be burdened with functions which may come in conflict with its own special objective. It is in this context that the Reserve Bank of India and the Government of India are examining the issue whether the management of public debt can be delinked from RBI.

Second, the emergence of an autonomous central bank does not mean that the 'state of bliss' has arrived. It only enables the central bank to pursue a consistent monetary policy over a long time. Then the onus of responsibility for the conduct of monetary policy will rest on the shoulders of the Reserve Bank, where it should logically rest. In an open economy, the task of the central bank will be rendered more difficult if it does not have the autonomy and discretion to make changes quickly in response to external shocks.

There was a time when it was said that central banking was neither a science nor an art but a craft. This is at best a half-truth. Central banking has never been a case of applying well known remedies to well-known problems. 'Rules versus discretion' has been a subject of long-standing debate in monetary policy. Rigid rules such as those implicit in gold standard will give to central banks no room for manoeuvrability. On the other hand, total discretion with respect to objectives and instruments will make monetary policy indeterminate. That is why the new phrase 'constrained discretion'. This will require the central banks to be transparent and explicit with respect to objectives and strategies, while leaving the freedom to them to choose the timing and nature of their actions. This is the type of autonomy towards which every central bank should move.

Oration 6:
2002 K.R. Narayanan Oration

Message from the President
of the Republic of India

I am delighted to know that the K.R. Narayanan Oration instituted at the Australia South Asia Research Centre (ASARC) of The Australian National University during the visit to this centre by my predecessor-in-office during 1994 has now become a regular feature of the Centre's calendar and that eminent personalities from various fields of life have delivered these orations on topics of immediate relevance to India.

I am happy to note that ASARC is continuing with its high tradition of inviting those personalities who have made outstanding contributions in their sphere of work, which is relevant to India. It is in this light that I see the name of Professor Meghnad Desai of the London School of Economics who is delivering this year's oration on 'Democracy and Development: India 1947–2002'. Professor Desai needs no introduction. We are all aware of the intellectual prowess and the policy analytical framework, which he has brought to bear upon contemporary development economics and the related social sciences. Having seen the birth and the early days of independent India first hand, I am sure there can be no better person to walk the august audience through the first 50 years of our Independence and the working of our democracy and its institutions.

This will be an excellent opportunity for our friends in ASARC and in Australia at large to get to know about India's experience of working a democracy after over 200 years of subjugation under alien rule. We have identified five areas where India has a core competence for an integrated action for transforming India into a developed nation: 1) agriculture and food processing — we have set a target of 360 million tons of food and agricultural production, other areas of agriculture and agro-food processing would bring prosperity to rural people and speed up economic growth; 2) reliable and quality electric power for all parts of the country; 3) education and health care — we have seen, based on experience that education and health care are inter-related; 4) information and communication technology — this is one of our core competences, we believe this area can be used to promote education in remote areas and also to create national wealth; and 5) strategic sectors — this area, fortunately, witnessed growth in nuclear technology, space technology and defence technology.

These five areas are closely inter-related and lead to national, food and economic security. A strong partnership among and between R&D academics, industry, business and the community as a whole with government departments and agencies will be essential to accomplish this vision. The key to success is in various forms of connectivity such as physical, electronic, knowledge, and economic. I am sure Professor Desai's oration will also give the audience sufficient intellectual queries and knowledge. I wish the event all success

A.P.J. Abdul Kalam
New Delhi
2002

Democracy and Development: India 1947–2002

Meghnad Desai

It gives me a particular pleasure to be giving the Narayanan Oration at The Australian National University. President Narayanan is a perfect example of how despite numerous obstacles merit will shine through. His life exemplifies the progress India has made, warts and all, over the entire 20th century but especially since Independence. Names of Harold Laski and Jawaharlal Nehru play a major part in his early story. On a personal note, he has also showed me immense kindness but perhaps more because I teach at his alma mater than for anything personal to me.

It is also a great pleasure to come back to ANU where I twice spent a term teaching in 1980 and 1984 and where I claim many friends. Australia has taken a great interest in South Asia as the centres here and in other Australian universities testify.

India Since 1991

It is 11 years since India had the economic shock of its life and had to rethink its economic policy and rearrange its economic institutions. It was nearly 10 years ago that I had the opportunity to welcome the drastic change and wish that it would be more rather than less drastic, not a popular position among my economist friends in India at that time (Desai 1993). This is thus a good opportunity to see how far India has got in its response to the shock of near bankruptcy in early 1991.

But a lot more has also happened to India in its political life since 1991. Indeed it is hard to say whether it is the political or the economic map that has changed more in the last 10 or more years. In various articles written over these years I have also tried to chart the political dynamics of the 1990s (see various references in the Bibliography). While there was always implicitly a political background to my economic comments and an economic background to my political comments, I would like to take this opportunity of the Narayanan Oration to try a synthesis.

The separate strands which need to be synthesised are as follows:

- In its first phase lasting just over three decades (1947–80), India's economic policy was driven by a model of national self-sufficiency. It was built around, indeed pioneered, an Import Substitution Industrialisation (ISI) strategy. It also chose (and this is separate strictly from ISI) a capital-intensive program hoping that matters of employment creation, consumer goods supply especially foodgrains would take care of themselves. Political developments in the mid and late 1950s forced a situation in which the planning authorities had to reverse the neglect of agriculture. The Green Revolution, which occurred by accident in the 1960s, corrected the earlier urban biases of the Second and Third Five-Year Plans but the poor performance of the manufacturing sector — in terms of inefficiency, excess capacity and low quality — persisted in both the private and public organised sectors. The growth rate was low relative both to early aspirations (Bombay Plan for instance) and to the rates achieved by other countries. This was the so-called Hindu Rate of Growth: 3.5 per cent per annum and 1.3 per cent per capita.

- Over this period 1947–80, India's political life exhibited a lot of stability and a solid, indeed unique achievement among post-colonial polities in creating and sustaining a vibrant political democracy. Single Party Dominance nurtured this democratic life except during the infamous Emergency, which was brief and was reversed by that very democratic process it tried to subvert. The dominant vision of nationalism was built around secularism, non-alignment and socialism. There was however beginning to be an assertion of the various regional, caste and religious — by and large 'subaltern' forces — in the federal polity. Indeed the Janata Government of 1977–79 reflected this.

- During the 1980s, there was a decade of restoration of Single Party Dominance but a relaxation of the imperative of economic self-sufficiency. There was borrowing from abroad — from the

IMF, from foreign commercial banks and then from NRIs. But the economic institutions of permit-license Raj did not change and there was no relaxation of domestic economic policy in parallel with foreign borrowing. Growth rate went up to 5.5 per cent, 3.5 per cent per capita.

- The decade of the 1980s stored up much trouble for political life later on. Secularism was compromised into a parallel populism with accommodation of the orthodoxies of the two major religions as Rajiv Gandhi's decisions on Shah Bano case and the *shilanyas* at Ayodhya showed. The subaltern elements continued to grow powerful at regional levels.

- The 1990s ruptured the old model in two ways. Economic dirigisme — often mislabelled socialism — became untenable as India could not repay its commercial borrowings without drastic reform. At the same time the end of Congress dominance unleashed forces — implementation of the recommendations of the Mandal Commission with all it meant about valorisation of caste distinctions, rise of the Hindutva parivar, *dalit* militancy — which ended for the decade and more any hope of a single-party government. In a strange combination, the arrival of globalisation saw India modernise and liberalise on the economic front but become less secular and more ethnically divided than before politically. Modernity in India thus took a different path from what its champions in the early days after Independence had charted for it. It is not a secular socialist democratic India but a liberal, increasingly Hindu nationalist democratic India that is shaping its own future.

- On the economic front the reform forced upon India by the trauma of 1991 has proved irreversible and effective. Despite much hesitation, the reform process has persisted and raised the growth rate nearer to 6.5 per cent for GDP and 4.5 per cent per capita. The liberalisation process has been slow relative to countries of Eastern Europe but it has been consensual. Even as politicians compete in populist rhetoric about protecting the jobs and the poor, it is clear that no possible combination of parties exists which upon gaining power would or even could reverse the liberalisation process.

- There is one solid continuity despite the change in party dominance and in economic philosophy over the last 55 years. This is the nationalist program of a militarily strong India. Even as India preached peace and non-alignment in 1950s it built up its military production capacity especially its atomic and nuclear research. Whether Congress or BJP, whether Nehru, Indira and Rajiv Gandhi or Vajpayee, the determination to make India militarily strong has been common. There is no peace party in India. Indeed, it can be seen now that the ISI strategy and the insistence on self-sufficiency arose from a defence policy that meant India to be a powerful regional power. The election of President Narayanan's successor has crowned that policy with official recognition.

It is this cluster of trends that I wish to explore. The decline of secularism and socialism, the rise of liberalism and religiosity, the persistence of nationalism as a force even as its nature has changed. Democracy has been the universal solvent in this process. In order to appreciate the importance of Indian democracy, it is necessary to go back to the early history of Independent India.

The Revolution of 1946–49: The Constituent Assembly in Action

The decision to adopt universal adult franchise with a Westminster style parliamentary system was a revolutionary decision of the Constituent Assembly. It was not inevitable nor was it a conservative decision. Given the experience of almost every other post-colonial country with constitutional change, it is a miracle that the Constituent Assembly (the Assembly hereafter), elected as it was on a restricted franchise got it so right. But this choice revolutionary as it is, profoundly constricted and shaped the subsequent trends.

The Assembly rejected the Gandhian option — a decentralised village republic with local autonomy and indirect democracy with an obviously weak Centre. A strong Centre was basic to Indian nationalism as its one great fear was, indeed is, of India breaking up into many nations. In the wake of Partition, a weak Centre was not going to be chosen whatever the Father of the Nation may say. The Assembly also firmly ruled out any role for the feudal order — the hundreds of native princes, for whom a role was envisaged in the 1935 Government of India Act. Unlike Malaysia, India did not give these kings even a ceremonial role. In copying the Westminster system, it replaced the Crown by an elected President with similar powers. It also rejected a single party polity which must have been tempting as it was for many African and Asian countries under the spurious rationalisation that multi-party democracy was a Western luxury that a poor country could ill afford. The Communist alternative was also rejected. Private property, including foreign property, was not disturbed but could be subject to state takeover with compensation. Land was not confiscated or nationalised but land reform was made feasible.

The democracy that was chosen was radical in other ways as well. There was to be no recognition of any ethnic, religious or caste basis of citizenship. There were to be no separate electorates, no religious qualification for holding office, nor a literacy test. Women were given the vote on the same terms as men when even in the developed countries, e.g. France, women's suffrage had only recently (i.e. 1945) been granted. But by the same token there were no guarantees of minority rights qua minority; no consociational arrangement in a formal sense whereby a minority had veto rights over drastic abridgements of its rights by the Majority vote Minorities, like majorities were treated qua Westminster as collections of individuals rather than ethnic blocks and therefore were to be looked after as part of the democratic process by legislative or by executive actions. Thus despite its being elected from a small and restricted franchise which could have made it conservative, the Assembly chose an individualist atomistic model of democracy for India rather than one grounded in caste, religion and language identities. Secularism was the implicit guarantee that a religious minority had nothing to fear from majority rule. Religion was not to be a subject which could be legislated about.[1]

It will be my contention that this bold revolutionary choice was crucial in shaping subsequent choices and indeed in making some of these subsequent choices less bold than they could have been. In making the Constitution, ethnicity-blind and religion-blind, the Founding Fathers were rejecting the trauma which had led to the Partition and hoping to avoid further fragmentation. But they were also denying reality, not only of the country at large but even of their own personal identities. Indians were individuals of course like anyone else but they also lived in a vital sense their ethnic, religious regional, linguistic identities. These identities were not to be left behind when they entered the political arena. Nor were these identities an invention of the colonial masters or a badge of poverty or underdevelopment ready to disappear at the first whiff of economic progress as Nehru in his more passionate moments thought.

---

1   Lijphart (1996) has argued that India's polity is de facto consociational. I have my doubts.

Indian democracy was shaped by these ignored identities as they asserted themselves in the daily course of electoral politics. At the elite level, their own orthodox upbringing, their upper caste loyalties if they were Hindus, their relatively prosperous state meant that the choices taken were their choices. But they were also the progeny of Macaulay and had absorbed western ideas of progress and equality, of liberty and the greatest good of the greatest number. They may have lived much as their fathers did at home but they thought and spoke the Englishman's language.

Social Conservatism and Economic Radicalism

Two crucial choices were made early in the years after Independence. One was to be socially conservative and not use the State apparatus to abolish the caste system with its inegalitarian logic of hierarchy and status. Primary education and adult literacy were state subjects and thus left to stagnate in those conservative states in the Hindi heartland where literacy, especially female and *dalit* literacy, were seen to be threats to the social order. Although untouchability was made illegal in the Constitution, the attendant evils of caste were left undisturbed. Muslim society was even more delicately handled. As far as Hindu society was concerned an attempt was made mainly at Nehru's behest to codify and systematise Hindu Family Law, though he met with resistance in his desire to modernise it from the then President Dr Rajendra Prasad. But Muslim Law was out of bounds even for Nehru. Thus political independence and the revolutionary decision to adopt democracy did not result in any state-led political program of social reform. Indian society was allowed to reform itself in a *laissez-faire* way.

In the economic sphere, on the other hand, radicalism was the order of the day. India had, by 1947, one of the oldest modern industries in the Third World (though it was not so called till later). It had the largest group of native modern capitalist entrepreneurs, the largest jute industry, a cotton textile industry which was globally competitive and was the seventh largest industrial country in terms of volume of industrial output. But the perception of the nationalist movement was that India had been deindustrialised by British rule and that industrialisation was the first priority. Free trade and foreign capital imports were to be shunned. India would become a self-sufficient industrialised country by relying on planning led by the State.

This was not particularly surprising both in terms of the thinking of the Congress as moulded by Nehru and the climate of the times. Free market ideology was on the retreat and many thought that capitalism too was on its way out. India had been much taken by the Soviet example and indeed even by the German example of planning in a mixed economy. What was not necessary, however, to this strategy was to neglect if not punish the Industries already established, especially the cotton textile industry and shifting resources to machine building. There was rampant export pessimism, unjustified as subsequent investigations showed (see articles in Ahluwalia and Little (1998) by Bhagwati, Desai and Sen). The strategy failed to take advantage of India's early start in modern industry and reinvented many of the things which were there but were tarred with foreign brush.

Thus India created a dependent entrepreneurial class in place of one that had survived foreign rule, depressed modern consumer goods industries and fostered small-scale ones which were capital wasting and inefficient, built at an enormous expense a basic goods sector with a long lead time before it could bring better consumer goods to the people and failed to generate industrial employment. The public sector, mainly in services, became the biggest provider of employment in the modern sector. Jointly the private and public organised industrial sector became a stagnant and highly privileged pool of a limited number of employees. Together the public services and the organised industrial sector employed 15 per cent of the labour force. This was called socialism (Desai 1993).

The strategy was wasteful of scarce capital and quite perverse in its determined neglect of the rules of efficient allocation. It is one thing not to get prices right but quite another to deliberately get them wrong. Restrictions on interest rates, multiple exchange rates, subsidies to inefficient industries, taxation on movement of agricultural commodities which constituted a tax on agriculture, perks to labour in the organised sector and de facto taxation of the informal sector by a lack of subsidies, etc. All this was done by an elite fully economically educated but determined to flout the rules of western economics.

The results were predictable — slow growth of output and employment and persistence of poverty and inequality through the first phase of 30 years. With slow growth of jobs in the private sector, government jobs at all levels became much sought after and the democratic electoral system was harnessed to provide patronage. The first task of government became provision of jobs through the public fisc and then the sale of permits and licences.

Triangulation Indian Style

Thus we get a unique triangular interaction. Economic radicalism leads to slow growth biased towards elite jobs. Social conservatism strengthens caste, regional and religious loyalties. Political democracy allows the mobilisation of these loyalties in an electoral competition to capture governments at State and then at Central levels. This capture then translates into jobs for the newly included. Yet the economic surplus does not expand by this route. So the system crashes in the 1970s under the weight of its own demands. A way out had to be found. It was the economic radicalism which began to be abandoned because that was the only way surplus could be enhanced. This is the way the model unfolded itself.

The interaction of social conservatism and economic radicalism in the context of political democracy produced a most interesting mutation. To get the fruits of patronage, non-elite groups had to get organised and they did this through their caste and regional identities. Linguistic states had to be created during the 1950s in response to popular pressure from the local capitalists as well as local middle classes who wanted public jobs and public contracts. Next came in the 1960s the pressure from the rural areas to divert resources to agriculture. This happily bore fruits in the form of the Green Revolution with input subsidies as well as price guarantees for outputs. But even then the discontent due to slow growth continued. This broke into a flood of protest from tribal *dalit* and lower caste groups in the 1970s, and were brought together under the Lokayan banner. This was what unhinged Indira Gandhi and led to the Emergency. Groups previously downtrodden were finding their voices and using the unreformed social structures of caste and religion to make their claims on the surplus. But the surplus was not expanding due to the elitist policies being followed.[2]

---

2   See for a most thoughtful account of the lower orders' entry into politics Christophe Jaffrelot (2002).

The Escape from Triangulation

The Janata government was the transition between the first and the second phase. By itself ineffective, it mirrored the subaltern groups which had come to stake their claim to power. But Janata had no organising vision to unite these groups as the elite vision of Nehruvian nationalism had. What Mrs Gandhi learned from her defeat was that the new India could not be run on old elite lines. She reinvented the Nehruvian vision keeping the rhetoric of socialism and secularism but changing the content.

The two major changes were that in the economic sphere she abandoned self-sufficiency as a goal but retained dirigisme (socialism). Foreign loans were taken but the economy not restructured. On the political side she used both Hindu and Muslim imagery to garner Hindu vote banks, and of course Muslim ones too. The foreign loans and some liberalisation on import account led to higher growth. The Green Revolution was also now routinely yielding good harvests so food imports were no longer an item on the balance of trade. Of course not all the regional and linguistic loyalties could be bought off. The demand for Khalistan was a demand too far and Indira Gandhi gave her life in her determination to combat that.

What was happening on the ideological front was less obvious but no less important for that. Indian nationalism had suffered a body blow with the Partition. The India that Nehru had 'discovered' during his final prison term was not the India that he came to be the leader of. He gave a new vision to the nation — of a non-aligned, secular modern, even socialist India. But the war with China shattered the non-alignment. Pragmatic consideration forced Indira Gandhi to replace secularism by parallel and simultaneous flattery of Hindu and Muslim religiosity. Socialism hung by a slim thread of dirigisme but one reinforced by foreign loans. Elsewhere Asian countries were marching ahead economically; China had abandoned Maoism in favour of Deng's pragmatism. Even Pakistan was no inferior to India in terms of income levels or industrial performance.

What was going to be India's vision of nationhood if the modernist Nehruvian vision with its secularism, socialism and non-alignment was no longer adequate? There were two rival models on offer. One was the religious Hindutva model which had been shunned aside in favour of the Congress one early in the independence movement which now began to be revived by the Jan Sangh/BJP. The other model — less articulated — was the one which came to the forth in the first Round Table Conference in 1929. This was the India of regions, languages, religious and ethnic identities. This was how the British saw India but the Congress rejected this vision in favour of a 'unity in diversity' vision. But this vision somewhat subaltern was what would have ruled India had the Cabinet Mission's plan been accepted. India would have remained united, unpartitioned but would have been a confederation. With provincial autonomy for big states like Panjab and Bengal and Sind, local nationalisms would have flourished.[3]

In the years since 1947, it was this vision which strengthened itself as linguistic and caste parties became electorally successful. It is these forces which have become the challenge to the Hindutva vision. Under the leadership of Mulayam Singh Yadav or Laloo Prasad Yadav or Karunanindhi/Jayalalitha or Chandrababu Naidu this confederate vision is also secular and can align either with the Left or the Centre Right (Congress). As the Congress hegemony fell apart at the end of the 1980s, this vision became a pillar of Indian politics.

The decisive change did not come with Rajiv Gandhi but after his defeat. He confirmed the abandonment of social reform by capitulating on the rights of Muslim women in the Shah Bano case and yielded to Hindu pressure on *shilanyas* for the potential Ramajanmabhumi temple on the site of the Babri mosque. It was electoral cynicism but it did not pay. But what a decade of growth at 5.5 per cent did was to create opportunities in the private sector which the old elite could exploit. It began to disengage from public sector jobs. There were better perks in the private sector. This created room for meeting the next explosion in subaltern demands which V.P. Singh tried to accommodate by undertaking to implement the Mandal recommendations.

The Crisis of 1991 and the New Dispensation

The uplift in the economic growth rate during the 1980s had been bought with foreign borrowings but without restructuring the economy. The economy's autarchic orientation continued and this meant that insufficient export income was generated to pay back the foreign debt.

---

3   See for a fuller discussion Desai (2000).

Had the borrowings been invested in exportables and India been given an open economy orientation, then repayment would have been easier. Had the capital come as equity rather than debt, the repayment would have not been a problem. But borrowings were made in debt form to retain political control over resources and this proved to be fatal. The economy crashed as it became unable to service its debt.

The political system crashed at the same time in as much as neither V.P. Singh nor Chandrashekhar could sustain a majority. The Budget for 1991 had to be postponed and central bankers had to scurry around raising money to pay back debt. The election of 1991 did not settle the issue though Congress (without Rajiv Gandhi) came back to power without a majority. A break away from the old model was now urgent in the economic sphere. Of the three sides of the triangle — social, political and economic — it was the economic which was the easiest to change quickly. But the change rapid as it was soon became mired into a reluctant transformation. The two other dimensions constrained the speed and thoroughness of the abandonment of the old dirigiste model in favour of economic liberalism.

Through the 1990s and into the 21st century, coalition governments persisted. In its first 42 years after independence, India had six prime ministers of whom three had ruled for 38 years. In the next 13 years there have been six more prime ministers. Political continuity in the sense of one-party dominance has now gone. Economic self-sufficiency as an ideal has also been abandoned. The contending visions of nationhood have resulted in a marked rise in political and communal violence. There are caste wars in Bihar, Hindu Muslim violence in 1992/93 and again in Gujarat in 2002 with smaller episodes in between. There is violence against *dalits* and Christians from those who prefer a Hindu India.

At the same time India has remained a democracy in a most resilient fashion. For someone who grew up when the world was worried about After Nehru who?, the question today seems absurd. Coalition governments have carried on Westminster politics in a most Indian fashion. Politics is more consensual, less elitist but at the same time more corrupt and self-serving. Democracy is too deeply entrenched now to imagine any other form of governance in India. Which by the same token makes it very difficult to imagine any drastic change in the second pillar of social conservatism. Thus castes are valorised as are regional and religious divisions. They are cards to play in the electoral game. Political power is the solvent which brings gains of patronage to communities which have little chance in the liberal market order for economic gain. Of course by resorting to political patronage, these 'backward' castes and scheduled castes dig themselves deeper into the mire of dependency. This strengthens the appeal of conservatism. The fact that some caste leaders spout secular or socialist slogans does not make them modern in any sense.

Thus the burden of keeping the show on the road, of plastering the differences together falls on the economic dimension. Economic reform over the last 10 years has been slow, hesitant but consensual. The strategy of implementing reform through the democratic process has meant that unlike in Eastern Europe there has been no shock therapy, no convulsion. The reformers of today were the dirigistes of yesterday. There is continuity. Thus the growth rate has gone up only modestly (relative to East Asian countries) to between 6 and 6.5 percentage points. There has been a slow trickle of FDI and India's export performance remains modest. The rate of privatisation has been slow for a long time though it has perked up in the last year or so. Infrastructure development is urgent as is the need for restructuring of public sector infrastructure provision if FDI is to be attracted. Budget deficits of the Centre and the states together are too large and represent a waste of savings.

But then the deficits are the price of the twin pillars of social conservatism and political democracy. Coalition politics and the patronage politics of social factions combine to make government expenditure a variable outside political control. Despite the misgivings of IFIs and credit rating agencies, Indian finance ministers carry on with the deficits as they are, knowing full well that any effective curbing of government spending would end any coalition. The same is the case with corruption and the crime/politics nexus. The quality of public life has gone lower as India's democracy has become more inclusive. The costs of this democracy now constitute a non-negligible burden on India's growth rate. If even half of the deficit now running at 10 per cent of GDP is avoidable, we are speaking of around 2 per cent per annum in GDP growth rate.

The Prospect

In one sense India is super stable and very resilient against drastic reform, social or economic. The strength of India's democracy vouches for its super stability. The revolutionary choice of the Constituent Assembly in 1946/1949 has had counter-revolutionary consequences, much as it happened in 19th-century France following the French Revolution. The country is immune to radical change. If there is a danger anywhere it comes from the overarching ideology of nationalism. Let me spell this out.

There are, as I said, above three competing visions of Indian nationhood (Desai 2000). The Nehru vision of secularism, socialism and non-alignment is now moribund if not dead. The BJP Hindutva vision is in ascendance. It is non-secular, non-socialist though uncomfortable with foreign capital. The third alternative is the confederate nationalist one which is deeply embedded in caste, language and religion. It is secularist and dirigiste if not socialist. (The Left parties — CPI, CPM — are a small presence in Lok Sabha and perhaps disproportionately large in India's political and intellectual life. They can be clubbed together with either the Congress or with the third cluster of confederationist parties.)

At present, Congress is secularist but against economic liberalisation. This is partly because it is in opposition and partly because the older vested interests in the socialist model are housed in the Congress. The rhetoric is all about the poor and anti-Western multinationals. The BJP and its parivar is split on economics. The RSS is anti-foreign capital and anti-reform. But the parliamentary wing of the BJP is led by people who have made their peace with economic reform. This is again because they are in office and not in opposition. But the old Jan Sangh was always derided as a party of shopkeepers and merchants. It has anti-dirigiste instincts. Of course being in electoral competition, the financing of patronage makes every party love the public sector. The third cluster is anti-capitalist in most of its rhetoric.

The dilemma facing India is that it can have a secular but anti-reform coalition or a non-secular but economically liberal coalition. The latter variant is in power now but it may lose the next election to a combination of Congress and a number of smaller parties. Only a Grand Coalition of the type German politics has seen, one between Congress and BJP may overcome this dilemma. I have been long an advocate of such a coalition which everyone considers quite utopian.

Such a coalition would become a reality only for one reason. If India is to be a militarily powerful force in Asia comparable to China then it does need to accelerate its economic growth. While the obsession with Pakistan lasts, China is not clearly perceived as a challenge. But sooner or later

Indian nationalists of whatever cluster will realise that China is the only serious competitor for India — a rival not an enemy. To catch up with China could yet become a nationalist ambition. To achieve that India will have to set aside its fear of economic change and its parochial concerns with religious divisions.

References

Ahluwalia, I. and Little, I. (eds) (1998), *India's Economic Reforms and Development: Essays for Manmohan Singh*, Oxford University Press, Oxford.

Ayres, A. and Oldenburg, P. (eds) (2002), *India Briefing: Quickening the Pace of Change*, M.E. Sharpe, Armonk, NY.

Desai, M. (1993), *Capitalism, Socialism and the Indian Economy*, EXIM Bank Lecture, Mumbai.

Desai, M. (1995), 'Economic Reform: Stalled by Politics?', in P. Oldenburg (ed.), *India Briefing 1995*, M.E. Sharpe, Armonk, NY.

Desai, M. (1996), 'India's Triple Bypass: Economic Liberalism, the BJP and the 1996 Elections', *Asian Studies Review*, 19(3).

Desai, M. (1998), 'Development Perspectives: Was There an Alternative to Mahalanobis?', in I. Ahluwalia and I. Little (eds), *India's Economic Reforms and Development: Essays for Manmohan Singh*, Oxford University Press, Oxford.

Desai, M. (2000), 'Communalism, Secularism and the Dilemma of Indian Nationhood', in M. Leifer, *Asian Nationalism*, Routledge, London.

Desai, M. (2002), 'Death, Development and Democracy in India 2002', *Encyclopaedia Britannica Hindu*, Delhi.

Jaffrelot, C. (2002), 'The Subordinate Caste Revolution', in A. Ayres and P. Oldenburg (eds), *India Briefing: Quickening the Pace of Change*, M.E. Sharpe, Armonk, NY.

Leifer, M. (ed.) (2000), *Asian Nationalism*, Routledge, London.

Lijphart, A. (1996), 'The Puzzle of Indian Democracy: A Consociational Interpretation', *The American Political Science Review*, 90(2): 258–68.

Oldenburg, P. (ed.) (1995), *India Briefing 1995*, M.E. Sharpe, Armonk, NY.

Oration 7:
2003 K.R. Narayanan Oration

Political-Economy and Governance Issues in the Indian Economic Reform Process

Pranab K. Bardhan

I am grateful to ASARC for the invitation to deliver the 2003 Narayanan Oration and am happy to be here at The Australian National University. I do not know ex-President Narayanan personally but we have a good common friend (K.N. Raj) from whom I had often heard glowing accounts about Dr Narayanan. Exactly 20 years back I gave the Radhakrishnan Lecture[1] at Oxford University, and I now have great pleasure in getting this opportunity to honour another distinguished south Indian ex-President.

My subject today is political economy and governance issues in Indian economic reform. Political economy is concerned with distribution of economic and political power, and inequality in this distribution poses important questions in a democracy. In 1949, as the Indian Constitution was getting ready and the debates in the Constituent Assembly were being wound up, B.R. Ambedkar, a founding father of the Indian Constitution, said in a speech in that Assembly:

---

1   See Bardhan (1984).

On the 26th of January, we are going to enter a life of contradictions. In politics we will have equality and in social and economic life, we will have inequality ... How long shall we continue to live this life of contradictions?

More than 50 years later in India we still live this life of contradictions, although there have been many changes, some of which would even have taken Ambedkar by surprise.

I will start with some historical and social factors which provide the context for Indian democracy and have shaped its complex unfolding in the last five decades, and then relate these to the various disjunctures between economics and politics that have developed in the ongoing economic reform process in the last decade or so.

The historical origins of democracy in India are sharply different from those in much of the west, and these differences are reflected in the current functioning of democracy in India, making it difficult to match the Indian case to the canonical cases in the usual theories of democracy. At least five of these differences are:

1. While in Europe democratic rights were won over continuous battles against aristocratic privileges and arbitrary powers of absolute monarchs, in India these battles were fought by a coalition of groups in an otherwise fractured society against the colonial masters. Even though part of the freedom struggle was associated with ongoing social movements to win land rights for peasants against the landed oligarchy, the dominant theme was to fight colonialism. And in this fight, particularly under the leadership of Gandhi, disparate groups were forged together to fight a common external enemy, and this required strenuous methods of consensus-building and conflict management (rather than resolution) through co-opting dissent and selective buyouts. Long before Independence the Congress Party operated on consensual rather than majoritarian principles. The various methods of group bargaining and subsidies and 'reservations' for different social end economic categories that are common practice in India today can be traced to this earlier history.

2. Unlike in western Europe democracy came to India before any substantial industrial transformation of a predominantly rural economy, and before literacy was widespread. This seriously influenced the modes of political organisation and mobilisation, the

nature of political discourse, and the excessive economic demands on the state. Democratic (and redistributive) aspirations of newly mobilised groups outstripped the surplus-generating capacity of the economy, demand overloads sometimes even short-circuiting the surplus generation process itself.

3. In western history the power of the state was gradually hemmed in by civil society dense with interest-based associations. In India groups are based more on ethnic and other identities (caste, religion, language, etc.), although the exigencies of electoral politics have somewhat reshaped the boundaries of (and ways of aggregating) these identity groups. This has meant a much larger emphasis on group rights than on individual rights.[2] A perceived slight of a particular group (in, say, the speech or behaviour of a political leader from another group) usually causes much more of a public uproar than crass violations of individual civil rights even when many people across different groups are to suffer from the latter. The issues that catch public imagination are the group demands for preferential treatment (like reservation of public sector jobs) and protection against ill-treatment. This is not surprising in a country where the self-assertion of hitherto subordinate groups in a hierarchical society takes primarily the form of a quest for group dignity and protected group niches in public jobs.

4. In western history, expansion of democracy gradually limited the power of the state. In India, on the other hand, democratic expansion has often meant an increase in the power of the state. The subordinate groups often appeal to the state for protection and relief. With the decline of hierarchical authority in the villages and with the moral and political environment of age-old deference to community norms changing, the state has moved into the institutional vacuum thus left in the social space. For example, shortly after Independence popular demands of land reform legislation (for the abolition of revenue intermediaries, for rent control and security of tenure), however tardy and shallow it may have been in implementation, brought in the state to the remotest corners of village society. With the advantage of numbers in electoral politics as hitherto backward groups get to capture state power, they are not too keen to weaken it or to give up the loaves and fishes of office and the elaborate network of patronage

---

2   One of the early leaders who carried in him the tension between individual and group rights was Ambedkar himself, a formidable constitutional lawyer concerned with individual liberty, but who was also a major spokesman of an oppressed caste group.

and subsidies that comes with it.[3] This serves as a major political block to the (largely elite-driven) attempts at economic liberalisation of recent years, as we will discuss later.

5. For a large federal democracy India, by constitutional design, differs from the classical case of US federalism in some essential features. Not merely is the federal government in India more powerful vis-a-vis the states in many respects (including the power to dismiss state governments in extreme cases and to reconstitute new states out of an existing state in response to movements for regional autonomy), but it has also more obligation, through mandated fiscal transfers (via the Finance Commission and the Planning Commission), to help out poor regions. In classical federalism the emphasis is on restraining the federal government through checks and balances, in India it is more on regional redistribution and political integration. Stepan (1999) has made a useful distinction between 'coming-together federalism' like the US, where previously sovereign polities gave up a part of their sovereignty for efficiency gains from resource pooling and a common market, and 'holding-together federalism' as in multinational democracies like India or Belgium or Spain, where compensating transfers keep the contending nationalities together and where economic integration of regional markets is a distant goal, yet incompletely unachieved even in more than 50 years of federalism.

Given these social and historical differences in the evolution of democracy in India its impact on inequality and poverty has been rather complex. In the history of western democracies extension of franchise has been associated with welfare measures for the poor. In the more recent data for a large number of countries cross-country regressions have found a positive association between democracy and some human development indicators[4] (relevant largely for the poor) or incomes of the lowest quintile of income distribution.[5] What has been the performance over time of the Indian democracy in terms of economic inequality and poverty? If we examine inequality in terms of the Gini coefficient there has not been much change overall. According to household consumer expenditure data collected by the National Sample Survey, during 1983 to 2000

---

3   In some sense this is familiar in the history of American municipal politics in big cities when one after another hitherto disadvantaged ethnic group captured the city administration and distributed patronage.

4   See Przeworski, Alvarez, Cheibub, and Limongi (2000).

5   See Lundberg and Squire (1999).

for example, rural inequality in consumption decreased a bit whereas urban inequality increased somewhat. Poverty has fallen significantly, though. In 1983, 46 per cent of the population was below the Planning Commission poverty line, whereas in 1999–2000 this figure was about 29 per cent. Despite this fall, India remains the largest single-country contributor to the pool of the world's extremely poor, illiterate people. Anti-poverty programs constitute a substantial part of the budgets of federal and state governments, but it is widely noted that a large part of them do not reach the real poor. The poverty figures are based on NSS consumption data and not data on income. Some fragmentary data on income suggest that the Gini coefficient for income distribution remains quite high, around 0.41 (and the Gini coefficient for asset distribution substantially higher). Some people contend that in the last decade or so the top 1 per cent of the population has become much richer, and their income or consumption is not captured in the usual survey data.

On the other hand, democracy has clearly brought about a kind of social revolution in India. It has spread out to the remote reaches of this far-flung country in ever-widening circles of political awareness and self-assertion of hitherto subordinate groups. These groups actually have increased faith in the efficacy of the political system and they vigorously participate in larger numbers in the electoral process. In the National Election Study[6] carried out by the Centre for the Study of Developing Societies, the percentage of respondents who answered positively to the question, 'do you think your vote has effect on how things are run in this country?', went up between 1971 and 1996 from 48.4 per cent to 58.7 per cent for the total population, from 45.7 per cent to 57.6 per cent for 'backward caste' groups (designated as OBC in India), from 42.2 per cent to 60.3 per cent for the lowest castes (designated as scheduled castes), and 49.9 per cent to 60.3 per cent for Muslims (only later data can show if this figure has now changed for Muslims in view of the recent happenings in parts of the country).

Yet, this faith in the efficacy of the political system is very inadequately translated into concrete results on economic progress for the median member of the poor disadvantaged groups. Let us explore this particular disjuncture between economics and politics in India a bit further. The politicians are seldom penalised by the Indian electorate for endemic

6   See Yadav (2000).

poverty; poverty is widely regarded among common people as a complex phenomenon with multiple causes, and they ascribe only limited responsibility to the government in this matter. In any case the measures of government performance are rather noisy, particularly in a world of illiteracy and low levels of civic organisation and formal communication on public issues. As we have indicated before, a perceived slight in the speech of a political leader felt by a particular ethnic group will usually cause much more of an uproar than if the same leader's policy neglect keeps thousands of children severely malnourished in the same ethnic group.[7] The same issue of group dignity comes up in the case of reservation of public sector jobs for backward groups which, as we have said before, fervently catches the public imagination of such groups, even though, objectively the overwhelming majority of the people in these groups have little chance of ever landing those jobs, as they and their children drop out of school in large numbers by the fifth grade. Even when these public job quotas mainly help the tiny elite in backward groups, as a symbol and a possible, though distant, object of aspiration for their children, they ostensibly serve a valuable function in attempts at group upliftment.

Particularly in north India there seems to be a preoccupation with symbolic victories among the emerging lower-caste political groups; as Hasan (2000) points out, with reference to BSP, a politically successful party of the oppressed in UP, these groups seem less concerned about changing the economic-structural constraints under which most people in their community live and toil. Perhaps this is just a matter of time. These social and political changes have come to north India rather late; in south India, where such changes have taken place several decades back, it may not be a coincidence that there has been a lot more effective performance in the matter of public expenditures on pro-poor projects like health, education, housing and drinking water. This reflects the fact that in south India there has been a long history of social movement against exclusion of lower castes from the public sphere, against their educational deprivation, etc. in a way more sustained and broad-based than in north India. One may also note that the upper-caste opposition to social transformation is somewhat stronger in north India, as demographically upper castes constitute in general a somewhat larger percentage of the population than has been the case in most parts of south India. So new political victories of lower castes

---

7   For a formal analysis of the role of visibility in influencing government resource allocation across multiple public goods in an electoral framework, see Mani and Mukand (2000).

in north India get celebrated in the form of defiant symbols of social redemption and recognition aimed at solidifying their as yet tentative victories, rather than in committed attempts at changing the economic structure of deprivation.

From this major disjuncture between politics and economics in India let me now move on to the various kinds of disjuncture that have appeared in the Indian scene between the policy of economic reform and the ongoing political and administrative processes. Economists often ignore these, and are surprised when things do not proceed in the way they want. In the last two decades, particularly since the early '90s, India has launched a widely heralded process of economic reform with a view to unleashing the entrepreneurial forces from the shackles of the nightmarish controls and regulations that have hobbled the economy for years. Yet many commentators have noted our ways of lumbering, proceeding two steps forward, one step backward. We need to have a better understanding of why reform is so halting and hesitant, why there is no substantial and durable political constituency for reform (outside the small confines of India's metropolitan elite), why even the few supporters of reform underplay it at election time. In the rest of this lecture I shall point to 10 different kinds of disjuncture that may be linked to this phenomenon.

1. Any process of sustained economic reform and investment requires a framework of long-term policy to which the government can credibly commit itself. But the political process in India seems to be moving in the opposite direction. While becoming more democratic and inclusive in terms of incorporating newer and hitherto subordinate groups, it is eroding away most of the structures of institutional insulation of long-run economic management decisions against the wheeling and dealing of day-to-day politics. There are very few assurances that commitments made by a government (or a leader) will be kept by successive ones, or even by itself under pressure. A political party that introduces some reforms is quick to oppose them when it is no longer in power.

2. With the extensive deregulation of the last two decades it was expected that corruption that is associated with the system of permits and licences will decrease. There are no hard estimates, but by most anecdotal accounts corruption has, if anything, gone up in recent years. Although there may have been some decline in smuggling, black market in foreign exchange, or real estate. Some of the newer

social groups coming to power are quite nonchalant in suggesting that all these years upper classes and castes have looted the system, now it is their turn. This has implications for the milking of the remaining obstructive regulations, particularly at the level of state governments (for example in matters of water and electricity connections to factories or enterprises, and in land acquisition and registration). As elections become more and more expensive the demands on business from the politician-regulator are unlikely to relent.

3. Much more than economic reform the major economic issue that captures public imagination, as we have noted before, is that of job reservation for an increasing number of 'backward' groups, which is accepted by all political parties. In the last decade of market reform more and more of the public sector job market has been carved up into protected niches. Cynics may even argue that the retreat of the state, implied by economic reform, is now more acceptable to the upper classes and castes, as the latter are losing their control over state power in the face of the emerging hordes of hitherto subordinate groups, and they are opting for greener pastures in the private sector and abroad. As these hitherto subordinate groups capture state power they are not likely to easily give up the lucrative benefits of office and the elaborate network of patronage distribution that goes with it. This is more acutely the case at the state government level where these groups are more secure in power.

4. There have been few substantive reforms in the agricultural sector, and the non-agricultural informal sector has been hurt by the credit crunch. Yet these two sectors constitute 93 per cent of the total labour force. No wonder they are not enthused by the reforms carried out so far. In fact even organised farm lobbies (with few exceptions) have not been very active in demanding reforms of agricultural controls like those on storage and distribution and on domestic and foreign trade. They may be worried that the dismantling of the existing structure of food, fertiliser, water and electricity subsidies in exchange of receiving, say, international agricultural prices may be too complex and politically risky a deal. In any case the high administered procurement prices for grains have now eroded India's earlier (largely unexploited) competitive advantage in world grain markets.

5. Political power is shifting more to regional governments and regional parties, which makes national coordination on macro-policy more difficult. For example, fiscal consolidation in general and a substantial

reduction in the budget subsidies in particular are difficult when the national government depends on the support of powerful regional parties that assiduously nurse their parochial interest lobbies with a liberal use of subsidies (implicit or explicit). As the logic of economic reform and increased competition leads to increased regional inequality, it is not clear how the Indian federal system will resolve the tension between the demands of the better-off states for more competition and those of other states (which a politically weaker Centre can ill afford to ignore politically) for redistributive transfers. Can, for example, a coalition government at the Centre, dependent for its survival on the large number of MPs from weak states (like Bihar or UP), ignore their redistributive demands to compensate them for losing out in the inter-state competition for private investment? It is also the case that a large number of entry taxes on goods imposed by governments even in otherwise leading states in economic reform (for example, Maharashtra, Tamil Nadu) are making the goal of reformers to unify an integrated all-India market that much more distant.

6. While the political power of regional governments is increasing, at the same time their fiscal dependence on the Centre is also increasing. (Between the middle 1950s to middle 1990s, the fraction of states' current expenditures financed by their own revenue sources declined from around 70 per cent to around 55 per cent.) A significant part of the central transfers is discretionary (examples are the numerous central sector and centrally sponsored schemes); these and discretionary subsidised loans are often used by the Centre more for political influence in selected areas than for the cause of fiscal or financial reform or of poverty removal.

7. Reform would have been more popular if it was oriented to aspects of human development (education, health, child nutrition, drinking water, women's welfare and autonomy, etc.). Reformers usually are preoccupied with problems of the foreign trade regime, fiscal deficits and the constraints on industrial investments in the factory sector, and they believe that once these are handled right, trickle-down will take care of the issues that concern the masses. In particular, the reformers have paid little attention to the crucial problems of governance in matters of achieving human development, which will be inexorably there even if trade, fiscal and industrial policy reforms were successful. Ravallion and Datt (2002) show from an analysis of household survey data across 15 states over 1960 to 1994 that non-farm growth is less effective in reducing poverty in states with poorer initial conditions in

terms of rural development, human resources and land distribution. For example, nearly two-thirds of the difference between the elasticity of headcount poverty index to non-farm output for Bihar and Kerala is attributable to the latter's substantially higher initial literacy rate. If the administrative mechanism of delivery of public services in the area of human development remains seriously deficient, as it is today in most states, chances of constructing a minimum social safety net are low, and without such a safety net any large-scale program of economic reform will remain politically unsustainable, not surprisingly in a country where the lives of the overwhelming majority of the people are characterised by a brutal lack of economic security. Of course, decentralisation of governance which the 73rd and the 74th constitutional amendments in the early 1990s ushered in most of the country (around the same time as serious economic reforms were also launched) has raised hopes for better delivery of public services, sensitive to local needs. In some sense this is quite a landmark in administrative reforms. But so far the progress in this respect has been disappointing in most states, both in terms of actual devolution of authority and funds, and the outcome variables of services actually delivered. Let me just quote from one general evaluation, by Pal (2001): 'With some exceptions in Kerala, Madhya Pradesh, Tripura and West Bengal, nothing worthwhile has been devolved to the *panchayats*. The bureaucracy at all tiers of *panchayats* is holding the balance.' Note also that in Kerala and West Bengal decentralisation with regular *panchayat* elections started long before the constitutional amendments. In many states not just the bureaucracy (which often has overlapping functions with the *panchayats*) has been reluctant to let go, the local MLAs, in order to protect their patronage turf, have hijacked the local electoral and administrative process (even in otherwise better-run states like Tamil Nadu). In Andhra Pradesh, a state supposedly at the forefront of economic reform, the Chief Minister is reportedly using information technology to further centralise (and personalise) the administrative process. Even in the relatively successful case of West Bengal the major role of *panchayats* has been in identifying beneficiaries of government programs and the management and implementation of local infrastructure projects like roads and irrigation, funded by tied grants from the Central or state government. There is no serious involvement of the *panchayat* in the management or control of basic public services like primary education, public health and sanitation or in raising local resources.

Of course, prior land reforms in Kerala and West Bengal have made the *panchayats* somewhat less prone to capture by the village landed oligarchy as compared to parts of north India.

8. Another potential link between economic reform and decentralisation largely unutilised in India relates to small-scale, particularly rural, industrialisation. (In fact, rural non-farm employment grew at a much slower rate in the '90s than in the '80s). The Chinese success in the phenomenal growth in rural industries is often ascribed to decentralisation, by which the Central and provincial governments gave 'positive' incentives to the local government-run village and township enterprises (by allowing them residual claimancy to the money they make) and 'negative' incentives to keep them on their toes (in the form of refusing to bail them out if they lose money in the intense competition with other such enterprises). In India decentralisation is usually visualised only in terms of delivery of welfare services, not in terms of fostering local business development, and yet if this link could be established, economic reform would have been much more popular, as local informal-sector industries touch the lives of many more people than the corporate sector. A program of economic reform that involves curbing the petty tyranny and corruption of the small industry inspectors (who currently act as serious barriers to potential entry), encouraging micro-finance and marketing channels, and providing the 'positive' and 'negative' incentives of Chinese-style decentralisation, has the potential of opening the floodgates of small-scale entrepreneurship in India. Examples of successful cooperative business development with the leadership of the local government, though rare in India, are not entirely absent. Take the case of the Manjeri municipality in the relatively backward district of Malappuram in north Kerala, with not much of a pre-existing industrial culture. In this area the municipal authorities, in collaboration with some NGOs and bankers, have succeeded in converting it into a booming hosiery manufacturing centre, after developing the necessary skills at the local level and the finance. This and other award-winning *panchayats* in Kerala dispel the common presupposition that civic bodies in the villages and small towns of India do not have the capability to take the leadership in developing and facilitating skill-based small-scale and medium-scale industries.

9. It is anomalous to expect reform to be carried out by an administrative setup that for many years has functioned as an inert, arbitrary, heavy-

handed, often corrupt, uncoordinated monolith. Economic reform is about competition and incentives, and a governmental machinery that does not itself allow them in its own internal organisation is an unconvincing proponent or carrier of that message. Yet very few economists discuss the incentive and organisational issues of administrative reform as an integral part of the economic reform package. We have an administrative structure dominated by bureaucrats chosen on the basis of a generalist examination (rank in that early entry examination largely determines the career path of an officer no matter how well or ill-suited s/he is in the various jobs s/he is scuttled around, each for a brief sojourn), and promotions are largely seniority-based not merit or performance-based. There are no well-enforced norms and rules of work discipline, very few punishments for ineptitude or malfeasance, and there are strong disincentives to take bold, risky decisions. Whether one likes it or not, the government will remain quite important in our economy for many years to come, and it is difficult to discuss the implementation of economic reform without the necessary changes in public administration including incentive reforms, accompanied by changes in information systems, organisational structure, budgeting and accounting systems, task assignments, and staffing policies. In these matters there is a lot to learn from the (successes and failures of) innovative administrative reform experiments that have been carried out in many developing countries in the last decade or so.

10. Finally, in large parts of the country the judiciary (particular at the lower end) is almost completely clogged by the enormous backlog of cases and the legal system is largely paralysed by delay and corruption. Even more important, the institutional independence of the police and criminal justice system is regularly undermined by politicians of whichever is the ruling party. As result, the rule of law, which is as much the foundation stone of a regime of market reforms as of political democracy, is often sadly missing. (The N.N. Vohra Committee Report of a few years back, now shelved, clearly spelled out the nexus between politicians, bureaucrats, the mafia, and even some members of the judiciary.) This politicisation of police and the administrative system is also the institutional background of the state-abetted carnage in Gujarat last year. This shameful chapter of recent Indian history took place in a state which is supposed to be a leader in economic reforms, indicating an alarming disjuncture between politics and economics in India today.

But much more than hostility of certain religious groups is involved here; what is basically at stake is a political failure of the Indian state. In large parts of India sectarian interests are fishing in the troubled waters mainly caused by a failed state, when the state cannot deliver the essential services (health, education, a minimum safety net and the rule of law). When public schools, for example, do not deliver education to the poor, they sometimes are compelled to send their children to the schools run by Hindu fanatics or madrasas run by Muslim fanatics. Market reformers, instead of trying to organise the retreat of the state, should devote a large part of their energies to the cause of reform of the state machinery, to administrative and judicial reform to make the state more accountable to the common people, and to prevent the hijacking of the police and the criminal justice system by the politician-criminal nexus.

In this lecture I have started with a delineation of the different social and historical context of Indian democracy, compared to the West, how it adds complexity to its relation with problems of inequality and poverty. In this discussion I have underlined the various kinds of disjunctures that have appeared, and unless these are addressed not much reform or reduction of poverty and inequality will be sustainable, in spite of the many strides of undoubted social and economic progress the country has taken over the last five decades.

References

Bardhan, P. (1984), *The Political Economy of Development in India*, Oxford University Press, Oxford (expanded edition, 1998, New Delhi).

Hasan, Z. (2000), 'Representation and Redistribution: The New Lower Caste Politics of North India', in F.R. Frankel et al. (eds), *Transforming India: Social and Political Dynamics of Democracy*, Oxford University Press, New Delhi.

Lundberg, M. and Squire, L. (1999), 'Growth and Inequality: Extracting the Lessons for Policymakers', Working Paper, World Bank, Washington DC.

Mani, A. and Mukand, S.W. (2000), 'Democracy and the Politics of Visibility', Working Paper, Vanderbilt University.

Pal, M. (2001), 'Documenting Panchayat Raj', *Economic and Political Weekly*, 36(36): 3448–50.

Przeworski, A., Alvarez, M., Cheibub, J.A. and Limongi, F. (2000), *Democracy and Development: Political Institutions and Material Well-being in the World, 1950–1990*, Cambridge University Press, Cambridge.

Ravallion, M. and Datt, G. (2002), 'Why Has Economic Growth been More Pro-poor in some States of India than Others?', *Journal of Development Economics,* 68(2): 381–400.

Stepan, A. (1999), 'Federalism and Democracy: Beyond the U.S. Model', *Journal of Democracy*, 10(4), 19–34.

Yadav, Y. (2000), 'Understanding the Second Democratic Upsurge: Trends of Bahujan Participation in Electoral Politics in the 1990s', in F. Frankel et al. (eds), *Transforming India: Social and Political Dynamics of Democracy*, Oxford University Press, New Delhi.

Oration 8:
2004 K.R. Narayanan Oration

Message from the President
of the Republic of India

I am delighted that The Australian National University is holding the 2004 Narayanan Oration on the theme 'India: On the Growth Turnpike' on 27 April 2004.

Today the GDP growth rate is about 8 per cent; it has to grow to 10 per cent and then be sustained for a decade. This is possible only by enriching 70 per cent of our population which lives in 600,000 villages. To realise this transformation, the nation is poised for the execution of PURA (Providing Urban Amenities in Rural Areas) program. This program aims at bridging the rural urban divide and achieving balanced socioeconomic development. PURA consists of four connectivities: physical, electronic, knowledge, all three of which lead to economic connectivity. This will enhance the prosperity of the village clusters. Economic connectivity will generate markets and production establishments for serving them. PURA has all the ingredients to be a business enterprise with global dimensions.

My greetings and felicitation to all those associated with the university. I wish the oration all success.

A.P.J. Abdul Kalam
New Delhi
2004

India: On the Growth Turnpike

Vijay L. Kelkar[1]

I

It is a great honour and privilege for me to be invited to deliver the 2004 Narayanan Lecture at The Australian National University. ANU is one of the premier universities of the world, and to speak at this great university itself is an honour. Further, to be associated with Dr Narayanan, one of our great Presidents, amplifies the honour manifold.

Dr K.R. Narayanan, a noble son of India, exemplifies all that is good in India. He was President in the year when I was involved in budget-making as the Finance Secretary. As you know, in India, it is the President who as the head of state sends the budget to Parliament for its consideration. Hence, it is customary for the Finance Minister and the Finance Secretary to brief the President on the Budget before he gives his assent to its transmission to Parliament.

As it was my first time, I was nervous, but I was told that this would be a short and pleasant affair. The President was very warm and gracious but he asked some penetrating questions, particularly about what this budget would mean to a common citizen, and how it would accelerate growth. I was very impressed by his grasp of complex economic issues.

---

1   The views in this lecture are mine and not of my employers. It draws heavily upon the collaborative work in progress with Arbind Modi, Ajay Shah and Arvind Subramanian. I am grateful to Centre for Monitoring Indian Economy (CMIE) and National Council of Applied Economic Research (NCAER) for access to their databases.

He emphasised the need for policies that foster accelerated growth and address problems of equity. Today, in my lecture, I will endeavour to discuss some aspects of these great questions.

II

My lecture is titled 'India: On the Growth Turnpike'. The term 'turnpike' — which is typically North American — refers to an expressway and, today, I propose to present logic and evidence which suggests that economic growth in India will considerably accelerate further in the coming decade.

Macroeconomic Trends and the Setting

A lot has been said and written about India's exciting growth story, which can be dated to the beginning of the 1980s. Let me start with the most interesting and important facts about India's growth experience.

From the early 1980s onwards, India got strong GDP growth, averaging 5.7 per cent over the last 24 years. This year, in 2003–04, GDP growth is expected to be 8.2 per cent, and GDP is expected to reach $625 billion. India's high GDP growth is sharply visible when GDP comparisons are done on a purchasing power parity basis. As of 2001, India came in at fourth place, with output of $3 trillion. It is likely that by 2004, India will reach third place, displacing Japan. That will give us a global ranking of US, China and India in that order.

Looking back, it seems to me that we had two broad phases in our growth experience: before 1980, and after. Before 1980, GDP growth had a mean of 3.5 per cent with a standard deviation of 3.5 per cent. In the 24 years after 1980, the mean rose to 5.7 per cent, and the standard deviation dropped to 1.9 per cent.

Many people have noticed India's high sustained growth over the last 24 years. But the low volatility of GDP growth is equally striking. For a comparison, over 1960–99, the median value for industrial countries was 2.18. For developing countries, it was 4.28. So we have had two big changes around 1980 as a breakpoint: mean GDP growth went up, and GDP growth volatility went down.

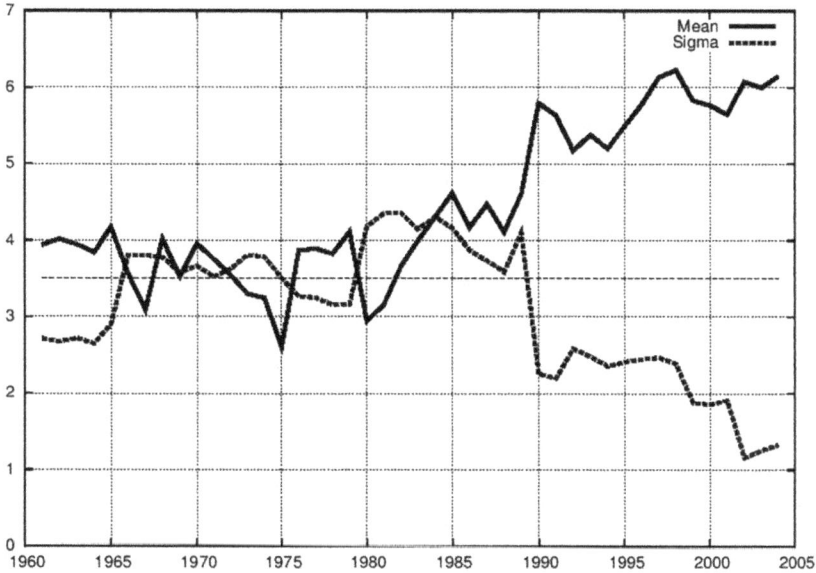

I find it useful to look at the acceleration of growth in India using the tool of 'rolling window' growth rates, where at each point, we compute the average growth over the last decade. A decade is a broad enough window, which allows us to smooth out the fluctuations caused by an unusual monsoon or two. So every year, we look back at the last 10 years, and compute the mean and standard deviation of GDP growth over that decade.

This graph gives us new insights into familiar facts about the acceleration in India's GDP growth.[2] We departed from the 'Hindu rate of growth' of 3.5 per cent in 1982, and reached levels like 6 per cent from 1996 onwards. In this lecture, I am going to argue that we will go further up to substantially higher growth rates in the years to come.

We have also obtained a sharp reduction in GDP growth volatility. Along with this, inflation and interest rates have also come down sharply. We seem to have thus created an extremely benign macroeconomic environment, with low inflation, low interest rates and high GDP growth.

---

2   J. Bradford Delong (July 2001), 'India since Independence: An Analytic Growth Narrative'; Dani Rodrik and Arvind Subramanian (2004), 'From Hindu Growth to Productivity Surge: The Mystery of the Indian Growth Transition', NBER Working Paper No. 10376, March.

	GDP growth (%)		Years to double
Period	Aggregate	Per capita	Per capita GDP
1972–1982	3.5	1.2	57
1982–1992	5.2	3.0	23
1992–2002	6.0	3.9	18

Let me talk about this in a different way — as growth of per capita GDP. While GDP growth has accelerated, population growth rates have gone down slightly. These have combined to give an even sharper acceleration of GDP growth per capita. In the 1970s, this was 1.2 per cent and it went up to 3.9 per cent in the 1990s.

I want to emphasise that 1.2 per cent and 3.9 per cent both sound like small numbers, but there is a huge difference between the two in terms of their human impact. At 1.2 per cent a year, per capita GDP takes 57 years to double. A man sees one doubling in his adult life. At 3.9 per cent a year, per capita GDP takes 18 years to double. A man who lives to 72 sees three doublings as compared with the standard of living that he saw at age 18. This is an enormous difference!

Why did India Exhibit Resilience to Shocks?

A remarkable feature of India's growth experience has been its resilience to shocks. In many countries, short periods of high growth appear to be punctuated by years of poor growth.[3] Largely speaking, this has not been the case in India over the last 25 years. This is reflected in the figure above, which shows a sustained increase in average GDP growth rates, coupled with a sharp *decline* in GDP growth volatility from the decade 1980–1990 onwards.

This resilience of growth in recent decades is an important change when compared with preceding decades. In 1973 and 1979, growth in India was adversely affected by oil shocks. In the later period, this vulnerability appears to have been greatly reduced.

---

3   William Easterly (2001), 'The Lost Decades: Developing Countries' Stagnation In Spite of Policy Reform 1980–1998', World Bank, February.

This aspect is important in understanding India's growth experience. It is important to address the questions: Why has India's growth been so consistent? Why has growth accelerated from decade to decade, without encountering the difficulties which are observed in many other developing countries? Why has India exhibited such resilience to shocks?

One could maintain a hypothesis that the Indian economy was exposed to smaller external shocks in the period after 1980; that this drop in volatility is an artefact of a benign external environment. However, this is just not true. In these years, the economy has faced many shocks, including international financial crises, security tensions, international sanctions, etc. From roughly 1995 onwards, the world has emphatically not been a quieter place. Hence, the drop in GDP growth volatility seems to reflect a genuine improvement in macrostability and not a lack of shocks.

Another possible hypothesis is rooted in currency flexibility. A broad consensus that appears to be emerging in the literature suggests that greater flexibility in exchange rates is conducive to enhanced macrostability. A recent paper by Edwards and Yeyati[4] finds that terms of trade shocks are exacerbated in countries with more rigid exchange rate systems. In their empirical work, under flexible exchange rates, the effects of terms-of-trade shocks on growth are approximately half of those under pegged regimes. They also find that under inflexible exchange rate regimes, output growth is more sensitive to negative than to positive shocks.

If the economic reforms in recent decades had moved towards greater currency flexibility, then this could have been pointed to as a key source of improved resilience. However, a series of recent papers[5] have demonstrated that in India's case, currency flexibility has been broadly unchanged since 1979. Hence, a *change* in the currency regime does not constitute a feasible explanation for this decline in GDP growth volatility.

---

4   Sebastian Edwards and Eduardo Levy Yeyati (2003), 'Flexible Exchange Rates as Shock Absorbers', NBER Working Paper No. 9867, July.

5   Carmen Reinhart and Kenneth S. Rogoff (2002). 'The Modern History of Exchange Rate Arrangements: A Reinterpretation', NBER Working Paper No. 8963, June; Ila Patnaik (2003), 'India's Policy Stance on Reserves and the Currency', ICRIER Working Paper No. 108, September; A. Guillermo Calvo and Carmen M. Reinhart (2002), 'Fear of Floating', *Quarterly Journal of Economics*, 117(2): 379–408.

One element of an explanation appears to be the improvement in price flexibility that took place in many *other* areas of the Indian economy. While price flexibility on two important markets — currency and food grains — did not go up, price flexibility rose sharply in the 1990s in myriad other areas such as interest rates, steel, cement, etc. In these areas, price volatility had been stifled in the traditional command-and-control paradigm of economic policy, and prices were freed up in the 1990s. This is expected to have improved the ability of the economy to adjust to shocks through changes in prices. A second explanation that we offer relates to the maturing processes of democracy, which I will come to later.

Globalisation

One of the most important phenomena about the Indian economy in the 1990s was the growth of international trade. We see striking changes in the one-decade period following 1991–92. India has engaged in unilateral removals of barriers to trade, and this process has been assisted by our WTO obligations.[6]

Through these, gross trade flows almost tripled over this period from $56.7 billion in 1991–92 to $155.5 billion in 2001–02. Expressed as a fraction of GDP, the trade GDP ratio went up from 21.3 per cent to 33.1 per cent over this 10-year period. This was a fairly rapid pace of change for a structural parameter like the trade/GDP ratio.

A key feature of India's experience with trade has been the rapid growth of services exports. Over this decade, merchandise exports grew by 145 per cent but services exports grew by 275 per cent.

This high growth of services exports has been based on two distinct components. In the earlier period, invisibles revenues were primarily obtained through remittances from Indians working outside India. In recent years, improvements in telecommunications have implied that many services, which were previously non-tradable, could now be produced in India as part of global production chains. Export-oriented services production in India ranges from high volume production of low-end services like accounting, all the way to services that require

---

6   Arvind Panagariya (2004), 'India's Trade Reform: Progress, Impact and Future Strategy', India Policy Forum, NCAER, March.

highly specialised and high-wage staff, like research and development. For example, research laboratories located in India by major US companies have filed for over 1,000 patents with the US Patent and Trademark Office.

The high degree of public awareness about India's success in these IT-enabled services exports has led to a widespread perception that India is faring extremely well in services exports but has failed in obtaining growth in manufacturing exports. This perception is inconsistent with the high growth which is *also* seen with merchandise exports. Particularly in the last five years, growth rates of manufacturing and services exports have been rather alike.

India's success on exports growth has made a big difference to the overall outlook on the external sector. We began the decade of the 1990s with a BOP crisis. Today, India is widely seen as having an extremely strong position on the external sector. This was achieved through several elements: currency depreciation, export buoyancy, and policies of avoiding foreign currency debt. Our foreign currency reserves are now roughly as big as our external debt, so there can be little question of a BOP crisis shaping up.

Political Economy of Growth

One of the most interesting features about India's growth is the way it has been achieved under a democratic framework. There is a view that democracy impedes economic growth and India would eliminate poverty faster if we are willing to sacrifice freedom and democracy.

I quite disagree with this perspective. I believe that democracy is a 'growth fundamental', that we have come where we have come *because* of democracy, and not despite it. I found one insightful way of thinking about this in a 1988 paper by Dani Rodrik,[7] which offered an interesting framework for understanding resilience of output growth, when faced with external shocks.

---

7   Dani Rodrik (1999), 'Where Did All the Growth Go? External Shocks, Social Conflict, and Growth Collapses', *Journal of Economic Growth*, 4: 358–412.

$$\Delta \text{ growth} =$$
$$- \text{ external shocks x} \quad \frac{\text{latent social conflict}}{\text{Institutions of conflict management}}$$

This 'equation' seeks to explain the impact on GDP growth of a given external shock. This is linked to three explanations:

1. The size of the external shock matters — bigger external shocks should obviously give a bigger impact on growth.
2. The extent of 'latent social conflict'. Rodrik defines this in terms of ethnic and religious heterogeneity.
3. Rodrik focuses on 'institutions of conflict management' as the tool through which countries are better able to absorb external shocks.

Going by his definition, India has substantial 'latent social conflict', given the ethnic and religious diversity present in the country. Yet, we know that the output loss associated with shocks in India was small. How did this happen?

By Rodrik's argument, this suggests the high quality of the institutions of conflict management in the country. This is achieved through political institutions, and the functioning of democracy. As is well known, India is the world's largest democracy. Freedom of speech, regular elections, and an independent judiciary have characterised India's 57-year post-independence experience.

While India started out with very strong majorities for a single party (the Congress) in Parliament, over the decades, the political system has learnt how to obtain consensus through coalition governments. For example, in recent years, bipartisan support was essential for every piece of legislation. Milestones in economic legislation, such as the Electricity Act, the Foreclosure law, or the Fiscal Responsibility and Budget Management Act, would not have been possible without bipartisan support.

In many countries, the introduction of market-oriented reforms has been highly unpopular with the larger populace. This appears to have not been a constraint in India. One litmus test of this problem is found in the labour market. One revealing statistic about this is the number of strikes and the man days lost through strikes in 1992 and 2002. Major changes in economic policy have been actually accompanied by a sharp *diminution* in the incidence of unrest on the part of organised labour.

How was such a consensus in favour of market-oriented reforms forged? In the early period, market-oriented reforms may have appeared relatively novel and required consensus building to support embarking on relatively unknown territory. These innovations in policy were better accepted in India, as compared with the experience of many other countries, since they were crafted through the processes of a participatory democracy. In recent years, the consensus in favour of market-oriented reforms has been cemented by the results which better economic policy has delivered. One of the reasons for this has been the better sequencing of reforms which enabled 'early harvest' of the benefits.

The most important area of progress is that of poverty reduction. A shocking fact, embedded in Indian history, is the stagnation of the headcount of the poor at 320 million for the two-decade period from 1973 to 1993. From 1993 to 1999, in a short six-year period alone, the headcount of the poor dropped by 60 million. Taking into account various factors, it can be said that 100 million people have been brought out of poverty by the growth process of the last decade. This is an astonishing achievement, and it has had a positive impact on the political acceptance of economic reforms.[8]

As mentioned before, per capita GDP now shows three doublings in an adult life, as compared with one doubling in an adult life that used to be observed earlier. These changes have been accompanied by a reduction in the volatility of GDP growth, which has helped alleviate fears about the vagaries of the free market. All these changes have been manifestly visible in the political system and public discourse, and have helped cement the consensus in favour of economic reforms.

While democratic institutions are very valuable things to have, this is not to say that it is easy for a country to learn how to operate democratic institutions. Many countries have lost high GDP growth rates for a decade or more, in learning to make the transition from dictatorship to democracy. By now, India appears to have absorbed the costs of learning to operate vibrant democratic institutions.

---

8   Surjit S. Bhalla (2003), *Not as Poor, Nor as Unequal, as You Think: Poverty, Inequality and Growth in India, 1950–2000*, Final Report of research project 'The Myth and Reality of Poverty in India', Planning Commission, Government of India, December.

Recent Themes in Reforms

A lot has been written about the economic reforms process in India. I would like to once again be brief and selective, and talk about a few big things that are going on.

I think the general principles that are driving the reforms process may be summarised as follows. We are trying to focus on *incentives*, and give the right people the right incentives to do the right things. We are trying to reduce frictions and transactions costs, so as to enable more transactions and more trading. We are trying to harness network externalities and obtain increasing returns to scale. Finally, we are trying to emphasise the 'mesoeconomic reforms', to put a focus on that in-between space between the macro and the micro, which consists of major institutions and 'rules of the game'.

Deepening Globalisation

Let me start with *globalisation*. As emphasised above, our trade/GDP ratio went up sharply from 22 per cent of GDP to 33 per cent of GDP over a 10-year period. India has digested the lessons of the 1960s and 1970s, about the enormous distortions and harmful political economy that is induced by protectionism. So we have made much progress in doing unilateral trade liberalisation, and in exploiting the WTO process. We have eliminated quantitative restrictions, and brought down the peak customs rate on manufactured goods from over 150 per cent to a present level of 20 per cent.

What is particularly striking is that this year, with elections impending, we were able to sharply cut tariffs, and this was criticised by some observers as a 'populist' thing to do! This highlights the sea change that has taken place in India's attitude towards trade integration with the world economy. India, which was once described as a 'hesitant globaliser', has become a 'willing globaliser'!

The elimination of QRs, and the drop in the peak rate from 150 per cent to 20 per cent, was obviously costly for many firms and individuals. There are real costs that have to be paid in terms of obsolete business plans, and factors of production had to shift into areas where India has a comparative advantage. In my view, this is a subtle reason behind the upsurge of bad loans in the banking industry in the mid-1990s.

However, the difficult part of our adjustment to eliminating tariffs and QRs now seems to be behind us, and we are well on our way to single digit tariffs. It is striking to observe that while the multilateral discussions about trade reforms are still talking in terms of multi-decade horizons for adjustment, India has been able to move much faster, and unilaterally make progress on trade reforms.

Going from the current account to the capital account, there is now a broad consensus that capital controls are ineffective when there is a large and free current account. There are simply too many opportunities for moving capital across the globe by over-invoicing, under-invoicing, transfer pricing by multinational corporations, and trade in gold. Hence, India has steadily made progress on freeing up the capital account, particularly in the last five years. For foreign institutional investors, we are 100 per cent convertible. Indian firms can take up to 100 per cent of their net worth out of the country. Domestic citizens can take up to $25,000 out of the country, which is a lot when compared with the per capita income. The opening up of the capital account has enormous implications for the conduct of Indian macro-policy. The impossible trinity is now with us, so that a restrictive currency policy comes at the price of monetary price autonomy. Hence, this is a new and exciting phase for Indian macroeconomics.

As an aside, I want to highlight some non-economic factors which have been at the foundation of India's success in rapid integration into the world economy. These consist of our strong IT and telecom sectors, our use of English, and our vibrant democracy. Our strengths in IT and telecom have helped us to exploit the Internet, which is an important highway of globalisation today. Our use of English has meant lower transaction costs in interacting with the global economy. Our democracy has helped us avoid the difficulties and hindrances that come into the picture when repressive regimes try to block ideas from flowing in through the Internet. For example, we in India have multiple competing private sector Internet service providers, with high speed lines that reach into the outside world, with no large government effort at censorship or selective blocking of content.

Infrastructure Sector: Unfolding Mesoeconomic Reforms

Let me turn to infrastructure. In the early 1990s, infrastructure was high on our minds. The public goods of transportation and communications were clearly a bottleneck to efficiency, and to internal and international trade. In the presence of those constraints, our ability to harness gains from trade was limited, owing to the high transactions costs of engaging in trade. Our inefficiencies in transport and communications ultimately filtered into the exchange rate, where the rupee had to devalue enough to obtain rough parity on the current account.

India chose to go down the path of moving towards competitive markets in infrastructure, with private sector production, under a framework of sound regulation. I believe that this was the right path to go down. But as we all know, this is a difficult path to take. There are truly subtle difficulties in finding the right policy mix, the right 'rules of the game' which provide sound incentives to private firms to produce adequate quantities of these goods, while at the same time avoiding monopolistic profit rates. I look at the difficulties in California on electricity, and in the US on broadband telecom, and I sympathise with the problems that they are facing.

For many years, all economists, including myself, used to be somewhat pessimistic about the way things were going on in infrastructure sector in India. From 1991 onwards, the State ceased to invest in infrastructure, but the new policy framework had not fallen into place! So we were stranded between the two stools.

Today, it increasingly looks like the light is at the end of the tunnel on our infrastructure problems.[9] I believe we have made good progress on telecom, roads, ports, electricity and aviation. The big piece where we have yet to obtain real progress is railways.

In *telecom*, we have obtained a revolution by having competition between multiple, private telephone companies. We are now at 40 million mobile phones, and are growing at the rate of 2 million mobile phones every month. Little shops offering internet access are now all over the country. Every visiting card that I encounter has an email address on it. We are one of the world's first countries to shift to a 'unified licensing', where

---

9   *Indian Economic Survey* (2003–04), Chapter 9, p. 206.

the licensing is neutral to telecom technology. I believe we are the only market in the world where the two major technologies for mobile telephony — GSM and CDMA — are locked in grim competitive battle, with customers reaping the rewards of this competition. Total phone subscribers are at 71 million, and what was once thought to be an ambitious target for teledensity that should be achieved by March 2005 was actually achieved in December 2003. Given the existing pace of hectic growth, it looks rather likely that an additional 100 million lines will be added over 2004–05 and 2005–06. This would take teledensity from 7 per cent today to 17 per cent by March 2006.

In *roads*, we have embarked on an enormous project to build new highways, which will take the sustained mean velocity up from 30 km/h to 80 km/h. I believe these new roads will generate a new phase of growth in India, by harnessing what I call 'internal gains from trade'. I believe this is the classical gains-from-trade story, being repeated *within* the country, when firms 1,000 km apart are able to trade for the first time, thanks to the lowered transactions costs. I think the full impact of these roads on investment, and the geographical distribution of production, will play out in the next five years.

We have yet to make the leap to eight-lane expressways, where we will get sustained mean velocities of 160 km/h. But we have a big step forward in terms of learning new institutions, revenue sources, and contracting mechanisms, through which four-lane highways are now very much in our grasp.

In the area of *ports*, we have made progress by contracting out the operations of ports to international firms who have specialised expertise on this subject. Remarkably enough, we find that when a public sector terminal competes with an international operator in the same port, the performance of this public sector terminal also improves! The turnaround time at ports dropped by half, from 7.5 days in 1996–97 to 3.5 days in 2001–02. These new ideas in contracting are being steadily applied across the country, giving a revolution in how the ports sector works.

These improvements in ports, roads and telecom sound nice. But are they large enough to make a *material* difference? Or are they high rates of growth on a very bad base? It is important to focus on the end result of better infrastructure, which should be more efficient firms. Using the CMIE Prowess database, we observe the 4,000 largest manufacturing companies in India. For these firms, working capital as per cent of sales went down dramatically from 13 per cent in 1996 to a level of 3.5 per cent today. This is a striking change, which reflects both the opportunities of being more efficient using the new infrastructure, and the competitive forces which are pushing firms to think more carefully about how they manage inventories.

In the area of *electricity*, the big change is the Electricity Act, which has setup a path-breaking pro-competitive framework whereby producers and consumers of electricity can interact in an unfettered market. We are already seeing myriad changes in the electricity sector in India as a consequence of this simple fact: that producers and consumers of power are now free to contract with each other across the country. Once again, I see this as a story of going from stifled markets to gains from trade.

Financial Sector Reforms: A Quiet Revolution

A major area of focus in the economic reforms has been the financial sector. Joseph Stiglitz has observed that finance is 'the brain of the economy'. The financial sector controls the efficiency with which incremental capital formation is converted into incremental GDP.

India has made good progress in building a sound regulatory framework for banking, insurance and the securities markets. Many countries, all over the world, have experienced problems with banking. Obtaining safe and sound banking is genuinely difficult, given the extreme leverage of banks, the opacity of their assets, and the moral hazard induced by a safety net. Difficulties in banking escalate into major macroeconomic problems when the banking system is itself large, when compared with GDP. In India today, bank deposits are just 48 per cent of GDP, and net non-performing assets are just 2.3 per cent of assets. Hence, there is little possibility of difficulties in banking derailing the economy.

In recent years, much detailed work has taken place on strengthening the banking system. Banking has become more competitive through a steady pace of entry by domestic and foreign banks, and has been steadily transformed by the introduction of new technology such as Real-time Gross Settlement System (RTGS). Banking has also benefited, as all creditors have, from the strengthening of creditors' rights which began in 2001. This continues to be an active area for new work in developing legal structures and institutional mechanisms.

India's financial system differs from that of many developing countries and it is more in line with the Anglo-Saxon model, with large and liquid public securities markets, and with bank deposits being relatively small when compared with GDP. There has been a particularly remarkable revolution in the stock exchanges in terms of a completely new design replacing traditional notions about how the market should be organised.[10] India's NSE and BSE are the third and sixth largest exchanges of the world, measured by the number of trades in 2001 and given the present trends, it is likely that in 2004, NSE will surpass NYSE in terms of the number of trades or transactions. India was a pioneer in shifting to T+2 settlement. India is unique by world standards in the extent to which non-transparent transactions have been proscribed: all trades match on the transparent order-matching screen on the equity market.

Equity derivatives trading was launched in India in June 2000, and now has daily turnover of $4 billion. This was one of the most successful launches of equity derivatives trading in the world.[11] India's success on the stock exchanges is a poster child of our ability to overcome difficult problems of political economy and entrenched interests, to obtain revolutionary change, and rise to the front ranks of the world. These institutions are precious assets today, and will be key building blocks in the next steps of modernising the financial sector, and improving transparency and competition, in the years to come.

In coming decades, enormous flows of savings are going to be intermediated through the financial sector. It is extremely important that the financial sector should be thoughtful and effective in delivering equity and debt capital into those firms in India which convert it into the highest possible GDP growth. This is particularly important because, as we will argue ahead, there is a good likelihood that the savings rate in India will grow significantly in the coming decade. The financial sector is of crucial importance in converting these vast flows of savings into a maximal impact upon GDP growth.

---

10 Ajay Shah (1999), 'Institutional Change on India's Capital Markets', *Economic and Political Weekly*, XXXIV(3–4): 183–94; Ajay Shah and Susan Thomas (2000), 'David and Goliath: Displacing a Primary Market', *Journal of Global Financial Markets*, 1(1): 14–21.
11 Susan Thomas (2003), 'Derivatives Markets in India 2003', *Invest India*, Tata McGraw-Hill.

We know, from the experience of other countries, that this process can go wrong. We need to continue to work on carrying through the reforms in the financial sector. We have many strengths in what has taken place in finance, particularly on the equity market, but a lot remains to be done in banking and the debt market.

A new frontier in financial sector development lies in pension sector reforms. From 1998 to 2003, an intensive effort took place in India to think about alternative strategies in pension reforms, and to design an institutional architecture that would be well suited to solve the unique problems of the Indian setting.[12] This led to important cabinet decisions in 2003 which are now being implemented.

The basic thrust of these reforms is to build a defined contribution pension system where workers would get a range of investment choices and fund managers. Centralised record-keeping infrastructure is envisaged, which gives scale economies, keeps down transactions costs, and maximises the contestability of the market for fund management services. This new pension system has been mandatory for all new recruits to the central government from 1 January 2004 onwards. It marks the dawn of a new breed of sophisticated institutional investors in the country, who will be sources of investment into debt and equity issued by the projects of the future.

Accelerating Privatisation

Privatisation has been a major new theme of reforms in recent years. Major successes, where control of a company has been sold off, include VSNL, BALCO, CMC and Maruti. The true significance of privatisation lies not in the proceeds, but in the impact upon productivity. There are 276 public sector companies at the central level. They contributed Rs 2.28 trillion of 'value added' in 2001–02. Of these, there are 47 companies with *negative* value added — i.e. GDP would go up if these firms ceased to exist. Each 1 per cent of increase in value added by these PSUs amounts to Rs 22.8 billion of additional GDP. The international experience suggests that the value added could go up by 20 per cent to 40 per cent after privatisation. Thus privatisation alone could generate

---

12 Anand Bordia and Gautam Bhardwaj (2003), 'Rethinking Pension Provision for India', *Invest India*, Tata McGraw-Hill Series; Ajay Shah (2005) 'Issues in Pension System Reform in India', in Priya Basu (ed.), *India's Financial Sector: Recent Reforms, Future Challenges*, Macmillan, pp. 205–24.

a direct impact worth 2 per cent to 4 per cent increase in GDP. In addition, there would be many positive indirect effects of privatisation. Interestingly enough, considerable privatisation efforts are now taking place at the level of state governments also. Of the 919 companies owned by state governments, 33 have been privatised and 69 have been closed down in recent years.

Link to Productivity Growth

In my discussion about recent themes in reforms, I have highlighted four big areas: globalisation, infrastructure, privatisation, and the financial sector. It is important to reflect on the consequences of success in these four areas: these successes will give improvements in *productivity*. For a given level of labour and capital, progress in each of these areas will give higher output growth.

Areas of Concern

There are two major areas of concern in this happy picture. The first is the problem of successful resolution of fiscal consolidation issues, and the second is that of regional disparities.

Fiscal Consolidation[13]

As you all know, one of the biggest problems faced in India is the fiscal deficit. The consolidated fiscal deficit, of the centre and the states, has been at stubbornly high levels for around 20 years now.

The essence of this problem has been a stagnation in the tax/GDP ratio. From 1990–91 to 2003–04, we did obtain progress on direct taxes, which went up from 1.9 per cent of GDP to 3.5 per cent. The phasing out of customs duties has inevitably given poor growth in indirect taxes, which went from 7.9 per cent of GDP to 5.7 per cent. The fiscal difficulties at the states have given a fresh impetus to state-level tax efforts, which have yielded some progress, with growth from 5.3 per cent of GDP to 6.3 per cent of GDP. However, the overall picture has been unchanged, with the

---

13   *Report of the Task Force on Direct Taxes*, Government of India, December, 2002; *Report of the Task Force on Indirect Taxes*, Government of India, December, 2002; Partho Shome (2002), *India's Fiscal Matters*, Oxford University Press.

tax/GDP ratio being stable at 15.5 per cent of GDP in 2003–04 and in 1990–91. The combination of large fiscal deficits with a stagnant tax/GDP ratio has given sharp growth in the debt/GDP ratio. From 1992 to 1998, the debt/GDP ratio was stable at 60 per cent of GDP, and that might have given some comfort. But after that, it has resumed an extremely rapid climb to the present level of 80 per cent of GDP. This has fuelled concerns about the possibility of India facing the problem of debt trap as interest payments have steadily become a bigger fraction of tax revenues.

Sometimes, India's fiscal problem is seen narrowly in terms of debt sustainability or a debt trap. I think this is a narrow perspective. The fiscal problem can be damaging to growth in coming years, even if it does not come to a debt trap. The reasons for this need to be reiterated:

- The high fiscal deficit has eliminated the room for manoeuvre in terms of counter-cyclical fiscal policy.
- It has sharply circumscribed the ability of the State to initiate new spending programs which could produce highly beneficial public goods.
- It has served to crowd out private investment, and thus reduce GDP growth.
- It has generated incentives for many distorted policies in the financial sector, where it has helped inhibit banking reform and the development of liquid markets for interest rates.

It is important to observe that the fiscal problems would have had an exacerbated impact on growth, by 'crowding out' private investment, if it had not been for the growth in household savings that was discussed earlier. Roughly speaking, government has taken 10 per cent of GDP in 1990 and in 2003. However, household savings grew from 18 per cent to 23 per cent, thus supplying an *additional* 5 percentage points of GDP to non-government investment in the country.

In many countries, 'downsizing government' — i.e. cutting government *expenses* — has been central to fiscal adjustment. In the case of India, central government expenses dropped from 18.9 per cent of GDP in 1986 to 15.6 per cent of GDP in 2001. These values do not appear to be particularly out of line by international standards, and are broadly consistent with the level of expenses that are required to produce public goods of the required quality and quantity.

Three difficult items of expenditure — i.e. interest payments, defence expenditures and subsidies — make up near 100 per cent of tax revenues. In addition, there are highly inflexible expenses such as pensions, transfers to states, etc. Hence, it appears that there is little flexibility in obtaining a fiscal adjustment by compressing expenditures. There is a great deal that can be gained in terms of improving the extent to which existing expenditures are refocused away from subsidies towards providing public goods, and improving the efficiency of provision of public goods. However, it is hard to visualise a drop in expenses which would be large enough to significantly contribute to the required fiscal adjustment.

This leads us to focus on improving tax revenues as the central policy instrument in the required fiscal adjustment. Hence, efforts towards the fiscal consolidation, that have been undertaken, are focused on the following elements:

- Enlarging the tax base by rationalising exemptions and expanding service tax.
- Process engineering of the tax system.
- Achieving a simple and rational tax system.
- Reduction in transactions costs; improved taxpayer services.
- Reduction in subsidies, with better targeting.

Have these efforts borne fruit? Many observers have pointed out that the tax/GDP ratio is still below the levels found in the late 1980s. This observation, taken in isolation, is sometimes interpreted as implying a failure of tax reforms in India. However, this aggregative fact masks important accomplishments in terms of obtaining change.

	1990		2001	
Source	Collections	%	Collections	%
Income tax (individual)	5,010	9.7	31,764	16.8
Income tax (firms)	4,729	9.2	35,696	18.9
Customs	18,036	34.9	47,542	25.2
Excise	22,406	43.4	68,526	36.3
Service tax			2,613	1.4
Others	1,455	2.8	2,463	1.3
Total tax collections	51636	100.0	188,604	100.0

The table summarises changes in the structure of tax revenues from 1990 to 2001.

The most important accomplishment was in the area of direct taxes, which grew by almost seven times over these 11 years. Direct taxes hence improved sharply from 18.9 per cent of collections to 35.7 per cent. This may be interpreted as a striking 'Laffer curve' outcome, where a sharp reduction in rates was accompanied by a sharp improvement in tax collections, by influencing incentives towards tax evasion and labour supply. Customs collections have lost ground, and will drop further, as India shifts away from protectionist policies. Taxing the services sector has now begun, in a small way.

These reforms anchor the fiscal consolidation envisaged in the *Fiscal Responsibility Act*,[14] and the commitments of state governments, which require elimination of the revenue deficit: from 5.83 per cent in 2002–03 to 0 by 2007–08. It is important to envision what the sources of a 5.83 per cent improvement could be. One example of a feasible combination could be as follows:

- An increase in direct taxes to GDP ratio of 1.5 percentage points.
- An increase in union excise duty (including services) to GDP ratio of 2 percentage points.
- State VAT will be implemented in the near future. It will replace many existing taxes, but across the entire transition, it is expected that this will yield an additional 1 percentage point of GDP.
- Reduction in subsidies and enforcement of user charges will yield 1 percentage point of GDP.
- A reduction in interest payments to GDP ratio of 0.5 percentage point is expected, as new debt, at contemporary low interest rates, replaced old, high-cost debt.

The Interim Budget presented in February this year indicates that fiscal consolidation is proceeding on this line, as the revenue deficit for the year 2003–04 has been projected to decline by 0.5 per cent. This has been due to combination of higher tax/GDP ratio and lower current expenditure.

---

14 *Fiscal Responsibility and Budget Management Act* (2003), No. 39 of 2003, *The Gazette of India Extraordinary*, Part II, Section 1, No. 43, August.

This fiscal consolidation will assist GDP growth in many indirect ways, including:

- reduction in the cost of capital
- enhanced equity
- improved allocative efficiency
- increased administrative efficiency
- reduced transactions costs
- enhanced transparency and accountability.

A successful implementation of this transformation of the tax system, and an elimination of the revenue deficit by 2007–08, is perhaps the most important single issue in public policy in India today. The tax reforms that are currently underway will enable the economy to meet the objective of fiscal consolidation. Successful fiscal consolidation will enable the economy to achieve other important social goals such as better environment protection, greater investment in health infrastructure, R&D and the agriculture sectors.

Regional Disparities

States	Per capita SDP 1999–2000 ('000 rupees)	Population 2001 (% of India)
Bihar	6.3	10.7
Orissa	9.2	3.6
Assam	9.6	2.6
Uttar Pradesh	9.8	17.0
Sum of these 4		33.9
India	15.6	100.0

A major problem that India faces is the large cross-sectional dispersion in economic development. There is a roughly 3:1 ratio in the per capita GDP, when we compare the richest states to the poorest states. Much attention has been focused on the 'BIMARU' states (Bihar, Madhya Pradesh, Rajasthan, Uttar Pradesh) which have high population density and low per capita output. The term 'BIMARU' is catchy because the word *bimaar* means 'sick' in Hindi. The table above identifies the four large states where per capita SDP was over 33 per cent below the national average. These four states make up 33.9 per cent of India's population.

Regional disparities in India have been present for at least a century, if not more. Under normal circumstances, the processes of the market economy should generate 'equalising differences', whereby firms move to low-wage areas in the quest for reduced costs thus equalising differences in wages and land prices. Similarly, individuals migrate to high wage areas, thus equalising wages, and increasing the land per capita in poor areas. These processes are expected to generate convergence of per capita GDP in the normal framework of growth theory.

It is important to emphasise that the forces of convergence depicted here are based on factor mobility. They operate over and above the conventional notions of convergence through trade, which are based on technological catch-up and trade in goods, without factor mobility. This worldview has faced a challenge from the empirical evidence of the 1990s, where there is some evidence of a lack of convergence. Some states, particularly the states of the West and the South, seem to have excelled in harnessing the opportunities of globalisation and the market economy. In other states, weaknesses in human capital and governance have generated reduced growth rates in the post-1990 period.

This has been a source of much concern on the part of many observers, from two points of view. First, it is argued that if the economic reforms of the 1980s and 1990s failed to ignite growth in Bihar, then there is a need to find a new policy mix which can achieve high growth in Bihar. Second, there are fears of mounting political stress that might come about if income disparities between rich and poor states widen further. There is a remarkable similarity between these problems in India and those that have been observed in China, where coastal provinces have progressed enormously compared with the interior.

These problems are undoubtedly important, and are going to be a central issue in Indian economics and politics in the years to come. While the above difficulties are real, there are also many forces at work which are steadily having an ameliorating effect.

Flexibility of the labour market: Factor mobility is a fundamental element of the process of equalising differences. As of today, roughly 90 per cent of India's labour force is in the unorganised sector, which is a classical labour market, undistorted by labour law. In addition, unlike China, India has no government restrictions on inter-state or rural-to-urban migration.

This innate flexibility of the labour market will assist the process of convergence. In the historical data, migration flows do not (as yet) account for substantial movements of the population. The reforms of the 1990s ignited high growth rates in some states. It is likely that migration flows have a lagged response to high wage differentials. By this logic, the 2011 census may be expected to show larger migration flows than were observed in the 2001 census.

Impact of new infrastructure on 'equalising differences': The development economics literature has emphasised the problems of land-locked states, which are unable to harness gains from trade through high costs of transportation.[15]

India's growth experience suggests that geography is important. At the same time, there are exceptions. Coastal states in India have fared well; however, Orissa is a coastal state. Land-locked states have fared poorly; however, Punjab and Haryana are land-locked.

Gains from internal trade are clearly an important mechanism through which poor states can obtain economic growth. This is critically related to costs of transportation. This suggests that the recent successes in infrastructure policy — particularly in roads, ports, airports, and telecom — are highly significant in thinking about regional disparities. The new roads being built by NHAI imply that vegetables produced in Bihar or Orissa can find markets in Calcutta. This constitutes a new impetus for the forces of convergence, as compared with the preceding post-independence experience.

Fiscal transfers: India has a well-developed system of fiscal transfers, through which taxes collected in rich states are transferred to poor states. This constitutes an important channel for convergence — one that is perhaps reminiscent of the 60-year story of North Italy and South Italy.

---

15   John Luke Gallup, Jeffrey D. Sachs, and Andrew D. Mellinger (1998), 'Geography and Economic Development', NBER Working Paper No. 6849, December.

While these rules have always been with us, the economic significance of these transfers improves in line with growth in GDP and in the tax/GDP ratio. Holding the fiscal rules intact, when the size of the pie goes up, larger per-capita flows are being sent into poor states. In the decade of the 1990s, India's GDP was roughly $350 billion and the tax/GDP ratio was roughly 12 per cent. GDP has already risen to $620 billion, giving a quantum leap in the expenditures of government. Looking forward, in a few years, if we envision GDP of $1 trillion and a tax/GDP ratio of 15 per cent, then there will be enormously larger resource flows through existing fiscal institutions, which will generate much larger spending in poor states.

Policy innovations: One important insight derived from the experience of economic growth in East Asia is the importance of 'regional role models'.[16] East Asian countries learned from each other. Across these countries, there was a significant amount of experimentation and real-world trials of alternative ideas, including choices of effective institutions, policies, and technologies. There was a contagion effect within this region with countries learning from each other's success stories.

In the decade of the 1990s, a similar phenomenon has begun with the states of India. States are now increasingly conscious of the importance of local public goods. The political leadership of many states is increasingly conscious of the need to find policy innovations which would improve the quality and quantity of local public goods.

The 1990s began with a certain heterogeneity of governance procedures in the states. The economic reforms of the 1990s have inevitably had a differential impact on various states; some states had policies which were more conducive to harnessing these opportunities. When the gap in per capita income widens, the political system has incentives to search for policy responses which would close the gap. Andhra Pradesh, Madhya Pradesh, West Bengal, and Kerala are all examples of states where there has been a distinct learning from the regional role models, and consequent changes in governance.

---

16 Nancy Birdsall et al. (1993), *The East Asian Miracle: Economic Growth and Public Policy*, World Bank, Oxford University Press, September.

In parallel to this learning from regional role models, there are two important policy innovations which are going to fully play out in the coming decade. The first is the move towards smaller states. It is widely conjectured that smaller states are more effective at catering to local variation in preferences and technology, and at ensuring greater accountability for public goods outcomes. Uttaranchal, Bihar, Jharkhand and Chattisgarh are important experiments in this regard. It is, as yet, too early to tell whether the outcomes play out in line with the conjecture. If governance does prove to be superior in smaller states, then (a) it will generate convergence, given that these four states are all below the national average, and (b) it suggests one policy avenue for improving governance in other large states in the future.

The second innovation is the devolution to local governments, as a consequence of the 73rd and 74th constitutional amendment. The underlying premise of Panchayati Raj is that when local citizens control public expenditures, there will be a greater likelihood of obtaining good *outcomes* in terms of producing public goods. There are three key elements of local autonomy: (a) transfer of functions and schemes, (b) transfer of staff, and (c) transfer of funds, and autonomous financial decision-making. As of yet, different states have made different degrees of progress on these three fronts. It is, as yet, too early to tell whether the outcomes play out in line with the underlying premise. If we do obtain improvements in governance by empowering local governments, then this would constitute one channel for convergence.

Empirical Evidence

How are we faring? There is some evidence that these effects are already at work and are reshaping the nature of regional inequalities in India. There are two striking illustrations which show the changes which are taking place:

- In a deliciously ironic development, the very phrase 'BIMARU', which symbolised backward states as of 1990, has become out of touch with the location of poverty traps! This symbolises the dynamism of regional economics in India. Rajasthan and Madhya Pradesh have made significant progress in the 1990s. Chattisgarh, Uttaranchal and western parts of Uttar Pradesh have lower poverty. The most difficult areas are now no longer the BIMARU states, but the eastern region comprising Orissa, Jharkhand, Bihar, and eastern parts of Uttar

Pradesh. This illustrates the *mutability* of poverty traps in India, and suggests that there *are* forces at work through which poor regions can obtain convergence.

- The second illustration concerns the BPO industry. If the idea of exploiting IT for services exports, in areas like call centres and accounting, had been described to an impartial observer in 1993, the prediction which would have been squarely made is that this would flourish in southern states, owing to the superior quality of local public goods. This would include issues such as education, reliable electricity, law and order and gender issues. Questions of law and order, and empowerment of women, are extremely important in this field, given the need for women to work the night shift. The impartial observer would have solemnly argued that North India was innately and deeply hamstrung when it came to women obtaining high education, participating in the labour force, and working at night.

The actual outcomes, from 1993 to 2003, have been inconsistent with the prediction that IT-enabled services would primarily be located in the peninsula. When we look back at the last 10 years, it is an undeniable fact that Gurgaon, Noida and Chandigarh have also emerged as the major centres of IT-enabled services exports. While locations like Bangalore, Madras, Hyderabad, Poona and Bombay have all also succeeded in this area, Gurgaon and Noida are probably the largest centres. This suggests that issues such as low labour cost dominated issues such as poor production of local public goods, which suggests that forces of convergence were effective.

The most interesting evidence about the question of convergence is found in data for investment projects outstanding.[17]

State	4/1995	10/2003	Change (%)
Delhi	313	5,966	1,804.8
Kerala	991	5,579	462.8
Chattisgarh	1,097	4,525	312.5
Madhya Pradesh	1,846	6,889	273.3
Tamil Nadu	2,491	6,941	178.6

17 Montek S. Ahluwalia (2002), 'State Level Performance under Economic Reforms in India', in Anne O. Krueger (ed.) *Economic Policy Reforms and the Indian Economy*, University of Chicago Press, Chicago.

State	4/1995	10/2003	Change (%)
Karnataka	3,528	8,265	134.2
Haryana	3,021	6,820	125.7
Maharashtra	4,409	8,957	103.1
Bihar	799	1,560	95.3
Andhra Pradesh	3,740	7,083	89.4
India	**3,258**	**5,510**	**69.1**
Rajasthan	1,852	2,771	49.6
Punjab	3,662	5,148	40.6
Orissa	6,073	7,432	22.4
Uttar Pradesh	1,302	1,544	18.6
West Bengal	2,408	2,686	11.5
Gujarat	12,531	11,950	-4.6
Jharkhand	3,908	3,643	-6.8

The table above exploits the CMIE database which tracks investment projects at hand as of a point in time. It juxtaposes the projects under implementation as of April 1995 (the first point in the CMIE database) versus October 2003 (the most recent date available). All values are expressed as rupees per capita.

This data is interesting from two points of view. Focusing on *levels*, we see states like Gujarat, which have above-mean output and above-mean investment. At the same, there also appear to be equilibrating forces at work. High growth in investment is seen in backward states like Kerala, Madhya Pradesh, Chattisgarh and Bihar. In a striking display of convergence, of the 10 states with above-average growth in per-capita investment, eight had a below-average *level* of per capita investment as of 1995. In addition, Punjab shows the opposite phenomenon. Low growth in investment is found in high income states like Punjab and Gujarat.

These trends are indicative of the possibility of meeting the objective of regional equity with well defined policies at the Central level and at the State level. Regional equity is going to be perhaps one of the most important issues for the political economy of growth in a federal system like India. We will need to be continuously mindful of this aspect and keep policies under review so as to achieve equity in outcomes across the States of our Union.

III

Growth Outlook: Contributions from Labour, Capital and Productivity

Let me now shift gears considerably. So far I have talked about the reform efforts, repeatedly alluding to the impact of reforms on efficiency, productivity and improved resource allocation.

But what about the perspective for the growth of inputs? Ever since Krugman's 1994 article[18] in *Foreign Affairs*, about the extent to which East Asian growth was 'merely' caused by a high flow of inputs in terms of labour and capital, all of us have had a heightened consciousness about both (a) the power of additional inputs in delivering high growth rates, and (b) the importance of asking whether there is productivity growth over and above this.

Labour

Let me start with labour. It is conventional to focus on citizens between age 15 and 64 as 'the working population'. The fascinating thing about India is that we will be one of the last large countries in the world to experience our demographic transition. Current projections show that from 2010 or so, the fraction of Chinese and of Koreans in the age group of 15–64 will start dropping. In the case of Japan, this fraction has been dropping from 1995 onwards.

In the case of India, we will experience 'demographic dividend' as the ratio of working population to the total population will grow all the way till 2050. In particular, a sharp drop in the dependency ratio from 59 per cent to 50 per cent is projected between 2005 and 2020. The dependency ratio is projected to drop to 47 per cent in 2040. It is only from 2040 onwards that India's dependency ratio is projected to go up. This will give robust fuel to the process of economic growth. This forecast for India reflects the existing young population structure, coupled with a deceleration of fertility, so that a large number of children are not expected to be added.

---

18 Paul Krugman (1994), 'The Myth of Asia's Miracle — A Cautionary Fable', *Foreign Affairs*, November/December.

A second change that is taking place on the labour force is equally significant for economic growth. This concerns the *quality* of the labour force. Every year, the human capital of the stock of labour goes up, through gains in education and gains in experience. Hence, we are likely to obtain improvements in the labour inputs to economic growth from three, distinct directions: (a) incremental workers, (b) incremental education, and (c) incremental experience of the existing stock of workers. All this is potent fuel for economic growth. The experience of Asia shows that the 'growth miracles' in Japan or in 'Tiger' economies of South-East Asia or in China occurred at the similar stage of demographic transition when the share of working population in total population grew sharply.

Capital

What about capital? One element flows directly from demographics. Children and old people tend to save less; saving is the highest in the working years. Using NCAER survey data,[19] we find that in 1994–95, while the overall savings rate was 20.3 per cent, this dropped to 16.9 per cent when the head of household was below 30. The highest savings rate, of 23 per cent, was found when the head of the household was in the 50s. In the case of urban households, these effects were more pronounced, with a savings rate of just 7.8 per cent when the head of household was below 30.

So the demographic projections which clearly point out that India will have a bigger fraction of the population in the age group from 15 to 64 simultaneously predict a higher savings rate in the future. Further, holding household characteristics identical, a larger number of children would induce higher consumption, so declining fertility is likely to induce higher saving.

A second factor that is at work is the sheer GDP growth. NCAER data shows that there are extremely low savings rates for low income households. Remarkably enough, as of 1994–95, only 1.9 per cent of all saving was done by households with income below the then prevalent median income. In 1994–95, the poorest 80 per cent of the population accounted for half the income, and this group accounted for 23.9 per cent of total savings. As a rough approximation, we may say that significant

---

19 Basanta K. Pradhan, P.K. Roy, M.R. Saluja and S.L. Shetty (2003), 'Household Savings and Investment Behaviour in India', NCAER, September.

savings behaviour only took place in the top quartile of the income distribution of 1994–95. Households in the top decile had a much higher savings rate, of 35.8 per cent, as compared with the general population.

Economic growth steadily pushes households above the absolute income threshold required to be in the top quartile by the income distribution as of 1994–95. Thus, every year, a large number of households graduate into the income group where saving will commence. The bottom 30 per cent of the 1994–95 income distribution has near-zero or negative saving. GDP growth shrinks this set of zero-savings households. The top quartile of the 1994–95 income distribution had high savings rates. GDP growth pushes more households into this set of high-savings households. Through this process, holding other aspects of the stochastic environment of the household constant, the high GDP growth rates that India has been experiencing are likely to generate a steady escalation of the savings rate.

The two arguments suggested above — about the impact of income growth and about the changing dependency ratio — have been at work for some time. If these arguments are on track, then it should have been the case that the savings rate in India should have been going up in recent years. The empirical evidence is consistent with this prediction, for household savings grew from 18 per cent to 23 per cent over the period after 1990. Looking forward, our arguments suggest that household savings will grow further in the coming 15 years. In addition, growing openness of capital account would mean greater inflow of foreign capital as the country becomes a 'willing globaliser' — i.e. more open to trade and investment. This means that in the coming decade, the supply of both domestic and foreign savings are going to sharply increase leading to a much higher rate of capital accumulation compared to the last two decades.

Outlook on Productivity

Paul Krugman noticed that East Asian growth had weak foundations in terms of productivity increases; that the high growth rates were primarily a combination of demographics (an increase in the working population) and capital being brought to bear on production. This is disappointing. The essence of development is improved technology; it is all about new ways of organising production, of injecting new scientific knowledge and new institutions into the economy. We expect that when economic development takes place, *productivity* should be transformed.

It is important to point out that many studies have taken place on productivity in India, and the consensus suggests that there *has* been significant TFP growth in India. The definitive measurement is by Bosworth and Collins in 2003,[20] who find that in the period after 1980, 2 per cent of the growth (out of a total of 5.73 per cent) was accounted for by productivity changes. This suggests that India's reforms process has been able to obtain results in terms of better incentives and competition, coupled with better public goods, inducing improvements in productivity.

The outlook for the acceleration in the TFP growth in the coming decade or two is very promising. This is for several reasons. The first is the impact of information technology. In the coming decade, the rate of diffusion of IT is going to be greater due to increased availability of hardware, telecom infrastructure and human capital. In the US and other countries, the diffusion of IT has had a well documented positive impact on productivity growth. The second reason is the beneficial impact of mesoeconomic reforms and privatisation of the infrastructure sector on productivity. The international experience has been that such mesoeconomic economic reforms have led to an all-round increase in productivity. The third element is the engines of increasing returns which will be accruing from network industries due to network externalities.[21] The new highway network and telecom networks are two prime examples of new network industries. In the US, both these network industries have had profound impact in accelerating growth in total factor productivity.

When we look back at the experience with growth across various countries over the last 200 years, each experience with rapid growth has been caused by accumulation of capital, coupled with a catching-up of scientific knowledge. Over the years, the technologies of information processing and dissemination have steadily improved. This suggests that the *diffusion of knowledge takes place faster and faster*. This is consistent with the fact that the more recent growth episodes, like those of China, Korea and Taiwan, have experienced higher growth rates when compared with the older growth episodes, like those of Russia, Japan and the US. Looking forward, India will benefit strongly from the great technological improvements in the diffusion of knowledge which have taken place in the last 25 years. When Korea was integrating into the world economy, and

---

20   Barry Bosworth, and Susan Collins (2003), 'The Empirics of Growth: An Update', Brookings Paper on Economic Activity 2: 113–79.
21   Oz Shy (2001), *The Economics of Network Industries*, Cambridge University Press, New York.

catching up with global scientific knowledge, the process of knowledge acquisition was slower than that found today in India, given the greater extent of information access through the Internet, voice calls, international travel, etc. This suggests that the speed of productivity change in India, in the next 20 years, could be higher than that seen in any experience with rapid economic growth in the last 200 years.

These arguments suggest that in the coming decade, it is not difficult to envisage a sharp increase of more than 50 per cent in the annual TFP growth a doubling of the TFP growth from the present trend of 2 per cent per annum. Such an increase would be in line with the international experience of dynamic economies.

On the Growth Turnpike

This brings me to my main thesis: that India may be about to embark on a new golden age of high economic growth. The key argument runs in these steps:

- There is a near inevitability that there will be a bulge in the working population, particularly till 2020. This effect will be further multiplied due to enhanced levels of skills — i.e. accumulation of human capital.
- It is likely that this demographic dividend, coupled with strong GDP growth, will fuel an increase in the savings rate.
- Thus India is likely to fare *better* than it did over the 1980 to 2000 period, in terms of putting factor inputs into the growth process.
- The policies of the recent years — particularly in infrastructure, reductions of protectionism, and building modern securities markets — will continue to fuel TFP growth.
- Being a 'willing globaliser' will attract greater flow of FDI and technology.
- In addition, India has already shown a track record for obtaining TFP growth over the 1980–2000 period. TFP growth will show further acceleration thanks to the impact of information and communication technologies upon the speed of knowledge diffusion and to the network externalities.

- These elements add up to a scenario where GDP growth in India over 2004–24 will be much higher than that seen over 1980 to 2004. In the coming decade or two, growth rate in India may surpass the 'miracle growth' rates achieved by other Asian countries. This is not surprising as India, compared to Japan, China and other high growth economies of Asia, will have advantage of an access to productivity enhancing IT, which was not available in earlier decades. This way, we will be cashing in on the 'latecomer's advantage'.

Concluding Remarks

Now, I would like to sum up. Thanks to painstaking policy reforms initiated over the last two decades by successive governments, I believe that India is at the threshold of 'a golden age of growth', with India's democratic framework being a key growth fundamental. It seems to me that, over time, India has paid the 'fixed costs' of democracy in terms of the creation of institutional infrastructure, traditions and conventions. Further, India's democratic system has also internalised what Prime Minister Vajpayee calls 'Coalition Dharma', showing that coalitions can provide stable government and push economic reforms. This means that in the future, the economy can reap the dividends from the resultant systemic stability. Thus, India — riding the wave of growth fundamentals such as demographic transition, human capital accumulation, improved incentive structures, diffusion of new technologies such as IT, total factor productivity accelerators through 'network industries', and an improved security environment — will be growing at growth rates which can be above 10 per cent per annum, i.e. double-digit growth rates. There is an ineffable sense of joy for me personally, and professionally, to see India embark on this growth odyssey, a journey that I call 'India: On the growth turnpike'.

Oration 9:
2005 K.R. Narayanan Oration

Message from the President
of the Republic of India

I am happy to know that the Australia South Asia Research Centre of The Australian National University is hosting the 2005 Narayanan Oration on the theme 'Science and Shaping our Agricultural Future' on 27 September 2005.

I visualise Village Knowledge Centres (VKCs) in *panchayats*, which would empower our rural communities. The VKCs would have computers and connectivity and would be windows to the world of knowledge that would reap the benefits of e-governance, tele-education, tele-medicine, e-commerce and e-judiciary initiatives. VKCs ultimately would be used to access village specific information to shape a prosperous future for these communities. An organisation of farmers by the farmers for agricultural farming and marketing is the need of the hour.

On this occasion, I extend my greetings and felicitations to all those associated with the Australia South Asia Research Centre and wish the oration all success.

A.P.J. Abdul Kalam
New Delhi
2005

Science and Shaping our Agricultural Future

M.S. Swaminathan

It is a privilege to deliver a lecture in honour of Dr K.R. Narayanan, immediate Past President of India. Dr Narayanan represents all that is best in Indian culture and democratic system of governance. He rose from the lowest to the highest position in Indian Society by virtue of his innate human and professional qualities. Dr Narayanan knows the pangs of hunger and has therefore been on the forefront of the hunger-free India movement. He encouraged scientists to work on problems relevant to the alleviation of poverty and eradication of hunger. I have therefore chosen the topic, 'Science and Shaping our Agricultural Destiny' for this lecture.

Introduction

From the beginning of time, technology has been a key element in the growth and development of societies. The spread of technologies has however been uneven throughout history. In food production, we have now reached the age of biotechnology and precision farming. Many of the technologies like improved seeds are scale neutral with reference to their relevance to farms of varying sizes but are not resource neutral. Inputs are needed for output and hence those who do not have access to inputs tend to get bypassed by technological transformation. Synergy between technology and public policy has therefore remained a pre-condition for technologies to confer benefit to all sections of the farming community, irrespective of the size of their holdings and their innate capacity to mobilise capital and take risks. Among factors of production, access to irrigation water has been a major determinant of technological change, since without assured irrigation, it is difficult to apply nutrients in quantities essential for high yields, even if genetic strains capable of high productivity are available.

Today, global agriculture is witnessing two opposite trends. In many South Asian countries, farm size is becoming smaller and smaller and farmers suffer serious handicaps with reference to the cost-risk-return structure of agriculture. Farm size in most industrialised countries is becoming larger and larger and farmers are supported by heavy inputs of technology, capital and subsidy. The recent breakdown of the Cancun negotiations of the World Trade Agreement in the field of agriculture reflects the polarisation which has taken place in the basic agrarian structure of industrialised and developing countries.

In India, average yields of major food crops remained well below 1 metric ton per hectare for centuries, until the introduction of high yielding varieties in the 1960s. To produce one metric ton of rice the rice plant needs at least 20 kg of nitrogen and appropriate quantities of phosphorus, potash and micronutrients. The native soil fertility was often below this level and hence yields tended to remain below a ton.

The steps taken after independence to improve the productivity of food crops fall under the following major categories:

- package of technology
- package of services in areas such as input supply and extension
- package of public policies in areas such as land reforms, rural infrastructure development, investment in irrigation, input and output pricing policies and assured and remunerative marketing.

Improvement of agricultural production through the productivity pathway is essential for both resource poor farmers and consumers. Casual agricultural labourers are the largest in number among the chronically poor and cultivators the second largest group. Most of the chronically poor were either landless or near-landless. The smaller the farm, the greater is the need for increasing productivity, so that the farm family has a higher marketable surplus. Productivity improvement also tends to reduce the cost of the commodity, thereby benefiting resource poor consumers. Above all productivity improvement is essential for safeguarding the remaining forests, since otherwise forest land will get converted to produce food. Thus, the productivity pathway of agricultural advance helps in strengthening ecological, livelihood and food security.

What we need is an evergreen revolution, which can help to increase productivity in perpetuity without associated ecological harm (Swaminathan 1996). Exploitative agriculture offers great dangers if carried out with only an immediate profit or production motive. The initiation of exploitative agriculture without a proper understanding of the various consequences of every one of the changes introduced into traditional agriculture, and without first building up a proper scientific and training base to sustain it, may only lead us, in the long run, into an era of agricultural disaster rather than one of agricultural prosperity (Swaminathan 1968). We need ecotechnologies rooted in the principles of ecology, economics, gender and social equity and employment generation. The vulnerable sections need job-led economic growth and not jobless growth.

In spite of striking agricultural progress and democratic decentralisation, chronic and transient poverty and poverty induced malnutrition are widespread. International and national media refer to this as the co-existence of 'grain mountains and hungry millions' (Swaminathan 2005). Section 2 outlines the issues in the context of food security and access, Sections 3 and 4 the transition from the green to gene to evergreen revolution in rice and wheat, Section 5 provides case studies that show how we can bridge the technological divide and Section 6 concludes.

Food Availability, Access, Absorption and Threats to Food Security

Food security was formerly considered essentially in terms of production. It was assumed that adequate food production would ensure adequate availability of food in the market as well as in the household. In the '70s, it became clear that availability alone does not lead to food security. It is becoming evident that even if availability and access are satisfactory, the biological absorption of food in the body is related to the consumption of clean drinking water as well as to environmental hygiene. Finally, even if physical and economic access to food is assured, ecological factors will determine the long-term sustainability of food security systems. We have to define food as physical, economic, social and ecological access to balanced diet and clean drinking water, so as to enable every child, woman and man to lead a healthy and productive life. The needs of each age group must be addressed (see cycle approach described by MSSRF 2001). Such an approach will involve the following steps (Swaminathan 2002a, 2002b).

Food Availability

This is a function of both home production and imports. There is no time to relax on the food production front. The present global surplus of food grains is the result of inadequate consumption on the part of the poor, and should not be mistaken as a sign of over-production.

Food Access

Lack of purchasing power deprives a person from access to food even though food is available. Inadequate livelihood opportunities in rural areas are responsible for household nutrition insecurity. For example, India today has over 30 million tonnes of wheat and rice in government godowns; yet poverty induced hunger affects over 200 million persons. It is endemic in south Asia and sub-Saharan Africa (Ramalingaswami et al. 1997; WFP 2001). Macroeconomic policies, at the national and global level, should be conducive to fostering job-led economic growth based on micro-enterprises supported by micro-credit. Where poverty is pervasive, suitable measures to provide the needed entitlement to food, should be introduced. The State of Maharashtra introduced, nearly 25 years ago, an Employment Guarantee Scheme to assist the poor to earn their daily bread during seasons when opportunities for wage employment are low.

Food Absorption

Lack of access to clean drinking water, poor environmental hygiene and poor health infrastructure, lead to poor assimilation of the food that is consumed. Nutrition security cannot be achieved without environmental hygiene, primary health care and clean drinking water security. Culinary habits also need careful evaluation as some methods of cooking may lead to the loss of vital nutrients.

Threats to Food Security

The most important among the internal threats to sustainable food security is the damage to the ecological foundations essential for sustained agricultural advance, like land, water, forests and biodiversity. Second, in the areas of farm economics, resource flow to the agriculture sector is declining and indebtedness of small and marginal farm families is rising. Input costs are increasing, while factor productivity is declining. Third, a *technology fatigue* has further aggravated farmers' problems, since the smaller the farm the greater is the need for sustained marketable surplus, in order to have cash income. Linkages between the laboratory and the field have weakened and extension services have often little to extend by way of location, time and farming system specific information and advice (chapter on 'Wake Up Call' in the NCF 2006).

The external threats include the unequal trade bargain inherent in the WTO agreement of 1994, the rapid expansion of proprietary science and potential adverse changes in temperature, precipitation, sea level and ultraviolet ß radiation. Though it is now over 10 years since the WTO regime started operating in agriculture, serious attempts are yet to be made to launch in rural areas movements for quality literacy (sanitary and phytosanitary measures and codex alimentarius standards of food safety), trade literacy (likely demand-supply and price situation), legal literacy (IPR, Farmers' Rights) and genetic literacy (genetically modified crops). No wonder the prevailing gap between potential and actual yields even with technologies currently on the shelf is very wide (Table 1).

Table 1: Comparative crop productivity (kg/ha)

Crop	USA	China	India
Maize	8,900	4,900	2,100
Paddy	7,500	6,000	3,000
Soybeans	2,250	1,740	1,050
Seed cotton	2,060	3,500	750
Tomato	6,250	2,400	1,430

Source: 'Wake Up Call' chapter in NCF (2006).

In the area of technology, there is also need to bridge the growing digital and genetic divides. Post-harvest technology is poor and there is little value addition particularly in the case of fruits, vegetables and spices including a wide range of tubers and medicinal and aromatic plants. Sustainable intensification, ecologically, economically and nutritionally desirable diversification and value addition to the entire biomass are important for raising small and marginal farm families above subsistence level. All this will call for initiating an era of knowledge intensive agriculture. Modern information communication technologies (ICT) afford an opportunity for launching a knowledge revolution in rural India.

Technological Transformation of Productivity, Profitability and Sustainability: Rice

Asia grows most of the world's rice output and 90 per cent of rice is produced by small farmers who depend on it for their livelihood and food security. The role of rice in national and global food security systems will increase, not only because of increases in population and purchasing power, but also because of likely changes in climate and sea level rise due to global warming. An immediate task is bridging the gap between potential and actual yields, widely prevalent in several rice growing countries and particularly in different parts of India. This is possible even at currently available levels of technology, through mutually reinforcing packages of technology, services and public policies. In the decades ahead, more rice will have to be produced under conditions of shrinking per capita arable land and irrigation water availability and expanding biotic and abiotic stresses. Due to breeding efforts based on an appropriate integration of Mendelian and molecular techniques, the ceiling to yield is being raised continuously (Figure 1).

Aided by biotechnology, the greatest potential for productivity gains in yield ceiling in the future lies in rainfed environments (Peacock and Chaudhury 2002). Integrating genetic efficiency with genetic diversity of diverse gene pool through pre-breeding and participatory breeding should be encouraged (Figure 2). Hybrid rice, 'super rice' and 'super hybrid rice' are likely to dominate the rice world in the future. What is however important is the initiation of research which can lead to the standardisation of methods of feeding the rice plant for higher yields in an ecologically sustainable manner. Research on breeding and feeding for higher yields should proceed concurrently.

Potential yield (t/ha)

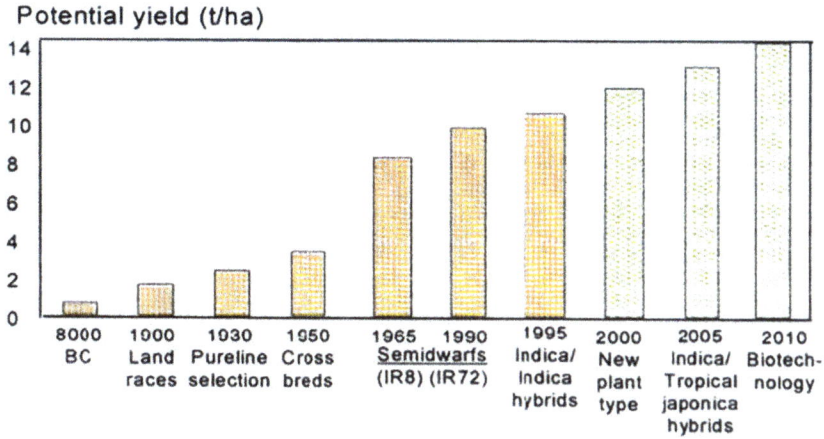

Figure 1: Progress in the yield potential of rice

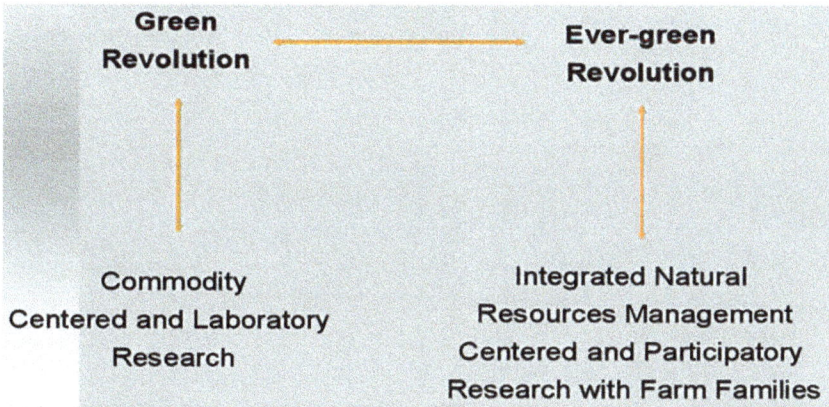

Figure 2: Paradigm shift: Adding the dimension of environmental sustainability

We have several simple and elegant tools that enable us to manipulate the rice genome to elicit desirable responses — tolerance to pests and diseases, moisture stress, salinity-alkalinity, heat, increased photosynthetic efficiency, dry matter accumulation, and source sink partitioning. Rice gene sequence information is widely viewed as an invaluable asset for developing products and technologies. Because of advances in molecular mapping and breeding, there are new opportunities for improving the nutritive qualities of rice, with particular reference to iron, vitamin A and other micronutrients. Under an expanding intellectual property rights (IPR) regime, it is important that research for public good receives the needed support at the national and international levels so that the resource

177

poor can gain from it. Farmers have to achieve revolutionary progress in productivity, quality and value addition. The emerging ecological, economic and social challenges have to be met through partnerships among rice researchers and developmental organisations, committed to the cause of improving the productivity, profitability, sustainability and stability of rice farming systems.

Pingali et al. (1997) have described in detail the steps needed to increase rice production in Asia to meet future needs. If global warming and the associated changes in temperature, precipitation and sea level rise do occur, the position of rice in national and global food security systems will increase, since rice has the ability to grow under very diverse environmental conditions. Rice is by far the best-adapted crop to lowland soils that are prone to flooding during wet season. They draw attention to the following challenges facing rice research and development agencies:

- Productivity gains from the exploitation of Green Revolution technologies are close to exhaustion.
- In the absence of further technical change, Asian farmers face increasing costs per tonne of rice produced.
- Adverse agricultural externalities are increasing due to lack of holistic perspective of the farm resource base management.
- Despite an anticipated decline in per capita rice consumption, aggregate Asian demand for rice is expected to increase by 50 to 60 per cent during the 1990–2025 period due to population increase and poverty reduction.
- Economic growth and the commercialisation of agricultural systems could reduce the competitiveness of rice relative to other crops and other farm enterprises.
- An upward shift in rice yield frontier is necessary to meet future rice requirements and to sustain farm-level profits.

Compounding these problems, there are potential dangers arising from the diminishing investment in research in institutions devoted entirely to national and international public good and the expanding intellectual property rights (IPR) regime. The question now is how much more improvement can we bring about in productivity without ecological harm? In other words, can we launch an evergreen revolution in rice in the new millennium, marked by sustained advances in productivity, profitability, stability and sustainability of rice farming systems (Swaminathan 1996,

2000, 2002a). How can we also increase the role of rice in the nutritional security of families dependent on it for their dietary energy supply? How can rice production be insulated from the adverse impact of potential changes in precipitation, temperature and rise in sea level? Above all, how can we maintain and strengthen international cooperation in rice improvement?

Increasing Production and Productivity

Bridging the Yield Gap

Due to imperfect adaptation to local environments, insufficient provision of nutrients and water, and incomplete control of pests, diseases and weeds the present average rice yield is just 40 per cent of what can be achieved even with technologies currently on the shelf. There is considerable scope for further investment in land improvement through drainage, terracing, control of acidification, etc. in areas where these have not already been introduced. While irrigated areas are making good progress, there is need for more attention on intensive research and development in rainfed, low land and upland areas. Ensuring that benefits from technology accrue to resource poor or marginal farmers will require special efforts as outlined in the case studies in Section 5.

An integrated approach is necessary to remove the technological, infrastructure and social and policy constraints responsible for the productivity gap and in some cases, productivity decline. Reducing the cost of production through eco-technologies and improving income through efficient production and post-harvest technologies will help to enhance opportunities for both skilled employment and farm income. Public policies should not only pay attention to agrarian reform and input and output pricing, but also to reaching the unreached in technology dissemination through training, techno-infrastructure and trade. A constraints analysis of the type shown in Figure 3 should be undertaken. Public policy on anticipating and avoiding production constrains research on facilitating adoption of new technology by small farmers should receive as much attention as agronomic research.

Future agricultural production programs will have to be based on a three-pronged strategy designed to foster an evergreen revolution, which leads to increased production without associated ecological and social harm. These strategies include defending the gains already achieved, extending the gains to rainfed areas and making new gains through farming systems diversification and value addition.

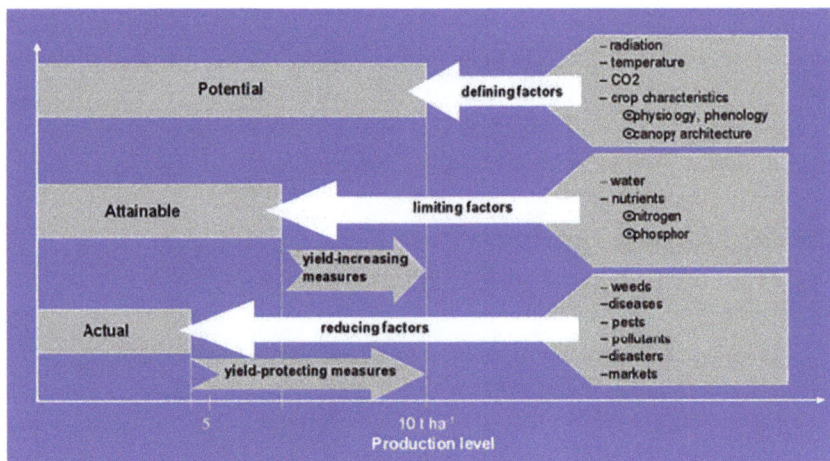

Figure 3: Yield gap — constraints analysis
Source: Modified from Rabbinge et al. (1994).

Defending the Gains Already Achieved

There is need for stepping up maintenance research for ensuring that new strains of pests and pathogens do not cause crop losses and prevent the introduction of invasive alien species. Water harvesting, watershed development and economic and efficient water use can help to enhance productivity and income considerably. Where water is scarce, high value but low water requiring crops should be promoted. As pulses and oilseeds are important income earning and soil enriching crops, they should be included in rice farming systems.

Extending the Gains

There is need to develop and disseminate eco-technologies for rainfed and semi-arid, hill and island areas, which have so far been bypassed by modern yield enhancement technologies. Regional imbalances in agricultural development are growing based largely on the availability of assured irrigation on the one hand and assured and remunerative marketing opportunities on the other. The introduction of eco-regional technology missions that look at all the links in the chain and work towards the stipulated goal, aimed at providing appropriate packages of technology, the specific farm infrastructure services required by the technology (techno-infrastructure), and input and output pricing and marketing policies, will help to include the excluded in agricultural progress. Technologies for elevating and stabilising yields are available for semi-arid and dry farming areas (Ryan and Spencer 2001). Therefore the emphasis should be on farming systems that can optimise the benefits of natural resources in a sustainable manner and not merely on cropping systems. Dry farming areas are also ideal for the cultivation of low water requiring but high value pulses and oilseeds.

Making New Gains

Farming systems intensification, diversification and value-addition should be promoted. Watershed and wasteland atlases should be used for developing improved farming systems, and designing what crops to grow based on soil structure so as to provide more income and jobs. Value addition to primary products should be done at the village itself. This will call for appropriate institutional structures which can help provide key centralised services to small and marginal farm families and provide them with the power of scale in eco-farming involving techniques like integrated pest management, integrated nutrient supply, scientific water management, precision farming, etc., as well as in marketing. A quantum leap in sophistication of management of all production factors will be required to sustain yield gains from the present levels to the commercially feasible threshold of about 80 per cent yield potential (Swaminathan 2001).

Small Farm Management

Institutional structures, which will confer upon farm families with small holdings, the advantages of scale at both the production and post-harvest phases of agriculture, are urgently needed. For example, thanks to the cooperative method of organisation of milk processing and marketing, India now occupies the first position in the world in milk production. Strategic partnerships with the private sector will help farmers' organisations to have access to assured and remunerative marketing opportunities.

Vital Areas for Sustainable Advances in Rice Productivity

There are great opportunities for achieving higher yields per unit of land; provision of water at the right time to rice farmers enabled them to shift to precision farming methods. The five vital areas of research, development and extension, which need attention from the point of view of achieving environmentally sustainable advances in rice productivity, are soil health and fertility management; water management; integrated plant health management; energy management; and post-harvest management (for more details see Swaminathan 2004).

Evergreen Revolution

As earlier mentioned, this implies improvement of productivity in perpetuity without associated ecological harm. Rice scientists should foster an evergreen revolution in rice through partnerships for the development and dissemination of precision farming technologies. The major goals that were proposed for the FAO sponsored International Network for an Evergreen Revolution in Rice by Swaminathan (2002b) are as follows:

- Initiate an Integrated Gene Management program.
- Improve productivity per unit of input, particularly of nutrients and water and thereby reduce the cost of production.
- Substitute to the extent possible knowledge and farm produced inputs for capital and market-purchased chemicals.
- Enhance the ecological and social sustainability of high-yield technologies.
- Increase farmers' income and opportunities for skilled employment.
- Establish an information grid and farmer-participatory knowledge system for empowering women and men engaged in rice farming with new knowledge and skills, thereby conferring on rice farmers the strengths of Knowledge Societies.

Research Strategies and Priorities

These strategies include Integrated Gene Management (IGM), integrated efforts in feeding and breeding rice for high productivity, information empowerment, overcoming hidden hunger caused by micronutrient deficiencies and promoting rice as a substrate for oral vaccines.

The IGM program in rice should be based on conservation, sustainable use and equity in sharing benefits. The over 100,000 strains available today in rice is the result of the conservation ethics of farm and tribal families. Most of them are from Asian countries. India is the largest contributor to this collection followed by Laos (Appa Rao et al. 2002).

Overcoming Hidden Hunger Caused by Micronutrient Deficiencies

The challenge of micronutrient deficiencies in diet is becoming great especially for the chronically poor. Iodine, Vitamin A and iron deficiencies are serious in many parts of the developing world. Worldwide, iron deficiency affects over one billion children and adults. Recent analyses from the United States Institute of Medicine (Earl and Woteki 1998; Burkhardt et al. 1997; Swaminathan 2002a) highlight the effect of severe anaemia in accounting for up to one in five maternal deaths. Maternal anaemia is pandemic and is associated with high MMR; anaemia during infancy, compounded by maternal under-nutrition, leads to poor brain development. Iron deficiency is also a major cause of permanent brain damage and death in children and limits the work capacity of adults (Smith and Haddad 2000; Swaminathan 2002b). There is not enough appreciation of the serious adverse implications to future generations arising from the high incidence of low birth weight (LBW) among newborn babies. LBW is a major contributor to stunting and affects brain development in the child. The new millennium will be a knowledge century, with agriculture and industry becoming more knowledge intensive. Denial of opportunities for the full expression of the innate genetic potential for mental development even at birth is the cruellest form of inequity that can prevail in any society (Smith and Haddad 2000). We must take steps to eliminate as soon as possible such inequity at birth leading to a denial of opportunities to nearly one out of every three children born in South Asia, for performing their legitimate role in the emerging knowledge century.

Wherever rice is the staple, a multi-pronged strategy for the elimination of hidden hunger should be developed by rice scientists. IRRI has undertaken research on enriching rice genetically with iron and other micronutrients. Fortification, promotion of balanced diets, new semi-processed foods involving an appropriate blend of rice and micronutrient-rich millets as well as genetic improvement, could all form part of an integrated strategy to combat the following major nutritional problems in predominantly rice-eating families:

- protein-energy malnutrition
- nutritional anaemia (iron deficiency)
- vitamin A deficiency
- iodine deficiency

- dietary deficiencies of thiamin, riboflavin, fat, calcium, vitamin C and zinc.

Swaminathan (2002a) suggested that the International Rice Commission could include nutrition security aspect as an integral part of the International Network. We must fight the serious threat to the intellectual capital of developing countries caused by low birth weight children and hidden hunger (UN Commission on Nutrition). Some of the research areas worthy of attention in this context are described below.

Breeding for Nutritional Quality

Nutritive quality is as important as cooking quality for countries in tropical Asia, where rice is the principal source of dietary protein, vitamin (B_1) and minerals (Fe, Ca) (Juliano and Villareal 1993). Rice provides about 40 per cent of the protein in the Asian diet. Among the cereal proteins, rice protein is considered to be biologically the richest by virtue of its high digestibility (88 per cent), high lysine content (±4 per cent) and relatively better net protein utilisation. Yet, it is nutritionally handicapped on account of two factors viz: (i) its inherently low protein content (6–8 per cent); and (ii) inevitable milling loss of as much as 15–20 per cent. Unlike in other cereals, increased protein content in rice does not result in decreased protein quality as all of its fractions (glutelin 65 per cent, globulin and albumin 15 per cent and lysine-cysteine rich prolamin 14 per cent) are rich in lysine and other essential amino acids. Even a marginal increase of 2 percentage points of protein, therefore, would mean 10–15 per cent increase in the nutritionally rich protein intake in our diet.

Genetic Engineering Approaches for Correcting Micronutrient Deficiencies

Breeding for Nutritional Improvement was recommended at the 19th Session of the International Rice Commission, which called for an increase in focus on strategies to combat malnutrition (Philip et al. 2000; Gopalan 2001). There are four categories of direct interventions believed to be successful in reducing micronutrients malnutrition: supplementation, fortification, dietary diversification and genetic enhancement. Nutritional status of populations will focus on the potential for improving malnutrition, primarily micronutrient malnutrition through genetic improvement.

Golden Rice

About 250 million people worldwide are deficient in vitamin A. Over 5 million children in South and South-East Asia are reported to suffer from the serious eye disease 'xerophthalmia' every year, and about 500,000 of them eventually become partially or totally blind due to deficiency of vitamin A. Besides affecting vision, vitamin A deficiency predisposes children to varied respiratory and intestinal diseases resulting in high mortality. Researchers from Swiss Federal Institute of Technology inserted these genes from daffodil and a bacterium into temperate rice plants to produce a modified grain, which has sufficient b carotene (precursor of vitamin A) to meet total vitamin A requirements in a typical Asian diet (Ye et al. 2000). Golden rice technology was made available to developing nations for research. If this technology can be moved to the production stage, it could represent an important contribution to improved human nutrition. In particular, rice fortified genetically with vitamin A and iron will be very useful to improve the nutritional status of pregnant and nursing women.

Iron Deficiency

Iron deficiency anaemia (IDA) is the world's most common nutritional deficiency. It affects pregnant and nursing women and young children most commonly. IDA in mothers predisposes to still births, neonatal mortality, anaemia and low birth weight in infants, and increases the risk of maternal mortality (Swaminathan 2002a; Earl and Woteki 1994). Regular intake of iron or administration of iron prevents anaemia. Daily supplementation with iron-folic acid tablets is a low-cost and effective intervention.

Technological Transformation of Productivity, Profitability and Sustainability: Wheat

The rediscovery of Mendel's laws of genetics in 1900 opened up a new era in crop breeding in general, and wheat breeding in particular. Although the art of plant breeding is as old as the beginning of agriculture nearly 12,000 years ago, systematic research in the areas of genetics and cytogenetics, which commenced in the early part of the 20th century, created uncommon opportunities for improving the productivity, profitability, stability and sustainability of wheat production. Even before

Mendel (1822–1884), plant hybridisers like Kolreuter, Knight, Gartner and Burbank were able to produce improved varieties of crops through careful observation and selection. The concept of sustainability to which we now attach great importance was recognised long ago as essential for sustained agricultural progress.

During the past 100 years, Mendelian genetics has helped not only to exploit naturally occurring genetic variability but has also accelerated the process of generation, manipulation and combination of new variability. We are now in a state of transition from Mendelian to molecular breeding. Breeder's eye for selection and for spotting the winner will continue to play an important part in successful plant breeding.

It is projected that global demand for wheat will increase by 40 per cent by the year 2020. Also, 67 per cent of the world's wheat consumption will be in developing countries. Between 1961 and 1990, yield increases accounted for 92 per cent of the additional cereal production in developing countries. In the years ahead, there is no option except to produce more from less per capita land and water resources. Can we sustain the yield revolution in wheat? It will be useful to consider this issue in the context of the genetic pathways which led to the wheat revolution of the 20th century.

Progress in Yield Improvement

Wheat is a crop of great antiquity. We can identify at least four major phases in the evolution of wheat breeding during the 20th century.

Phase I (1900–30): Early Days of Mendelian Genetics

Soon after the re-discovery of Mendel's laws of genetics in 1900, systematic work on the genetics of resistance to stem, leaf and stripe rusts started. Selection from naturally occurring genetic variability also began.

During the early part of the 20th century, the major breeding challenges were in the area of resistance to rusts and grain quality improvement. A study of the yield improvement achieved between 1900 to 1930 in USA shows only limited progress. The emphasis was more on stability of production through disease resistance than on achieving quantum jumps in yield.

Phase II (1930–60): Enlarging the Base of Theory and Its Application

This period was marked by the introduction of cytogenetic knowledge and tools in wheat improvement. This phase of wheat improvement was characterised by widening the gene pool used by breeders, incorporation of genes for the semi-dwarf plant type, shuttle breeding and breeding to meet the challenge of physiologic specialisation in pathogens.

Phase III (1960–80): The Green Revolution Phase

This phase is also generally referred to as the Green Revolution era. It was characterised by revolutionary progress in improving wheat production and productivity in several developing countries like India and Pakistan. The introduction of the semi-dwarf plant type enabled the wheat plant to yield well under conditions of good soil fertility and irrigation water management. Farmers who were used to harvesting 1 to 2 tonnes of wheat per hectare started harvesting over 5 t/ha (Swaminathan 1993). In view of the widespread interest in this remarkable transformation in India's agricultural destiny, it will be useful to summarise some of the highlights.

During 1942–43, the Indian subcontinent witnessed a severe famine in Bengal resulting in the death of nearly 3 million children, women and men. This prompted Jawaharlal Nehru, the first Prime Minister of Independent India to remark in 1948, 'everything else can wait, but not agriculture'.

In 1964, a National Demonstration Program was started in farmers' fields, both to verify the results obtained in research plots and to introduce farmers to the new opportunities opened up by semi-dwarf varieties for improving very considerably the productivity of wheat. When small farmers, with the help of scientists, harvested over 5 tonnes of wheat per hectare, its impact on the minds of other farmers was electric. The clamour for seeds began and the area under high-yielding varieties of wheat rose from 4 hectares in 1963–64 to over 4 million hectares in 1971–72. A small government program became a mass movement (Swaminathan 1993). Wheat production in India rose from 10 million tonnes in 1964 to 17 million tonnes in 1968. In 1999, Indian farmers harvested about 72 million tonnes of wheat, taking India to the second position in the world in wheat production.

Greater interdisciplinary collaboration among breeders, plant pathologists, agronomists, physiologists, soil scientists, entomologists, nemotalogists, economists and other social scientists, climatologists and policymakers was the principal factor responsible for the success of the green revolution. The green revolution era can also be termed 'the golden age in interdisciplinary and international collaboration' in wheat improvement for sustainable food security. The concept of shuttle breeding transcended continental boundaries and a global college of wheat scientists emerged. Above all, the green revolution showed how to generate synergy between technology and public policy.

Phase IV (1980–2000): Transition from Mendelian to Molecular Breeding

The last 20 years have witnessed great progress in using sophisticated approaches to wheat breeding. Hybrid wheat is reaching the possibility of large-scale commercial cultivation. The use of genetic-cytoplasmic male sterility and of chemical hybridising agents (CBA) are responsible for progress in the commercial exploitation of hybrid wheat. Different management practices such as lower seed rate, raised bed planting, split nitrogen application and different row width are being tried to enhance the expression of hybrid superiority. The cultivation of hybrid wheat is slowly gaining in momentum in South Africa, Australia (New South Wales), China, Argentina and France. The use of wild relatives in genetic engineering is growing (Khush and Baenziger 1998). The global average yield of wheat is 2.5 t/ha; the low average yield of wheat is because of large areas of wheat being under rainfed conditions. Progress in improving yield is however steady. So far, advances in yield improvement have been associated with increases in harvest index (i.e. grain/straw ratio). Further advances will depend upon greater biomass production and not merely on partitioning the phytosynthates.

Challenges Ahead

At the dawn of the 21st century, we can look back with pride and satisfaction on the revolution, which farm men and women have brought about in our agricultural history during the 20th century. The Punjab farmer, hardworking, skilled and determined, has been the backbone of the revolution.

While we can and should rejoice about the past achievements of farmers, scientists, extension workers and policymakers, there is no room for complacency. We will face several new problems, of which the following are important.

- First, increasing population leads to increased demand for food and reduced per capita availability of arable land and irrigation water.

- Second, improved purchasing power and increased urbanisation lead to higher per capita food grain requirements due to an increased consumption of animal products.

- Third, marine fish production is tending to become stagnant and coastal aquaculture has resulted in ecological and social problems.

- Fourth, there is increasing damage to the ecological foundations of agriculture, such as land, water, forests, biodiversity and the atmosphere and there are distinct possibilities for adverse changes in climate and sea level.

- Fifth, while dramatic new technological developments are taking place, particularly in the field of biotechnology, their environmental, food safety and social implications are still being debated.

- Finally, gross capital formation in agriculture is tending to decline in both public and private sectors during the present decade. The rate of growth in rural non-farm employment has been poor.

Since land and water will be shrinking resources for agriculture, there is no option in the future except to produce more food and other agricultural commodities from less per capita arable land and irrigation water. In other words, the need for more food has to be met through higher yields per unit of land, water, energy and time. It would therefore be useful to examine how science can be mobilised for raising further the ceiling to biological productivity without associated ecological harm. It will be appropriate to refer to the emerging scientific progress on the farms as an evergreen revolution, to emphasise that the productivity advance is sustainable over time since it is rooted in the principles of ecology, economics, social and gender equity and employment generation.

The Green Revolution based on Mendelian genetics has so far helped to keep the rate of growth in food production above population growth rate. The green revolution was however, the result of public good research supported by public funds. The technologies of the emerging gene revolution based on molecular genetics in contrast, are spearheaded by proprietary science and can come under monopolistic control. How can we take the fruits of the gene revolution to the unreached? This is a challenge, which we need to address.

I would like to list five major challenges, which will confront the wheat scientists during this century.

Equity

The Convention on Biological Diversity (CBD) stipulates that plant exploration, collection and introduction should be based on the principles of prior informed consent and equity in benefit sharing. Therefore exchange of wheat genetic resources in the future will be possible only on the basis of Material and Knowledge Transfer Agreements.

Ecology

Ecological sustainability of high productivity will be an important determinant in relation to the choice of technologies. For example, if hybrid wheat can enable us to produce 8–10 t/ha, over 300 kg of nitrogen will be needed by the crop. It is obvious that if the nutrient needs of hybrid or other high-yielding wheat varieties are to be met entirely through mineral fertilisers, there will be serious environmental problems including nitrate pollution of ground water. Hence, success in achieving high productivity on a sustained basis will depend upon our ability to develop new methods of feeding the plant. Research on breeding and feeding should be carried out concurrently by a team of breeders, physiologists, agronomists and soil scientists.

Concerns Relating to Genetically Modified Organisms (GMOs)

There are growing public and political concerns relating to GMOs. The concerns relate to food and environmental safety and bioethics. It is essential that these concerns are carefully addressed through a mechanism for risk-benefit analysis, which inspires public confidence. An integrated disease management strategy should be developed to ensure that GMOs with novel genetic combinations for disease resistance do not break down due to the emergence of new physiological strains of pathogens. Also, regulatory procedures should be transparent and should inspire public confidence. There is also need for integrating molecular breeding with organic farming methods.

Expansion of Proprietary Science

The world is witnessing an expansion of proprietary science governed by Intellectual Property Rights (IPR). Public good research supported from public funds, in contrast, is shrinking. What will be the impact of such a situation on international varietal or other trials organised by CIMMYT? Is the golden age of cooperative research coming to an end? How can we find a balance between public good and private profit?

Climate Change and Safeguarding Genetic Diversity

Will molecular breeding resulting in 'super wheats' lead to a high degree of genetic homogeneity in farmers' fields? We know that genetic homogeneity will enhance genetic vulnerability to biotic and abiotic stresses. Hence, we should foster an integrated program of pre-breeding and participatory breeding. Pre-breeding will help to generate novel genetic combinations, while participatory breeding with farm families will help to combine genetic efficiency with genetic diversity. Numerous location specific varieties can be developed in this manner. This will be the most effective way of meeting challenges arising from potential changes in temperature, precipitation and sea level as a result of global warming arising from the growing imbalance between carbon emissions and absorption.

Sustaining and Strengthening Agricultural Progress

In a predominantly agricultural country like ours, agricultural progress serves as the most effective safety net against hunger and deprivation. There is need for intensifying our efforts to improve agricultural productivity, quality and income. An urgent need in this area is the strengthening of institutional structures, which can help to confer on small and marginal farmers, the ecological and economic benefits of scale at both the production and post-harvest phases of farming. The following are some of the institutional structures whose reach has to be extended.

Without socially relevant and beneficial institutional structures, the extrapolation domain of successful experiences and development efforts will remain limited.

Table 2

S. No	Sector	Institutional Mechanism
1.	Dairy	Cooperatives
2.	Poultry	Egg Coordination Council
3.	Integrated on-farm and off-farm employment	Biovillages
4.	Power of scale to small producers	Small Farmers' Agri-business Consortium
5.	Technological upgrading of production and post-harvest sectors	Agri-clinics Agri-business centres
6.	Group action for micro-enterprises supported by micro-credit	Market-driven self-help groups
7.	Timely and affordable credit	Kisan credit cards, integrated informal and formal banking systems
8.	Operation of minimum support price	Food Corporation of India and State Food Corporations, as well as assured buy-back arrangement and contract farming by the private sector

Dr K.R. Narayanan inaugurated the JRD Tata Ecotechnology Centre at the M.S. Swaminathan Research Foundation (MSSRF) in 1998. In the second part of my lecture, I shall briefly summarise the work done in MSSRF on issues relating to linking ecological security with food and livelihood security in a mutually reinforcing manner.

In 2005, MSSRF whose work has always received encouragement and support from Dr K.R. Narayanan will be completing 15 years of work in the areas of research, education, capacity building, mentoring, policy advocacy and networking. In retrospect, the decision made in 1990 to choose integrated coastal zone management for priority attention with a view to linking the ecological security of coastal areas and the livelihood security of coastal communities (both fisher and farming families) in a mutually reinforcing manner has proved to be a wise one. The Coastal System Research (CSR) program of MSSRF was designed to give concurrent scientific attention to sea and land surfaces along the shoreline. The CSR program was initiated in anticipation of potential adverse changes in sea level as a result of global warming. An early scientific step in this process was the conservation of mangrove genetic resources and the rehabilitation of degraded mangrove wetlands in Tamil Nadu, Andhra Pradesh, Orissa and West Bengal. Such mangrove forests served as 'bio-shields' during the Tsunami attack on 26 December 2004. They had also served a similar purpose during the super cyclone in Orissa in 1999. These observations have helped to generate at both the political and public levels interest in the development of bio-shields along the shoreline.

The following are among the major contributions of the CSR program during 1990–2005.

- Restoration of degraded mangrove wetlands along the east coast of India: the area restored by MSSRF scientists alone comes to 1475 ha of degraded area restored with the help of 5240 families organised in 33 village mangrove councils. Nearly 7 million saplings were planted.
- Conservation strategy for mangrove genetic resources in the Asia-Pacific region and the establishment of a Genetic Garden for meeting the challenge of sea level rise at Pichavaram, Tamil Nadu.
- Genome mapping of mangrove species (*Avecinnia marina*) and the identification and transfer of genes for sea water tolerance from *A.marina* to rice, mustard and pulses.
- Development of a trusteeship mode of management of the Gulf of Mannar Biosphere and helping to create the first Biosphere Trust in the world, with the support of the Global Environment Facility and the governments of Tamil Nadu and India.
- Development of integrated Bio-shield – Biovillage – Village Knowledge Centre Programmes in coastal areas.
- Development of a code for the participatory management of mangrove ecosystems, involving cooperative action among fisher and farm communities and Forest and Fisheries departments.
- Development of a comprehensive strategy for the rehabilitation of Tsunami ravaged coastal areas in Tamil Nadu, Pondicherry, Andhra Pradesh, Kerala and the Andaman and Nicobar Islands.
- Drawing national and international attention to the urgent need for conserving mangrove wetlands and promoting the adoption of a Charter for Mangroves.
- Organising national and international training programs for creating a cadre of well-trained mangrove forest managers.
- Preparation of comprehensive atlases of the mangrove forests of Tamil Nadu, Andhra Pradesh and Orissa.

- Standardisation and popularisation of mangrove propagation methods based on both vegetative and micro-propagation techniques; and helping local communities to undertake the raising and planting of mangrove forests.
- Preparation of a tool kit for raising bio-shields in coastal areas.
- Establishment of the first community developed and managed artificial reef in the Gulf of Mannar area based on the technology developed by the Central Marine Fisheries Research Institute.
- Developing eco-agriculture strategies for coastal drylands through participatory evaluation and propagation of varieties of pulses developed at the Bhabha Atomic Research Centre through mutation breeding, and the establishment of green belts and genetic garden of horticultural crops for sustainable food and livelihood security.
- Launching a Fish for All movement at Kolkata in December 2003 in association with the World Fish Centre (ICLARM) located in Penang, Malaysia, to promote sustainable capture and culture fisheries movements.
- Advocacy for the adoption of aquarian reform measures designed to promote harmony between artisenal and mechanised fisheries as well as aquaculture and agriculture.

The CSR approach helped MSSRF to propose a comprehensive and integrated strategy for launching a 'Beyond Tsunami' program based on concurrent attention to ecological, livelihood, agronomic, psychological and educational rehabilitation. The experience gained by MSSRF in developing integrated coastal zone management procedures helped a National Committee set up by the Ministry of Environment and Forests under my Chairmanship to review the Coastal Regulation Zone Notification of 1991, to propose 12 basic guiding principles for the sustainable and scientific management of the coastal zone. Some of these are:

- Ecological and cultural security, livelihood security and national security should be the cornerstones of an integrated coastal zone management policy.
- The coastal zone would include an area from territorial limits (12 nautical miles), including its sea-bed to the administrative boundaries or the biological boundaries demarcated on the landward side of the sea coast. The coastal zone management should also include

the inland tidal water bodies influenced by tidal action and the land area along such water bodies. This area should be taken up for an integrated, cohesive, multi-disciplinary and multi-sectoral coastal area management and regulatory system.

- Regulation, education and social mobilisation should be the three major components of a participatory and sustainable Coastal Zone Management strategy. Panchayati Raj institutions in coastal areas should be fully involved in the educational and social mobilisation programs.

- Coastal regulation needs to be based on sound scientific and ecological principles and should safeguard both natural and cultural heritage. Heritage sites need particular care and should be conserved in their pristine purity. These include areas of environmental significance, rich in biodiversity and scenic beauty. Bird sanctuaries, parks and breeding grounds of migratory birds should be protected.

- The precautionary approach should be used where there are potential threats of serious or irreversible damage to ecologically fragile critical coastal systems and to living aquatic resources. Scientific uncertainty should not be used as an excuse for the unsustainable exploitation of coastal resources — both living and non-living.

- Ecological economics should underpin economic activities, so that present day interests and future prospects are not antagonistic. Significant biological, cultural and natural assets should be considered incomparable, invaluable and irreplaceable and should receive overriding priority in the allocation of resources for coastal area protection and conservation.

- Coastal policy and regulations should be guided by the principles of gender and social equity as well as intra-generational and inter-generational equity, (i.e. the interests of future generations). They should be based on Mahatma Gandhi's dictum, 'Nature provides for everyone's needs, but not for anyone's greed'. All stakeholders should be involved in decision making. Precious biological wealth, coming under Marine Biosphere Reserves, should be managed in a trusteeship mode, with all the stakeholders protecting the unique natural wealth of biosphere reserves as trustees and not as owners. A case study should be made on how the Gulf of Mannar Biosphere Trust is functioning, so that the Trusteeship pattern of sustainable management by the principal stakeholders can be replicated.

- The regeneration of mangrove wetlands, coral reefs and sea grass beds as well as the promotion of coastal forestry and agro-forestry will confer both short- and long-term ecological and livelihood benefits. Carbon sequestration through coastal bio-shields will make an important contribution to promoting a balance between carbon emission and absorption, in addition to offering protection during coastal storms and calamities like tsunami. An important lesson taught by the tsunami disaster is that the rehabilitation of degraded mangrove forests and the raising of coastal plantations of salicornia, casuarinas, Vetiver and appropriate species of halophytes will represent a 'win–win' situation both for nature and coastal human habitations. No further time should be lost in initiating a national coastal bio-shield movement along the coasts of the mainland of India as well as islands. This can be a priority task under the National Rural Employment Guarantee and Food for Work Programmes.

- The severe loss of life and livelihoods as well as property caused by tsunami in Andaman and Nicobar Islands and in the coastal regions of Tamil Nadu, Kerala, Andhra Pradesh and Pondicherry teaches us that short-term commercial interests should not be allowed to undermine the ecological security of our coastal areas. Human memory tends to be short and neglecting the lessons of tsunami will be equivalent to writing off the future of coastal communities.

Based on the experience gained during the last 15 years, it is proposed to establish in Chidambaram a Resource Centre for Integrated Coastal Zone Management, for the purpose of imparting training in the erection of bio-shields, the development of biovillages and the establishment of Village Knowledge Centres. Tool kits for these purposes have already been prepared.

In addition to the above, steps have been taken in association with the Tata Relief Committee and the World Fish Centre (ICLARM) to establish a Fish for All Training and Resource Centre at Akkarapettai village near Nagapattinam for imparting training in all aspects of capture and culture fisheries through the principle of learning by doing. The centre will give attention to capacity building of fisher women and men in every step in the chain of capture/culture to consumption.

During 2004–05, MSSRF's strategic and participatory research to meet the challenges of climate change, which has been so far confined to the coastal zone, was extended to the arid and semi-arid areas of Andhra Pradesh and Rajasthan with financial and technical help of the Swiss Agency for Development Cooperation (SDC) and in partnership with Action for Food Production (AFPRO) and the National Institute of Agricultural Extension Management (MANAGE). This project will help to study vulnerability to adverse changes in temperature and precipitation and develop mitigation and adaptation strategies. Such proactive measures are essential to prevent human suffering resulting from agricultural collapse during drought and flood. The climate change program will take into account the impact of radiation, carbon dioxide concentration in the atmosphere, temperature and precipitation. It will also help to understand and chronicle traditional coping mechanisms, so that these can be conserved and strengthened. Computer simulation models on the impact of variations in temperature and precipitation will be developed and contingency plans to mitigate the adverse impact of climate change will be introduced.

Besides developing a methodology for conserving the Gulf of Mannar Biosphere Reserve for posterity through a multi-stakeholder trusteeship system of management, MSSRF has evolved during the last 15 years three other major institutional innovations in areas of significance to sustainable food and livelihood security and poverty eradication. These are described briefly below.

Community Nutrition and Water Security System

This system introduced in the Koraput district of Orissa consists of organising field gene banks (in situ on-farm conservation), seed banks, genetic enhancement through participatory breeding, water banks (i.e. water harvesting and saving in farm ponds), and grain banks.

This system helps to enlarge the food basket by facilitating the inclusion of millets and other under-utilised but nutritious crops in the Community Grain Bank. Such a decentralised community-managed nutrition security system helps to foster concurrent attention to conservation, cultivation, consumption and commerce. The tribal community of Koraput pioneering this system was given the Equator Initiative Award by UNDP at the World Summit on Sustainable Development held at Johannesburg in 2002.

Currently there are 2,34,676 village *panchayats* in 31 States and Union Territories. In addition, there are traditional councils in Meghalaya, Mizoram and Nagaland. Each of these *panchayats*/local bodies can spearhead the Community Food and Water Security movement. This will be the fastest and a sustainable method of making hunger history.

Fostering Job-Led Economic Growth

The most serious challenge facing India is overcoming the famine of jobs or sustainable livelihood opportunities in rural India. MSSRF, whose mandate is imparting a pro-poor, pro-nature and pro-woman orientation to technology development and dissemination, designed and developed the biovillage model of sustainable human well-being for this purpose in 1992. The biovillage concept involves the technological upgradation of agriculture and agro-based enterprises in villages through ecotechnologies developed by blending frontier technologies like information and biotechnologies as well as space, nuclear and renewable energy technologies with traditional ecological prudence. Thus, the biovillage based on the economics of human dignity, capitalises on the benefits conferred by ecotechnology to both the environment and the rural economy. By giving simultaneous attention to on-farm and non-farm employment, the biovillage promotes job-led economic growth and helps to transfer poor families from the primary to the secondary and tertiary sectors of economic activity. This model is now being adopted both in other parts of India and other countries like Bangladesh and Mozambique.

With the help of the Technology Information Forecasting and Assessment (TIFAC) program of the Government of India, a business plan was prepared for establishing Rice BioParks. A wide range of economically viable business activities were identified for producing value-added products from rice straw, husk, bran and grain. Business plans were prepared for nearly 28 different enterprises.

Thus, the biomass of cultivated plants can provide opportunities for new enterprises. Similarly, the production and marketing of the biological software essential for sustainable agriculture, such as biofertilisers, biopesticides, vermiculture, etc., could help self-help groups (SHG) of women and men to enhance their income. MSSRF organised a workshop for sharing experiences on SHGs. It became clear at the workshop that SHGs can become economically sustainable only if they have backward linkages to technology and credit, and forward linkages to markets and management. MSSRF has developed an accounting software for helping SHGs to maintain both accuracy and transparency in accounting.

With the help of the Central Food Technology Research Institute, Mysore, training in post-harvest processing was given to trainees from Ladakh to help them prepare value-added products from apricot and seabuckthorn. Similarly, technical advice was given to the Sher-E-Kashmir University of Agricultural Science and Technology of Kashmir in Srinagar for establishing a Womens' Biotechnology Park at Srinagar on the lines of the one functioning in Chennai.

Under the International Year of Rice Year Programme, consultations were held at Koraput in Orissa, Pattambi in Kerala and Shillong in Meghalaya for reviewing the current status of research on medicinal and aromatic rices. Detailed scientific strategies were developed for the improvement of the Navara rice of Kerala and Kalajeera rice of Koraput through participatory breeding and knowledge management. In all such programs the role of women in conservation and enhancement of genetic resources was given specific attention.

Centre

The third major institutional innovation developed by MSSRF for transforming the rural economy is the computer-aided and internet connected Village Knowledge Centre.

The work undertaken by MSSRF in setting up community-centred and managed Village Knowledge Centres (VKC) in Pondicherry villages since 1998 based on modern information and communication technologies (ICT) with financial support from IDRC of Canada has shown that ICT helps to improve the timeliness and efficiency of farm operations and enhances income through producer-oriented markets. Also, experience has shown that bridging the digital divide is a powerful method of bridging the gender divide. Knowledge connectivity therefore confers multiple economic and social benefits. The VKC operates on the principles of social inclusion and giving voice to the voiceless. The information provided, which includes location-specific data on entitlements to different government schemes, is demand-driven and is in the local language. For example, in Union Territory of Pondicherry there are over 150 schemes designed to help the poor; yet nearly 20 per cent of families are below the poverty line. After the onset of the digital age, knowledge on entitlements and how to access them has grown rapidly. The VKC will be a powerful instrument for operationalising the provisions of the *Right to Information Act* (2005).

Encouraged by the ability of rural women and men to take to ICT like fish to water, MSSRF initiated in 2003, two major steps to take ICT to every one of the over 600,000 villages in India by 15 August 2007, which marks the 60th anniversary of 'our tryst with destiny', to quote Jawaharlal Nehru. The first is the organisation of a National Alliance for Mission 2007: Every Village a Knowledge Centre which provides a platform for partnership to all committed to the cause of extending the power of ICT to rural India. The National Alliance has now over 150 members comprising Central and State government agencies, business and industry, academia and non-governmental and mass media organisations.

The second is the establishment of the Jamsetji Tata National Virtual Academy for Rural Prosperity with generous support from the Tata Education Trust. The Internet – community radio combination is a powerful method of reaching the unreached in terms of delivery of dynamic information. Public policy in promoting the use of community radio should be based on the following principle enunciated by the Supreme Court in its judgment delivered in December 1995, 'Air waves constitute public property and must be used for advancing public good'. This is the same principle enshrined in the Dandi March movement of Mahatma Gandhi in relation to sea water, which is the basis of MSSRF's program on sea water farming for coastal area prosperity.

At a recent meeting held at MSSRF, Panchayati Raj leaders have assured that they will provide space, electricity and telephone connection for establishing VKCs in the Panchayat premises. Thus, all the 234,676 village *panchayats* in 31 States and Union Territories as well as Traditional Councils in the North-East States can be brought together under the umbrella of the National Alliance. A hub-spokes model will help to reach all villages from Panchayat VKCs. Such Centres can be operated by ICT SHGs of rural women and men. MSSRF is assisting NABARD to organise about 10,000 ICT SHGs in 10 States of the country during 2005–06.

Besides connectivity and content, capacity building is essential for ensuring local ownership of VKCs. This is where the Jamsetji Tata National Virtual Academy (NVA) of MSSRF hopes to play a key role. The President of India, Dr A.P.J. Abdul Kalam inducted the first 137 Fellows of the NVA drawn from 15 States on 11 July 2005 at New Delhi. Microsoft is providing generous support for capacity building under its Unlimited Potential program.

The Fellows of NVA are rural women and men who have studied up to the 10th class or up to the first degree. They serve as Master Trainers and undertake the training of other rural women and men as well as children. These grassroots academicians will be the torchbearers of the rural knowledge revolution. Another significant development in taking the benefits of the space age to the rural poor was the inauguration by the Prime Minister of India, Dr Manmohan Singh on 18 October 2004 of an ISRO–MSSRF joint initiative in setting up Village Resource Centres (VRCs) which can link rural families to the best available sources of knowledge in medicine and health care, education, agriculture, markets and government programs. This program which initially linked MSSRF (Chennai) to VRCs in Thiruvayaru, Sempatti and Thangachimadam in Tamil Nadu is being extended to Chidambaram, Pudukottai, Pondicherry, Nagapattinam and Kanyakumari during this year. With the help of the Indian Space Research Organisation, additional centres are being opened in tsunami-affected areas and in farmers' 'distress hotspots' in Kerala, Andhra Pradesh, Maharashtra and Karnataka. These are areas where suicides by farmers occur. Those operating the computer aided knowledge system at such centres will be either wives or daughters or sons of those who were driven to take their lives. This will help to provide a sense of realism and urgency in achieving a match between content and the need to save livelihoods and lives. While VKC operates at the village level, the VRC is designed to cover a block and thereby serve as a resource centre for all the villages in the block.

The Prime Minister of India has announced a well-funded Bharat Nirman program to accelerate progress in providing urban amenities in rural areas and to bring an additional 10 million hectares under assured irrigation. Knowledge connectivity should be the backbone of the Bharat Nirman program, since it is fundamental to deriving maximum benefit, in terms of a better quality of life in villages, from the investment on roads, telephone connectivity and other forms of physical connectivity. The involvement of *panchayats* and *gram sabhas* in providing the needed logistic and policy support will ensure the efficient functioning of VKCs. To begin with VKC should be tools of information, knowledge and skill empowerment of rural families, particularly of the economically and socially under privileged sections of the society. This is a fundamental responsibility of government. Hence, the initial expenses should be met from the Bharat Nirman Programme and the Universal Service Obligation (USO) Fund. By the end of this decade (i.e. by 2010), the VKCs will become vibrant centres of economic activity and will provide opportunities for outsourcing of assignments from urban to rural areas. They will then become not only economically self-reliant but will help to create a wide range of skilled jobs for youth in villages. A VKC-centred Bharat Nirman will be the most effective method of fostering rural and agrarian prosperity and arresting the unplanned migration of the rural poor to urban areas resulting in the proliferation of urban slums. Therefore, knowledge connectivity through VKCs should be the corner stone of a New Deal for Rural India.

What motivates the scientists and scholars of MSSRF are the words of the Poet Rabindranath Tagore:

> With your mind intent, cross this sea of chaos
> And sail to that shore of new creation.

References

Appa Rao, S., Bounphanousay, C., Schiller, J.M. and Jackson, M.T. (2002), 'Collection, Classification, and Conservation of Cultivated and Wild Rices of the Lao PDR', *Genetic Resources and Crop Evolution*, 49: 75–81.

Burkhardt, P.K., Beyer, P., Wünn, J., Klöti, A., Armstrong, G.A., Schledz, M., von Lintig, J. and Potrykus, I. (1997), 'Transgenic Rice (*Oryza sativa*) Endosperm Expressing Daffodil (*Narcissus pseudonarcissus*) Phytoene Synthase', *The Plant Journal*, 11(5): 1071–78. onlinelibrary.wiley.com/doi/pdf/10.1046/j.1365-313X.1997.11051071.x

Earl, R. and Woteki, C.E. (eds) (1994), *Iron Deficiency Anemia: Recommended Guidelines for the Prevention, Detection and Management among US Children and Women of Childbearing Age*, Institute of Medicine, National Academies Press, Washington DC.

Gopalan, C. (2001), *Combating Vitamin A Deficiency and Micronutrient Malnutrition through Dietary Improvement*, M.S. Swaminathan Research Foundation, Chennai (mimeographed).

Juliano, B.O. and Villareal, C.P. (1993), *Grain Quality Evaluation of World Rices*. IRRI, Manila.

Khush, Gurdev S. and Baenziger, P. Stephen (1998), 'Crop Improvement: Emerging Trends in Rice and Wheat', in V.L. Chopra, R.B. Singh and A. Varma (eds), *Crop Productivity and Sustainability — Shaping the Future*, Proceedings of the 2nd International Crop Science Congress, pp. 113–25.

M.S. Swaminathan Research Foundation (MSSRF) (2001), *Community Grain Bank: An Instrument for Local Food Security*, MSSRF, Chennai.

NCF (National Commission on Farmers) (2006), *Serving Farmers and Saving Farming, 2006: Year of Agricultural Renewal, Third Report*. agricoop.nic.in/sites/default/files/NCF3%20%281%29.pdf

Peacock, K. and Chaudhury, A. (2002), 'The Impact of Gene Technologies on the Use of Genetic Resources', in J.M.M. Engels, V. Ramanatha Rao, A.H.D. Brown and M.T. Jackson (eds), *Managing Plant Genetic Diversity*, IPGRI, pp. 23–31.

Philip, James et al. (2000), 'Ending Malnutrition by 2020: An Agenda for Change in the Millennium', *Food and Nutrition Bulletin*, 21(13): 88.

Pingali, P.L., Hossain, H. and Gerpacio, R.V. (1997), *Asian Rice Bowls: The Returning Crisis*, CAB International in association with IRRI, p. 341.

Rabbinge, R., Leffelaar, P.A. and Van Latesteijn, R.C. (1994), 'The Role of Systems Analysis as an Instrument in Policy Making and Resource Management', in P. Goldsworthy and F.W.T. Penning de Vries (eds), *Opportunities, Use, and Transfer of Systems Research Methods in Agriculture to Developing Countries*, Systems Approaches for Sustainable Agricultural Development series, Kluwer Academic Publishers, Dordrecht, The Netherlands, pp. 67–79.

Ramalingaswami, V., Johnson, U. and Rohde, J. (1997), 'Malnutrition: A South Asian Enigma', in Stuart Gillespie (ed.), *Malnutrition in South Asia*, Rosa Publication 5, UNICEF, Nepal.

Ryan, J.G. and Spencer, D.C. (2001), *Future Challenges and Opportunities for Agricultural R&D in the Semi-Arid Tropics*. ICRISAT, Patancheru.

Smith, L.C. and Haddad, L. (2000), *Overcoming Child Malnutrition in Developing Countries: Past Achievements and Future Choices*. International Food policy Research Institute, Washington DC.

Swaminathan, M.S. (1968), 'The Age of Algeny, Genetic Destruction of Yield Barriers and Agricultural Transformation', Presidential Address, Agricultural Science Section, 55th Indian Science Congress, Varanasi, January.

Swaminathan, M.S. (ed.) (1993), *Wheat Revolution: A Dialogue*, p. 164, Macmillan India Ltd, Madras.

Swaminathan, M.S. (1996), *Sustainable Agriculture: Towards an Evergreen Revolution*, pp. 232. Konark Publishers Pvt Ltd, Delhi.

Swaminathan, M.S. (2000a), 'Bridging the Nutritional Divide', *The Little Magazine*, II(6), available at www.littlemag.com/hunger/swami.html.

Swaminathan, M.S. (2000b), 'An Evergreen Revolution', *Biologist*, 47(2): 85–9.

Swaminathan, M.S. (2001), 'Food Security and Sustainable Development', *Current Science*, 81: 948–54.

Swaminathan, M.S. (2002a), 'Building a National Nutrition Security System', Paper presented at India-ASEAN Eminent Persons Lecture Series 11, January, FAO, Bangkok.

Swaminathan, M.S. (2002b), 'Nutrition in the Third Millennium: Countries in Transition', Plenary Lecture 17th International Congress on Nutrition Vienna, 27–31 August.

Swaminathan, M.S. (2004), 'Technological Change and Food Production: Implications for Vulnerable Sections', Working Paper 20, CPRC-IIPA, New Delhi.

Swaminathan, M.S. (2005), 'India's Greatest Living Industry: Hundred Years Later', IARI New Delhi, IARI Centenary Lecture, 16 March.

United Nations Commission on the Nutrition Challenges of the 21st Century (2000), 'Ending Malnutrition by 2020: An Agenda for Change in the Millennium', *Food and Nutrition Bulletin*, 21(3), Supplement, Final Report to the ACC/SCN by the Commission on the Nutrition Challenges of the 21st Century, United Nations University Press.

World Food Programme (WFP) (2001), *Enabling Development: Food Assistance in South Asia*, p. 316, Oxford University Press, New Delhi.

Ye, X., Al-Babili, S., Kloti, A., Zhang, J., Lucca, P., Beyer, P. and Potrykus, I. (2000), 'Engineering Provitamin A (ß-carotene) Biosynthetic Pathway into (Carotenoid-free) Rice Endosperm', *Science*, 287: 303–5.

Oration 10:
2006 K.R. Narayanan Oration

Message from the President
of the Republic of India

I am delighted to find that The Australian National University, Canberra is organising the K.R. Narayanan Oration with the theme 'India's Space Enterprise: A Case Study in Strategic Thinking and Planning'. I am happy that this oration is being delivered by Dr K. Kasturirangan, one of the foremost space scientists in India. Former President of India K.R. Narayanan was a noted statesman and strategic thinker who has contributed to the development of India in different spheres.

Indian space program has its origin with the unveiling of the vision by Dr Vikram Sarabhai as early as 1962. He visualised the importance of space application for societal upliftment through communication and remote-sensing satellites for a country like India with 600,000 villages spread in remote corners of the nation. Now 700 million people 70 per cent of our population live in the rural areas. Dr Vikram Sarabhai gave a roadmap to build expertise to achieve the ultimate goal of building India's own launch vehicles and satellites and ability to launch them from Indian launch station by Indian scientists in partnership with academic institutions and industry.

Over the last four decades, the vision of Dr Sarabhai has been translated into mission mode programs by Professor Satish Dhawan and his nurtured leaders like Dr U.R. Rao and Dr K. Kasturirangan and now Dr G. Madhavan Nair. Today India is self reliant in space technology with its own satellite for remote-sensing and communication applications.

The benefits of space program are now reaching the society through tele-education, tele-medicine, e-governance, meteorology, communication and broadcasting, resource assessment and disaster management. This has been realised through strategic thinking and meticulous planning. Further, India is poised to send a probe for lunar exploration and develop reusable launch vehicles. This will lead to manned missions and mining in planets through international collaborations. The leadership attributes and qualities developed through India's space program have found significant applications in many socioeconomic programs of the country.

Considering that half of the world population is yet to experience the excitement of space program, I am sure this Oration will generate a renewed interest by these countries in space missions through international cooperation drawing the benefits of expertise and experience available with countries like India.

I greet the organisers of K.R. Narayanan Oration and wish the participants success in the mission of promoting science and technology for societal upliftment.

A.P.J. Abdul Kalam
New Delhi
2006

India's Space Enterprise: A Case Study in Strategic Thinking and Planning

K. Kasturirangan

It is a matter of proud privilege and honour for me to be invited to deliver the 2006 Narayanan Oration at the Australia South Asia Research Centre (ASARC) of The Australian National University (ANU). It is with profound regret and sorrow that we had to confront Mr K.R. Narayanan's demise recently on 9 November 2005. Whenever I met him, he left in me an indelible impression of his awe-inspiring and deep erudition and his extraordinary passion and commitment to uplift underprivileged segments of the society. Nonetheless, he also pursued relentless efforts to achieve excellence in all walks of life. His holistic approach to science and technology has been candidly revealed in his speech on the eve of Golden Jubilee celebrations of the Indian Republic:

> We cannot and ought not halt movement in the trajectories of our modern progress. Factories will and must rise, satellites must and will soar to the heavens, and dams over rivers will rise to prevent floods, generate electricity and irrigate dry lands for cultivation. But that should not cause ecological and environmental devastation and the uprooting of human settlements, especially of tribals and the poor. Ways and methods can be found for countering the harmful impact of modern technology on the lives of the common people. I believe that the answer to the ill-effects of science and technology is not to turn our back on technology, but to have more science and technology that is directed to human needs and for the betterment of the human condition.

It is my good fortune that I could pay my own humble tribute to this noble soul through this oration instituted in his honour. I also thank the ASARC of ANU and its Executive Director, Professor Raghbendra Jha, for this invitation.

Early History

Modern space science had its beginnings around 1946 when scientists started the deployment of instruments to the outer fringes of the earth's atmosphere using balloons and rockets to study radiations from outer space as well as geophysical phenomena. In spite of the professed scientific goals for the first earth satellite missions, the launch of SPUTNIK on 4 October 1957 by the then Soviet Union added a new dimension (Logsdon 2001) to the Cold War between the US and the Soviet Union. The early scientific satellite missions of the US also had implicit goals of pursuing US interest in establishing the international legal principle that national sovereignty did not extend to the altitudes at which the satellite would orbit. Thus there was no obstacle in international law to the over flight of a reconnaissance satellite over Soviet territory. Against this backdrop, it is significant to note that the early inspiration for the Indian space program came not from any military objectives, but from the interests of a large scientific community who have been actively engaged in research programs related to geophysics and astrophysics. When Vikram Sarabhai and Homi Bhabha suggested support to space science and technology for possible application to Indian problems, in 1962, the Sputnik era was just five years old. Pandit Nehru's approval for the application of space technology in India was an act of extraordinary foresight and courage. This decision in the absence of experience with operational systems, the newness and complexity of the technology and the high risks involved, could have only been based on a vision of the future and an abiding faith and confidence in the Indian scientists and people.

The Vision

The vision of space that Dr Vikram Sarabhai gave for India is extraordinary for its realism and pragmatism, unique for its deep insights into the socioeconomic context of the country, extensive in the level of details and identification of different dimensions and remarkable for the display of his own conviction. In the annals of our science and technology endeavour, very rarely has one come across such a vision that has withstood the test of time — in this case over more than four decades. Some glimpses of his vision (Sarabhai 1979) are in order at this juncture, as an early example in strategic thinking.

The vision recognised that promotion of space research, besides contributing to societal benefits and enrichment also results in intangible benefits coming out of the need to develop high technologies for economic development and security. The vision also identified space's unique ability to create leadership and the benefits of international collaborations. Further, it could help develop the nucleus of a new culture where a large group of persons in diverse activities learn to work together for the accomplishment of a single objective. Establishing a synchronous satellite over the Indian Ocean to improve meteorological forecasting, critical to agricultural operations and evolving national plans using space technologies for resource survey were also visualised as important for India. The vision called for an exciting development of a synchronous direct television broadcasting satellite that could serve as the most powerful means of mass communication to reach a large segment of the population in an economically depressed region of the world. Early in the conceptualisation of a satellite-based communication and broadcasting system, issues of system choice including the financial implications and the economic benefit were recognised as important. The establishment of strong linkages with key user agencies was central to this vision. Dr Sarabhai's emphasis on self-reliance made it the life current of the Indian space program and enabled the program to overcome numerous challenges in the course of its journey towards operational applications of space. His vision was not merely restricted to technology and application, but also to the attendant needs of new organisational structures on one side, and the fundamental issue of the role of humans in space on the other (Sarabhai 1966).

Development of this vision itself was spread over a decade from 1961. This period was characterised by consultation among the various stakeholders (ISRO Report 1972) — using professionals across the world as sounding boards — for detailed assessments of the different dimensions of the envisaged program through experimentation, analysis and simulation that factored in the socioeconomic context of the country. In retrospect, it is gratifying to note that such an elaborate and carefully formulated vision helped to grow the program, in a directed manner over the next three decades without any major deviations, except for small mid-course corrections on some specific parts of the program. It is also of interest to note that this entire decade accounted for an expenditure, that is less than 1 per cent of the total investment in the space program up to 2006 (constant price basis).

Present Dimensions of Indian Space Program

The Indian space program today is a large integrated program, which is self-reliant and applications driven, maintaining vital links to the user community and committed to excellence in scientific endeavours.

The program developed capabilities to produce world-class satellites and launch vehicles and to apply them in diverse areas relevant to national development. India has established two operational space systems. The Indian National Satellite (INSAT) system, currently made up of nine satellites in orbit is one of the largest domestic satellite communication system in the world. The Indian Remote Sensing satellite (IRS) system, with a constellation of seven satellites, comprises some of the best satellites in the world for generating information on natural resources. Space launch vehicles developed by India are aimed towards providing autonomous launch capability to orbit these classes of satellites. India's Polar Satellite Launch Vehicle (PSLV) is well proven through eight successive successful flights and it provides the capability to orbit remote-sensing satellites of the 1.4-tonne class in polar sun synchronous orbits. The Geo-synchronous Satellite Launch Vehicle (GSLV), capable of launching 2 to 2.5-tonne class of INSAT satellites, has been operationalised with three successful flights in a row, making India one of the six countries in the world to demonstrate capabilities for geo-stationary satellite launch.

Both IRS and INSAT satellites have benefited the country in various areas of national development. INSAT satellites are the main stay for the TV broadcasting and provide connectivity to more than 1,100 TV transmitters. They also network radio stations, provide rural area communications, business communications and tele-education and tele-medicine services. They are also used to relay cyclone warnings, gather meteorological data, assist weather forecasting for emergency communication support during disasters and providing search and rescue support. The imageries and data from the IRS satellites are used for vital applications such as locating zones for availability of ground water in habitations having no access to drinking water, monitoring agricultural crops, providing advisories to coastal fishermen on potential zones for fishing, planning water shed, rural development and waste land management programs as well as disaster management support.

Front ranking scientific investigations are being carried out in the fields of astronomy, atmospheric sciences and long-term climatic research using satellites, balloons, sounding rockets and ground instruments. India has also embarked on an ambitious planetary exploration program, the flagship mission of which is Chandrayaan-1. This mission aims to place a satellite around the Moon for physical and chemical mapping of the lunar surface.

India has forged bilateral cooperative arrangements with more than 20 countries, including Australia, China, France, Germany, Russia and USA. The scope of the international cooperation is multidimensional in nature, which includes conduct of joint missions, offering opportunity for flight of instruments on board Indian satellites, exchange of meteorological data and offering education and training in the area of space. It is worth noting that six scientific instruments from the USA and Europe are being flown in India's Lunar Mission Chandrayaan-1. India has established a Centre for Space Science, Technology and Application Education for Asia and Pacific, affiliated to the UN and is offering well-structured educational programs.

An entity called Antrix Corporation has been established to promote commercial use of the space assets of ISRO and to help Indian space industries achieve global competitiveness. Global marketing of IRS data, launching of four foreign small satellites by PSLV, leasing of INSAT transponder capacity to commercial operators including INTELSAT, supply of spacecraft subsystems and mission support services of Indian ground stations are some of the highlights of the Antrix space business. It has also recently established an alliance with Europe's leading satellite manufacturer, EADS Astrium, to jointly manufacture communication satellites using the INSAT bus for selling in global markets.

India piloted a satellite communication policy in 1997 paving the way for use of INSAT capacity by private users and for private ownership of communications satellite assets. Further, a comprehensive remote-sensing data policy on acquisition and distribution of remote-sensing data for civilian users is also in place. Remote-sensing data from satellites have been accepted as legal evidence in many States of the country for purposes such as environment impact assessment for site clearances, forest encroachment and infrastructure development.

Linkages with academia have also been an important aspect of Indian space program. More than 80 universities and academic institutions of higher learning are involved in a variety of research projects related to space science, technology and applications.

In a nutshell, these multifaceted contributions from the Indian Space program, which has been developed and run with modest budgets, make it particularly significant in the modern context.

Evolving Strategies

The evolution of the Indian space program over the past four decades represents a systematic and phased approach to building knowledge, technological capacity and an organisational system to ensure effective application of sophisticated technologies to national development (Dhawan 1985; Kasturirangan 2001).

Beyond the first decade of vision and initiation, the space program evolution can be broadly categorised under three distinct phases. The first phase related to proof of concept demonstration, the second dealt with the realisation of end-to-end systems at an experimental level that then led into the current operational phase. In what follows, we discuss briefly some of the examples of strategic thinking and planning while progressing through these phases.

Proof of Concept Phase

The proof of concept phase of the Indian space program was characterised by the use of foreign space systems, configuring the ground system to suit national needs and conditions as well as working closely with the potential user community. We illustrate the nature of the activities in this phase through three examples.

The first is an experiment to develop, test and manage a satellite-based instructional television system, to demonstrate the utility of satellite television for mass communication with a specific emphasis on remote rural areas communications. Known as the Satellite Instructional Television Experiment (SITE), it used the American satellite ATS-6 specially moved over Indian Ocean to conduct this experiment in 1975–76. The responsibility of design, development, deployment, operation and maintenance of ground equipment was entirely that of India and it involved nearly 2,400 direct reception television stations in six clusters. India also undertook development of instructional programs, in the areas of family planning, agriculture, national integration, primary education, and teacher training. While departmental boundaries are often difficult to cross in a bureaucratic system, in a multi-disciplinary project such as SITE, it often became necessary to work across conventional boundaries and sort out the interface problems. SITE gave very valuable inputs as to how TV, a new extension tool, can be integrated into the existing organisation of the user agencies. Social research and evaluation design was also carried out for impact survey of target populations. Further, the experiment helped arriving at cost estimates for a national operational satellite system.

The second example related to the Satellite Telecommunication Experimental Project (STEP). This project, undertaken primarily to understand the issues of interfaces between space and ground systems for communication, was conducted with a Franco-German satellite, Symphonie. STEP helped in concretising our initial thinking on 'Disaster Warning Systems', radio networking concepts and transportable terminal developments, and provided vital inputs to the planning of INSAT.

The third example relates to space-based earth observation system. Landsat, launched by USA in 1972 provided an unique opportunity to test out the utility of a satellite-based earth observation system for obtaining timely, accurate and precise information of earth resources. The exercise of establishing ground systems, integrating space-based data with conventional aerial and ground-based data and working closely with user community, such as the Geological Survey of India, Agriculture, Forestry and Water resources users provided several crucial insights for planning the future operational remote-sensing systems.

In summary, the proof of concept demonstrations enabled evaluating the potential of the vantage point of space for addressing the country's developmental needs and issues of scalability at the national level. An important outcome was the evaluation of uniqueness of space in providing new services, or for assessment of their superiority vis-à-vis conventional approaches. Further, this phase enabled a short turn around time and a low cost strategy for evaluating the concepts, the systemic issues including technologies, the institutional frameworks and the user interfaces.

Experimental Phase

The experimental phase was identified with a strategy to derive an end-to-end experience in the realisation of space systems where the potential of its use at the national level had already been clearly demonstrated in the proof of concept phase. Here the strategy took due cognisance of the fact that space systems are inherently complex, carry high risks and are investment intensive. Further the creation of a heritage in hardware, human resource and methods are critical to develop confidence for operational systems. There was also a need to minimise the impact of probable early failures in the public mind and the political system. This phase additionally facilitated competence building at the core level, helped in the detailed evaluation of issues for scaling the effort to the national level and set the rules relating to the overall practices in system engineering. The overall demonstration of the systemic approach in this phase paved the way for the country to create national systems at a much larger scale with bigger and more sustained investments. We briefly discuss the nature of two satellite missions, Bhaskara and Apple, that were accomplished based on these considerations.

The Bhaskara Satellites (two of which were built and launched in 1979 and 1981), were earth observation satellites with a low resolution of 1 km operating in two spectral bands. The Bhaskara program at a cost of Rs 60 million, and spread over six years gave valuable experience of building imaging camera systems, realising satellite platform to take pictures from space, receiving the image information and processing these on the ground through appropriate ground infrastructure. Further, the mission enabled evaluating application interface methodologies with users in resource areas such as vegetative cover, geology and hydrology.

The Ariane Passenger Payload Experiment (APPLE) conducted in 1981, provided experience in satellite communications, including building of a body stabilised geo-synchronous satellite. The involvement of the user agencies early in the program, had a very significant influence on the adoption of the satellite communication technology in operational communication systems of India in the subsequent years.

The experimental phase also saw some very significant progress in the design and development of launch vehicles. Systematic efforts in building capabilities, studies of configurational options, issues of phasing the program, development of relevant infrastructure were all part of both the proof of concept and the experimental phases. The strategy for developing the launch vehicle was dictated by the country's decision to have autonomy in accessing space. Before going for the realisation of a full-fledged launch capability, the need to have a phased development was recognised as necessary both for building competence and for developing the needed confidence. Successful realisation of India's first launch vehicle SLV-3, with a modest payload capability of 40 kg and initiation of the augmented capability version ASLV with 150 kg payload capability took place in this phase. Valuable experience and inputs from both SLV-3 and ASLV, provided the basis for planning, configuring and implementing strategies for the current operational launch vehicles, the PSLV and GSLV (Gupta 2006).

The proof of concept and experimental phases together accounted for an expenditure of 8 per cent of the total expenditure as on 2006 (constant price basis).

Operational Phase

The operational phase called for certain unique strategies and decision making. Let me give a couple of examples in this connection. Encouraged by the lessons of the SITE experiment and recognising the potential of a space-based communication and broadcasting system for meeting the developmental needs of the country (Kale et al. 1971), India decided to go for a space-based communication and broadcasting system. Taking into account, the time frame for indigenous design and development of an operational Indian National Satellite (INSAT) and recognising the urgency to initiate services in this area, India decided to go for a bought out option for the first-generation INSAT systems, even as we embarked on the design and development of the second-generation systems. The four satellites of the first generation were thus procured, launched and operated for providing space-based communication and broadcasting services for meeting national needs. The subsequent three generations of satellites, many of which are currently in service, were all designed and built indigenously. The strategy adopted was different in the case of earth observations. Although the then operating foreign satellites were used for developing the remote-sensing applications in the country, the special requirements of earth observations, peculiar to our country as well as cost and strategic considerations called for an indigenous design and development route for the realisation of operational remote-sensing satellite systems. 'Bhaskara' missions provided the necessary confidence to undertake such an effort. The implementation of this strategy has resulted in India's own world class IRS series of satellites.

Another example is about the decision, in the early phase itself, to de-couple the time frame for the development of the launch vehicles from their role in providing operational support for satellite launches. Considering the complexities and the longer time frames for the development of launch vehicles, India consciously decided to seek launch support services for operational satellites from outside agencies. Such a strategy enabled the timely establishment of space services and also provided specific inputs for sizing the launch systems for these classes of satellites. The present capabilities of PSLV and GSLV and their future versions are based on the evolutionary requirements coming out of the IRS and INSAT programs.

The above considerations, relating to the introduction of high technology systems for meeting developmental and other innovative service goals, therefore called for pragmatic strategies. This in turn required understanding and analysing the complex interplay of several issues. First was a detailed assessment and evaluation of alternate approaches to arrive at the most optimal solutions. The second was to decide on exercising buy or build options taking into account the time frame for the introduction of services. In the case of buy options, a parallel indigenous development plan was created to achieve self-reliance goals.

Coming to the organisational systems (Kasturirangan 2001; Narasimha and Kalam 1988), experience from earlier experiments involving broadcasting, communication and remote-sensing, and dealing with the user communities, provided valuable inputs for the creation of innovative formal institutional frameworks. In the case of remote-sensing, the institutional framework involved setting up of the Planning Committee of the National Natural Resources Management System (NNRMS), which at the overall level is mandated to provide directions for the creation of space-based remote-sensing capabilities for the country. NNRMS consists of secretaries of the line departments of the Government of India dealing with natural resources and is headed by a member of the Planning Commission. Such a structure enables the involvement of major user communities to address issues of ensuring the use of such systems in their own areas of thematic applications, while at the same time facilitating the incorporation of this new and powerful technique into conventional approaches. Similarly the INSAT Coordination Committee, with the Secretaries of the user departments (Information and Broadcasting, Communication, Information Technology, and Science and Technology) working along with the Secretary of the Space Department, was created as an apex body to address the development of space communication, broadcasting and meteorology and planning their utilisation. In the context of space science, the Advisory Committee On Space Sciences (ADCOS) represented by some of the leading space scientists in the country provides directions for space science research. The three structures identified above have no parallel anywhere else in the world and have played a crucial role in sustaining the various space endeavours. Being user driven also means the beginning of a culture of accountability and transparency. Another important aspect is that the overall space program in India is overseen by a high-level body, known as the Space Commission, chaired by the Head of the space organisation and reporting directly to the Prime Minister. This structure ensures that the space program derives strength from the highest level and that the policy directions are duly integrated by different government agencies.

Another aspect of the organisational strategy was to create an industrial base for supporting the space program (Dhawan 1983, 1988) and for carrying out relatively routine operations, while the space agency concentrated on pushing the internal output up the value chain by enhancing the quality and content of research and development output. This also enabled us to progressively increase the strength of highly qualified professionals without increasing the overall size of the organisation. Also, in successive five-year plan periods, the organisation could deliver increasingly larger number of complex missions, as illustrated in the Figure 1.

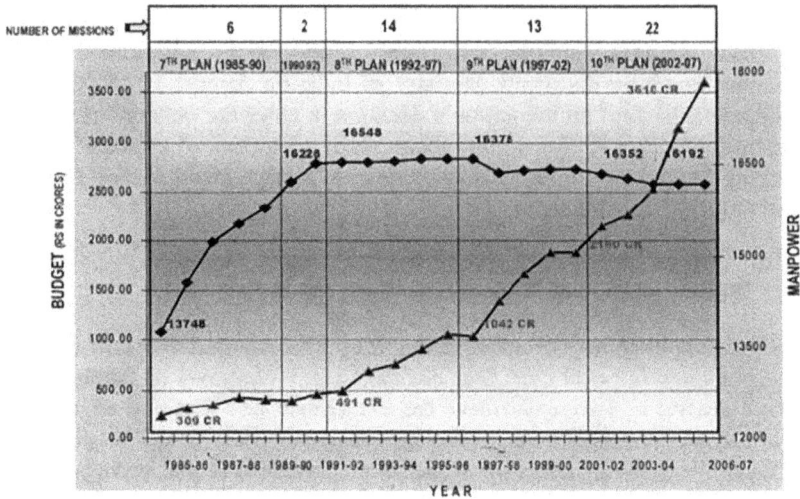

Figure 1: Growth of budget, manpower and missions

There have also been instances where the justification for initiating a new activity based on measurable direct benefits is lacking. At the same time the intangible benefits that could come from some of these programs could be convincing or not so convincing. An interesting case in point is the recent Indian initiative for planetary exploration Chandrayaan-1 (Kasturirangan 2004a). We had to go through an elaborate process of consultation and justification with the scientific community, academics, the political system and the public media before this mission was given the go ahead. The steps that were taken are shown in Figure 2.

This process, spread out over four years, culminated in the announcement by the Prime Minister of India on 15 August 2003 (India's independence day) on the nation's decision to enter the new era of planetary exploration. This is also a good example of a practice of ethics of decision making in science involving consultation of a large cross-section of society and ensuring transparency.

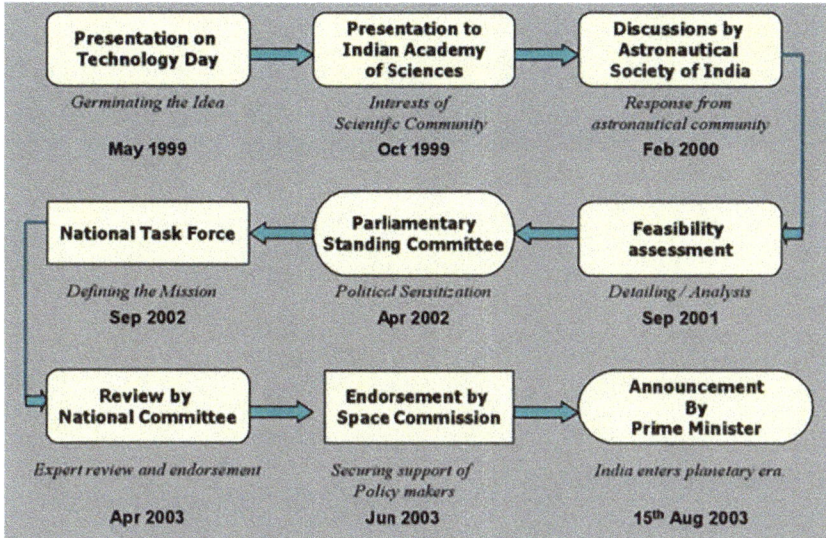

Figure 2: Decision-making process of Chandrayaan-I

Relevance of Space to South Asia

Although applications of space technology have taken deep roots in society and practiced for well over four decades, many countries in the developing world are yet to fully experience the excitement and take full advantage of space systems. In this context, the experience of India could be relevant for a developing country wanting to realise a cost effective and socially relevant program.

Turning to the development needs and priorities in South Asia, it is not difficult to realise that an appropriate application of space technology and creation of services based on space technology are highly relevant. South Asia comprising Afghanistan, Bangladesh, Bhutan, India, Maldives, Nepal, Pakistan and Sri Lanka have a combined population of 1.45 billion, which is about 22 per cent of the global population. Because of the agrarian focus of a predominant proportion of their populations, efficient use of natural resources such as land and water assumes great importance. The high population density places tremendous pressure on environment, requiring sound strategies for sustainable management (Rao 1995). There is also the issue of a divide between urban and rural areas in terms of access to health and education facilities. Common to all these countries, there is the major issue of response to natural disasters that are adversely impacting their economic growth. For ensuring equity-oriented development in such situations, there is a need to adopt high technologies such as space.

Some of the space technology inputs that relate to the needs of South Asia in terms of providing solutions are highlighted below (Kasturirangan et al. 2004).

Table 1

Needs	Areas where space technology can help
Improving food security	Water shed management Optimal land use strategy plan Control of land degradation Drought mitigation and proofing Recovery of irrigation systems Monitoring of crops and cropping systems Ground water targeting Siting water harvesting structures Fisheries forecasting
Infrastructure development	Road connectivity analysis Selection of site Land use mapping/monitoring Urban mapping Community Information kiosks VSAT communications network
Health and education – bridging gaps and improving quality	Tele-medicine network Tele-education network
Disaster management and response	Cyclone warning (land falls) Flood damage assessments Flood plain GIS/flood zoning analysis Drought monitoring Landslide zoning
Environment management	Vegetation monitoring Forest mapping, forestation plans Coastal zone regulation monitoring Mining impacts Urban sprawl and land use monitoring Monitoring desertification Weather watch Water conservation and management Atmospheric pollution monitoring

It is pertinent to note that information inputs from space technology lead to better decision-making and interventions. Both long-term and short-term goals are to be set in order to realise practical solutions in the shortest possible time and to build capacity for sustaining the programs. An appropriate organisational nucleus has to be created to plan and implement space activities.

A conceptual framework for use of space for development is shown in Figure 3.

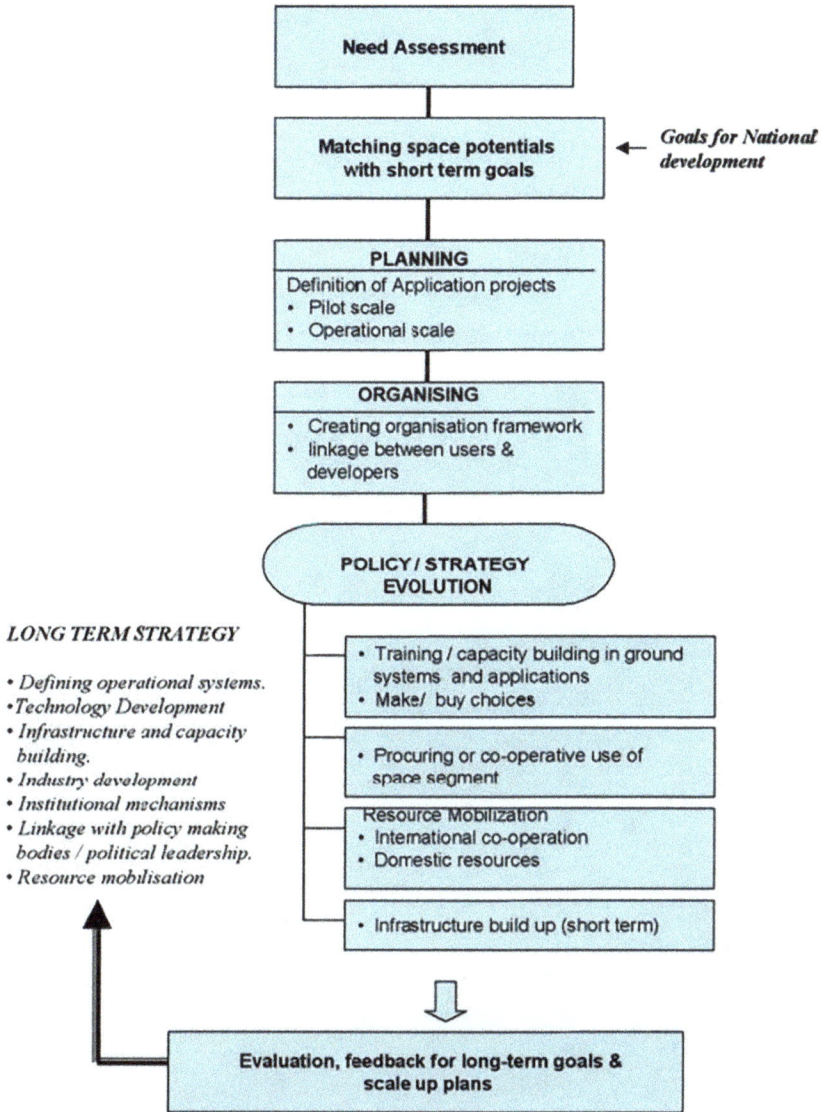

Figure 3: A conceptual model for use of space for development

Use of space technology, with an accent on capacity building, is sine qua non for its progress. The conceptual framework given above is based on the experience of India, and the relevant strategies described in the earlier sections are quite relevant for wider application in the region as well as other developing parts of the world.

Economic Aspects of India's Space Program

By the early '90s, all the four major components of the space program, namely, Satellite Communications, Meteorology, Earth Observations and Launch Vehicles had entered the operational stage.

The Satellite-based Communication Services (SATCOM) Policy of 1997 and the remote-sensing-based value-added services envisaged opening of the space industry to the private sector. Therefore it was considered timely and appropriate to commission a study on the economic aspects of the Indian space program through the Madras School of Economics (Sankar 2006; Sankar et al. 2003; Sankar, private correspondence).

Space Expenditures

Accumulated space expenditures since inception to the last fiscal year ending on 31 March 2006 amounted to US$7 billion. These expenditures category-wise are given in Figure 4.

As is obvious from the figure, 39 per cent investment is on launch vehicles, 36 per cent on satellite communications and meteorology, 14 per cent on earth observations, 6 per cent on space sciences and the balance on other items. About three-quarters of the total expenditure was incurred towards development of technology in the case of launch vehicles, whereas in the case of satellite communications, meteorology and earth observations, three-fourth of the investment is for building operational systems based on service needs of the country.

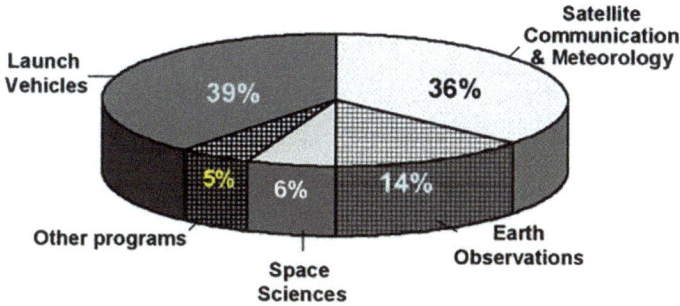

Total investment up to March 2006 : US$7 billion

Figure 4: Category-wise investment in Indian Space Program

The space expenditure of India as a percentage of gross domestic product (GDP) today stands at 0.09 per cent. Compared with the current annual government space budgets of US$2.5 billion for Japan, and US$1.5 billion for France, India's space budget is US$0.6 billion.

Methodology

For the purposes of economic analysis, it is useful to classify space activities into two stages: (i) design, development, testing, manufacturing and launch of spacecrafts into desired orbital slots (construction stage); and (ii) applications of satellite services to different uses (exploitation stage). The output basket of the space program contains a mix of private goods, public goods, social goods and strategic/incommensurable goods. Research in space sciences, most meteorological services and information are public goods. Equity considerations are important in provision of certain goods — for example, access to public telephone, access to radio and TV. The social goals dominate in public sector radio and TV programs. Use of the space program as an instrument for guaranteeing strategic, political, scientific and economic leadership yields strategic and incommensurable benefits. The methodology adopted for the two stages, category-wise, is given in Figure 5.

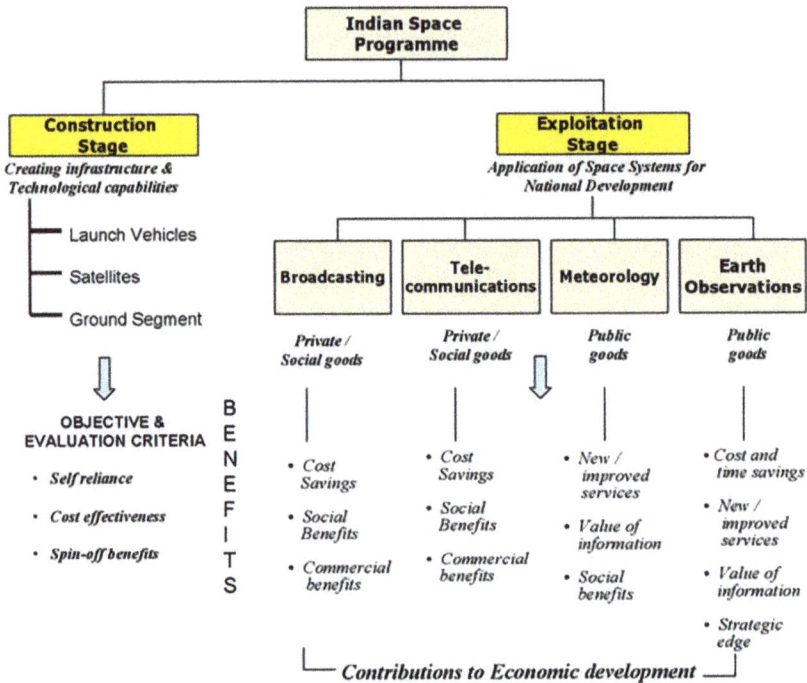

Figure 5: Framework of economic analysis

Construction Stage

Regardless of the nature of goods/services provided and whether it is produced by a public firm or private firm, cost minimisation is a valid criterion. The economic costing methodology requires (i) a rational basis for allocation of costs among the payloads of a multi-purpose satellite; (ii) apportionment of common and joint costs amongst various ongoing programs of the organisation/institution; (iii) investment expenditure, their time pattern and cost of capital; and (iv) output streams, their time pattern and discount rates for present value.

The global market for communication transponders is generally competitive with many private and public suppliers and many customers buying the transponders. Government-induced market distortions are relatively less in this market. Hence, the international market prices can serve as a benchmark for assessing the cost effectiveness of INSAT transponders. A detailed study on economic costing of INSAT transponders with 10 per cent cost of capital on investments and

5.5 per cent discount factor on future returns has brought out the cost advantage of INSAT transponders by at least 25 per cent of the prevailing international prices. The cost performance of INSAT system has been considered to be commendable keeping in view the relatively high capital cost in India and the dependence on some foreign components in the production of the satellites.

A comparative analysis of remote-sensing satellites and launch vehicles is rather difficult due to non-availability of reliable estimates of the costs of foreign systems and also due to differences in capabilities. However, preliminary estimates show that the costs of Indian Remote Sensing Satellite (IRS-1D) is very much lower than the reported costs of similar LANDSAT and SPOT satellites. Similarly, the development cost of India's PSLV and GSLV is US$1.3 billion as compared to about US$4 billion for the European Ariane 1 to 4, though there are some capacity variations in these systems.

Exploitation Stage

For measurement of the benefits, the role of satellite technology is considered under three different categories: (a) where the technology is unique; (b) where the technology is a substitute to existing technologies; and (c) where the technology is complementary to existing technologies. In the second case, one can measure cost savings due to satellite technology compared with the existing technology. If the technology is superior to the existing one, one has to estimate the incremental value of the improvement. Where the space technology is used in conjunction with many other technologies, one has to rely on a cost allocation procedure or a benefit sharing method or on expert opinion to estimate the benefit attributable to the space technology.

The INSAT system has played a key role in augmenting broadcasting, telecommunications and meteorological services in the country and has contributed immensely to economic and social development. Satellite communication technologies are terrain and distance independent and they enable governments to achieve goals such as the development of backward and remote areas at low costs and in a short time and thereby achieve technological leapfrogging.

Television

The major benefits of the INSAT system to Doordarshan (public TV) are expansion in area coverage from 14 per cent in 1983 to 78 per cent in 2005, population coverage from 26 per cent in 1983 to 90 per cent in 2005, increase in the number of channels from two to 32, remote area coverage, satellite news gathering, dissemination of weather and cyclone warning and use of TV as a media for training and education.

A detailed analysis show that for enhancing the population coverage further from 90 to 100 per cent with the distribution of a bouquet of 20 DD channels by the public broadcaster Doordarshan, the capital cost and annual operating cost through terrestrial technology is Rs 34,560 million and Rs 5,184 million respectively while a satellite-based solution with direct reception at homes, would involve a capital cost of Rs 6,380 million and annual operating cost of Rs 357 million. Thus, given the unique physiographical feature of India, the satellite communications is the least-cost option for achieving 100 per cent population coverage.

The growth of satellite TV has also aided in the emergence of new economic activities. The advent of satellite TV contributed to the growth of several industries like the manufacturing of TV sets, cables, receiving antenna and other equipment and program production. There are about 100,000 cable TV operators and about 35 million cable TV households in the country. The gross earnings of cable TV operators is nearing Rs 10 billion.

Telecommunications

Remote-area communication is an important objective of public policy. There is considerable cost savings due to use of satellite technology compared with the alternative of optical fibre cable network in remote-area communication. The cost of connecting 393 remote areas, currently served by INSAT, by optical fibre cable would be Rs 23,580 million while the comparable cost for satellite technology would be Rs 10,460 million. It may be noted that there are 30,000 remote villages of similar nature needing connectivity. The other uses of satellite technology are alternative media back up for terrestrial services, business communications, portable terminals for disaster management, tele-medicine and satellite-aided search and rescue.

Apart from the cost-saving, there are many external benefits which are diffused economy-wide. In the case of Andaman and Nicobar, rapid expansion of telecom since the mid-'90s facilitated the integration of Andaman and Nicobar with the mainland thereby boosting the growth of industry, trade and tourism and raising the growth rate of gross state domestic product to more than 8 per cent.

Meteorology

Satellites have made significant contributions to the generation of meteorological information by extending observation to oceans and remote areas on land, enabling generation of new types of observations, facilitating new concepts of data assimilation into models, reducing costs of a few types of observations and enhancing the reliability of certain types of data.

Meteorological services are recognised as public goods. The major contributions of satellite technology are in the areas of weather technology (cloud motion vector, wind-sea surface temperature and outgoing long wave radiation) and tropical cyclone (identification of genesis and current position, intensity of change and transmission of cyclone warnings). A comparative study of 1977 (before INSAT) and 1990 (after INSAT) cyclones which hit Andhra Pradesh, shows that even though the two cyclones are similar, due to the successful tracking of the cyclone in 1990 with the INSAT imaging instrument (VHRR) and the success of preparatory steps taken by the government, the loss of lives in 1990 was only 817 compared with 10,000 in 1977. This is an important incommensurable benefit of satellite technology.

Remote-Sensing

The advantages of remote-sensing are synoptic coverage, multi-spectral capability, multi-temporal capability and digital capture of data. Remote-sensing technology is being used in three different situations. It is an exclusive tool for estimation of snow melt run-off, rapid assessment of areas affected by natural disasters, identification of potential fishing zones in offshore areas and mapping of inaccessible areas. It is a substitute tool to conventional methods in mapping of land use, waste lands, and urban land use; preparing ground water prospect maps, watershed development plan, coastal zone management plan, etc.; and in monitoring forest cover, urban sprawl, status of environment, etc. It is a complement in cases like area and crop forecasting and urban development plans. Its advantage is that it yields unbiased, timely and enhanced information. Based on case studies of applications of remote-sensing in India's development programs, Table 2 provides estimates of investments, direct returns, and economic benefits.

Apart from the major benefits enumerated above, the policy of self-reliance has also enabled internal competence building and technology development and spin-offs to non-space sectors. For example, the spin-off outputs till 2005 include 224 technology transfers, 165 patents, 10 trademarks and 17 copyrights. ISRO has nurtured a symbiotic partnership with more than 500 Indian firms. The flow of funds to industry currently is about 40 per cent of the space budget. This partnership has generated significant spin-off effects to the industries in terms of improved manufacturing processes, quality control and management practices.

Table 2: Investments and benefits in remote-sensing

A	Investments		Rs (millions)	
	Operational Missions		10,080	
	Data Reception, Processing and Applications		5,540	
B	**Direct returns**			
1.	Returns from sale of satellite data and value-added products by NDC		1,600	
2.	Returns from ANTRIX through access fees and royalty		600	
3.	Opportunity cost (cost of foreign satellite data equivalent to IRS data used).		~5,000	
4.	Cost-saving due to value addition		~12,000	
5.	Cost-saving due to mapping using RS data		~11,000	
C	**Economic benefits**		**Rs (millions)**	
	Program	Nature of benefit	Estimate from case studies	Potential benefit to the country in the long-run
1.	National Drinking Water Technology Mission	Cost-saving due to increase in success rate	2,560 (5 States)	5,000–8,000
2.	Urban Area Perspective / Development / Zonal / Amenities Plan for Cities / Towns	Cost saving in mapping	50.4 (6 Cities)	16,000–20,000
3.	Forest Working Plan	Cost saving in mapping	2,000 (200 Divisions)	11,860

4.	Potential Fishing Zone Advisories	Cost-saving due to avoidance of trips in non-PFZ advisories	5,450	16,350
5.	Wasteland Mapping: Solid Land Reclamation	Productivity gain	990 (UP)	24,690
6.	Integrated Mission for Sustainable Development: Horticultural Development in Land With and Without Shrub	Gross income	Rs 0.20 to 0.40 (per hectare)	13,000–26,000
7.	Bio-prospecting for Medicinal Herbs	Value of Indian life-saving drugs		800

Note: US$1 = Rs 45.

Concluding Remarks

Space, in India, has become deeply intertwined with many facets of the national developmental endeavour. As we continue into the 21st century, the relevance of space as demonstrated by India is becoming even more applicable to a large number of countries across the world, faced with the daunting problems of development and improving the quality of life. Further, the growing role of space in addressing issues of environment and sustainability of development as well as in the formulation of the related policies, treaties and conventions adds to the importance of this endeavour on a global scale (Kasturirangan 2004b). It is in this context that I thought it worthwhile to provide a model for organising space research activities addressing particularly the peculiar problems of a developing country. Our approach to growing a world class space program highlights the fact that bold and imaginative adoption of new technologies to accelerate the process of development is realistic even with modest investment. Space, thus, is well within the reach of the developing world, and even more important could be a sustainable endeavour. What is needed is a vision, forward looking leadership and above all the political will. I hope the pragmatic approaches, elucidated here, will serve to inspire embarking on such an exciting and meaningful venture by countries not touched by its innovative consequences.

Turning the spotlight again on India and her dreams to transform herself into a developed nation in the very early part of 21st century, it is pertinent to note that the mix of strategies and planned approaches evolved so far by Indian space program have the potency to fire a powerful vision of future space endeavours. In its core part, this vision will continue to orient space activities towards societal needs such as education, health services, sustainable management of resources and environment, disaster management support and so on, possibly with new generations of thematic satellite constellations. Further, it could embrace new steps for expanding the horizons of knowledge through front-ranking missions for space exploration in a way that strengthens international cooperation. Future space missions will also be strong instruments for new advances in technology bringing in new synergies such as those between air and space, energy and matter, and living and non-living objects. Our vision has to cater to younger generation, whose population will be over one half of a billion, for technological leadership, environmental stewardship and economic prosperity (Kasturirangan 2004c). While the strategic framework of the Indian space endeavour will evolve further in response to the changing environment India could even leverage space capabilities in bringing greater global integration in many other human endeavours. It is important to recognise the values that gave those strategies potency and vitality. Striving always to keep Space relevant to the public, transparency, accountability, drive for excellence, cost-effectiveness and team culture are the backbones of the strategy. They are responsible for the success of the Indian Space Enterprise and indeed for effectiveness of its strategic thinking and planning.

Before I conclude, it is appropriate to recall the extraordinary directions provided by the successive leaderships of the organisation: M.G.K. Menon, Satish Dhawan and U.R. Rao; scientists with vision and deep understanding of the role of technology in national development. The culture of team spirit is a special attribute of the space program. We recall with pride the yeoman contributions made by our present President H.E. Dr A.P.J. Abdul Kalam in creating and nurturing this culture when he headed the India's prestigious first launch vehicle project SLV3. The success story of space program is also a tribute to the sustained enthusiasm, dedication and hard work of men and women of ISRO/DOS and other cooperating agencies.

To all of them and to the political system symbolised by the late Shri K.R. Narayanan, we owe the credit for touching the lives of millions of people towards a sustainable improved quality of life.

References

Dhawan, S. (1983), 'Space and Industry', Shri Ram Memorial Lecture, New Delhi, 7 February.

Dhawan, S. (1985), 'Application of Space Technology in India', Aryabhatta Lecture, Indian National Science Academy, 2 August.

Dhawan, S. (1988), 'Prospects for a Space Industry in India', Lala Karamchand Thapar Memorial Lecture, New Delhi, 26 February.

Gupta, S.C. (2006), *Growing Rocket Systems and the Team*, Prism Books Private Limited, Bangalore.

ISRO Report (1972), 'Indian Program for Space Research and Applications', Seminar, 7–12 August.

Kale, P.P. and Sarlez, William F. Jr (co-chairs) (1971), 'INSAT Satellite Systems', study by MIT and ISRO, published by ISRO.

Kasturirangan, K. (2001), 'Space: An Innovative Route to Development', 4th JRD Tata Memorial Lecture, Assocham, 31 August.

Kasturirangan, K. (2004a), 'Environment from Vantage Point of Space', Third Darbari Seth Memorial Lecture, New Delhi, 19 August.

Kasturirangan, K. (2004b), 'Space — A Vision for the Next 25 years', 40th Founder Memorial Lecture, Sriram Institute for Industrial Research, New Delhi.

Kasturirangan, K. (2004c), 'Space Science in India — Two Recent Initiatives', Sir Jagdish Chandra Bose Memorial Lecture, delivered at the Royal Society, London, 14 December.

Kasturirangan, K. and Becker, F. (co-chairs)(2004), 'Space to Promote Peace', IAA Commission — V Study Group Report, Paris, September.

Logsdon, J.M. (ed.) (2001), *Exploring the Unknown: Selected Documents in the History of US Civil Space Program, Volume V: Exploring the Cosmos*, NASA History Series, NASA, Washington DC.

Narasimha, R. and Kalam, A.P.J. (eds) (1988), *Developments in Fluid Mechanics and Space Technology*, Indian Academy of Sciences, Bangalore.

Rao., U.R. (1995), *Space Technology for Sustainable Development*, Tata McGraw Hill Co., New Delhi.

Sankar, U. (2006), *The Indian Space Programme: An Exploratory Analysis*, Oxford University Press, New Delhi.

Sankar, U. et al. (2003), 'Economic Analysis of Indian Space Program: An Exploratory Study', Madras School of Economics, Chennai, November.

Sarabhai, V.A. (1966), 'Exploration in Space: Sources of Man's Knowledge', National Program of Talks Series.

Sarabhai, V.A. (1979), *Sarabhai on Space — A Collection of Writings and Speeches*, ISRO, Bangalore.

Oration 11:
2007 K.R. Narayanan Oration

Message from the President
of the Republic of India

I am happy to know that The Australian National University, Canberra, has been organising an annual K.R. Narayanan Oration by eminent Indian personalities. The theme of this year's oration 'Coping with Climate Change: Is Development in India and the World Sustainable?' is indeed topical.

Climate change is a global challenge with strong economic, environmental and social dimensions. Both the developed and developing countries have to act in accordance with a common but differentiated responsibilities and capabilities. In order for developing countries to address climate change, access to appropriate technology is a key requirement. Collaborative research between institutions of developing and developed countries is the need of the hour. Institutions such as the Asia-Pacific Partnership on Climate and Clean Development, of which both India and Australia are members, are useful in this context though they are not a substitute for the Kyoto Protocol.

India is a signatory to the Kyoto Protocol and has been undertaking measures to reduce greenhouse gas emissions. While the government cannot compromise on the commitment for economic and industrial development of the country, it remains committed to addressing issues relating to our environment. Several measures have been taken by the government to reduce pollution, including emission of greenhouse gases.

I wish to take this opportunity to convey my greetings to the people of Australia, particularly the staff and students of The Australian National University. I also thank all those associated with the oration and wish the event every success.

Pratibha Patil
New Delhi
8 August 2007

Coping with Climate Change: Is Development in India and the World Sustainable?

R.K. Pachauri

I feel deeply privileged at being asked to deliver the 11th K.R. Narayanan Oration. For me this is also a significant moment personally, because I had the privilege of knowing Shri K.R. Narayanan very well. I met him first when he was minister of state for science and technology in the Narasimha Rao government in 1986. He was again a member of parliament, when, in 1992, The Energy and Resources Institute (TERI) was asked to develop the Indian segment of the Rockefeller Foundation supported program on Leadership for Environment and Development (LEAD). I asked Shri Narayanan to become a member of the steering committee of the program in India and he readily agreed. I kept in touch with him both when he was vice-president and then later president of the Republic. It was a unique honour for me to receive the Padma Bhushan from him, and I shall never forget the joy and pride on his face and his words on the occasion when he said 'it is a special pleasure for me to pin this recognition on your chest'. He was truly one of the most shining models of humane, erudite and dignified leadership that our country has seen, and I feel this oration is a fitting tribute to his memory.

The theme of my talk today I hope reflects not only Mr Narayanan's dedication to social causes and the protection of the environment, but something that is of critical importance to the future of India and the world in view of new knowledge that has now become available, and on which awareness has grown dramatically.

The concept of sustainable development was really enunciated and popularised through the report of the Brundtland Commission, and it is appropriate that we are focusing today on a report that was released 20 years ago. However, the importance of sustainability in development policies and practice has not been realised until recently. As is often the case, it is only the occurrence or the threat of a crisis that spurs human society to unusual actions and changes in pathways. In the case of sustainable development, I think the wake-up call has really come from the sudden growth in awareness and understanding of the scientific realities of climate change. I feel privileged to acknowledge that much of what is happening today is the result of the findings of the three working groups of the Intergovernmental Panel on Climate Change (IPCC). But some of the issues that are generic to all aspects of sustainable development and the reality of climate change really go back in time, since industrialisation began. For well over a century, human society derived growing satisfaction and, in some sense, exhibited a state of euphoria from the availability of a multitude of goods and services that industrialisation and its spread provided to different countries and communities.

It was only some 50 years ago that concerns about the unfettered advance of industrialisation and all that it brought, particularly in the nature of environmental damage, received attention, and it was felt that the implications of unregulated growth needed careful reappraisal. The clarion call perhaps was sounded first by Rachel Carson who published her pioneering book *Silent Spring* in 1964. This courageous lady withstood various personal attacks and the might of the powerful chemical industry in the US while highlighting the dangers of unlimited use of pesticides for a variety of purposes. She was essentially emphasising the need to evaluate externalities that were created by industrial processes and from specific products and their use, which, while providing benefits in one sense, could cause enormous harm to society in several other respects. Incidentally, this year, 2007, happens to be centenary of Rachel Carson's birth, but I am not too sure whether we have honoured the memory of this great pioneer in this period adequately. A country like India needs to learn from her example and ensure that we do not emulate the excessive use of chemicals and pesticides that were prevalent in developed countries 50 years ago.

The next stage of concern underlying sustainability issues related to development was attained when the Club of Rome published their influential study *Limits to Growth* in 1972. It is noteworthy that this particular report sold 30 million copies in more than 30 translations. This has undoubtedly become the largest selling book in this general field that the world has produced. An updated version was published on 1 June 2004, which brought in several refinements to the earlier study. The central thesis of *Limits to Growth* was based on the finite nature of several natural resources that the world had become accustomed to using on a large scale. The Club of Rome cautioned the world against the belief that these resources could be exploited and used at increasing levels without the danger of some discontinuity and disruption in the future. Significantly, the first oil price shock took place in 1973, which led to sudden concerns about the finiteness of oil on which the world had become increasingly dependent and about issues of energy security, a subject that haunts us perhaps to a much greater degree today. *Limits to Growth* also emphasised the problem of environmental pollution, but, in most of the material presented, the book focused on environmental quality at the local level. The world had to wait another 15 years before concerns about human induced climate change received due attention. This is when the IPCC was established and undertook the task of assessing all aspects of climate change by mobilising the best scientific talent and relevant expertise from across the globe.

Today, I would like to present some major findings from the Fourth Assessment Report (AR4) of the IPCC contained in the contributions of the three working groups whose reports have been approved by the panel. In November, we hope to complete the Synthesis Report, which will provide a synthesised assessment of the major findings of the three working groups and form a relevant basis for policymaking and agreements in this area. A major finding of the Working Group I Report was:

> Warming of the climate system is unequivocal, as is now evident from observations of increases in global average air and ocean temperatures, widespread melting of snow and ice, and rising global mean sea level.

Several other pieces of knowledge have been revealed in the three reports based on the advancement of scientific understanding and knowledge that has taken place since the Third Assessment Report (TAR) was brought out in 2001. First, 'most of the observed increase in globally averaged temperatures since the mid-20th century is *very likely* due to the observed increase in anthropogenic greenhouse gas concentrations'. This contrasts significantly with the findings of the TAR, which considered it 'likely' that the climate system had changed because of human actions. The change in these qualifying terms represents a substantially higher level of probability attached to this finding in the AR4. Future projections of climate change are shown in Figure 1.

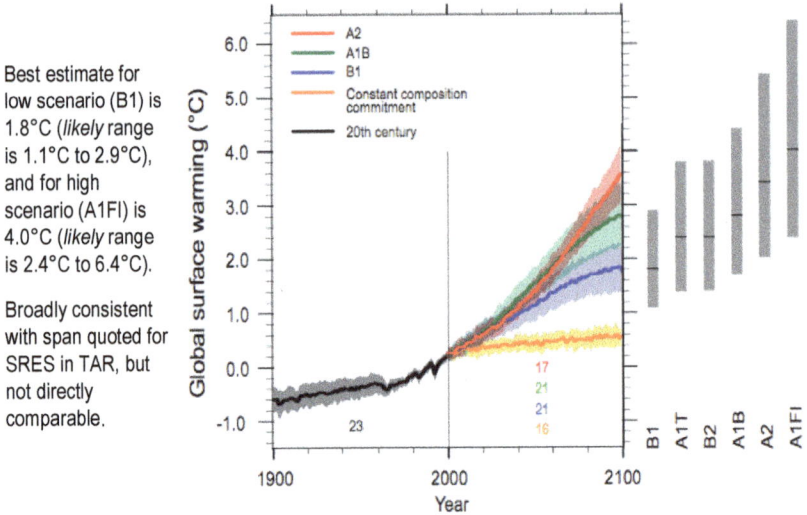

Best estimate for low scenario (B1) is 1.8°C (*likely* range is 1.1°C to 2.9°C), and for high scenario (A1FI) is 4.0°C (*likely* range is 2.4°C to 6.4°C).

Broadly consistent with span quoted for SRES in TAR, but not directly comparable.

Figure 1: Projections of future changes in climate

The AR4 has also advanced our understanding of the impacts of climate change on which we now have much greater regional detail as well as desegregation of sector-wise and ecosystem-wise impacts. Some of these impacts are not merely significant in terms of their threat to species but would clearly have unfavourable effects on economic activities as well.

India, for example, is vulnerable to the impacts of climate change to a substantial degree. One major observation of concern relates to the melting of the Himalayan glaciers. This, of course, is a worldwide problem, but an issue of considerable significance to Indian society, since the large population located in the northern part of the subcontinent relies on water from rivers originating from Himalayan glaciers. The change in glacier mass balance across the globe is shown in Figure 2, wherein the decline in the Asian High Mountain region mass balance as shown is significant.

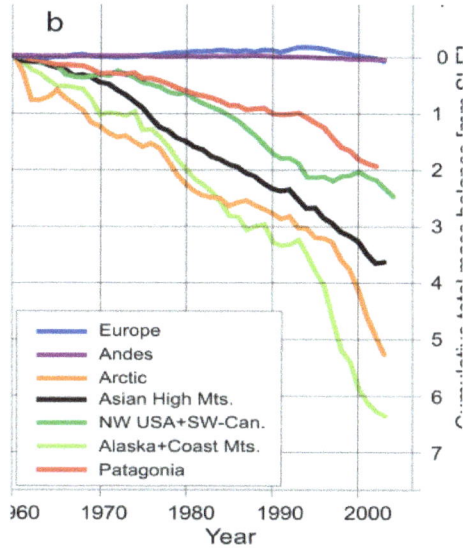

Cumulative loss of glacier mass in many regions.

During the 20th century, glaciers and ice caps have experienced widespread mass losses and have contributed to sea level rise.

Legend:
- Europe
- Andes
- Arctic
- Asian High Mts.
- NW USA+SW-Can.
- Alaska+Coast Mts.
- Patagonia

Figure 2: Glacier mass balance

Any reduction in the flow of rivers in northern India will not only reduce water supply for irrigation and other purposes, but would also adversely affect recharge of groundwater in the region. The economic implications of these could be serious. The IPCC AR4 has also brought out the fact that annual precipitation in lower latitudes including parts of South Asia has been declining, and is likely to decline in the future as well. Yet, at the same time, extreme precipitation events are likely to increase in frequency and intensity. Overall, India would see more frequent floods as well as droughts. This would affect agriculture adversely. But the more serious effects on agriculture are already evident in the decline of yields of crops such as wheat and rice, resulting from an increase in temperature, particularly during certain periods of the crop cycle. It is estimated that a 0.50°C rise in winter temperatures can reduce the yield of wheat by 0.45 tonnes per hectare against an average yield of 2.6 tonnes per hectare currently.

This would have serious implications for food security in India and the ability of the country to ensure adequate nutrition for a growing population. No doubt adaptation would be a critical part of response strategies to climate change in India, but given the existence of 300 million people who are undernourished today, the magnitude of the threat of hunger is likely to grow in the future. While agriculture contributes less than 30 per cent of GDP in the country, it affects the lives and livelihoods of a very large number of people, most critically those who are involved in rainfed agriculture. Nearly two-thirds of the area of land under agriculture is still rainfed. The scarcity of water that is likely to grow would affect not only agriculture, but also industry, household consumption and other areas. The gross per capita water availability in the country is projected to decline from 1,820 cubic metres per year in 2001 to 1,140 cubic metres per year in 2050. India, therefore, has to bring about a major transformation in its management of water resources.

The challenge of supplying enough food for India's growing population is becoming more difficult because the global food scenario does not look bright. Global food stocks in recent years have shown a substantial decline, with no prospects for improvement in view of growing demand for food grains worldwide and stagnation in productivity of major crops. There are over 850 million people in the world who do not have enough nutrition. As many as 54 nations do not produce enough to feed their people and, against the prospect of growing food prices in the global market, their economic prospects would also suffer. India would be no exception to this possibility.

The nature and intensity of the impacts of climate change for different levels of temperature increase are shown for specific sectors and ecosystems in Figure 3.

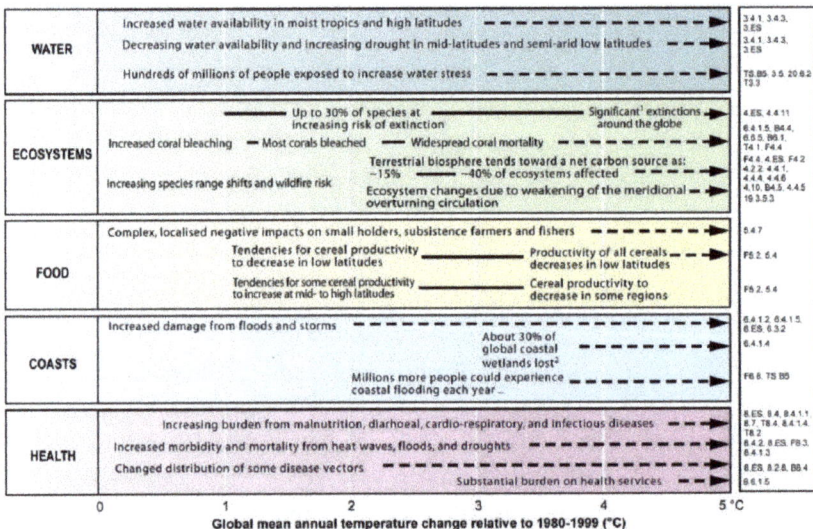

Figure 3: Global mean annual temperature change

One of the most serious aspects of climate change is the equity dimensions of the problem. The largest responsibility for the increase in concentration of greenhouse gases (GHGs) in the atmosphere lies with developed countries, but the worst impacts and the highest vulnerability applies to several developing countries. The Asian megadeltas, which include cities such as Dhaka, Kolkata and Shanghai, would be some of most vulnerable spots against the projections of rising sea levels, with prospects of coastal flooding and other serious consequences that would affect large numbers of people and property. It is entirely possible that some of the prosperous cities in Asia would suffer seriously from the human and economic consequences of extreme events that would have a major impact. With the growing vulnerability of these habitats, economic loss and human misery would increase. The city of Mumbai within a span of two years has suffered two incidents of heavy precipitation descending in a short period of a few hours on each occasion, the economic consequences of which are being felt now and are likely to continue for several years.

Under the UN Framework Convention on Climate Change (UNFCCC), negotiations are currently in hand for a new agreement beyond 2012. Not only is it urgent for the world to reduce emissions of GHGs adequately to stabilise the Earth's atmosphere and climate system, but also essential is the need to address the equity aspects of this threatening problem. The international community has provided hardly any resources for adaptation measures in the most vulnerable countries, such as small island developing states where the very survival of human beings is at stake. A country like India, therefore, has not only to raise its voice on the inequitable nature of actions and responses to climate change between developed and developing countries, but also ensure that in its own path of development it pursues the objectives of sustainability. The co-benefits of such an approach are so overwhelming that, even in the absence of climate change, they would be justified for reasons of energy security, reduced local pollution and, in several respects, the creation of new employment.

The problem of climate change, therefore, provides a unique moment of opportunity when a large developing country such as India can show exemplary resolve to follow a path distinctly different from that adopted by the world's developed nations. By doing so, India would not only serve its own people well but also, and at the same time, create a powerful model for the rest of the world to emulate, which is clearly the most compelling way of ensuring that human society gets off the unsustainable path of increased GHG emissions and heightened levels of climate change in the future.

It was on Earth Day in 1995 that TERI launched a major project called GREEN India 2047. This was in response to a desire within the institute to attempt something of value to celebrate 50 years of independence. After considerable discussion and debate, it was decided that the institute should carry out a study to assess the damage and degradation that had occurred in India's natural resources and the environment during the first 50 years of independence, which was to end on 15 August 1997. On the eve of Independence Day 1997, the results of this major study were released and a presentation made before the then Prime Minister of India Mr I.K. Gujral and several of his colleagues in the Council of Ministers.

Several of the findings of that assessment were of deep concern and, as Mr Gujral said on the occasion, these should 'jolt us into action'. It was found, for instance, that over 10 per cent of the country's economic output was being reduced on account of damage and degradation in the country's environment and natural resources. Between 11 and 26 per cent of agricultural output was being lost on account of soil degradation. It was also estimated that approximately 2.5 million people were dying annually on account of air pollution, of which indoor air pollution was the largest cause. Updates have been carried out of the original study including one that was completed in 2006, wherein several changes were documented, some of which were in the right direction and others were actually accentuating existing problems. Ongoing analysis also indicates that, particularly in rural India, the poor are far more dependent on common property resources than urban communities. Consequently, the depletion or degradation of natural resources leads to hardship and deprivation for the poorest sections of society. India is a large and diverse country and disparities of income are significant and widening. In the case of agriculture, the largest numbers of farmers are those that are essentially engaged in subsistence farming. Any reduction in the availability of natural resources or rainfall, therefore, affects the lives and livelihoods of this section of society directly. The GREEN India 2047 study was not merely an effort to present a doomsday scenario, which clearly emerged in the business as usual projections that were developed for the year 2047. The project also attempted to provide answers and solutions to the current dilemma of achieving high rates of economic growth while also rejuvenating the country's natural resources, the quality of which had been degraded over the years.

The popular approach in developing countries is to emphasise that their governments cannot and will not accept any targets or commitments to limit emissions of GHGs. The overlap between mitigation measures for improving local environmental quality and managing emissions of GHGs is so large that several actions need to be taken for domestic rather than global considerations. Consequently, the time has come to identify so-called 'no regrets' measures that would help to address local environmental problems primarily, and would also produce large global benefits, by which India can justly claim that it is undertaking its share of the 'common but differentiated responsibility' that is defined in the UNFCCC. Overall, the world has to implement reduction of emissions with some sense of urgency. Table 1 shows the period within which a peaking of emissions should be attained for different levels of concentration of GHGs. Beyond the peak, a decline in emissions becomes essential. And the cost of action is dwarfed by the consequential costs of inaction. For the stabilisation level shown in the first row of this table, the total cost globally in 2030 will not exceed 3 per cent of global GDP.

Table 1: Long-term mitigation (after 2030)

Stab level (ppm CO_2-eq)	Global mean temp. increase at equilibrium	Year CO_2 needs to peak	Year CO_2 emissions back at 2000 level	Reduction in 2050 CO_2 emissions compared to 2000
445–490	2.0–2.4	2000–15	2000–30	−85 to −50
490–535	2.4–2.8	2000–20	2000–40	−60 to −30
535–590	2.8–3.2	2010–30	2020–60	−30 to +5
590–710	3.2–4.0	2020–60	2050–2100	+10 to +60
710–855	4.0–4.9	2050–80		+25 to +85
855–1130	4.9–6.1	2060–90		+90 to +140

Overall, it is time that India defines a totally new path of development that ensures efficient use of natural resources and a shrinking footprint on the ecosystems of this planet. The importance of this reality is being realised increasingly by the Indian people and government. It is no surprise, therefore, that, as revealed in a recent survey, 60 per cent of the country's population is concerned about climate change — a concern that ranks second only to the fear of terrorism. Similarly, it is an indication of the increased attention that the Government of India is providing to this problem that the prime minister has set up an Advisory Council on

Climate Change, chaired by him and with members from the Union Council of Ministers as well as representatives and experts from outside the government.

Given the rapid growth of the Indian economy, urgent shifts towards a sustainable path of development are essential. Otherwise, investments and infrastructure would be created that would use natural resources unsustainably, to the detriment of coming generations and leading to a stage where the economy itself would suffer adversely. What is good for India would also be good for the world, and it is in realisation of this fact that India has to emerge as a model that other nations would like to emulate. By establishing a benchmark, India would also gain economic advantage, since the processes, technologies and products that it develops for attaining a sustainable path of development would provide a competitive advantage that would open markets globally for Indian suppliers who would access opportunities overseas. It is appropriate to recall Gandhiji's famous words 'Be the change that you want to see in the world'.

While I have the privilege of delivering this talk in Australia, may I also say that the global community and posterity demands that Australia also seize this opportunity for reassessing its position and act resolutely on the basis of scientific evidence and actual observations to chart a new path of development. Indeed, Australia can be a major example for other developed countries and particularly for its neighbours in Asia, which are at various stages of development towards economic prosperity and growing rapidly. A shared vision in this respect between India and Australia can have much greater global appeal and potential than if the two countries act in this regard entirely on their own. I would, therefore, plead for a closer relationship of development issues with a sense of urgency. A churning of conventional thinking and reappraisal of past practices and policies is essential.

Shri K.R. Narayanan, at the major summit organised by TERI in 2000, pointed out the perils of 'voluptuous consumption' that the world was pursuing and advised participants to see the merit of Gandhian principles in which lie abounding benefits to the human race. If India were to seriously alter its path of development and create a new model of sustainability, then that would be an appropriate tribute to the memory of Shri K.R. Narayanan and a timely acceptance of Gandhian thought.

Oration 12:
2008 K.R. Narayanan Oration

Message from the President
of the Republic of India

I am happy to learn that The Australian National University, Canberra, is organising the annual K.R. Narayanan Oration on the theme of 'Why Environmentalism Needs Equity: Learning from the Environmentalism of the Poor to Build Our Common Future' by Ms Sunita Narain, Director of the Centre for Science and Environment.

India attaches great importance to the conservation of the environment. The government as well as non-governmental organisations are making efforts to do so even while ensuring continued development for the country. A number of measures have been taken to reduce pollution, including increased uses of liquefied gas in public transport, higher standards for emissions from industries and transport and relocation of polluting industries. The government is also focused on conservation of forests and optimal utilisation of water resources.

The issue of greenhouse gas emissions and climate change is currently dominating global attention. We are also concerned about this. We need to look at energy mixes that are sustainable in the long run and explore viable ways of using new and renewable sources of energy. While our demands for energy are growing as a developing country, we have clearly stated that India would not exceed the level of per capita greenhouse gas emissions of developed countries. Our National Action Plan on Climate Change released in June establishes eight missions focusing on solar energy, energy efficiency, sustainable habitats, water resources management, ecosystems, agriculture, a 'Green India' and research.

I wish the oration every success.

Pratibha Patil
New Delhi
16 September 2008

Why Environmentalism Needs Equity: Learning From the Environmentalism of the Poor to Build Our Common Future

Sunita Narain

I am honoured to deliver the 12th K.R. Narayanan Oration. It is a special occasion because our former president K.R. Narayanan was a very special person. Most of us, who knew President K.R. Narayanan, will remember him as an erudite, compassionate, thoughtful politician, who knew his mind and stood by his beliefs. We will remember him for his integrity and for his intellectual might.

I remember him for all this and even more. I remember him for making the system 'bend' to make space for issues, people, ideas and what was right. He did this in his own style, giving of himself to what he believed in. Most importantly, he did this not by standing *against* the system, but by standing *with* the system. For me, he was the ultimate subversive: he made power good.

In the mid-1990s, when K.R. Narayanan was vice-president, my colleague Anil Agarwal, of whom he was very fond, asked if he would release a book on air pollution. But this was no ordinary book, which is ordinarily released in such ordinary functions of our leaders. The book was titled *Slow Murder*. It indicted the most powerful industrialists in the country for manufacturing highly polluting vehicles and demanded change with the stridency of an angry rebel. This was also the time when the air of Delhi was toxic and dirty. It was also the time when nobody cared about issues of air pollution and its effects on our health and our bodies.

K.R. Narayanan not only agreed to release the book, he agreed to do it from his own palatial and powerful vice-presidential house. In one stroke, the profile of the concern changed. It became acceptable. It became powerful. Since then, government has taken strong steps to combat air pollution in our cities, with some success. But I will discuss more on this later.

Later, Agarwal went back to K.R. Narayanan — this time in the grandeur of the president's house, to request him to inaugurate a workshop on traditional water harvesting. Again, you could say: so what is new? This was the time when rainwater harvesting was a non-issue, which was discounted by technocrats and policy. K.R. Narayanan agreed to inaugurate the meeting and to present awards to the unsung engineers and water managers of rural India; he also agreed publicly to learn from this knowledge. After speaking to the rural engineers who had built structures to hold and recharge rainwater in different ecosystems, he declared publicly that the most powerful house in the country would adopt their humble science and undertake water harvesting. And he did. My fondest memory is of him inspecting the rainwater harvesting recharge wells of the president's estate, accompanied by his bewildered but respectful government engineers. Today, rainwater harvesting has caught the imagination of the nation. Today, rainwater harvesting is seen as an integral solution to building a water secure India.

Still later, he agreed enthusiastically to visit the dusty and still unknown villagers who had done rainwater harvesting and brought their river to life. His visit to Alwar (a district in Rajasthan state) to recognise the achievements of the village of Bhaonta brought with it the pomp of the state — the governor, chief minister and others trekking to the river to see the water that gave it life.

Standing at the river, which had become perennial because of the water harvesting structures made by village communities, K.R. Narayanan said:

> I would like to congratulate the people of this village. Not only have the people revived their river, they have also established democratic institutions to manage their resource. Their initiative and self-reliance is an example and an inspiration to the rest of India.

Today, we need this voice of authority and reason more than ever in the world, as we hurtle towards growth, which can be divisive and destructive or can bring prosperity for all.

The Age of Environment

This is the time when the world is confronted with the knowledge of impending and potentially devastating climatic changes. It is also the time when the world realises that the model of consumption of a few cannot be supported for the majority. It is also the time when we, in India, are realising the pain of environmental degradation of our air, water and forests. This, then, is the time of crisis.

It is also the age of environment. Today, environmental concerns — domestic and global — are defining the way of our economy and our everyday life. The world is battling different but linked developments. The oil price is rising, crippling economic growth as we know it and forcing governments to look for new answers to conservation. Prices of food are skyrocketing, leading to conflict in poor countries dependent on imports and putting pressure on poor communities struggling at the margins of survival. In addition, we see the beginning of signs of climate change in many parts of the world in the form of intensified tropical cyclones, variable and extreme weather events such as heavy rains leading to floods, bitter cold spells and frost that causes crops to fail.

But this is also the time of opportunity. This is the time when we can use the ingenuity and inventiveness of science and society to find ways to 'leapfrog' to the future. We can reinvent the pathway of growth so that we can have economic wellbeing without the pain of pollution and degradation.

The world has to search for new answers to its growth paradigm. For this, it literally has to reinvent what growth and development mean. The question we need to explore is: will these answers lie in the activism of the poor, who are dependent on the environment for their survival, or in the prescriptions of the consuming middle classes? It is also a fact that the movements of the poor and dispossessed against environmental degradation are demanding more than simple technological changes to suit the new generation of needs. They want hard and uncomfortable issues of access to natural resources to be resolved; they want equity and justice to be the bedrock of the environmental movement of the future.

These movements — emerging from the bottom of the world's pyramid, often led by village communities and remarkable individuals — are today showing the way to the future. These movements are products of democracy, as change in any society is a product of negotiation and innovation.

In vast parts of the poor world, where these voices are becoming shouts, environmental warriors have a different relationship with their environment. They live on and off their environment — the land, the forests — and use its resources — medicinal plants, building material, firewood to cook and fodder to feed their animals. They get their water from streams, rivers and ponds. Here the destruction of the environment affects livelihoods and lives, not just lifestyles. High population pressure also means that there is no piece of land or water that is not used — and used with intensity — for daily survival. In these circumstances, if the environment is degraded or the margins of subsistence threatened further, conflict is inevitable. This is why dissent and dialogue has to be part of the alternative model of growth.

Nature's Way or Our Way

A few years before he died, environmentalist Anil Agarwal wrote that the 21st century was going to be the century of the environment. Technological change, he said, would be driven by environmental imperatives. Agarwal believed that any nation that forgot to invest in environmental science and technology would imperil its economy and the lives and health of its people. He also said that, in future, human technologies would be forced to mimic nature's cycles and gentleness. Today we must recognise these words and act on them.

Let us look at the evolution of science itself in the 20th century. Scientists during the last century essentially asked four important questions. At the start of the century, the biggest question in the minds of scientists like Albert Einstein or Neils Bohr was: 'What is Matter'. By the middle of the 20th century, scientists had begun to ask two other important questions, namely: 'What is Life' and 'What is the Universe'. It was around the 1950s that Francis Crick and James Watson unravelled the structure of DNA. This discovery led to enormous developments in life sciences and, more recently, we have begun to see the emergence of biotechnologies based on the knowledge gathered by life scientists in a very big way. But, by the last quarter of the 20th century, scientists had begun to ask yet another critical question: 'What is the Web of Life'.

This last question is not just about scientific curiosity but human necessity. The fact is that modern technologies and processes of production, so critical to our economies, have adverse impacts on our environment. This technological paradigm is beginning to go beyond the carrying capacity of the Earth's environment and could easily destroy numerous critical geochemical cycles such as the carbon cycle and the nitrogen cycle. Science for ecological security is, therefore, our imperative.

It is here that we will have to learn from nature itself, Agarwal had argued. Nature uses weak forces rather than concentrated forces to do its work. For instance, very tiny temperature differences can transport massive quantities — as much as 4,000 million hectometres or 40,000 billion tonnes — of water from the oceans and travel across thousands of kilometres to deposit it as rainfall over India. But humans still use concentrated energy sources like coal or oil, which then create enormous problems like local air pollution and global climate change. In the years ahead, we will have to learn from nature and move towards much weaker sources of energy — like solar energy, for example.

It is for this reason that the world must begin to listen to the creativity of the action being proposed and practised in its vast but remote parts. These actions are driven with the understanding that progress for countries of the South will not lie in the models practised in other regions of the world. They will have to find new answers to old problems, from growing food without destroying soils to building factories without destroying rivers to building cities without drowning in excreta. And all this will have to be done with limited financial resources and even more limited choices of technology. This can only be done if the world begins to combine the confidence of the literate with the humility of the knowledgeable.

Environmentalism of the Poor: Localisation and Growth

India's environmental movement, like so much else in the country, is about managing contradictions and complexities — between rich and poor, between people and nature.

But the movement in India has one key distinction, which holds the key to its future. The environmental movements of the rich world happened after periods of wealth creation and during periods of waste generation. So, they argued for containment of the waste but did not have the ability to argue for the reinvention of the paradigm of waste generation itself. However, the environmental movement in India has grown in the midst of enormous inequity and poverty. In this environmentalism of the relatively poor, the answers to change are intractable and impossible, unless the question is reinvented.

Just consider the birth and evolution of the green movement. Its inception dates back to the early 1970s with former Indian prime minister Indira Gandhi's famous words at the Stockholm conference on environment that 'poverty is the biggest polluter'. But, in this same period, the women of the Chipko movement in the Himalaya showed that the poor, in fact, cared about their environment. In 1974, years before the environment became fashionable, the women of this poor, remote village, stopped loggers from cutting their forests. In other words, this movement of the poor women was not a conservation movement per se, but a movement to demand the rights of local communities over their local resources. The women wanted the first right over the trees, which they said were the basis for their daily survival. Their movement explained to the people of India that extractive and exploitative economies were the biggest polluter, not poverty.

This is because in vast parts of rural India, as in vast parts of rural Africa and other regions, poverty is not about the lack of cash, but the lack of access to natural resources. Millions of people live within what can be called a biomass-based subsistence economy, where the *gross nature product* is more important than the *gross national product*. Environmental degradation is not a matter of luxury but a matter of survival. In these cases, development is not possible without environmental management.

In the environmental movement of the very poor, there are no quick fix techno-solutions that can be suggested to people who are battling for their survival. In this environmentalism, there is only one answer: we must find a way reduce needs and increase efficiency for every inch of land, every tonne of mineral and every drop of water used. It will demand new arrangements to share benefits with local communities so that they are persuaded to part with their resources for a common development. It will demand new ways to growth.

I say this because it is also clear that the environmental movement of the relatively rich and affluent is still clearly looking for small answers to big problems. Today, everyone is saying, indeed screaming, that we can 'deal' with climate change if we adopt measures such as energy efficiency and some new technologies. The message is simple: managing climate change will not hurt lifestyles or economic growth — it is a win–win situation in which we will benefit from green technologies and new business.

For instance, biofuels — growing fuel, not food, on land to run the cars of the rich — is one such techno-fix. There has been no discussion on whether biofuels, already competing for land with food crops and raising prices, will indeed reduce emissions when vehicle numbers are increasing. With biofuels under criticism for raising food prices and depleting water resources, the next generation technical solution is on the cards: hybrid cars. I am not against either biofuels or hybrid cars. But I know these are small parts of the big change we need. The transition to a low-carbon economy is not just about technology but also about redistributing economic and ecological space. This change will hurt, as indeed will climate change itself; variable weather events that are destroying crops are already hurting the most vulnerable and powerless.

Relearning Knowledge: Water

It is also clear that these new answers will lie in learning the frugality and rationality of societies, and in relearning technologies. Take water management. For many countries of the South, water insecurity, which on the one hand leads to declining agricultural productivity and on the other leads to waterborne disease and death, has become the biggest limiting factor for growth. Today, water management is the starting point for getting rid of poverty in the world. Water security is the starting point for food security.

Countries of the water-stressed South have to plan not for drought relief, but for a relief against drought. This will demand a new paradigm of water management. It will demand realising that water and culture go together and that water shortage is not about mere failure of rain. It is about the failure of society to live and share its water endowment.

But, to get the water-practice right, we first have to deal with the poverty of the professional mind, which, over time, has become fossilised and rigid in its outlook. We literally need a movement for water literacy so that we can build a new understanding based on past traditions and wisdom of our people, who had learnt to survive and indeed make best use of their environment.

Take the fascinating case of ancient Rome and Edo (the ancient Japanese city, on which modern Tokyo is built). Romans built huge aqueducts that ran for miles to bring water to their settlements. These aqueducts even today are the most omnipresent symbols of that society's water management. And many experts have praised the Romans for the meticulousness with which they planned their water supply systems.

But, no, these aqueducts represent not the intelligence but the utter environmental mismanagement of the great Romans. Rome was built on the river Tiber. The city did not need any aqueducts. However, as the waste of Rome was discharged directly into the Tiber, the river was polluted and water had to be brought from long distances. Water outlets were few as a result and the elite appropriated these using a system of slaves. By contrast, the inhabitants of Edo never discharged their waste into the rivers. Instead, they composted the waste and then used in the fields. Because they used common and shared rivers, Edo had numerous water outlets and a much more egalitarian water supply.

When we turn our backs on the water around us, we are following Rome: out of sight, of mind; flush it and who cares — but care we must.

Dying Wisdom: Building New Practice

Ancient Indians understood the speed with which water, the world's most fluid substance, disappears. They understood that the mathematics of water is simple: if you harvest just 100 millimetres of rainfall on just 1 hectare of land, you will receive as much as 1 million litres of water. But, on the other hand, if we do not capture this rainfall, the wettest place on Earth will have water shortages.

Research published by the Centre for Science and Environment (CSE) in the mid-1990s showed that countries like India must learn from their traditional community-based water management systems so that they can build ways to the future. In today's India it is imperative that groundwater is recharged so that the rate of abstraction is not greater than the rate of the water infiltration. The traditional water systems were designed to ensure that rainwater was stored in millions of disaggregated and diverse structures, which would in turn lead to local recharge of water into the ground. It is this distributed water harvesting that will build water security.

In other words, India must rework the paradigm of water management so that it is designed to harvest, augment and use local water resources so that it leads to local and distributed wealth generation. It is also clear that local and distributed water infrastructure will require new forms of institutional management, as water bureaucracies will find it difficult to manage such vast and disparate systems. It is here that countries like India must learn from their traditional community-based water management systems so that they can build ways to the future.

These ideas have captured the imagination of policy planners in the country. It is now well established that water management strategies will need to devolve power to local communities so that they can build structures for local water conservation and practise its use for efficiency and equity. This protest, alternative practice and policy research has converged into policies to build local water structures under employment guarantee schemes in which the state guarantees the right of employment to the poor. This employment is used to build water conservation structures so that drought relief can become relief against drought.

The Great Water Leapfrog

The problem becomes more intractable as the country progresses and moves from using water in traditional sectors like agriculture to industries and urban areas. It is for this reason that a country like India is considered a traditional water economy that has to make the transition to a modern water economy. In other words, the water sector has to become part of the formalised economy, with formal institutions and mechanisms for its management and pricing.

The point to understand is what this modern and formal water economy means in the rest of the world and what it will mean for countries like India. In the industrialised world, industry and urban households use over 70 per cent of the water resources, while agriculture gets the remaining

30 per cent. In traditional water economies like India, the reverse is true: agriculture consumes over 70 per cent and industry and urban areas the rest. The point is not where we are, but where we are heading.

The fact is that urban areas and industrial centres in countries like India are now putting greater pressure on water resources. Cities across the country need more water for their growing population and, more importantly, their growing affluence. Their growing demand leads to pressure to source water from further and further away. The capital city of Delhi will get water from the Tehri dam, over 300 km away in the Himalaya; the software capitals of the country, Hyderabad, will get water from Nagarjuna Sagar Dam on the Krishna River 105 km away; and Bangalore will get water from the Cauvery, about 100 km away. The desert city of Udaipur used to draw water from the magnificent Jaisamand Lake but it is drying up and so the city is desperately seeking a way out of this new thirst.

The problem is that the 'informal' water economy of rural India — its agriculture-dependent population — still exists. The economy has not transformed from being agriculture-dependent to one that is manufacturing and service sector driven. The water crisis is about the management of these competing needs: the vast rural economies, which need water for their food and livelihood security, and the newer growth economies of modern and industrial India. This water competition is leading to low intensity conflicts between different users. For instance, when the southern city of Chennai wanted to source its drinking water from the Veeranam Lake some distance from the city, farmers agitated against the withdrawal for the thirsty city. When the Gujarat city of Rajkot needed water, farmers drew fire and were killed. In 2005, in two separate incidents in Rajasthan, farmers were killed as they rioted against water withdrawal from their neighbouring reservoir or canal for distant cities.

It is because of this imperative that water policy has to shun the dogma that dictates against the pricing of water and its efficient management. Cities and the industries of rich India must begin to pay for the water they use. But pricing and markets will not suffice. It is also equally imperative that water management paradigms and their technologies are reinvented for this poor-rich world.

These rich cities of the poor world will have to invest in efficiency so that they do not become water wasteful and then learn the science and art of efficiency. Conversely, they will also have to invest in managing and treating their wastewater. Today, cities extract from cleaner upstream sources and discharge their waste — sewage and industrial effluents — downstream, which in turn leads to increased problem of polluted water and ill-health for poorer users of the rivers. The capital intensity of the modern sewage system — its transportation and eventual treatment before disposal — is such that it cannot be afforded by all users, and even all urban areas. How will the modern cities of India grow without creating water waste and pollution? How will these cities innovate so that they can practise the technologies of recycling and re-use even before their counterparts in the industrial world? The challenge is to reinvent a modern waste management system that re-uses every drop of water discharged, at costs that can be afforded by all.

There is no denying India's water sector needs to be reformed, indeed transformed, so that it can provide clean and adequate water to all. But what has to be accepted is that there is no established model for this transformation. A country like India has to leapfrog over the modern economic paradigm, to create its own — hybrid — version of the water future. Modern water policy will have to be built on the premise that scarcity is not about the lack of resources but about being wise about the use of resources.

Defining the Challenge of Economic Growth

Years before India became independent, Mahatma Gandhi was asked a simple question: would he like free India to be as 'developed' as the country of its colonial masters, Britain? 'No', said Gandhi, stunning his interrogator who argued that Britain was the model to emulate. He replied: 'If it took Britain the rape of half the world to be where it is, how many worlds would India need?'

Gandhi's wisdom confronts us today. Now that India and China are threatening to join the league of the rich, the environmental hysteria over their growth should make us think: not just about the impact of these populated nations on the resources of our planet, but also — again, indeed, all over again — of the economic paradigm of growth that has led to much less populated worlds pillaging and degrading the resources of this only Earth.

Let us be clear. The Western model of growth India and China wish most feverishly to emulate is intrinsically toxic. It uses huge resources — energy and materials — and it generates enormous waste. The industrialised world has learnt to mitigate the adverse impacts of wealth generation by investing huge amounts of money. But let us be clear that the industrialised world has never succeeded in containing the impacts: it remains many steps behind the problems it creates.

Take the example of local air pollution control in cities of the rich world: economic growth in the postwar period saw it struggling to contain pollution in each of its cities — from London to Tokyo to New York. It responded to the growing environmentalism of its citizens by investing in new technology for vehicles and fuel. By the mid-1980s, the indicators of pollution, measured then by the amount of suspended air particulates, declared the cities to be clean. But, by the early 1990s, the science of measurement had progressed. Scientists confirmed the problem was not particulates as a whole, but those that were tiny and respirable, capable of penetrating the lungs and the circulatory system. The key cause of these tiny toxins — this respirable suspended particulate matter — was diesel fuel used in automobiles. So vehicle and fuel technology innovated. It reduced sulphur in diesel and found ways of trapping the particulates in vehicles. It believed new-generation technology had overcome the challenge.

But this is not the case. Now Western scientists are discovering that, as the emission-fuel technologies reduce the mass of particles, the size of the particles goes down and the number emitted goes up, not down. These particles are even smaller. Called nanoparticles (measured in the scale of a nanometre or one-billionth of a metre), these particles are not only difficult to measure, but also — say scientists — could be even more deadly since they easily penetrate human skin. Worse, even as technology has reduced particulates, the trade-off has been to increase emissions of equally toxic oxides of nitrogen from these vehicles.

The icing on the cake is a hard fact: the industrialised world may have cleaned up its cities, but its emissions have put the entire world's climatic system at risk and made millions of people, living at the margins of survival, even more vulnerable and poor because of climate change. In other words, the West not only continues to chase the problems it creates, but also externalises the problems of growth to others, those less fortunate and less able to deal with its excesses.

It is this model of growth that the poor world now wishes to adopt. And why not? The world has not shown any other way that growth can work. In fact, it preaches to us that business is profitable only when it searches for new solutions to old problems. It tells us its way of wealth creation is progress and it tells us that its way of life is non-negotiable.

But I believe the poor world must do better. The South — India, China, and all its neighbours — has no choice but to reinvent the development trajectory. When the industrialised world went through its intensive growth period, its per capita income was much higher than the South's is today. The price of oil was much lower, which meant the growth came cheaper. Now the South is adopting the same model: growth that is highly capital intensive (and, therefore, socially divisive) and material and energy intensive (and, therefore, polluting). The South does not have the capacity to make investments critical to equity and sustainability. It cannot temper the adverse impacts of growth. This is deadly.

Let's stay with the challenge of air pollution. Some years ago, the organisation I work with argued that the city of Delhi should convert its public transportation system to compressed natural gas. The move to gas would give us a technology jump-start, as it would drastically cut particulate emissions. Delhi today has the world's largest fleet of buses and other commercial transport vehicles running on gas. The result is that the city has stabilised its pollution, in spite of its huge numbers of vehicles, poor technology and even poorer regulatory systems to check the emissions of each vehicle. In other words, Delhi did not take a technology-incremental pathway of pollution control on the basis of fitting after-treatment devices on cars and cleaning up fuel. It leapfrogged in terms of technology and growth.

Now, with ever-increasing numbers of private vehicles crowding the roads of our cities and pollution attacking the lungs of people, the question remains: Can we reinvent the dream of mobility so that it does not become a nightmare? Can we make new ways to build a future city that combines the convenience of mobility and economic growth with public health imperatives? In this hybrid-growth paradigm — which combines the best of the new and old — cities would run on public transportation, using the most advanced of technologies. Even as the whole world looks for little solutions to pollution and congestion, the city of the South must reinvent the answer itself.

In other words, we have to rethink the options for our energy and economic security. The South will have to find ways of leapfrogging so that we can have progress without the curse of pollution and inequity. Like the resource challenge, this will also demand enormous creativity so that we can reinvent the economic treadmill of the world.

Equity Provides the Basis of Change

This is the challenge that we in India are discussing to find ways ahead. We know that our cities are on a different development trajectory: people still drive in buses or bicycle or walk to work. In these cities, the car has not replaced the bus, the bicycle or the pedestrian. It has only marginalised them, crowded them out. In Delhi, for instance, even now, 60 per cent of people commute by buses, which occupy less than 7 per cent of the road space, while cars, which crowd over 75 per cent of the roads, transport only 20 per cent of the people. Our cities can and must develop an alternative vision for growth.

The question is: Can these cities leapfrog — from cities with few buses to cities with few cars? Can they build a mobility plan based on swanky buses, trams, bicycle paths and pedestrian walkways? In other words, can they do everything today that modern cities — from Berlin to Vancouver — of the old rich world want to do tomorrow?

In Delhi, policy is now working towards creating a new mobility model. It is building a bus rapid transit system, BRT as it is called, on a 15 km road in the heart of Delhi. This system creates a central lane for buses to drive without obstruction, and segregates the remaining road space between cars (two or three lanes), bicycles and pedestrians. The project is built on the premise that road space must be equitably allocated to the users of the road. It is also investing in a metro and augmenting its bus system, buying 6,000 new buses for its roads.

But we also know that equity is a policy prescription that is easy to talk about and difficult to implement. In Delhi, as well, whereas everybody agrees that public transport is important, the first bus corridor has been contested, not just because of its technical glitches, but also because it is seen as taking away road space from users of cars. As cars have already taken over the road space, the scarce space has to be reallocated and this creates tension. But equity is a prerequisite when it comes to managing scarce resources in a sustainable manner. The city will have to learn to share its economic and ecological space if it wants a sustainable future.

Climate Change: Equity is a Prerequisite

Climate change is definitely the biggest challenge of our century. However, currently its sheer complexity and urgency is defeating us.

For the past 16 years — the first intergovernmental negotiation took place in Washington DC in early 1991 — the world has been haggling about what it knows but does not want to accept. It has been desperately seeking every excuse not to act even as science has confirmed and reconfirmed the fact that climate change is both real and related to carbon dioxide and other emissions, which are related to economic growth and wealth in the world. In other words, it is human made and it can devastate the world as we know it.

The fact is that science is not just certain but 'unequivocal' that climate change and its devastation are now inevitable. Along with understanding the still obtuse science, we must begin to put a human face to the climate change that is beginning all around us. We must see climate change in the faces of the millions who have lost their homes in the Sidr or Nargis cyclones, which ripped through Bangladesh and then Myanmar. After all, science has clearly established that the intensity and frequency of tropical cyclones will increase as the Earth heats up. We need to see climate change in the faces of those who lost everything in the floods caused by intense rainfall events. We need to know that the thousands of people who died in these events did so because the rich have failed to contain the emissions necessary for their growth.

When I say this, I know, climate-sceptics and purist-scientists will combine to argue that it is difficult to prove cause and effect. After all, we cannot say that this cyclone in Bangladesh is related to climate change. It is a natural disaster, not a human-made crime. Climate complexity is clearly at the edge of chaos here. The fact is we will never be able to make certain predictions or direct correlations between events that we see around us and the warming that is now inevitable. But, when the world is unequally divided between the polluters and the victims, clearly prevarication and denial will be the name of the game.

Talk Not Action

As the call for action is becoming more strident and more urgent (as it must), the world is looking for small answers and petty responses. On the one hand, there is a well-orchestrated media and civil society campaign to paint China and India as the dirty villains on the block. If they 'cry' about their need to develop, the response is to tell them that they are most vulnerable: 'We cannot afford to waste time in the blame game. Even if, in the past, the Western world created the problem, *you* must in *your* interest take the lead in reparations.'

The West's hysteria is growing. But so is their inaction. The irony is that these countries had agreed in 1997 to make a small cut in their gargantuan emissions in the interest of us all. These emission cuts were nowhere close to what was needed, then or now, to avert climate change. The fact (which is mostly unsaid) is that these countries have done nothing, absolutely nothing, to contain their emissions. Between 1990 and 2005 — when they agreed to cut emissions — rich country emissions increased by 11 per cent and emissions from the growth-related energy sector increased by 15 per cent. They have reneged on their commitment. They have let us all down.

Energy Is the Key

It is the world's need for energy — to run everything from factories to cars — that is the cause of climate pain. The fact also is that, after years of talk, no country has been able to de-link its growth with the growth of carbon dioxide emissions. No country has shown how to build a low-carbon economy, as yet. No country has been able to reinvent its pathway to growth, as yet.

This then is the challenge. After years of talk, the proportion of new renewable energy — wind, solar, geothermal, biofuels — comprises just about 1 per cent of the world's primary energy supply. It is misleading to say that renewable sources add more electricity than nuclear power. It is an old renewable — hydroelectric power — that makes the world light up.

What is tragic is that the world is hiding behind the poverty of its people to fudge its climate maths. The renewable sector is made up of biomass combustion — the firewood, cow dung, or leaves and twigs used by the desperately poor in our world to cook their food and light their homes. It is this that is providing the world its space to breathe.

We are the Change

What then is the way ahead?

First we must accept that the rich world must reduce emissions drastically. Let there be no disagreements or excuses on this matter. There is a stock of greenhouse gases in the atmosphere that has built up over centuries in the process of creating nations' wealth. It is a natural debt. This has already made the climate unstable. Poorer nations will now add to this stock through their drive for economic growth. But that is not an excuse for the rich world not to take on tough and deep-binding emissions reduction targets. The principle has to be that they must reduce so that we can grow.

The second part of this agreement is that poor and emerging rich countries need to grow. Their engagement will not be legally binding but based on national targets and programs. The question is to find low-carbon growth strategies for emerging countries, without compromising their right to develop.

This can be done. It is clear that countries like India and China provide the world with the opportunity to 'avoid' additional emissions. The reason is that we are still in the process of building our energy, transport or industrial infrastructure. We can make investments in leapfrog technologies so that we can avoid pollution. In other words, we can build our cities on public transport; our energy security on local and distributed systems — from biofuels to renewables; and our industries using the most energy (and, therefore, pollution) efficient technologies.

We know it is in our interest not to first pollute, then clean up; or first to be inefficient, then save energy. But we also know that technologies that exist are costly. It is not as if China and India are bent on first investing in dirty and fuel-inefficient technologies. We invest in these, as the now rich world has done, to make money, which can then be invested in efficiency.

As yet, the rich world has found small answers to existential problems. It wants to keep its coal power plants (even as it points fingers at China and India). It wants to build new coal power plants. It believes it can keep polluting and keep fixing. This time, the answer it has hit upon is carbon capture and storage — to pipe the emissions underground and hope the problem will just go away. In this way, it hopes it can have its cake and eat it too.

It also wants to keep its cars and add more. Or drive more. It can do this by simply growing fuel and pumping it into vehicles. It does not matter if this biofuel is a small blip in the total consumption of oil: all the corn in the US can only meet 12 per cent of current US petrol use. It does not matter if there is not enough land to grow food and fuel in the world. The cynics will say, after all, that corporations rule the oil and food business. Scarcity will only increase their business. But the realists should say that the 'illusion' of solutions is the opiate of the rich. This way they do nothing while creating an illusion of action — and turn their attention to the countries that are just learning the mind-matter game.

In spite of fact that science tells us that drastic reductions are needed, no country is talking about limiting their consumption: this is not ironical. Every analysis proves that efficiency is part of the answer but it is meaningless without sufficiency. Cars have become more fuel efficient so people drive longer and have more cars. Emissions continue to grow.

The New Deal

If we know that the emerging world can leapfrog to make the transition to cleaner technology, why is this not happening? Why is it that the world talks big but gives small change?

When the Kyoto Protocol was being negotiated, the world decided to invent the clean development mechanism (CDM) to pay for the transition in the poorer world. But the mechanism was designed to fail. The obsession was to get the cheapest emission reduction options for the rich world. As a result, the price of the certified emission reduction (CER) unit used in this transaction has never reflected the cost of renewable and other high technology options. It is a cheap and increasingly corrupt development mechanism. It is also a convoluted development mechanism, in which rules bind governments not to think of big change. In fact, current CDMs provide disincentives for governments in the South to drive policies for clean energy or production. Any policy, which is already designed for good is bad in the CDM portfolio. It is not additional and it will not qualify for funding.

The world must realise the bitter truth. Equity is a prerequisite for an effective climate agreement. The fact is that without cooperation, this global agreement will not work. It is for this reason that the world must seriously consider the concept of equal per capita emission entitlements so that the rich reduce and the poor do not go beyond their climate quota. We need climate responsible action. We need effective action.

Rights-Based Agenda

In 1990, the Washington based World Resources Institute (WRI) published a report that showed that annual greenhouse gas emissions of the developing world almost equalled those of the industrialised world, and that, in fact, the emissions of the developing world would overtake the industrialised world's emissions in the near future. However, CSE found that the methodology used by WRI to compute the responsibility of each nation favoured the polluter.

Under the WRI methodology, each nation was assigned a share of the Earth's ecological sink, but the assignment was proportional to the nation's contribution to the Earth's emissions. The sinks are natural systems, oceans and forests, which absorb emissions. Global warming is caused because emissions exceed this natural capacity of the Earth to clean pollutants. WRI had estimated that the world produced 31,000 million tonnes of carbon dioxide and 255 million tonnes of methane every year. It then estimated that the sinks of the Earth naturally assimilated 17,500 million tonnes of carbon dioxide and 212 million tonnes of methane annually. On this basis, it then computed a 'net' emission of each nation by allocating a share of the sinks to each nation based on its gross emissions contribution.

CSE, in its critique, argued that there were two main types of 'sinks' where carbon dioxide is reabsorbed by the biosphere: the oceans and terrestrial sinks. While terrestrial sinks, such as forests and grasslands, may be considered national property, oceanic sinks belong to humankind. They can be regarded as common global property. CSE then apportioned the sinks on the basis of a country's share in the world's population, arguing that each individual in the world had an entitlement to the global commons. This allocation, based on individual rights to the Earth's natural cleansing capacity, changed the computation of nations' responsibility drastically. For instance, under the WRI methodology, the US contributed 17 per cent of the world's net emissions, while the CSE methodology computed that it actually contributed roughly 27.4 per cent. Similarly, China's contribution of net annual emissions decreased from 6.4 per cent (WRI estimate) to 0.57 per cent, and India's from 3.9 per cent to just 0.013 per cent.

This allocation of the Earth's global sinks to each nation, based on its population, created a system of per capita emission entitlements, which, taken together, were the 'permissible' levels of emissions for each country. This, according to CSE, would create a framework for trading between nations, as countries that exceeded their annual quota of carbon dioxide could trade with countries with 'permissible' emissions. This would create financial incentives for countries to keep their emissions as low as possible and to invest in zero-carbon trajectories.

We have also argued that, as much the world needs to design a system of equity between nations, nations of the world need to design a system of equity within the nation. It is not the rich in India who emit less than their share of the global quota. It is the poor in India, who do not have access to energy, who provide us the breathing space. India, for instance, had per capita carbon emissions of 1.5 tonnes per year in 2005. Yet, this figure hides huge disparities. The urban-industrial sector is energy intensive and wasteful, while the rural-subsistence sector is energy-poor and frugal. Currently, it is estimated that only 31 per cent of rural households use electricity. Connecting all of India's villages to grid-based electricity will be expensive and difficult. It is here that the option of leapfrogging to off-grid solutions based on renewable energy technologies becomes most economically viable. If India's entitlements were assigned on an equal per capita basis, so that the country's richer citizens must pay the poor for excess energy use, this would provide both the resources and the incentives for current low energy users to adopt zero-emission technologies. In this way, too, a rights-based framework would stimulate powerful demand for investments in new renewable energy technologies.

This rights-based agenda is critical in the resolution of the climate change challenge. The fact is that climate change, more than anything else, teaches us that the world is one; if the rich world pumped excessive quantities of carbon dioxide into the atmosphere yesterday, the emerging rich world will do so today. It also tells that the only way to build controls is to ensure that there is fairness and equity in the agreement, so that this biggest cooperative enterprise is possible.

Strengthen Global Democracy

In conclusion, there is no doubt we live in an increasingly insecure world. Indeed, the state of insecurity in the world is made more deliberate, more wilful, because of the intentional and unintentional actions of nation-states and governments — all in the name of development and global justice. So, if the rich world is increasingly paranoid about its defence from the failed, bankrupt and despotic states of the developing world, the poor are insecure because they are increasingly marginalised and made destitute by the policies of the rich. The challenge of climate change is adding a new level of insecurity for the world's people. It is also equally clear that a business as usual paradigm of growth will lead the world towards a vortex of insecure people, communities and nations.

It is here that the countries of the South face even greater challenges. They will need to rebuild security by rebuilding local food, water and livelihood security in all villages and cities of their world. And, in doing this, they will have to reinvent the capital and material intensive growth paradigm of the industrialised North that deepens the divide between the rich and the poor. They will have to do things differently in their own backyards. But, more importantly, these countries will have to become the voice of the voiceless, so that they can demand changes in the rules of globalisation in the interest of all.

Sustainable development needs to be understood as a function of deepened democracy. As every society makes mistakes, it is the process of decision-making about sustainable development that will lead to fast rectification and resolution. Sustainable development is, therefore, not about technology, but about a political framework, which will devolve power and give people — the victims of environmental degradation — rights over natural resources. The involvement of local communities in environmental management is a prerequisite for sustainable development.

The South's quest for an alternative growth strategy will have two essential prerequisites.

First, a high order of democracy, so that the poor, marginalised and environmental victim can demand change. It is essential to understand that the most important driver of environmental change in these countries is not government, laws, regulation, funds or technology per se. It is the ability of its people to 'work' democracy.

But democracy is much more than words in a constitution. It requires careful nurturing so that the media and the judiciary, and all other organs of governance, can decide what is in the public, and not private (read corporate), interest. Quite simply, this environmentalism of the poor will need more credible public institutions, not less.

Second, change will demand knowledge and new and inventive thinking. This ability to think differently needs confidence to break through the historical 'whitewash' — the arrogance of old, established, ultimately borrowed ideas. A breakthrough — a mental leapfrog — is what the South lacks the most. The most adverse impact of the current industrial growth model is that it has turned the planners of the South into cabbages who believe they have no answers. The current model has only problems, for which the solutions lie in the tried and tested answers of the rich world.

It is also important that this environmentalism of the poor — built from the bottom up and based on principles of equity and human need — influence the world. To combat climate change, it is essential that the world learns from these movements about the need to share resources so that we can all tread lightly on the Earth, and so that we can all remember, not forget.

In closing, I would like to quote from President K.R. Narayanan. In his address to the nation, on the eve of India's Republic Day, 25 January 2001, he said:

> Let it not be said by future generations that the Indian Republic has been built on the destruction of the green earth and the innocent tribals who have been living there for centuries. A great socialist leader has once said that a great man in a hurry to change the world who knocks down a child commits a crime. Let it not be said of India that this great republic in a hurry to develop itself is devastating the green mother earth and uprooting our tribal populations. We can show the world that there is room for everybody to live in this country of tolerance and compassion.

This is the message the world must learn, fast.

Oration 13:
2009 K.R. Narayanan Oration

Message from the President
of the Republic of India

I am happy to learn that the Australia South Asia Research Centre (ASARC) is organising the 13th K.R. Narayanan Oration on the theme 'Rocket Science, Other Science: A Trajectory of Indian Science and Technology from 20th to the 21st Century' at The Australian National University, Canberra on 2 November 2009.

Since independence, Indian scientists have made noteworthy achievements in the field of science and technology, especially in successfully developed launch technology and launch vehicles. I hope that the oration will highlight the ways in which science and technology can be used for development of society.

I wish the oration all success.

Pratibha Patil
New Delhi
23 October 2009

Rocket Science, Other Science: A Trajectory of Indian Science and Technology from the 20th to the 21st Century

Roddam Narasimha

The untapped resource of technical and scientific knowledge available in India for the taking is the economic equivalent of the untapped continent available to USA 150 years ago.[1]

I feel greatly honoured at having been invited to present the 2009 K.R. Narayanan Oration at this renowned university. Shri Narayanan was a person that I came to know, and quickly learned to respect, especially during the period (1986–89) that he was union minister for Science and Technology in Delhi — a period that started shortly after my own tenure at the National Aerospace Laboratories (NAL) began at Bangalore. It was both a pleasure and a privilege to have a minister of Shri Narayanan's erudition, with keen appreciation of the role that science and technology (S&T) could play in India's development, and a regard and sense of friendship that he and the scientific community shared with each other. When, in 1986, NAL embarked on a parallel computing project, Shri Narayanan was one of the closest friends and supporters we had. This friendship continued even after he became president of the Republic, and I have the fondest memories of his visits to the National Institute

---

1   Milton Friedman (1955), Report to the Union Ministry of Finance.

of Advanced Studies and the Jawaharlal Nehru Centre for Advanced Scientific Research, where he showed once again his warm and almost personal interest in the future of Indian S&T and the men and women who pursued science in India.

It is a privilege, therefore, for me to be able to pay a tribute to a great diplomat, scholar, gentleman and friend of science, and I am grateful to my hosts at the Australia–India Council and the Australia South Asia Research Centre at The Australian National University (ANU) for providing me an opportunity to do so.

It seems appropriate to use this occasion to sketch a personal view of the path that India has followed in S&T since 1947, the year that signalled the end of British rule, although (as I shall argue briefly later) the roots of national policy in this period are intimately connected with developments in Indian science in the first half of the 20th century. This lecture, however, is not intended to be a comprehensive survey of all the significant developments that took place during this period. Some of them have already formed the theme of previous Narayanan orations. Instead, I shall describe the path that has been followed in areas in which I have myself been involved in some way, in particular aerospace and computer technologies.

***

Let me begin with space. The first, and indeed the most remarkable, aspect of India's space program is how long ago it started. The Indian National Committee on Space Research was established in 1962 as a part of the Department of Atomic Energy by Homi Bhabha, with Vikram Sarabhai as the committee's chairman. I shall return to the great impact that these two leaders have had on Indian S&T in the last half-century, but let me only note here a Bangalore connection. The speed with which space research was made part of the national agenda was perhaps in part due to the visions that Bhabha and Sarabhai shared on the way to build S&T in India. Both had been at the Physics Department of the Indian Institute of Science during the war years — Bhabha having been prevented from resuming his career at Cambridge by the war, and Sarabhai having been forced to wait to go to Cambridge to complete his doctoral degree. As Amrita Shah says in her fine biography of Vikram Sarabhai:

> It is tempting to speculate that Vikram and Bhabha, the two
> princes of Indian science, used their youthful days in Bangalore
> to spin dreams for the future ... sharing their precocious hopes
> in the rambling wild landscape of the IISc or sealing a blood
> pact under the bright lights of the West End [Hotel] ... because
> of the uncanny sureness with which they set about their plans and
> the suggestion of complicity in so many of their actions.[2]

The modest National Committee set up in 1962 was eventually to
lead to what is probably India's most striking technology development
program today.

Vikram Sarabhai came from a well-known and wealthy family of
businessmen and industrialists in Gujarat, but chose science as his career.
When he first invited me in 1964 for a personal discussion at Trivandrum,
two things struck me. The first was the dramatic Nike–Apache launch
from the beautiful, unspoiled palm-fringed beaches near Veli Hill. And the
second was the company that Sarabhai was travelling with. It included not
only some of the engineers and scientists who were then working with him,
and a group of distinguished foreign scientists, but also artists, journalists
and various other friends. Sarabhai asserted that India was not doing
space for prestige, and, like the good businessman he was, insisted that
sound economic evaluation of the required resources was necessary before
embarking on the program. He also saw space science and technology as
offering an opportunity for India to leapfrog from its backwardness and
poverty. In the debate that still sometimes goes on between the virtues
of leapfrogging vs those of piggybacking, Sarabhai (like most scientific
leaders of his time in India) was definitely for leapfrogging. Having trained
as a physicist who was used to balloons for cosmic ray work, it was natural
for him to think of sounding rockets as providing another tool that would
help his research. The first rockets launched in Trivandrum had to do with
the upper atmosphere and the so-called electro-jet, a huge river of electric
current that flows over the magnetic equator that lies across the southern
tip of India.

Unfortunately, Sarabhai died when he was only 52. He was succeeded by
Satish Dhawan, my own guru when I was a student at the Indian Institute
of Science, and it was left to him to set up a space establishment in the
country that would realise Sarabhai's dreams. In 1972, this establishment

---

2   Amrita Shah (2007), *Vikram Sarabhai: A Life*, Penguin, New Delhi.

took shape in the form of a Space Commission (a high-level policymaking body) and a Department of Space (part of the government administrative machinery), which in another few years took charge of the Indian Space Research Organization (ISRO) (the technical executing arm) as well. In succeeding years, Dhawan went on to build the superb technology delivery system that ISRO has now become in India.

Dhawan vigorously and single-mindedly pursued the idea of using space technology for national development, and presided over a program that eventually led to a series of satellites for communication, meteorology, broadcasting, natural resource survey, education, and, more recently, cartography, ocean resources and health, etc. He showed his deep commitment to developmental goals by preserving space as an open, purely civilian organisation. In 1975–76, he used the US satellite ATS–6 for a Satellite Instructional Television Experiment (SITE), which broadcast a series of educational TV programs on such subjects as health, family planning and agriculture to more than 2,500 villages in the country — and in many different languages. For its time, SITE was seen as the largest societally motivated experiment ever conducted in the world using satellite technology.

Dhawan also was an unusual man. Even as he led big science he retained great respect for little science. He was keenly sensitive not only to social issues but also to environmental ones. So it was no wonder that he handled, in a most sensitive spirit, the displacement of the inhabitants (including the cattle!) of Sriharikota Island, which houses ISRO's satellite launch complex at what is now the Satish Dhawan Space Centre. He found birdwatching at the Sriharikota Range very relaxing and, even as he built and ran his space empire, made time to write a little gem of a book about bird flight. He spent much time charting the future of the space program in India, often with sketches and charts drawn in his own hand. And he realised that the program often called for unconventional methods.

The visionary commitment of these founding fathers slowly got translated into reality. On 19 April 1975, India's first satellite — called Aryabhata, after the great Indian astronomer-mathematician (fifth century CE) — was launched from the Soviet Union. On 18 April 1980, the Rohini satellite was launched by India's own launch vehicle SLV–3 from the Sriharikota Range. On 10 April 1982, the first Indian geostationary satellite INSAT–1A was launched from the US and, on 17 March 1988, the first Indian remote-sensing satellite IRS–1A followed. So, by the

1990s, the program was beginning to achieve the objects that it had set for itself. By 1997, India had launched eight satellites on its own rocket launch vehicles (and 12 more on others') by the time it could put its own automobile on the roads (India in 1998). So there *had* been some leapfrogging. With the more recent successes of the Polar Satellite Launch Vehicle (PSLV) and the geostationary launch vehicle (GSLV), the country now has what seems like a robust launch capability in satellites up to the 3–4-tonne class for geostationary orbits. India's entry into interplanetary exploration has been signalled by Chandrayaan 1, a remote-sensing lunar orbiter. Although prematurely terminated recently, it has acquired much new data on the lunar surface and, in particular, provided the strongest evidence yet of the presence of water on the moon. And the rest of the world is taking notice of these developments. The US magazine *Aviation Week and Space Technology* (*AWST*), the most widely read periodical in the field, has at various times run stories on India's 'prolific space program', called it 'world class' and pointed out that it is run on a 'shoestring budget' (currently of the order of about US$1 billion a year).

***

To understand the early genesis of the Indian space program, we must appreciate that, in the India of the 1950s and 60s, there was widespread faith in the idea that modern S&T could solve many of the nation's old problems. Most Indian scientists believed this, and Jawaharlal Nehru, the first prime minister of the country, was a most eloquent and powerful advocate of the idea. Soon after the end of British rule, India set out (under Nehru's inspiration) on a spree of establishing new laboratories, agencies, industries and academic institutions. As Nehru happily laid one foundation stone after another, he confessed that he would much rather be the director of one of those laboratories, if he had the competence, than be the prime minister of the country. He advocated science with almost religious zeal. He saw dams, factories and laboratories as modern temples; and when he inaugurated the Indian Science Congress year after year, he would say that he had come to 'burn incense at the altar of science'. In 1958, he had parliament pass a Scientific Policy Resolution that declared government's determination to participate fully in the march of science, which Nehru called 'probably mankind's greatest enterprise today'.

Nehru's vision was that science and, in particular, what he called the scientific temper, was an instrument for nothing less than civilisational revival. This vision was shared by virtually all Indian scientists of that time. Among these the most dynamic and charismatic was Homi Bhabha (1909–66), who set up the country's atomic energy program — which, incidentally, became first the father of the country's space program (as we have already seen) and, later, a model for it when it became independent. Bhabha invented, with Nehru's encouragement, the administrative and scientific mechanisms that made it possible to pursue national science and technology goals in a focused way.

How was it that in 1947 Nehru and people like Bhabha could have had such extraordinary faith in the path of science, as well as the confidence that its pursuit would, first of all, be feasible and, secondly, successful? One part of the answer to these questions lies in Nehru's own unique educational background, for he studied natural science at Cambridge before his forays into law and politics. Even more important was the knowledge that, in the first half of the 20th century, a number of Indian scientists had begun to make such outstanding contributions as to attract attention all over the world. The remarkable thing about these scientists was that they were all nationalists in some sense — not in a jingoistic or xenophobic way, but rather as those intent on recovering lost civilisational pride. The most famous of these was C.V. Raman, who won the Nobel Prize for physics in 1930 (it is said that he had tears in his eyes when he had to sit under a Union Jack during the Nobel ceremonies). Then there was Meghnad Saha, who, through his well-known thermodynamic analysis of ionisation, was a pioneer in theoretical astrophysics; Satyendra Nath Bose, who invented quantum statistical mechanics even before quantum mechanics had been properly founded; and M. Visweswaraya, an engineer who promoted new industry as the *dewan* (chief minister) of the Maharaja of Mysore, and became India's most eloquent and passionate advocate for industry and technology, often crossing swords on these subjects with Mahatma Gandhi. Earlier, Jagadish Chandra Bose had made a microwave device that was the precursor of Marconi's radio. Then there was S. Ramanujan, the one least directly influenced by Western scientific thinking, but also the one to make the most striking impact on it by his vast outpouring of extraordinary mathematics. He was not just a much better mathematician than the rest, but (to borrow a description used by Mark Kac in another context) he was a magician. The methods he used to obtain his extraordinary results can only be ascribed to deeply rooted cultural instincts and weapons that he trained on modern mathematics, rather than on anything much he learnt directly from the West as method.

As I said, the confidence that people like Nehru and Bhabha had in the potential of Indian science was inspired by the knowledge that some Indian scientists had done outstandingly well against heavy odds. That faith was clearly shared by the well-known American economist Milton Friedman (Nobel Prize 1976), one of whose opening sentences in his 1955 report to the Union Finance Ministry provides the theme of this oration.

***

It is useful to realise that Indian policy in many of its major technology programs has for long been based on what may be called the low-slow-steady approach. The funding in any given year may not be very high, but budgetary support has been steady, and the country showed that it had the patience to learn everything from scratch as a technology was painstakingly developed. This policy has paid rich dividends. We thus have not only a very good foundation but even an impressive superstructure in some of the fields in which the country has invested.

But times have changed. The economic reforms initiated in the early 1990s have, over the last 15 years, taken root. These reforms have been responsible for spectacular growth in many ways. From the point of view of a Bangalorean, IT and the software business come most immediately to mind. Growth in some of these areas cannot be attributed to direct government support or planning. They just prospered because of government's new economic policies. But as economic growth picks up pace in the country, time becomes a more important value than it was before. The need now is to make things faster and cheaper and hence to create wealth. So we should ask ourselves what set of policies we might now adopt that will do for the future what, 30–40 years ago, Sarabhai and Dhawan did for the present.

I would like to suggest that there are a couple of options that the country may be ready to examine. (I must emphasise at this point that I do not speak here as a member of the Space Commission.) First, in line with the changed economic thinking, we may ask ourselves whether a much more vigorous commercialisation of space is feasible and necessary. ISRO has done a commendable job of involving private industry in their programs. But should we do that in an even bigger way, so that the publicly supported space program can direct its manpower to taking a lead in things that private enterprise will not or cannot do? For example, by developing entirely new technologies, say reusable launch vehicles;

science and research such as the recent unmanned mission to the moon, Chandrayaan 1; or the proposed new satellites for astrophysical and atmospheric research (Astrosat and Megha-Tropiques, respectively).

The potential for the use of satellite technology in providing almost universal access to education is immense, but in spite of the recently launched Edusat, the potential is inadequately tapped in India. This is in fact strange from one point of view, because 40–50 per cent of the Indian population is still illiterate and, in many ways, satellite telecasts might provide an excellent medium for raising literacy levels, diffusing a variety of skills, and making the methods and the wisdom of the best teachers in the country available to huge numbers of people.

***

I should mention in particular satellites for weather and climate research. The space program has already taken several initiatives in atmospheric and oceanic sciences. The INSAT series has provided imageries of the Earth in both visible and infrared parts of the electromagnetic spectrum, and offered communication channels for transmission of meteorological data. The geostationary satellite Kalpana, launched by PSLV, was meant exclusively for meteorological applications. Two Oceansats provide much data on the ocean surface, including sea-surface temperature and winds.

A major step forward will be taken in 2010 with the atmospheric research satellite Megha-Tropiques. As the name indicates ('Megha' is cloud in Sanskrit and 'Tropiques' is the tropics in French), the satellite is a collaborative effort between India and France devoted to the study of tropical convective systems. The tropics are driven by solar radiation and moist convection, so the satellite focuses on water cycle and energy budget issues in the tropical atmosphere, and will provide data over the tropical belt of approximately 30°S–30°N. A unique feature of the satellite is its repetitivity: the same tropical site is visited four to six times a day over the heart of the tropics, enabling valuable data to be acquired over the whole diurnal cycle.

The mission objectives are:

1. to collect a long-term set of measurements with good sampling and coverage over tropical latitudes, and to understand better the processes related to tropical convective systems and their life cycle

2. to improve the determination of atmospheric energy and water budget in the tropics on various time and space scales

3. to make detailed studies of special events like cyclones, floods, droughts, etc.

4. to carry out analyses that can improve forecasting skill on the monsoons

5. to provide to forecasting centres/groups real-time data that can be assimilated into operational or research models to enhance their performance.

The objectives are sought to be achieved through four payloads:

- MADRAS (microwave analysis and detection of rain and atmospheric structures)
- SAPHIR (sounder for atmospheric profiling of humidity)
- SCARAB (scanner for radiation budget)
- GPS radio occultation sensor (ROS).

MADRAS will provide data on rain above the oceans, integrated water vapour, liquid water in clouds, ice in cloud tops, etc.; SCARAB will provide short- and long-wave radiative fluxes; SAPHIR will provide humidity profiles; and the GPS ROS will provide temperature and water vapour profiles.

Megha-Tropiques promises to provide unique data sets. It follows TRMM (Tropical Rainfall Measuring Mission), the joint US–Japan tropical radar satellite, whose current life is set to end in 2010, and may well turn out to be the harbinger of the international Global Precipitation Mission, which envisages a whole constellation of satellites launched by several international partners.

The Megha-Tropiques will be launched from Sriharikota on ISRO's PSLV, and signals India's entry into joint international projects on earth science related issues using the best available space technology. The tropics are a frontier area of meteorology. The three major countries in the global tropical belt are India (approx. 8°N–36°N), Australia (approx. 11°S–39°S over the mainland) and Brazil (approx. 5°N–32°S). Given both the scientific challenge and the extraordinary relevance of the tropics to its own inhabitants and the rest of the world, more major international projects in the field are bound to contribute to the wellbeing of the planet.

Nearly half the land area and nearly half the population of the world live in the tropics. The tropics receive two-thirds of total world rainfall; they also receive relatively more solar radiation, and export the surplus to higher latitudes keeping them warmer than they would otherwise have been. Interestingly, meteorological connections exist between India and Australia, as foreseen in the 1920s by Sir Gilbert Walker who, as head of the India Meteorological Department, reported the significant correlation between rainfall in India and pressure at Port Darwin and south-east Australia, for example (envisaging what is today called ENSO, or the El Niño-Southern Oscillation phenomenon). Shouldn't India and Australia be working more closely in atmosphere–ocean science?

Such initiatives should become more feasible as the space program tends towards greater self-sustainability. Thanks to the progress achieved by Indian space scientists and technologists, that now no longer seems difficult to accomplish. Globalisation should make international projects more attractive, provided geopolitical considerations do not intrude. There is an excellent chance that such international ventures can in fact lead to both faster and cheaper projects and services for both collaborating parties. *AWST* talked about ISRO's shoestring budget; a study carried out at the Madras School of Economics[3] shows in specific cases how cost-effective the Indian program is. So we may need a two-pronged policy. On the one hand it could be more oriented to commerce and wealth creation (of which Sarabhai the scientist-businessman would surely have approved). Conversely, it could emphasise the vigorous use of satellites in education and scientific research (helping to enhance the value of our human resources), including in particular the earth system (of which Dhawan the humane technologist would have approved). This would still be part of the developmental process that ISRO's founding fathers placed before us. Commerce, basic science, education, land, water and the earth system as a whole can form a sustainable complex of goals.

These goals, in part new and in part only a new version of the original vision, can be pursued with confidence, because of the sustained achievements of the Indian space program in the last 40 years.

* * *

---

3   U. Sankar (2007), *The Economics of India's Space Programme*, Oxford, New Delhi.

I would now like to consider computer technology, which has some interesting parallels with space but also some striking differences. In the 1980s, it started with the need felt in India for high performance computing systems on a variety of national projects. However, it was soon discovered that, because of the technology embargoes prevailing at the time, it was not possible to import any of the supercomputers of that era to India (the exception was a Cray machine that was acquired by the National Centre for Medium Range Weather Forecasting at Delhi for numerical weather prediction).

In the early 1980s, some scientists both in Europe and US had started experimenting with parallel computing (i.e. achieving higher computing speeds by using a large number of processors that would work in parallel). During the time that I was at NAL we began a parallel computing effort in a small way in 1986. To our (and everybody else's) pleasant surprise, my colleague at NAL, Dr U.N. Sinha, was able to put together, before the end of the year, a small parallel computer that was already faster than the large mainframe that NAL had been using at that time. The demonstration of the way that the Flosolver (as the NAL parallel computer was called) could solve, for example, the transonic small perturbation equations faster than the mainframe removed all scepticism on the possibility of using parallel computers for tackling problems in fluid dynamics. (By the way, that scepticism was shared at the time by many experts in the West as well, and so was not limited to Indian scientists.) Through the Scientific Advisory Committee to Prime Minister Rajiv Gandhi, a proposal was made to the government in 1986 for pursuing a major national initiative in parallel computing. As is well known, Mr Gandhi was a great advocate of computers in the country at the time, and I recall that the less than 10 minutes that had been allotted to me to make a presentation to the prime minister extended to 90 minutes — because of his extraordinary interest in the project. At the end, Mr Gandhi said that the question was not whether we should make parallel computers but how fast we could make them and at what cost. (He was also all for leapfrogging.) Very quickly thereafter several parallel computer projects were undertaken in the country. These had different philosophies, and it was decided that each of them was valid in its own way and should continue with further development. I must mention here that Mr K.R. Narayanan, as minister for Science and Technology at the time, was a great supporter of the Flosolver project, and he kept asking me years later (even after he had become president of the Republic) how the project was going. What started as a small effort to acquire some additional computing power has now gone through six generations (Mark 7 is now operational), and has led to new technology development and new architectures (some of them patented). All this has been done at low costs compared to international levels, and with huge and enthusiastic student participation.

But as these computers went from one generation to the next, the most important applications also slowly changed. Currently, modelling of the atmosphere and the oceans takes precedence over the other applications. Considerable commercial interest has been shown in the possibility of using these computers for financial modelling. A separate project, through a scheme called the National Millennium Initiative for Technology Leadership in India and conceived by the Council of Scientific and Industrial Research, has selected modelling monsoons as a targeted application. Forecasts are now being continuously made and sent to the India Meteorological Department for their use.

An interesting aspect of the parallel computing effort in India is that, over the years, four distinct groups emerged, including one at the Centre for Development of Advanced Computing at Pune whose machines, known as the Param series, have probably had the widest use in the country (some of them even exported). Nevertheless, none of these efforts can be called a strong commercial success. At the time that the projects were undertaken, commercialisation was not ignored, but it would be correct to say that non-vulnerability to technological embargoes was an even more important consideration. After all, the first objective of Mrs Gandhi's Technology Policy of 1983 was 'to attain technology competence and self-reliance to reduce vulnerability'. To that extent, the projects have been most successful. But, in spite of serious efforts, it has not been possible to get the involvement of private industry in the project, although it has often shown considerable interest. The question of forging stronger links between the laboratory and the marketplace is one of major interest and continuing importance in India even today.

A similar problem has also affected another computing initiative relating to what came to be known as the Simputer. The roots of this project can be traced to a meeting that was organised by the National Institute of Advanced Studies (NIAS) as part of the first Bangalore IT.COM show (as the series came be known later), held in 1998 with the support of the late Mr Sanjoy Dasgupta who conceived the idea. As part of the first event, NIAS organised an international seminar that considered the future of IT in developing countries. In keeping with the broad objectives of NIAS, which in particular emphasise the bringing together of people in science, technology, the humanities and a variety of other sectors including business, industry and the political leadership, we included in the NIAS team that organised this event both distinguished academic scientists like Professor Vijay Chandru of the Indian Institute of Science, industry experts like Mr Vinay Deshpande, sociologists like Professor M.N. Srinivas and others. In fact, a Bangalore Declaration was passed at the meeting and had the wide approval of both the developing and the developed countries whose representatives were present at the meeting.

That declaration highlighted a major concern at the time, which was what has been called the digital divide. In trying to see how the problem represented by the divide — that is, between those who have access to (for example) the internet and those who do not — the idea emerged that what India needed was a small handheld computer that could sell for a few thousand rupees (something less than $100). This led to the concept of the Simputer, which excited worldwide attention. The *New York Times* called it the most significant innovation in computing technology in 2003, *Time* magazine said it was 'one of ten technologies to know on the planet', and the MIT *Technology Review* rated it among the top 10 innovations of the year. Some examples of the Simputer were made, the product was officially released and something like a thousand test pieces were sold on a very special application — to the great satisfaction of its fastidious customer. Nevertheless, the Simputer did not become a commercial success.

In retrospect, it has become clear that it is not enough to have a brilliant idea; to convert idea into reality in the marketplace takes a variety of other resources, capabilities and skills that together constitute what may be called the innovation ecosystem. This ecosystem has technology and the technologists as one component, but includes financing, promotion, advertisement, large-scale applications, the ability to take risks and accept failures and, increasingly, a globalised business model. That ecosystem is not yet in place in India, especially for the technologist–entrepreneur. So, interestingly, at the time the Simputer was first made, it could not break into the market, for whatever reason; it now looks as if there may be a resurrection: it has acquired a second life as newer applications are making demands for which it appears a very appropriate solution.

But the Simputer is only one of the most well-known instances of a good idea that did not reach the market. There have been others that have had a similar experience. It is to be hoped that, as the country breeds more technologist–entrepreneurs, the rest of the ecosystem that is needed to convert such ideas into wealth will quickly emerge.

Meanwhile, a major commercial entry into the supercomputer market is represented by the computer Eka, which the Tata Computing Research Laboratories in Pune have designed and constructed. At the time that it was put into operation (in 2007), the Eka was the fourth most powerful computer in the world; it remains to this day the most powerful in Asia. It is being used for scientific research, technology development, weather prediction and a variety of other applications. It appears that this project works to a different business model. Here much of the system may carry imported components, but the basic concept, the financial risk involved in the project and the business model supporting it are all completely Indian. The fact that private industry in India is now willing to undertake such projects (either moving away from piggybacking to leapfrogging, or making a pragmatic mix of the two) marks a significant departure in the way that technology development can take place in India. The Eka appears more ambitious than the interesting developments in some other sectors, for example, pharmaceuticals. Nevertheless, the number of industries that are beginning to see the *economic* advantages of technology development within India is slowly on the rise. In support of this view we may also quote the recent example of what may be the world's cheapest car, namely the Nano. The interesting thing about both Eka and Nano is that they are primarily inspired by the needs of the Indian market, with the realisation that success achieved there may well take the product to other parts of the world.

***

All these projects — whether in space or in computer technology — depend critically on management of the skills and knowledge 'available in India for the taking', as Friedman put it, and the world is slowly discovering this 'untapped' resource. If India has recently emerged as a major exporter of automobiles and automobile parts, it is because of the discovery that India offers cheap *skills* (rather than cheap labour). Several years ago, *Business Week* and a whole host of multinational corporations (led by GE) discovered similarly that India was about the most cost-effective location in the world for doing high-level R&D (research and development). India's scientific output, measured by the number of publications in well-recognised scientific journals, remains about the most cost-effective source of high-quality scientific research in the world. (But the total scientific output itself, although growing, remains stagnant at about 2.5 per cent of the global output.)[4]

We need stronger policies that recognise the natural advantage that India has in its youthful human resources, and provide all the supporting institutions and mechanisms — from education to counselling to encouraging technological entrepreneurship and domain scholarship — that can convert this untapped talent (the economic equivalent of the untapped American continent of the 19th century) into wealth and national wellbeing.

I have in this lecture tried to trace the way that science and technology have evolved in India in two sectors in which I have some direct personal experience. (I could have added others, like the aircraft industry, where the situation is quite different from its space cousin, but the overall conclusions would not change.) After the economic reforms of 1991, the rate of growth of the Indian economy has risen and has typically been in the range of 6–8 per cent in recent years. Business leaders are tackling more challenging and competitive technology-driven products and systems. The examples I have described show that there is plenty of talent in India to take on the most challenging tasks in modern technology (and that talent is not confined to the metropolitan centres and the national institutes: it is spread across the country). Both the public and the private sector have demonstrated this, especially in the last five to 10 years. This augurs well for the future. At the same time, we have instances where brilliant ideas have not made it to the marketplace. It is my personal view that the ecosystem that can make this happen — all those advanced services that include venture capital, market survey, globalised manufacturing, being first to the marketplace and many others — are not yet in place; it needs to be a part of national endeavour to correct the situation as early as possible. Something similar is true in the field of basic science as well: in spite of the many new initiatives taken to promote it, we are still a relatively small force in global science, and that relentless pursuit of excellence that leads to game-changing ideas has not yet become part of the Indian academic environment.

---

4   Roddam Narasimha (2008), Science, Technology and the Economy: An Indian Perspective, *Technology in Society*, 30(3–4): 330–8.

But things are changing rapidly, and we may expect further initiatives in coming years that will enable India to create systems that can tap its great human resources more effectively.

Thank you, once again, for inviting me to deliver the 2009 K.R. Narayanan Oration.

Oration 14:
2010 K.R. Narayanan Oration

Message from the President
of the Republic of India

I am happy to learn that the Australia South Asia Research Centre (ASARC) is organising the 14th K.R. Narayanan Oration on the theme 'India's Prospects in the Post-Crisis World', at The Australian National University, Canberra on 29 November 2010.

The Indian economy has weathered the global financial crisis of 2008–09 quite well. At a time when several other economies of the world have slowed down, India continues to register high rates of growth. This year, it is poised to continue its high growth trajectory. There is growing interest in the Indian economy and its development model. I have no doubt that the oration will go a long way towards addressing this interest, focusing on the challenges and the opportunities shaping the Indian economy and its growth and development in the years to come.

I wish the oration all success.

Pratibha Patil
New Delhi
18 November 2010

India's Prospects in the Post-Crisis World

Montek Singh Ahluwalia

It is a privilege for me to deliver the K.R. Narayanan Oration this year. I had the pleasure of knowing President Narayanan before he became president of India, and have very warm memories of his kindness and gentleness of character, and also his deep insight into social problems. I first met him in 1985 when he joined the government as minister of state for Planning in the government of Prime Minister Rajiv Gandhi. I happened to be a civil servant in the prime minister's office at the time and I remember asking him how it felt to move from a distinguished career as a diplomat into the very different world of politics. With his characteristic self-deprecating humour, he said: 'Well, I am now supposed to do Planning, but honestly, I often feel more planned against than planning.' I wondered at the time whether he was referring to the stress of being a planner — which is considerable — or the stress of being a politician. I imagine he had in mind a bit of both.

Since the Planning Commission is about to start working on the approach to the Twelfth Five-Year Plan, which begins in 2012, I thought it would be appropriate to focus this lecture on India's prospects and the challenges it faces at this point.

Building on a Strong Base

First, for four years before the global economic crisis of 2008–09, the Indian economy averaged a growth rate of about 9 per cent per year, an impressive performance by any standards.

Second, the economy has shown great resilience to unprecedented external shocks. It was certainly affected by the global crisis when the growth rate dropped to about 6.7 per cent in 2008–09, but it recovered quite smartly thereafter to 7.4 per cent in 2009–10 and is likely to reach 8.5 per cent or even a little more in 2010–11. This is at a time when most of the industrial world has negative growth and even many emerging economies experienced sharp slowdown. There is a very good chance of getting back to 9 per cent growth in 2010–11.

Third, India's economic prospects are viewed very favourably by global investors and this is reflected in the fact that India has become one of the favoured destinations for foreign direct investment (FDI). Total foreign investment in India in 2001–02 was about $4 billion; by 2009–10, it had increased to $37 billion.

Finally, most observers expect growth over the medium and longer term to be somewhere between 8.5 and 9 per cent. If these growth rates are maintained for the next 25 years, the Indian economy would become the third-largest economy in the world by 2035, when China is expected to be number one, and the US number two at market exchange rates. I should emphasise that India would obviously not be the third richest country in per capita terms; it would still only be a middle-income country, but the total size of the economy and, therefore, the domestic market would make it a much more significant player than it is today.

This positive performance in recent years and expectations for the future has generated large positive dynamics. Economists are familiar with the notion of 'animal spirits' as a catch-all phrase describing investor sentiment. There is no doubt that the strong growth performance of recent years has boosted animal spirits. It has created a 'can-do' attitude among many Indians, including, but not only, those in business, and has created a new sense of confidence — particularly among our younger population — that the global game is not necessarily weighted against newcomers.

Not surprisingly, this has reinforced expectations about what is possible in the future. Prime Minister Dr Manmohan Singh has spoken of India growing between 9 and 10 per cent per year, and the Planning Commission have been tasked to see whether and how the economy can be put on a 10 per cent growth path in the Twelfth Plan.

I propose to use this lecture to share my thoughts on what it would take for India to achieve a transition to rapid and inclusive growth. I mention inclusiveness because we have repeatedly emphasised that growth is not the sole objective of policy; growth is essential, but it must also be inclusive in the sense that its benefits must be experienced by the mass of the people. I will deal explicitly with this aspect of India's performance, and what it implies for policy, a little later in the lecture.

Prospects for the Future

One reason for being optimistic about the future is that India has been experiencing a steady acceleration in growth and it is tempting to conclude that this will continue. The growth rate in the 1990s was about 5.7 per cent and this increased to 7.7 per cent in the decade following the 90s, which is just ending. If we could achieve a 2 percentage point increase in the average growth rate over the preceding decade in a period that included a global crisis of exceptional magnitude, it appears reasonable to argue that raising the growth rate by another 2 percentage points in the next decade should not be impossible.

This approach is obviously oversimplistic because past performance cannot be projected mechanically into the future. There are many examples of countries that have done very well for a while and suddenly slumped. The best known example is Brazil, which grew at an average rate of 9 per cent for 20 years in the 1960s and 1970s, and then collapsed to an average of 2 per cent growth for the 1980s and 1990s. It has done much better in the current decade but, even so, the average growth rate has been only a little over 3 per cent per year. The South-East Asian high performers have also found it difficult to get back to the high growth they experienced before 1997.

This raises the question: will India be able to avoid a similar loss of momentum? This question is best answered by analysing the factors that accounted for India's improved performance in the past and assessing whether these factors will continue to operate or even strengthen in the years ahead. We also need to consider whether rapid growth itself will produce structural changes that raise new challenges. If so, continued growth in the future, to say nothing of acceleration in this growth, will depend not just on continuing the policies that have worked in the past, but also on the ability to provide credible responses to the new challenges. I will explore each of these questions in the course of the lecture.

The question of whether India will be able to accelerate beyond the 7.7 per cent growth rate achieved in the decade that is just ending is best answered by considering the determinants of growth, first on the supply-side and then on the demand-side.

Determinants of Growth on the Supply-Side

On the supply-side, the traditional growth accounting framework explains growth of GDP in terms of growth of primary inputs — that is, growth of capital and growth of labour (adjusted for labour quality), and, of course, total factor productivity. Let us look at each of these in turn.

The growth of capital inputs in an economy depends on investment and that in turn depends on the investment climate and the availability of savings, domestic and foreign. Consider the investment climate first: one can envisage a situation in which resources are available to finance investment but, for some reason, the entrepreneurial class does not actually believe that any of the available investment opportunities are worthwhile. In the absence of 'animal spirits' we will not get an increase in capital inputs. This is not likely to be a problem in India. India benefits from the existence of a vibrant entrepreneurial class, which has demonstrated its ability to expand investment, especially, corporate investment. It sees enormous opportunities ahead and is willing to undertake investment. It is, therefore, reasonable to assume that investment will take place provided financing is available. The government also recognises that future growth will be private sector–led and is committed to creating an environment that is pro-investment.

Viewed from this perspective, the prospects for investment over the next decade appear very favourable. Investment rates have been rising and, as a result, the investment rate today is already significantly higher than the average investment rate of the previous 10 years. If we can assume some further increase in the rate of investment in the years ahead, one can conclude that India's average investment rate in the next 10 years would be significantly higher than the average investment rate in the previous 10 years. The scope for such an increase depends largely on what happens to domestic savings and foreign resource flows and the prospects on both fronts are positive.

At the start of the decade of the 1990s the domestic saving rate in India was 23.7 per cent. The impact of economic reforms, rapid growth and rising per capita incomes, and probably also the demographic transition, led to a sharp increase in the savings rate to 36.4 per cent in 2007–08. This came down subsequently because of the crisis, but I expect that when the figures for the current year (2010–11) become available, it will have gone up again. The average savings rate in the decade just ending will probably be around 31 per cent but we will probably end the decade with a savings rate of around 35 per cent. This could easily go up by another 2 or 3 percentage points over the next 10 years, taking the savings rate at the end of the next decade to something of the order of 37–38 per cent. The average savings rate during the next decade, therefore, could be around 36 per cent or even a little higher. Higher domestic savings could, therefore, finance an investment rate that is about 5 percentage points of GDP higher than the average in the previous decade.

This domestic savings performance obviously should not be taken for granted. It depends critically upon the achievement of rapid growth, with a concomitant growth in corporate savings similar to the trend witnessed in the decade just ending. That outcome in turn depends on maintaining a macroeconomic environment that encourages domestic savings. A moderate rate of inflation is critical in this context as is a well-functioning financial system capable of channelling savings towards the right kinds of investments. Much also depends upon the fiscal position of the government, which should ideally be bolstered by some reduction in government dis-savings, which increased in recent years.

The projected availability of domestic savings can be supplemented by additional foreign capital flows. In the previous 10 years, the average current account deficit was about 1 per cent of GDP. Over the next 10 years, since the Indian economy is now much more open and global investors are taking an interest in investing in India, we could see a current account deficit rising to between 2.5 and 3 per cent of GDP. This implies an additional flow of savings for investment of 1.5–2 percentage points.

A current account deficit of 3 per cent of GDP is more than what has traditionally been thought to be a prudent level in India, which is closer to 2 per cent. However, it is not unreasonable to plan on a higher figure considering the fundamental change that has taken place in the global economy. With the industrialised world likely to grow more slowly, and with growth prospects in emerging market countries such as India being much higher, it is logical to expect that more investible resources would move from the slower growing economies to the faster growing emerging market economies. In that process, the flow of foreign resources to India could increase significantly, provided India's policies are perceived to be investor friendly by foreign investors. I have already mentioned that India has, in recent years, been viewed as a preferred FDI destination. The government of India has every intention of ensuring that it continues to be so. For the rest, whatever creates an investor-friendly environment for domestic investors will also attract foreign investors.

The combined effect of higher domestic savings and higher capital inflows could, therefore, increase the rate of investment by 6.5–7 per cent of GDP in the next decade over the level achieved in the decade just ending. An increase of this order would certainly contribute substantially to achieving a higher rate of growth of GDP.

Turning to the other key primary input — labour — India is favourably placed in one respect because of the demographic transition. The working-age population in India will be increasing over the next 30 years, whereas in all the industrialised countries, and also in China, it will be going down. However, I should point out that a growing workforce is not by itself an advantage. It is an advantage only if it occurs in an environment in which sufficient investment is taking place to absorb labour productively, and if the education and skill level of the workforce is consistent with employability. I have already argued that the prospects for higher levels of investment are good. As for the quality of the labour force, this calls for a major effort in education and skill development and, as it happens, these are among the major objectives of the government at present.

The government has recognised that India needs an across the board expansion and upgradation of quality in the educational system, including higher and technical education. We also need much faster expansion in a wide range of middle-level skills, which, in turn, calls for strengthening and modernising the skill-development system. Skill development has been neglected in the past but is now receiving concerted attention. The Twelfth Five-Year Plan will pay special attention to the need to expand the system of higher education and skill development and also to upgrade the quality.

Let me now turn to the third determinant of growth, that is, total factor productivity. Economists know that total factor productivity is as important in determining the rate of growth of an economy as the growth of primary inputs such as capital and labour. These primary inputs are extremely important. One almost certainly cannot have high growth without rapid growth in both capital and labour inputs. However, it is also true that one can have a lot of growth in capital and labour inputs without getting much of total growth, if the factor productivity side is not looked after. This is what happened in the 1960s and 1970s. Our overall growth rate was low, and a large part of the explanation lay in low or even negative productivity growth. Investment was taking place, but we were not getting growth because of poor performance in productivity. This, in turn, can be attributed to the economic inefficiency associated with the pre-reform economic system.

The economic reforms were designed to unleash productivity in the system by injecting much greater competition, both domestically and from abroad, and giving domestic entrepreneurship the freedom and flexibility it needed to invest and expand in search of profitable opportunities. Recent research has shown that the reforms did have the effect expected and total factor productivity became significantly positive in the post reforms period. This raises the question: will the pace of total factor productivity growth witnessed in the post-reform period continue and perhaps even accelerate? In tune, this question is usually transformed into the question: will the economic reforms continue and at what pace?

The Agenda for Reforms

It is well recognised in India that economic reforms are still a work in progress and much remains to be done. There is a substantial agenda of unfinished reforms, many of which are simply a logical extension of the reforms already undertaken. Their completion would improve the investment climate and add to productivity growth in the years ahead. Let me list some of the areas where reforms are in the pipeline.

India has already made a substantial transition from a fairly closed economy with high levels of protection before 1990 to a much more open economy, with much lower protective levels and a market-determined exchange rate. It is a major achievement that this transition has been achieved with none of the economic disruption often feared when economies open up. However, it is often pointed out that India still has somewhat higher tariff walls than other emerging market economies and more needs to be done to open up on the trade front. The comparison with other countries is not entirely fair. India's customs duties, which (with some exceptions) are now subject to a peak rate of 10 per cent are actually less protective than they seem as there is no countervailing duty to offset the sales tax levied by the state governments. If an amount equivalent to sales tax is netted out of the current customs duty to arrive at the actual 'protective duty', it would be much lower. Once the goods and services tax is in place, it will be possible to apply it to all imports, at which stage customs duties could be lowered by around 5 percentage points.

More importantly, the government has clearly signalled further movement towards reducing trade barriers as part of the Look East Policy, which is explicitly aimed at integrating the Indian economy more fully into the East Asian region. In pursuit of this policy, India has entered into a number of free trade agreements with countries in East Asia. They are not always called free trade agreements, being referred to as 'comprehensive economic cooperation agreements', but they amount to the same thing. Such agreements have been signed with Singapore, Malaysia, Thailand and one with ASEAN (Association of South-East Asian Nations) as a group. An agreement has been signed with Korea and negotiations with Japan have been completed and the agreement is expected to be signed in 2011. These agreements will ensure a steady decline in applied tariffs over the next five to seven years.

FDI has been extensively liberalised with most areas open to FDI up to 100 per cent. However, there are several areas where limitations on foreign ownership remain and where liberalisation is being considered. Insurance is one such area, with foreign investment currently limited to 26 per cent. The government has introduced legislation to raise this limit to 49 per cent, though the legislative process has yet to be completed. Investment in multi-brand department stores is another where FDI is currently not permitted at all. The Ministry of Industry has stated that this policy is currently under consideration for a possible relaxation.

Mining is another area, and one of keen interest to Australian business, in which changes in the law are being considered. A new law governing the mining sector is under consideration that aims at establishing a more transparent regime for assigning mining leases, with a fairer system of compensation for those displaced.

The development of infrastructure, particularly power, roads, ports, airports, telecommunications and railways, is an important part of the ongoing reform agenda in which progress is being made but there is need for further acceleration. These sectors are widely regarded as constraining India's industrial competitiveness and, therefore, its ability to accelerate growth. The Government of India recognises the enormous importance of infrastructure development in India and the government has a big role to play in promoting investment in infrastructure. However, although large investments in infrastructure are necessary, the task cannot be performed by the public sector alone. Public sector resources are scarce and have to be directed into other priority areas like education and health. The government has, therefore, outlined a mixed strategy of developing infrastructure through a combination of public investment and public–private partnership. Public investment in infrastructure will remain important but will be directed to areas in which the private sector is unlikely to come. The public sector effort needs to be supplemented by private investment wherever possible. The government has, therefore, launched a very major effort to attract private investment in all these areas.

Investment in infrastructure was estimated to be about 5 per cent of GDP in the base year of the Eleventh Plan (i.e. 2006–07). We had expected to raise this percentage to around 9 in the last year of the Eleventh Plan (i.e. 2011–12). The actual achievement is likely to be around 8 per cent. To maintain the momentum in infrastructure development, we estimate that the investment in infrastructure would need to increase further to say 10 per cent by the end of the Twelfth Plan (i.e. 2017–18). This implies that investment in infrastructure will increase from $500 billion in the five years of the Eleventh Plan period (i.e. 2007–08 to 2011–12) to about $1 trillion in the Twelfth Plan period (i.e. 2012–13 to 2017–18). What is more, whereas about 30 per cent of the investment in the Eleventh Plan period was projected to come from the private sector, the private sector share in the Twelfth Plan will have to increase to about 50 per cent.

The challenge for the government is to design a policy framework that will attract private investment on the scale required. The policy has evoked a positive response thus far and substantial investments have been made by the private sector in all these infrastructure sectors. However, the level of involvement will have to be increased substantially to achieve the higher levels of investment that will be necessary in the years ahead.

While private investment in infrastructure needs to be encouraged, it is also necessary to ensure a high degree of transparency in the terms on which private investment is invited into infrastructure in order to protect the interest of the consumers of the service and to prevent the emergence of crony capitalists. Since infrastructure sectors are typically regulated, and in some cases amount to giving the concessionaire a limited monopoly, there are a number of difficult questions that need to be addressed. Private investors need the assurance of an adequate return and, in many cases (e.g. road transportation), the revenue that can be earned from the project may not suffice to service the total capital cost. In such cases, the government has to provide a capital subsidy, but the subsidy must be provided in a transparent manner based on competitive bidding. Competition takes different forms in different sectors. In the roads sector, concessionaires are selected based on competitive bidding for the lump sum capital subsidy they would need to undertake the project. In the case of airports and ports, competitive bidding is done on the basis of revenue share. Managing the award of concessions in a manner that ensures transparency and is perceived to be fair is crucial, as any slippage in this process runs the risk of appearing to promote cronyism.

A long pending element of the unfinished reform agenda relates to labour market reform. Economists have repeatedly emphasised that the rigidity of labour laws in the organised sector, including especially the fact that retrenchment of labour needs government permission, which is typically not given, is a factor that discourages the growth of employment intensive industries in India. Many have argued that this makes it more difficult to absorb surplus labour into productive industrial employment and is, therefore, actually anti-employment and anti-inclusion. However, this is a politically sensitive area in which reforms face strong opposition from labour unions. The government has taken the view that labour reform is necessary, but we must work to develop a consensus with representatives of labour.

Economic reforms aimed at achieving microeconomic efficiency and at rationalising some sector-level policies have to be underpinned by a sound macro-economic environment characterised by fiscal sustainability and a well-functioning financial sector. India has had high levels of fiscal deficits in the past, with the combined deficit of the centre and state governments reaching 9.5 per cent of GDP in 2001–02. This was progressively brought down to just over 5 per cent in 2007–08 just before the global crisis. However, it expanded again to 9.6 per cent in 2009–10 because of a conscious policy of fiscal stimulus.

With recovery from the crisis now well established, the government has again outlined a path of fiscal correction that will reduce the fiscal deficit of the Central Government from 5.5 per cent of GDP in 2010–11 to 3.5 per cent by 2013–14. Allowing for a fiscal deficit of about 2 per cent for the states, the combined fiscal deficit of the centre and the states would be around 5.5 per cent in 2013–14. This order of deficit is high by international standards but it represents a substantial improvement from the current situation and is consistent with a steady reduction in the debt to GDP ratio given the high growth potential of the economy.

An important part of the fiscal reforms expected in the years ahead is the integration of domestic indirect taxes, which are at present imposed by the central and state governments separately on different tax bases, into a unified 'goods and services tax'. This will have separate central and state components but will be applied on a common base, with a provision to net out taxes at the input stage for the central and state component, respectively. This is an extremely important domestic reform initiative, which will contribute hugely to economic efficiency and also to revenue collection. However, it requires an amendment of the constitution and this calls for delicate political negotiation with the states. We had hoped that this process might have been concluded in 2010 so that the GST could be implemented with effect from 1 April 2011. It now looks as if it will take a little longer, but I am very hopeful that this reform will be implemented.

I could go on and list a number of other reform initiatives in the pipeline but the reforms mentioned indicate that we do have a well-defined agenda. Understandably, this leads observers to ask what is the time frame in which these reforms will be completed. I confess that it is difficult to set time lines in our system because of the nature of our democratic process. I have no doubt that the demonstrably favourable effect that the reforms have had on growth has created a broad constituency in support of the reforms, and we will see progress in this direction. However, progress is likely to be gradualist as it has been in the past.

The gradualism of Indian reforms has been much commented upon and a brief digression on this subject is perhaps appropriate. This gradualism has often led to impatience on the part of many observers and I confess I have often shared this feeling of impatience myself. However, it is important to recognise that gradualism is perhaps an inevitable consequence of the compulsions of the democratic process in a very large and heterogeneous country. The heterogeneity of the country has produced electoral outcomes that have produced coalition governments at the national level in the past 15 years. This environment does not lend itself to quick decision-making and rapid implementation. It puts a premium on consultation and consensus building, which often takes time. It is at times opportunistic. Reforms that are in the pipeline get done when it is felt that a sufficient consensus has been built. This inevitably makes reforms appear piecemeal rather than a coordinated advance on all fronts in an orderly sequence. This approach undoubtedly has costs.

The good news, however, is that though the pace of reforms has been slow, it has been steady and irreversible. We have now seen many changes of government, both at the centre and in the states. As governments have changed, parties that were earlier in opposition, and were strongly opposed to the economic program of the previous ruling party, have had the wisdom when they came to power not to change the broad direction of economic reforms.

A particularly encouraging feature of Indian elections in recent years is that governments that have a good record of economic performance can get re-elected on the basis of their performance. Ten years ago, the conventional wisdom was that the Indian electorate had a strong anti-incumbency bias, which meant elections typically led to incumbents being thrown out irrespective of performance. That is not what has happened in the last 10 years. Governments that have been seen to deliver have been re-elected, both at the centre and also in the states.

All of this suggests that the reforms we have seen will continue as governments at the centre and the states give greater priority to the development agenda. The pace of reforms will remain gradualist, but it will be steady. The favourable effect of reforms in generating higher productivity growth and, therefore, higher rates of growth of GDP can be expected to continue.

Demand-Side Constraints

The supply-side approach discussed above needs to be supplemented by analysis on the demand-side to establish that India will be able to generate a pattern of demand that can support higher growth. The most important demand-side constraint arises from the fact that the post-crisis world will be different from the world prior to the crisis. Growth in industrialised countries will be lower and the pace at which exports can increase to the US or Europe will be lower. This raises the question: if export prospects are likely to be weaker, how we can project more rapid growth for India? The answer is that we can do this if we can replace lost export demand with higher levels of investment demand, especially investment in infrastructure. India suffers from a significant deficiency in infrastructure and making up this deficiency will not only improve our competitiveness on the supply-side, but also will attract private investment.

The strategy of replacing export demand with investment demand implies that imports will increase and, with exports expected to be subdued, this in turn implies that the current account deficit in the balance of payments will widen. This, as I have mentioned, is actually happening. Three years ago we had near balance on the current account. Today, the current account deficit is expected to be around 3 per cent of GDP. The viability of this strategy depends critically upon our ability to finance a current account deficit of this order. As I have mentioned earlier in this lecture, we are in a situation where we can reasonably expect to finance a deficit of this order through long-term capital flows, including through FDI. India has only recently begun to attract global capital and, as such, it is 'under invested' compared with other Asian countries, given the size of its economy and its growth potential.

I conclude from this that whether we look at the supply-side or the demand-side, India is well positioned to experience a further acceleration in growth based on the continued pursuit of economic policies that have already yielded ample dividends.

New Challenges

Let me now turn to some of the challenges thrown up by rapid growth and the structural changes it produces. We have just begun the process of identifying these challenges for the Twelfth Plan so my list is necessarily preliminary, but, subject to that caveat, I would list the following: i) achieving inclusiveness; ii) dealing with problems arising from imperfect and non-transparent markets that encourage market manipulation, corruption and cronyism; iii) managing the energy demands of rapid growth; iv) management of water resources; and v) meeting the challenge of urbanisation. Some of these challenges are not new but they will each be exacerbated by rapid growth. Each of them is formidable and calls for major policy initiatives. Because of the limited time available, I can only comment briefly on each of these.

The Search for Inclusiveness

The need to ensure inclusiveness is a major and continuing challenge. When the reforms were first introduced, critics charged that the new economic policies would damage growth and also hurt the poor. No-one today doubts that the reforms have accelerated growth, but there is concern that the growth unleashed by the reforms has not been inclusive enough.

The concern for greater inclusiveness surfaces in many different forms and all of them are relevant. In one variant, attention is focused on whether those at the bottom of the income ladder benefit sufficiently from growth. This leads to efforts to enhance incomes of the poor through various poverty alleviation programs. However, low incomes are only one part of the problem. Many families, whose incomes are above the poverty line, lack access to such basic services as education, health, drinking water and sanitation, and, where they have access, the quality of the service is unacceptable. Providing such access is also an important part of any strategy of inclusiveness.

Inclusiveness, however, is not only about ensuring a defined minimum level of income and access to basic services. There are traditional concerns about inequality getting worse, or at any rate not getting better. There are also concerns about inequality across states and, in some cases, across regions within states. In the Indian context, inclusiveness also requires steps to overcome the exclusion experienced by social groups such as the Scheduled Castes and Scheduled Tribes, which have suffered historically from discrimination. These groups typically occupy the lower ranges of the income distribution and, as such, any strategy of poverty alleviation or even inequality reduction would definitely benefit them. But if inclusiveness is to aim at correcting for historical discrimination, and bring these groups on par with the rest of the population, it has to go beyond mere poverty alleviation and reduction in inequality to address the larger issue of achieving equal proportional representation for these groups along the entire income distribution. Defined in this way, 'group equality' is not necessarily linked to reduction in overall poverty or reduction in general equality; it can in principle be achieved leaving the incidence of poverty and the level of inequality unchanged.

Each of these distributional concerns is related to each other but is also quite distinct. It is perfectly possible for poverty to decline while inequality increases. Equally, inequality in the country as a whole may decrease or remain unchanged while inequality across states increases. Similarly, the economic conditions of the Scheduled Castes and Scheduled Tribes may improve but, if it leaves the gap between them and the others unchanged, it does not achieve social inclusiveness. Ideally, one would like to be able to claim an improvement in each of these multiple dimensions of inclusiveness, but that is not easy. This illustrates why it is so difficult to make an assessment about the inclusiveness of India's growth process thus far. However, I think an apt summary would be as follows:

1. Available data firmly establish that the percentage of the population below a fixed poverty line, defined in terms of real consumption per head, has been falling. This means real income and consumption have increased even at the lower levels. The view sometimes expressed that 'the rich have become richer and the poor have become poorer' is, therefore, simply not borne out by the facts. However, the pace of reduction in poverty is much slower than one would have expected. The percentage of the population below the poverty line has been falling at about 0.8 percentage points per year. The latest Planning Commission estimate of poverty, based on the revised rural poverty line recommended by the Tendulkar Committee, indicates that 37 per cent of the population was below the poverty line. If this percentage declines at 0.8 percentage points per year, it would take 25 years to reduce poverty by 20 percentage points! This is clearly unacceptable and it should be the objective of policy to ensure that future growth must be made more inclusive.

2. There is evidence that overall inequality in consumption has increased but the increase is not alarming. The Gini coefficient of consumption has increased only marginally between 1999 and 2000 and 2004 and 2005 to 0.25 for rural areas and 0.35 for urban areas. These measures

of inequality are fairly low. The ratio of urban to rural consumption has remained more or less constant, suggesting no change in rural–urban inequality.

3. Inequality across states has increased in recent years, but it is not true that the poorer states have become poorer or experienced stagnation. In fact, some of the richest states (e.g. Punjab) have been growing more slowly than average while some of the poorest states (e.g. Rajasthan, Bihar and Orissa) have shown an acceleration in growth. More rapid growth has been experienced in states that were in the middle range (e.g. Andhra Pradesh, Tamil Nadu and Gujarat).

4. The size of the population that still does not have access to basic services (e.g. education and health) is larger than the percentage of the population below the poverty line. For example, whereas the latest estimates of poverty show 37 per cent of the population below the poverty line in 2004–05, in 2007–08, 43 per cent of children dropped out of primary school by the age of 11, 47 per cent of women gave birth unsafely (i.e. without at least a skilled birth attendant), 47 per cent of children did not get full immunisation and 55 per cent of the population did not have toilets. It is important to note that all these indicators show improvement over time, suggesting that access to basic services is improving, but the extent of deprivation remains too high and, if the objective is, as it should be, to achieve universal coverage in these very basic facilities, we clearly have a long way to go.

5. As far as narrowing the gap between the Scheduled Castes and Scheduled Tribes and the others is concerned, there is no doubt that a narrowing is taking place, but the gap remains substantial in absolute terms. Accelerated progress in this area must be a major objective government policy and programs.

6. Equality of access to education is perhaps the most important factor for ensuring equality of opportunity, which is an important aspect of inclusiveness. The evidence here is mixed. On the one hand, enrolment in primary schools has increased significantly, being now almost universal, and is also now legally guaranteed by the *Right to Education Act*. However, dropout rates by the end of the primary level are 43 per cent. Besides, expanding access does not automatically ensure a narrowing in the quality of education across income classes, which is essential for improving opportunity. The quality of education in rural

areas suffers because of the difficulty in recruiting qualified teachers and, equally important, the difficulty in enforcing accountability among teachers once recruited.

7. Finally, perceptions about the extent of inclusiveness are affected by the perception of concentration of income and wealth at the upper end. The fact that India is reported to have the third-highest number of billionaires after the US and Russia is often quoted in the press, though the authenticity of the claim is doubtful given the unreliability of information on private wealth in many countries. However, it definitely feeds the perception that the gains of economic reforms have accrued disproportionately to a few.

Part of the problem is that public perceptions of inclusiveness are often determined as much by media projection as by a cold analysis of facts. An active media, including especially the electronic media that now has very wide reach, has tended to heighten the perception of disparity by dramatising both success at the top end and poverty at the other end, both of which are viewed as newsworthy. Unfortunately, the massive and perceptible improvement in living standards in the middle, and the associated rise of a substantial middle class, which is an important social phenomenon with many potentially positive spin-offs for development, is not viewed as newsworthy.

Taking all these factors into account, India's record on inclusion can, therefore, be described as mixed. The positive side is that there is significant improvement in many areas, but it is also true that achievements fall short of expectations. The shortfall is all the more disappointing because of the visible success on the growth front. Can India address the challenge of achieving greater inclusion in all these multiple dimensions? I have no doubt that it can, but to do so calls for conscious shaping of the growth strategy to achieve better outcomes.

Greater attention to growth in agriculture has to be an important part of the solution since around 50 per cent of the population draws the bulk of its income from agriculture and there is considerable evidence that growth in the agricultural sector has a greater impact on poverty than growth elsewhere. Growth of agricultural GDP was 3.6 per cent per year between 1980 and 1996 but it slumped to 2 per cent from 1997 to 2003. The government had set a target of bringing it up to 4 per cent in the Eleventh Plan. Early indications are that there is a turnaround in agricultural performance and agricultural growth may come up to

3.5 per cent in the Eleventh Plan. This will be better than in the Tenth Plan, but shall still fall short of the target. This is an area where we need to do more.

The key to achieving better agricultural performance lies in closing the gap between potential productivity per hectare and actual productivity. Estimates suggest that productivity for many crops can be increased by 80 to 120 per cent, provided technical and other inputs can be made available. Water is a key input, and better systems of water management and water application are critical. Most agricultural growth in the years ahead will come not from food grains but from horticulture, dairying and fisheries sectors in which the product is perishable and requires greater attention to post-harvest conditions including refrigerated transport to urban markets, food processing and exports. Development of these marketing linkages should be an important element of the strategy. Establishing better road connectivity in rural areas can play a major role in promoting agricultural production by improving linkages to markets.

Faster growth in agriculture must be combined with a much faster shift of labour from the agriculture to the non-agriculture sectors. Growth of high-quality, non-agricultural employment will contribute greatly to inclusiveness; therefore, policies for promoting growth of small and medium enterprises, including enterprises in rural and semi-rural areas, are especially important. Absorption of labour in non-agricultural employment would be greatly facilitated by education and skill-development policies aimed at improving the employability of the labour force. Labour market reform is also important in this context, though, as I have mentioned, it is a politically sensitive area in which progress thus far has been limited.

Market Manipulation and Crony Capitalism

Greater reliance upon market forces is a key component of the reforms and has yielded tangible benefits in terms of higher growth. However, it has also posed a new set of problems wherever markets are imperfectly regulated or non-transparent, thereby providing opportunities for manipulation, corruption and crony capitalism. These problems are by no means unique to India. Indeed, we have seen a string of corporate scandals in the industrialised world ranging from Enron, Worldcom, Parmalat and Madhoff etc., and a great deal of regulatory manipulation in the run-up to the financial crisis. Perhaps because of these developments, sensitivity to corporate wrongdoing has been heightened, and there is certainly a perception that the scale of such activity has increased in India. These developments need to be countered by appropriate policy initiatives if the reforms are not to be brought into disrepute.

Raghuram Rajan, in the Indian edition of his recent book *Faultlines*, draws special attention to two areas. One is the market for land that remains subject to extensive and highly discretionary control by state governments. These controls limit land development in cities as a result of which land values in the major cities are hugely inflated and there are large rents to be enjoyed by those who can obtain the relevant permissions to develop land. Since the grant of permission is discretionary and non-transparent, this inevitably leads to suspicion of corruption and cronyism. These areas of discretionary policy need to be reviewed and more transparent mechanisms put in place. Acquisition of agricultural land for industrial development, or for creating industrial parks, also presents a problem because the *Land Acquisition Act* is hopelessly outdated and provides for very inadequate levels of compensation, often below true market prices. Modernisation of this piece of legislation is urgently needed and this is currently under consideration.

The second area that deserves special attention relates to those sectors that have been opened up for private sector activity, but are subject to various types of discretionary controls and regulation. Telecommunications and mining are two such sectors in which allegations of corruption and cronyism surface frequently. The government is currently engaged in a major investigation of some decisions in the telecommunications sector.

The importance of taking corrective steps to minimise market manipulation and cronyism cannot be doubted. An environment that encourages cronyism will crowd out genuine entrepreneurship and this can only weaken growth potential. It also greatly undermines the social legitimacy of a private sector–led growth process. Wealth accumulated through genuine entrepreneurship that succeeds in creating in a competitive environment evokes much less resentment than wealth accumulated through cronyism and market manipulation.

Managing the Energy Challenge

Managing the energy requirements of rapid growth will be a major challenge for India in the years ahead as the global supply of conventional energy sources is almost certain to become much tighter. We will need to evolve a growth strategy that is much more energy efficient, thus reducing the energy intensity of GDP. We will also need to take steps to increase the domestic supply of energy from all sources, conventional and non-conventional.

Reducing the energy intensity of GDP calls for action on three fronts. First, we must align domestic energy prices to world prices. With energy prices below world prices as at present, it is difficult to believe that the full scope for energy efficiency can be achieved. Second, we must have a proactive policy of pushing energy efficiency through non-price mechanisms such as regulation and standard setting for appliances, equipment and buildings. Third, we need to bring about inter-sectoral shifts that economise on energy such as the shift from road to rail and from private to public transport in urban areas. The government is acting on all these fronts, but much more needs to be done.

As far as energy pricing is concerned, the government has adopted a general policy that energy prices must be aligned with world prices but this policy has not yet been fully implemented on the ground. Prices of petrol (gasoline) have been decontrolled. Prices of diesel are also proposed to be decontrolled, but this has yet to be implemented; it is expected that it will be done in phases. LPG (liquefied petroleum gas) and kerosene prices remain under control and are currently well below the normal level. The original rationale for keeping these prices under control was that increasing them would hurt lower income groups. However, the subsidy implicit in low prices is completely untargeted and a shift to a targeted subsidy is necessary. Coal prices have been decontrolled, but the nationalised coal companies have maintained domestic prices about 30 per cent below world prices at levels that are after allowing for coal quality. Prices of electricity are set by supposedly independent state regulators, but there is great resistance to selling prices at economic levels that will cover costs.

On the supply-side, we are doing what we can to expand domestic availability of petroleum and gas and also coal. Both petroleum and natural gas are open to investment by the private sector, including foreign investment. The coal industry is nationalised but private sector investment is allowed in captive coal mines (i.e. coal mines linked to power plants or steel and cement plants). This exception is an important window of flexibility and has led to sufficient investment in captive coal mines. The case for moving away from nationalisation and allowing private investment in non-captive mining is strong, though there are political sensitivities here. Expanding coal production in the future is also affected by the fact that much of India's coal reserves lie in forested areas where there are environmental limits on mining. Efforts are being made to reconcile these conflicting objectives in a rational manner. India is actively following a policy of investing in coal and oil assets abroad.

India has good prospects over the longer term for exploiting nuclear power. The recent agreement with the Nuclear Suppliers Group enables India to expand the program of setting up conventional first-generation reactors based on imported uranium. The spent fuel can be reprocessed and the reprocessed fuel and the plutonium generated in the process can be used in second-stage, fast-breeder reactors. This strategy will enable India to build up a stock of safeguarded plutonium to be used in the third-stage, thorium-based reactors, on which research is underway in the hope that commercial production will be feasible in the future. India has the world's largest supply of thorium and, if the technology for thorium-based reactors is commercially proven as expected, India could aim at having as much as 500,000 MW of nuclear generation capacity by 2050.

Along with efforts at expanding nuclear power, India is also engaged in developing solar-based generation using both photovoltaic (PV) and thermal solar technology. A program has been initiated to install 20,000 MW of solar power by 2020, consisting of equal amounts of PV and thermal capacity.

Since both nuclear power and solar power are more expensive than conventional thermal generation, the development of supplies from these sources will only produce energy at higher cost. Costs can be expected to come down as technology develops further, but in the next decade at least there is no doubt that energy costs will rise. There is an obvious need to absorb these costs through higher energy prices and this poses a challenge to policymakers. It is always difficult to raise prices, but unless this is done, energy supplies will not be financially viable and the incentives to reduce energy intensity of GDP will be weakened.

Managing Water Resources

The challenge of managing scarce water resources is, in some ways, even more daunting than the challenge posed by energy. This is because, unlike energy, we don't really have 'non-conventional' sources of water. India's available fresh water is the same as it was 5,000 years ago, and the population has grown and so has GDP. On some calculations, the per capita availability of usable fresh water in India is now close to the level normally associated with water stress. In many parts of the country, there is clear evidence of excessive withdrawal of groundwater, leading to a steady lowering of the water table.

Most studies indicate demand for water rapidly outstripping supply as GDP expands and with it the demand for water. There is room for expanding water supply by building storage dams, investing in improved groundwater recharge and also treating wastewater for re-use. However, a large part of the solution lies on the demand-side in improving efficiency of water use.

The good news is that water is very inefficiently used at present and there is considerable scope for saving water by increasing efficiency. About 80 per cent of India's water use is for agriculture and it is technically feasible, with better agricultural practices, to reduce water use in agriculture by 50 per cent. However, this is possible only by adopting more modern agricultural practices. Persuading millions of small farmers used to time-tested traditional methods is very difficult, requiring not only a great deal of effort to disseminate new technology but also extra resources. This transformation will have to be built into the development strategy for agriculture. It will also have to be supported by agricultural research directed towards evolving crops capable of dealing with water stress.

An important reason why the water crisis is more difficult than the energy crisis is because most people recognise that energy has to be paid for, whereas the pricing of water poses many problems. The National Water Policy states that water is scarce and we must conserve every drop, but as long as we are not able to price water to reflect its scarcity, it is difficult to incentivise economic use. Farmers, in particular, have long been used to regimes in which water is severely underpriced, even though the system does not actually assure them of the water they need in a predictable manner. Further, if left unchanged, it will definitely deliver less and less. There is an overwhelming need to adjust water prices both to encourage economic use and to ensure effective maintenance of irrigation systems, but this is politically difficult. The alternative is to put in a system that will equitably ration water for different uses so that available water can be distributed to different uses and variations in supply can be met by fair adjustment of allocations for different uses. In practice, we have to use both prices and better regulation.

Rational use of water calls for basin-specific strategies based on a scientific assessment of how available water resources in each basin can be allocated to different uses. It will be necessary to set up statutory water regulators to determine water allocation for different uses, such as household needs, agriculture and industrial use, with some method of varying entitlements for different uses in the event of variation in supply. A start has been made in some states (e.g. Maharashtra) but we have a long way to go.

I am told that we could learn from Australia's experience in the area of water management because water use in the Murray–Darling Basin showed many of the problems we are facing.

Managing the Urban Transition

A new challenge that the economy will face in the years ahead because of the acceleration in growth is that of urbanisation. The rate of urbanisation in India has been slow historically, but is expected to accelerate in future because of faster growth, especially non-agricultural growth. The urban population is currently around 30 per cent and is expected to reach 40 per cent by 2030, which means the urban population will increase from about 300 million today to 600 million by 2030.

An expansion in urban population on this scale requires a massive expansion in urban infrastructure, especially if we keep in mind that only about half of those currently in urban areas are adequately served even by today's standards. The resources needed to achieve this expansion in urban infrastructure are much larger than what the cities or local urban bodies can mobilise on their own.

Lack of resources for urban development is partly a reflection of the fact that cities and urban local bodies in India have very limited capacity to raise their own resources. Most of the revenue generated from economic activity in the cities accrues not to the city but to the central or state governments, and there is much less devolution to city government levels than there should be. For some urban services, such as water and sewerage or urban transport, it is possible to generate revenue on the basis of a user charge, but potential revenues are not realised because of a long tradition of fixing low user charges. There is scope for unlocking land value to finance urban infrastructure, but this avenue has not been adequately used.

Historically, cities all over the world have rarely financed all the infrastructure they need themselves. The national government has contributed in various ways and this will have to be done in India also. However, the cities have to take on a much larger part of the burden than they do today. The growing urban population has to be persuaded that they have to pay for urban services and this requires a mindset change not only among the city dwellers but also among politicians. The same is true about persuading state governments to devolve more resources from general revenue to urban local bodies.

In addition to the financing problem, urban infrastructure development is also impeded by the lack of capacity at the city level to manage and plan for infrastructure expansion. India is likely to have a large number of cities with populations exceeding 10 million by 2030. However, the system of local government in India is such that cities are not run by empowered city managements. Too often, critical decisions regarding the needs of metropolitan cities are made by state governments that respond not to the electorate in the cities but to the electorate in the state as a whole. In the process, the needs of the cities tend to be ignored and the city government is not adequately empowered to address these needs. A broad-based change in governance structures will be needed if cities are to manage the transition now facing them.

Before concluding, I should perhaps mention one other challenge and that is climate change. This is not just a challenge for India. It is a challenge for the global community as a whole. No country can solve this problem on its own for the simple reason that whatever we do individually to mitigate climate change, does not just help us, it helps everybody. Since the benefits of mitigation are externalised, we know that, left to themselves, countries will do much less to combat climate change than they should. Therefore, the solution to the climate change problem can only come from a collective decision, and a collective decision can only materialise if countries can agree on a fair distribution of the burden of action among countries. Unfortunately, the world is making less progress in agreeing on what is a fair distribution of the burden than one would have hoped.

I would like to emphasise, however, that we in India are not waiting for a global agreement before we act. We have taken a number of initiatives under a National Action Plan for Climate Change. The plan involves some action in the area of mitigation and some in the area of adaptation. I will not get into the details, but let me just say we have set a national target that we need to reduce the emissions intensity of GDP by 20 per cent between 2005 and 2020. That's not a reduction in the emission levels; it is a reduction in the emissions intensity of GDP, but that is extremely important. I should also clarify that this is not a binding commitment as part of an international agreement. It is a self-imposed national target, but I am quite certain that we will be able to meet it. Indeed, it is our hope that we will do even better in practice.

These are some of the challenges we have to face to ensure that India does achieve her full growth potential. I am sure there are others. We expect to outline them more fully as we move to finalise the Twelfth Five-Year Plan by 2012.

Oration 15:
2011 K.R. Narayanan Oration

Message from the President
of the Republic of India

I am happy to learn that the Australia South Asia Research Centre (ASARC) at The Australian National University, is organising the 15th K.R. Narayanan Oration on the theme 'India and the Global Financial Crisis: What Have We Learnt' by Dr Duvvuri Subbarao, Governor, Reserve Bank of India, at the university in Canberra on 23 June 2011.

The Indian economy has posted robust growth in recent years. While several other economies of the world have contracted, India has continued to fare better than other countries because of its domestic demand and investor-friendly policies. There is growing interest the world over in the Indian economy and our developmental model. I have no doubt that the oration will go a long way towards addressing this interest, focusing on the lessons learnt while tackling the challenges faced by the Indian economy and the opportunities shaping its growth and development in the years to come.

I wish the event all success.

Pratibha Patil
New Delhi
3 June 2011

India and the Global Financial Crisis: What Have We Learnt?

Duvvuri Subbarao

Thank you for inviting me to deliver the 2011 K.R. Narayanan Oration. It is an honour to which I attach a lot of value.

President Narayanan

Late President Narayanan was a distinguished diplomat, a reputed parliamentarian, a capable minister and, above all, an erudite scholar. Born at the very bottom of India's social pyramid, he rose to occupy the highest office in the country with no assets other than hard work, integrity and humility. 'A working President', as he described himself, he never allowed dogma to overwhelm his beliefs and convictions.

President Narayanan was in office from 1997 to 2002, a time when globalisation, as we are experiencing it in the current times, was taking root. At the banquet he hosted for visiting US President Bill Clinton in New Delhi in March 2000, President Narayanan remarked:

> Mr President, we do recognise and welcome the fact that the world has been moving inevitably towards a one-world ... But, for us, globalisation does not mean the end of history and geography, and of the lively and exciting diversities of the world.

This was a thoughtful remark. As much as globalisation may be inevitable, history and geography need not be destiny. If we learn the lessons of experience, we will not repeat the same mistakes. This, indeed, is the topic for my oration, and my tribute to late President Narayanan — to seek the lessons of the crisis that we have just gone through so that we can make this a better world of all of us.

Is This Time Different?

By all accounts, the 2008–09 crisis has been the deepest financial crisis of our times. It has taken a devastating toll on global output and welfare. Arguably, the fundamental causes of all financial crises are the same — global imbalances, loose monetary policy and high levels of leverage driven by 'irrational exuberance'. In that respect, this crisis has been no different.

Where this crisis has been different, however, is in its manifestation. Most recent crises had occurred in individual emerging economies or regions, and were, at their core, traditional retail banking or currency crises. The countries in trouble could be rescued by multilateral interventions; besides, the advanced countries provided a buffer for trade and financial support. In contrast, this crisis originated in the most advanced economy, the United States, and hit at the very core of the global financial system. With virtually no buffers to fall back on, the crisis rapidly engulfed the whole world. Much to their dismay, emerging market economies too were soon pulled into the whirlpool.

How was India Hit by the Crisis?

India was no exception. We too were affected by the crisis. Output growth, which averaged 9.5 per cent per annum during the three-year period 2005–08, dropped to 6.8 per cent in the crisis year of 2008–09. Exports, which grew at 25 per cent during 2005–08, decelerated to 12.2 per cent in the crisis year (2008–09) and declined by 2.2 per cent in 2009–10. In the pre-crisis years, we had capital flows far in excess of our current account deficit. In contrast, during the crisis year, net capital flows were significantly short of the current account deficit and this put downward pressure on the rupee. The exchange rate depreciated from 39.37 per dollar in January 2008 to 51.23 per dollar in March 2009.

Notwithstanding our sound banking system and relatively robust financial markets, India felt the tremors of the tectonic shocks in the global financial system. The first round effects came through the finance channel by way of the sudden stop and then reversal of capital flows consequent upon the global deleveraging process. This jolted our foreign exchange markets as well as our equity markets. Almost simultaneously, our credit markets came under pressure as corporates, finding that their external sources of funding had dried up, turned to domestic bank and non-bank sources for credit.

By far the most contagious route for crisis transmission was the confidence channel. For weeks after the Lehman collapse in mid-September 2008, everyday there was news of yet another storied institution crashing. In this global scenario of uncertainty, the lack of confidence in advanced country markets transmitted as hiccups to our markets too. The net result was that all our financial markets — equity, debt, money and foreign exchange markets — came under varying degrees of pressure. Finally, the transmission of the crisis through the real channel was quite straightforward as the global recession that followed the financial crash resulted in a sharp decline in export demand for our goods and services.

Why was India Hit by the Crisis?

There was dismay in India that we too were affected by the crisis, and this dismay arose mainly on two counts. First, the exposure of our banks to toxic subprime assets was marginal and their off balance sheet activities were limited, and so, the argument went, we should not have been affected by a financial sector crisis that originated from these causes. Second, India's growth is driven by domestic demand and a drop in external demand, it was contended, should have caused no more than a small dent in output growth. Yet, the crisis hit us, and did so more ferociously than we thought possible. The reason for this is globalisation: India is more integrated into the global system than we tend to acknowledge. Let me illustrate that point with some broadbrush numbers.

India's two-way trade (merchandise exports plus imports), as a proportion of GDP, more than doubled over the past decade: from 19.6 per cent in 1998–99, the year of the Asian crisis, to 40.7 per cent in 2008–09. Note that global trade declined by 11 per cent in 2009 as a result of the crisis in contrast to a robust average growth of 8.6 per cent during the previous few years (2004–07). Such a sharp collapse in world trade had an impact on our export demand, demonstrating that our trade integration was quite deep.

319

If our trade integration was deep, our financial integration was even deeper. A measure of financial integration is the ratio of total external transactions (gross current account flows plus gross capital account flows) to GDP. This ratio had more than doubled from 44 per cent in 1998–99 to 112 per cent in 2008–09, evidencing the depth of India's financial integration. In sum, the reason India was affected by the crisis, despite mitigating factors, is its deepened trade and financial integration with the world.

Managing Globalisation

What the experience of the crisis demonstrated clearly was the power of globalisation. Globalisation is a double-edged sword: it opens up incredible opportunities but also poses immense challenges. India surely benefited from opening up to the world but had also incurred costs on that count. The challenge for India, and indeed for all emerging market economies (EMEs), is really to minimise the costs and maximise the benefits of globalisation.

Lessons of Crisis

A lot is being written about how this crisis has been too important to waste — how we should learn the lessons of the crisis and apply them in a Schumpeterian creative destruction mode. Some people have, however, questioned the wisdom of drawing lessons even before the crisis is fully behind us. When Zhou Enlai, former Chinese prime minister, was asked what he thought of the French Revolution, he said it was too early to say. Historians who take a long view may agree with Zhou Enlai but practical policymakers do not enjoy that luxury. So, let me use the opportunity of this platform to draw out eight big picture lessons of the crisis.

Lesson 1: In a globalising world, decoupling does not work

The crisis challenged many of our beliefs, and among the casualties is the decoupling hypothesis. The decoupling hypothesis, which was intellectually fashionable before the crisis, held that, even if advanced economies went into a downturn, EMEs would not be affected because of their improved macroeconomic management, robust external reserves and healthy banking sectors. Yet, the crisis affected all EMEs, admittedly to different extents, bringing into question the validity of the decoupling hypothesis.

Some analysts argue against such an outright dismissal of the decoupling hypothesis and suggest a more nuanced evaluation. In fact, recent IMF (International Monetary Fund) research[1] illustrates that the transmission of distress from advanced economies to EMEs took place in three distinct phases. The first phase runs from the time early signs of the crisis appeared in mid-2007 until the Lehman collapse in September 2008. During this period, the growth performance of EMEs outshone that of advanced economies, indicating decoupling. The second phase, starting with the Lehman collapse until the first quarter of 2009, was one of 'recoupling' when advanced economies pulled EMEs into the downturn. The third phase started in the second quarter of 2009 when EMEs started recovering from the crisis ahead of advanced economies, suggesting a shift once again to decoupling.

So, have EMEs decoupled from the advanced economies? The answer has, necessarily, to be nuanced. A useful way to visualise decoupling in the wake of the crisis is to distinguish between 'trend' and 'cycle' decoupling. 'Trend' decoupling is reflected by the widening gap between the trend rates of growth of EMEs and of advanced economies. This is evidently owing to the growing weight of domestic factors, mainly consumption, in the EMEs' growth process. However, given that there is still significant integration between the two groups of countries, cycles are still coupled. From a 'lessons' perspective, what this means is that EMEs should focus on strengthening domestic drivers of demand and instituting automatic stabilisers to buffer themselves against cyclical shocks from advanced economies.

Lesson 2: Global imbalances need to be redressed for the sake of global stability

No crisis as complex as this has a simple or a single cause. In popular perception, the collapse of Lehman Brothers in mid-September 2008 will remain marked as the trigger of the crisis. At one level that may well be true. Indeed, I can visualise future textbooks in finance dividing the world into 'before Lehman' and 'after Lehman'. But, if we probe deeper, we will learn that at the heart of the crisis were two root causes — the build-up of global imbalances and developments in financial markets over the last

---

1   Ricardo Llaudes, Ferhan Salman and Mali Chivakul (2010), 'The Impact of the Great Recession on Emerging Markets', IMF Working Paper 237, October.

two decades. The received wisdom today is that these two root causes are interconnected, and that financial market developments were, in a sense, driven by global imbalances.

Global macro imbalances got built up because of the large savings and current account surpluses in China and much of Asia in the wake of the East Asian crisis a decade ago. These were mirrored by large increases in leveraged consumption and current account deficits in the US. In short, Asia produced and America consumed. Between the US consumption boom and the Asian savings glut, there is a raging debate on what was the cause and what was the effect. Regardless, the bottom line is that one was simply the mirror of the other and the two share a symbiotic relationship.

And how did these imbalances build up? The answer lies in globalisation — globalisation of trade, of labour and of finance. The world witnessed a phenomenal expansion in global trade over the last three decades; global trade as a proportion of global GDP increased from 34 per cent in 1980 to 51 per cent in 2007, just before the crisis hit.[2] Globalisation of finance was even more prolific, especially over the last decade. For the world taken together, the ratio of foreign assets and foreign liabilities to GDP rose from 133 per cent in 1994 to over 300 per cent in 2008.[3] The impact of the globalisation of labour was by far more striking. Emerging Asia added nearly 3 billion people to the world's pool of labour as it integrated with the rest of the world over the last two decades, thus hugely improving its comparative advantage. Together, the three dimensions of globalisation — trade, finance and labour — helped emerging Asia multiply by a factor its exports to the advanced economies. The result was large and persistent current account surpluses in the Asian economies and corresponding current account deficits in the importing advanced economies.

The chain of causation from these imbalances to the financial crisis is interesting, although not obvious. As Asia accumulated savings and simultaneously maintained competitive exchange rates, the savings turned into central bank reserves. Central banks, in turn, invested these savings not in any large, diversified portfolio, but in government bonds of the advanced economies. This, in turn, drove down risk-free real interest rates to historically low levels, triggering phenomenal credit expansion

---

2   Calculations based on IMF Direction of Trade Statistics, June 2010.
3   Calculations based on IMF Balance of Payments Year Book, 2010.

and dropping of the guard on credit standards, erosion of credit quality and search for yield, all of which combined to brew the crisis to its explosive dimensions.

It is argued that, if the US Federal Reserve had refused to supply the incipient demand for liquidity in the late 1990s and early 2000s, higher interest rates could have prevented the borrowing boom and the follow on widespread deterioration of financial standards and the subsequent meltdown. But this also would have meant lower growth in the US and the rest of the world. The short point is that, even as macroeconomic imbalances should not be allowed to proliferate, it is necessary to balance the need for global economic growth against the disruptions that follow the unwinding of such imbalances.

So, where do we go from here? The G20 is now actively engaged in the challenging task of redressing structural imbalances in the global economy. At their Pittsburgh Summit in September 2009, the G20 leaders agreed on a 'Framework for Strong, Sustainable and Balanced Growth' and committed to a 'Mutual Assessment Process' (MAP) that is a peer review of each country's progress towards meeting the shared objectives underlying the framework. Recognising that global imbalances that had narrowed during the crisis started widening again in the exit phase, driven mainly by the uneven recovery around the world, the G20 resolved that promoting external sustainability should be the focus of the next stage of the MAP and entrusted this task to a Framework Working Group (FWG).

India is privileged in co-chairing, together with Canada, the FWG for managing the task of developing the indicative guidelines for assessing and addressing persistent global imbalances. The FWG has adopted a two-stage approach: a limited number of indicators will guide the initial assessment process, while a broader set — including qualitative ones — will be used in the second stage to inform an in-depth external sustainability assessment. The success of this initiative is critical for redressing the problem of global imbalances.

Lesson 3: Global problems require global coordination

The crisis demonstrated the interconnectedness of the world through trade, finance and confidence channels. What originated as a bubble in the US housing sector soon snowballed into a crisis and radiated in two different ways: first, in a geographical sense, from the US to other advanced economies and then to the rest of the world; and, second, in a sectoral sense, from housing to all productive sectors. Even as each country started dousing the fires on its own, it was soon realised that the effort was in vain and that global coordination is a necessary condition for managing a global crisis.

From that perspective, the London G20 Summit in April 2009 will go down in history as a clear turning point when the leaders of the world showed extraordinary determination and unity. Sure, there were differences, but they were debated and discussed and compromises were made without eroding the end goal — that is, to end the crisis. This resulted in an agreed package of measures having both domestic and international components, but all of them to be implemented in coordination and, indeed, in synchronisation where necessary. The entire range of crisis response measures — accommodative monetary stance, fiscal stimulus, debt and deposit guarantees, capital injection, asset purchases, currency swaps — all derived in varying degrees from the G20 package.

Now, as we exit from the crisis, there are concerns and apprehensions that the vaunted unity that the G20 had shown during the crisis is dissipating. But might it also be a tad unrealistic to expect the degree of unity shown in managing the crisis to also be shown in addressing 'peacetime' issues? The focus of the G20 now is to flesh out the agenda for economic and financial restructuring at national and international levels so that the world can prevent, or at any rate minimise, the probability of another crisis of the type we have gone through. Differences of opinion, when the agenda is so broad, are not only to be expected, but may in fact have a positive influence in determining what is collectively optimal.

The common thread running through the entire G20 agenda is the need for global cooperation in solving our most pressing problems of today. The crisis has taught us that no country can be an island and that economic and financial disruptions anywhere can cause ripples, if not waves, everywhere. The crisis also taught us that, given the deepening integration of countries into the global economic and financial system, uncoordinated responses will lead to worse outcomes for everyone.

The global problems we are facing today are complex and not amenable to easy solutions. Many of them require significant and often painful adjustments at the national level. Because short-term national interests conflict with globally optimal solutions, it is quite understandable that there are differences of views within the G20. We must remember though, that in a world divided by nation-states, there is no natural constituency for the global economy. At the same time, the global crisis has shown that the global economy as an entity is more important than ever and that global coordination to solve global problems is critical.

Lesson 4: Price stability and macroeconomic stability do not guarantee financial stability

The years before the crisis were characterised by steady growth and low and stable inflation in advanced economies, and rapid growth and development in EMEs. The so-called 'Great Moderation' prompted a growing consensus around the view that the best practice in monetary policy framework is the pursuit of a single target (price stability) by means of a single instrument (short-term policy interest rate). The success of the Great Moderation fortified the argument that price stability is a necessary and (a nearly) sufficient condition for economic growth and for financial stability. Central bankers believed they had discovered the holy grail.

That sense of triumph was deflated by the unravelling of the crisis. As the global financial sector came to the brink of a collapse even in the midst of a period of extraordinary price stability, it became clear that price stability does not necessarily guarantee financial stability.

Indeed, the experience of the crisis has prompted an even stronger assertion — that there is a trade-off between price stability and financial stability, and that the more successful a central bank is with price stability, the more likely it is to imperil financial stability. The argument goes as follows. The extended period of steady growth and low and stable inflation during the Great Moderation lulled central banks into complacency. Only with the benefit of hindsight is it now clear that the prolonged period of price stability blindsided policymakers to the cancer of financial instability growing in the underbelly.

A dominant issue in the wake of the crisis has been the role of central banks in preventing asset price bubbles. The monetary stance of studied indifference to asset price inflation stemmed from the famous Greenspan orthodoxy, which can be summarised as follows. First, asset price bubbles are hard to identify on a real-time basis, and the fundamental factors that drive asset prices are not directly observable. A central bank should not, therefore, second-guess the market. Second, monetary policy is too blunt an instrument to counteract asset price booms. And third, central banks can 'clean up the mess' after the bubble bursts. The surmise, therefore, was that the cost-benefit calculus of a more activist monetary stance of 'leaning against the wind' was clearly negative.

The crisis has dented the credibility of the Greenspan orthodoxy. The emerging view post-crisis is that preventing an asset price build-up should be within the remit of a central bank. Opinion is divided, however, on whether central banks should prevent asset bubbles through monetary policy action or through regulatory action. On one side, there is a purist view questioning the efficacy of resorting to monetary tightening to check speculative bubbles. Opposed to this is the argument that a necessary condition for speculative excesses is abundant liquidity, and that controlling liquidity, which is within the remit of monetary policy, should be the first line of defence against 'irrational exuberance'.

No matter how this debate settles, a clear, if also disquieting, lesson of the crisis is that price stability and macroeconomic stability do not guarantee financial stability.

Lesson 5: Micro-prudential regulation and supervision need to be supplemented by macro-prudential oversight

The crisis has clearly demonstrated that a collection of healthy financial institutions does not necessarily make a healthy financial sector. This is because there are complex interconnections in the financial sector across banks, other financial institutions, markets and geographies, and a problem in any part of the system can rapidly transmit through the system, cascade across layers and develop into a crisis. Systemic safety can also be jeopardised by procyclicality. As the crisis demonstrated, there is a strong collective tendency among financial entities to overexpose themselves to the same type of risk during an upturn and become overly risk averse during a downturn. Importantly, individual institutions and, indeed, micro-prudential oversight too, fail to take into account the spillover impact of the actions of the rest of the financial system on them. This raises the paradox of the fallacy of composition. What is good from an individual institution's point of view can become disruptive, and even destructive, if all institutions act in a similar way.

That a bubble that started in the US housing sector snowballed into a major crisis is a vivid illustration of the risks arising from the interconnectedness of the global financial system and the risks of procyclicality. The lesson clearly is that as much as micro-prudential supervision is necessary, it needs to be supplemented by macro-prudential oversight to prevent systemic risk building up.

Macro-prudential oversight requires both analytical sophistication and good judgement. Regulators need to be able to analyse the nature and extent of risk and be able to make informed judgement on when and what type of countercyclical buffers they must impose. Both type I and type II errors — imposing buffers too early out of excessive caution or delaying imposition of buffers until it is too late to avert an implosion — can be costly in macroeconomic terms.

Lesson 6: Capital controls are not only unavoidable, but advisable in certain circumstances

As EMEs started recovering from the crisis earlier than advanced economies, they also began exiting from the crisis-driven accommodative monetary stance ahead of the advanced economies. This multi-speed recovery and consequent differential exit have triggered speculative capital flows into EMEs, resulting in currency appreciation unrelated to economic fundamentals. This poses complex policy management challenges. Currency appreciation erodes export competitiveness. Intervention in the forex market to prevent appreciation entails costs. If the resultant liquidity is left unsterilised, it could potentially fuel inflationary pressures. If the resultant liquidity is sterilised, it puts upward pressure on interest rates, which not only hurts competitiveness, but also, in a curious variation of the Dutch disease, encourages further flows.

Capital inflows far in excess of a country's absorptive capacity could pose problems other than currency appreciation. Speculative flows on the lookout for quick returns can potentially lead to asset price build-up. Also, in the current juncture, one of the driving forces behind hardening commodity prices in recent months is excess liquidity in the global system, which has possibly triggered financialisaton of commodities.

Quite unsurprisingly, the old debate about whether capital controls are a legitimate policy option has resurfaced again. This is a debate that has traditionally frowned on moderation. Critics maintain that capital controls are distortionary, largely ineffective, difficult to implement, easy to evade and that they entail negative externalities. On the other hand, supporters of capital controls argue that controls preserve monetary policy autonomy, save sterilisation costs and tilt the composition of foreign liabilities towards long-term maturities and ensure macroeconomic and financial stability.

The debate on capital controls resurfaced after the Asian crisis of the mid-1990s, especially as one of the root causes of the crisis was the open capital accounts of the East Asian economies. However, as the Asian economies recovered in quick order, regained their export competitiveness and started building up external reserves for self-insurance, the debate was not pursued to its logical conclusion, and the orthodoxy that capital controls are undesirable persisted.

The recent crisis has, however, been a clear turning point in the worldview on capital controls. Notably, the IMF put out a policy note[4] in February 2010 that reversed its long-held orthodoxy that capital controls are inadvisable always and everywhere. The note referred to certain 'circumstances in which capital controls can be a legitimate component of the policy response to surges in capital flows'. The World Bank[5] and the Asian Development Bank's *Outlook 2010* both echoed these views.

A useful way of assessing the capital account management of an EME is to draw a distinction between 'strategic' and 'tactical' controls. Strategic controls would involve defining a long-term policy indicating the inter se preference — or the hierarchy of preferences as it were — across different types of capital flows and the controls that will be deployed to operationalise that policy. Strategic controls give stakeholders a clear and predictable framework of rules to make informed choices and to manage risks, and they give policymakers sufficient levers to calibrate the flows; in essence, they define the boundaries of the playing field. Tactical controls, on the other hand, introduce barriers into the playing field itself. They are deployed opportunistically to stem a surge in inflows or outflows. By their very nature, tactical controls introduce a new element of uncertainty into the calculations of both domestic and foreign stakeholders.

India's approach to capital account management is typically strategic. For example, we have an explicitly expressed preference for long-term over short-term flows and equity over debt flows, and we have used both price-based and quantity-based controls to operationalise this policy. We have,

---

4   Jonathan D. Ostry et al. (2010), 'Capital Inflows: The Role of Controls', IMF Staff Position Note, SPN/10/04, 19 February.
5   World Bank (2009), *Global Monitoring Report 2009: A Development Emergency*, Washington.

of course, periodically recalibrated elements of the strategy in pursuit of capital account liberalisation. An important lesson from India's experience is that, even with relatively large swings in capital flows during the crisis, the pressure to use tactical controls did not build up because the strategic controls provided automatic buffers.

Even as we debate what EMEs should or should not do to manage excess capital flows, we should remember that, to the extent that lumpy and volatile flows are a spillover from policy choices of advanced economies, managing capital flows should not be treated as an exclusive problem of emerging market economies. How this burden is to be shared raises both intellectual and practical challenges. The intellectual challenge is to build a better understanding of the forces driving capital flows, what type of policy instruments, including capital controls, work and in what situations. The practical challenge is the need to reach a shared understanding on a framework for cross-border spillovers of domestic policies in capital-originating countries, and the gamut of policy responses by capital-receiving countries.

Lesson 7: Economics is not physics

A few months into the crisis, the Queen happened to be at the London School of Economics and asked a perfectly sensible question: 'how come none of the economists saw the crisis coming'. The Queen's question resonated with people around the world who felt that they had been let down by economics and economists. As economists saw their profession discredited and their reputations dented, the economic crisis soon turned into a crisis in economics.

What went wrong with economics? It now seems that by far the most egregious fault of economics, one that led it astray, has been to project it like an exact science. The charge is that economists suffered from 'physics envy', which led them to formulate elegant theories and models — using sophisticated mathematics with impressive quantitative finesse — deluding themselves and the world at large that their models had more exactitude than they actually did.

Admittedly, in a limited sense, there may be some parallels between economics and physics. But similarity in a few laws does not mean similarity in the basic nature of the academic discipline. The fundamental difference between physics and economics is that physics deals with the physical universe, which is governed by immutable laws, beyond the pale of human behaviour. Economics, in contrast, is a social science whose laws are influenced by human behaviour. Simply put, I cannot change the mass of an electron no matter how I behave, but I can change the price of a derivative by my behaviour.

The laws of physics are universal in space and time. The laws of economics are very much a function of context. Going back to the earlier example, the mass of an electron does not change whether we are in the world of Newton or of Einstein. But, in the world of economics, how firms, households and governments behave is altered by the reigning economic ideology of the time. To give another example, there is nothing absolute, for example, about savings being equal to investment or supply equalling demand as maintained by classical economics, but there is something absolute about energy lost being equal to energy gained as enunciated by classical physics.

In natural sciences, progress is a two-way street. It can run from empirical findings to theory or the other way round. The famous Michelson–Morley experiment that found that the velocity of light is constant led to the theory of relativity — an example of progression from practice to theory. In the reverse direction, the ferocious search now under way for the Higgs Boson — the God particle — that has been predicted by quantum theory is an example of traversing from theory to practice. In economics, on the other hand, where the human dimension is paramount, the progression has necessarily to be one way, from empirical finding to theory. There is a joke that if something works in practice, economists run to see if it works in theory. Actually, I don't see the joke: that is indeed the way it should be.

Karl Popper, by far the most influential philosopher of science of the 20th century, propounded that a good theory is one that gives rise to falsifiable hypotheses. By this measure, Einstein's General Theory was a good theory, as it led to the hypothesis about the curvature of space under the force of gravity that, indeed, was verified by scientists from observations made during a solar eclipse from the West African islands of Sao Tome and Principe. Economics, on the other hand, cannot stand the scrutiny of the falsifiable hypothesis test, since empirical results in economics are a function of the context.

The short point is that economics cannot lay claim to the immutability, universality, precision and exactitude of physics. Take the recent financial crisis. It is not as if no one saw the pressures building up. There were a respectable number of economists who warned of the perilous consequences of the build-up of global imbalances, said that this was simply unsustainable and predicted a currency collapse. In the event, we did have the system imploding — not as a currency collapse, but as a meltdown of the financial system.

We will be better able to safeguard financial stability both at global and national levels if we remember that economics is a social science and real world outcomes are influenced at a fundamental level by human behaviour.

Lesson 8: Having a sense of economic history is important to prevent and resolve financial crises

Let me finish with the last lesson, which is on a larger canvas: namely, that having a sense of economic history is important to prevent and to resolve financial crises. In their painstakingly researched book, *This Time is Different: Eight Centuries of Financial Folly*, Kenneth Rogoff and Carmen Reinhart argue that every time a crisis occurs and experts are confronted with the question of why they could not, based on past experience, see it coming, they would argue that past experience was no guide as circumstances had changed. Yet, this 'this time is different' argument does not hold. Reinhart and Rogoff put forward impressive evidence showing that over 800 years, all financial crises can be traced to the same fundamental causes as if we learnt nothing from one crisis to another. If only teaching in economics included the study of economic history, perhaps we could avoid repeating history, never mind as a farce or a tragedy.

Oration 16:
2012 K.R. Narayanan Oration

Message from the President
of the Republic of India

I am happy to learn that the Australia South Asia Research Centre (ASARC) at The Australian National University is organising the 16th K.R. Narayanan Oration on the theme 'The Indian Economy: Rising to Global Challenges' by Dr Kaushik Basu, Chief Economic Adviser, Ministry of Finance, Government of India, at the university in Canberra on 1 June 2012.

The Indian economy has emerged as the third-largest economy in Asia, a trillion-dollar economy that has joined the ranks of the top 10 economies of the world.

A noticeable feature of India's economic growth is that it is largely driven by domestic demand. While India's growth trajectory has been good in the recent past it has also be resilient. India has to maintain a high growth path for another 30 years to attain the status of a developed economy to fully satisfy the aspirations of its people. For this, several challenges need to be addressed — the challenges of poverty eradication, unemployment, bridging the rural–urban and regional divides and achieving inclusive growth that leads to sustainable development. India also needs to address critical challenges relating to energy, food and water security, and climate change. I have no doubt that the oration will give insights into these issues for the audience.

I wish the oration all success.

Pratibha Patil
New Delhi
28 May 2012

The Indian Economy: Rising to Global Challenges

Kaushik Basu

This is the revised version of the K.R. Narayanan lecture that I delivered in Canberra on 1 June 2012. At the time of the lecture, and up to 31 July, I was the Chief Economic Adviser to the Government of India, Ministry of Finance. The final revisions in preparing the written version were made on 25 August 2012. At the end of the lecture in Canberra there was a remarkably engaged discussion with the audience. This provided valuable inputs for my subsequent revision and in writing up the lecture as a paper. I am grateful to the members of my audience for their interest. I would also like to record my thanks to Supriyo De Priya Mukherjee for research assistance and advice.

Prelude

I feel honoured to be here in Canberra to deliver the K.R. Narayanan lecture both because of the person after whom this lecture series has been named and because of the amazingly distinguished list of speakers who have lectured in the series before me. I am grateful to Australia's High Commissioner to India, H.E. Peter Varghese, who first conveyed to me the invitation to deliver the lecture and also for the many engaging discussions I have had with him over the years concerning policymaking in India and Australia. I am grateful to the Indian High Commissioner to Australia, H.E. Biren Nanda, the Vice-Chancellor of The Australian National University, Professor Ian Young, Professor Raghbendra Jha, Australia's Department of Foreign Affairs and Trade, and to The Australian National University for the hospitality here in Canberra.

Kocheril Raman Narayanan was a remarkable man. He was born into a *dalit* family in a small village in Kerala's Kottayam district and spent his early years suffering all the ignominies that this implied in those times. His school experience exemplified this well. Given his superior intellect, school was where he faced for the first time the excitement of learning, but it was also a place where he faced discrimination and the embarrassment of his parents' frequent inability to pay his school fees, which meant that he had to sit outside the classroom. Among political leaders of that generation in emerging economies, there is often competition for how far one had to walk to get to school. With 15 km daily, Narayanan would certainly be among the leaders.

That a person would rise from this background to being a star student at the London School of Economics, a distinguished diplomat, India's ambassador to several countries and, ultimately, president of India, is a truly rare feat. I had direct interaction with him on only a few occasions, after I returned from the London School of Economics and began teaching in New Delhi. What impressed me most was his keen intellect — he was a favourite student of the famed Harold Laski — and his natural humility.

Ladies and gentlemen, I am honoured and humbled to be giving this lecture.

My lecture is about the Indian economy, its unexpected arrival on the global stage and the challenges and responsibilities that arise from this. But before launching into it, I want to say a word about Australia. In recent years, the Australia story has stood out as one of the success stories in the world. Contemporary Australia has managed to combine a culture of vibrant democracy, strong civil rights and a progressive social agenda, alongside a vibrant economy. Even though, as with the rest of the world, its growth has been slow in recent years, it nevertheless stands out as one of the best managed economies amid today's global gloom. Even during my brief visits to Australia, it has been evident what has contributed to this success. It is a progressive and inclusive economic policy agenda, along with an effort to draw some of the best professional minds to the task of designing and implementing economic policy. We all have a lot to learn from this.

I believe that the scope for collaboration and cooperation between India and Australia is enormous. The two nations have deep similarities, such as our democracy, our vibrant media and our commitment to secularism. We also share several common social problems such as that of having people, in fact some of the earliest settlers on our lands, who have been discriminated against historically, and of the consequent responsibility of trying to draw them and other discriminated groups into mainstream life. We are also two countries with deep commitments to higher education. There is a substantial flow of expertise, skills and students between the two nations. The potential for collaboration in this area is large. There is also increasing trade and the movement of capital in both directions between India and Australia. By further nurturing economic and strategic relations between the two nations, there is a lot to be gained by not just India and Australia, but by the world at large.

The India Story: Backdrop

The paper is concerned with India's growth and globalisation. Lest the reader misread my attention to these as a reflection of a fundamental normative concern, let me clarify that I view growth to be of value only for instrumental reasons. The ultimate aim of any nation should be to build an equitable, humane, secular and tolerant society, where human beings achieve a decent standard of living. As such, as policymakers, our focus should be on the poorest and weakest segments of the population. India should be deemed as doing well to the extent that the bottom segment is doing well. And, if the nation grows rapidly but the poorest people remain as poor and miserable as before, I would refrain from describing that as a success. In brief, we must learn to judge a nation by how its poorest and most miserable human beings have fared.

Growth is important because it enables us to do more for such people. If we grow rapidly but fail to distribute the spoils among the most wretched of the nation, we may lead the global growth charts, but by the values that this paper espouses, we will not be considered a success.[1]

The big story about India since the early 1990s has been its unexpectedly rapid economic growth. The trajectory of the Indian economy after 1994 shows a clear breaking of trend with what had happened prior

---

1   The formal analysis associated with this is fully spelt out in Basu (2001).

to that. While there had been an occasional year of high growth, like the 9 per cent growth in 1975–76 and 10.5 per cent in 1988–89, it is only from the mid-1990s that India seemed to have moved to a sustained high growth path, achieving approximately 7 per cent per annum growth for three consecutive years, beginning in 1994.

There would be some growth interruption in 1997, when the East Asian crisis came ashore in India, past our gates of capital control and slowed us down somewhat. Growth picked up further at the start of the 21st century. It moved up to around 8 per cent by 2003 and over 9 per cent by 2005, with the phenomenal growth of around 9.5 per cent during each of the three years 2005–08. There was a brief interruption again in 2008–09 as we were rocked severely by the global financial crisis that began with the subprime mortgage crisis in the US; but growth picked up quickly in response to a stimulus package that was implemented part deliberately but part unwittingly, and India grew by a remarkable 8.4 per cent in 2009–10 and 2010–11, despite the headwinds of a global slowdown.

This growth trajectory is a remarkable story, but what is even more remarkable and has not been commented on enough is India's globalisation since the early 1990s. While India was always an open society and polity, through a strange process of competitive politics and faulty thinking, the economy had become increasingly closed. The first Gulf War of 1990–91 and the subsequent economic crisis — one of the deepest that India had witnessed since the country's independence in 1947 — jolted India out of its closed-economy stupor. Reforms were undertaken to open up the economy and the subsequent globalisation that India witnessed stands out as a rare event.

In the mid-1990s, India's exports plus imports of goods as a ratio of GDP stood at approximately 18 per cent. By 2010–11, this had jumped to 37.5 per cent. In the mid-1990s, India's exports plus import of services was around 4 per cent of GDP. By 2010–11, this had risen to 12.9 per cent. In the middle of the 1990s, the gross capital outflows and inflows to India stood at approximately 15 per cent of the country's GDP. By 2010–11, this had risen to an astonishing 53.9 per cent (Government of India 2012).

With this rapid growth and even more rapid globalisation, India has been drawn to the global round table of policymaking and strategising more suddenly than anyone would have anticipated. We are today an important and verbose member of G20, BRICS (Brazil, Russia, India China, and South Africa) and other international clusters. Even though the verbosity may have nothing to do with growth performance and globalisation, but a sociocultural propensity of little consequence, the membership in these important global bodies and India's visible participation in them is testimony to our nation's rapid integration with the global economy. It is indeed remarkable that, in both the BRICS cluster and the G20, India is both a very prominent member and the poorest nation by a wide margin in terms of per capita income.

All these pose challenges and responsibilities that could not have been anticipated even 15 years ago; and it is these responsibilities and challenges that I plan to delineate, analyse and discuss in the remainder of this lecture.

Choppy Waters

Over the last year, the Indian economy's journey turned choppy, with growth in 2011–12 slowing down to 6.5 per cent, with the last quarter of that year registering a growth of 5.3 per cent. A sector-wise analysis is worrying because manufacturing — the one sector where our comparative advantage is arguably the greatest — has slowed down sharply. It is indeed a matter of some concern that India's share of the manufacturing sector in the GDP has declined from 16 per cent four years ago to 15 per cent. Over the last eight years, India's exports grew faster than in any comparable period in the independent nation's history. But this has also slowed down to virtually zero over the last three-quarters.

I do not believe there is any reason to treat the slowdown as anything more than a periodic downturn that occurs in any economy. This is not to absolve policymakers of mistakes and minimise the imperative of taking corrective measures, but recognition of the fact that mistakes do occur periodically in economic policymaking, which is not surprising given that economics is still a very young science and its prescriptions are often cast aside by considerations of politics.

A careful look at investor behaviour confirms that the last year is being treated as a periodic downturn and not a reflection of any long-run proclivity of the Indian economy. In the last financial year, 2011–12, foreign direct investment (FDI) into India was a record $46.8 billion. This outstrips the previous high by approximately $5 billion. This happened even while investment from foreign institutional investors (FIIs) dropped off sharply. Once we take account of the fact that FDI entails fixed costs by the investor and therefore reflects long-run bets being taken on the economy, and that FII money is relatively costless to bring in and take out, it is evident that the simultaneous occurrence of increased FDI and decreased FII inflows reflects concerns about the Indian economy in the short run and confidence in the Indian economy in the medium and the long run.

There are several reasons behind this recent slowdown in growth, but what is essential to remember is that we are no longer impervious to what is happening in the global economy the way we used to be in India's pre-globalisation days.[2] With the global economy slowing down sharply in 2011 and the first quarter of 2012, it is not surprising that India is also slowing down. Indeed, in terms of relative growth, India stands roughly where it did two years ago. In the first quarter of 2012, among the G20 countries, for instance, India recorded the third-highest growth, behind China (8.1 per cent) and Indonesia (6.3 per cent). With the exception of Australia, which grew by 4.3 per cent, most industrialised nations were virtually grinding to a halt. Indeed, the Eurozone nations collectively had a growth of 0 per cent.

One consequence of the rapid globalisation achieved by India over the last two decades, as noted above, is that from now on both global buoyancy and global depression will impact us with much greater severity than was the case earlier.[3] It is probably true that no country in the world, with the possible exception of North Korea, can escape the crisis that is paralysing the Eurozone economies. But what is also true is that the impact this time on India is harder than what would have been the case even a decade earlier.

As a consequence, we have to learn the art of making policy, ranging from monetary and fiscal measures to the making of law and regulation, in a relatively open economy. This is something new for us, because India has never been anywhere nearly as open as it is today in its six-odd decades since independence. In adjusting to this changed scenario, there will,

---

2   For an explicit discussion of how the global financial crisis affected India and a robust rejection of the decoupling hypothesis, see Subbarao (2011).
3   This is often further exacerbated by the fact that India runs a large current account deficit. Every time there is a slowdown in capital inflows, this creates a pressure on the exchange rate, resulting in depreciation of the rupee. This can give rise to troublesome volatility (Gokarn 2012).

of course, be some missteps — and some missteps (let me call them that) there have been. But, if India gets its act right, the opportunities that lie ahead for India are beyond what it has ever had in the past. India has the potential to be the forerunner among emerging and developing nations of the world.

If I were to use a somewhat blunt comparison with China, both nations began structural reforms in the late 1940s. Through ups and downs, China has managed to get its economic house in fair order and pursued good economic policies over the last three decades. India, on the other hand, has managed to get its political house in reasonable order. It has a functioning democracy, a vibrant media, a vocal civil society and an independent judiciary. Given that getting one's political house in order is arguably the harder task than getting one's economic policies in order, the expectation that India will rise through the current tribulations of the economy to a phase of steady and rapid growth seems like a reasonable forecast.

Proactive Policymaking

One reason why the Eurozone crisis has affected us so deeply and, in fact, more in terms of morale than actual economic indicators, is that India is new to the art of policymaking in an open globalised economy. For many years, the global aspect of making policy was so marginal to India that this was not an art in which we became well practised. Much of our policies, be they in international political relations or international economics, were reactive. A proposal came from some nation or some international body and we decided whether to go along with it or not.

The dramatic change in the structure of the Indian economy over the last decade or two has made it incumbent on us to move from being a reactive to a proactive agent in the international domain. There is a need to define our national prerogatives in the international arena and pursue these actively. India has to move from being a nation that accepts or rejects agenda developed by others to a nation that creates some of that agenda and begins to take up the role of initiator in some of these foreign policy and strategic economic matters. It is important for India to do some strategic thinking in terms of who should be our partners and friends in the global space and then take the first steps to bring these to fruition, instead of waiting for all the initiative to come from elsewhere. It is in this spirit, and not just to celebrate the location of the Narayanan lecture, that I suggested the need to promote greater economic and strategic engagement with Australia.

The need for proactive engagement is true in many different ways — ranging from policies in our neck of the woods to larger international issues such as the ones that come up in G20 meetings. Our neck of the woods refers to South Asia, where India needs to play a much more active role than it does currently. The scope for collaboration and trade in South Asia is vast. Trade routes opened up through India's north-eastern neighbours — such as Bangladesh and Myanmar — can energise our neighbouring economies and unleash the potential of India's own north-eastern states, which have, for far too long, relied on dole outs from Delhi. This is a region of India with high literacy and plenty of enterprise. Once we facilitate the development of the region, it will move on autopilot. There are lessons to be learnt from the success of cooperation in the Mekong Delta. Power generation using Nepal's unexploited potential for hydro power can help Nepal and India. All such projects require strategic activism, involving the Ministry of Finance, the Ministry of External Affairs and the Export Import Bank of India.

Done correctly, this can promote development not only in India but also in our neighbouring countries. Given that South Asia is among the poorest regions of the world, this is worthwhile from a purely global, humanitarian point of view. In addition, this can contribute to political stability and peace in the region.

But I put this thought on the table not merely for engagement with South Asia and South-East Asia but the world, and emphasise the need for India to take a more active role in choosing its strategic partners and promoting humanitarian global objectives.

Policy Imperatives

Before plunging into economics, let me deal with, and put aside, a matter that is essentially that of politics. Much has been made recently of the compulsions of coalition politics with many claiming that this is what is slowing down decision-making and reforms. Having to take one's coalition partners along means cajoling and compromise, often referred to in India as 'coalition dharma'. Whether or not this is used as an alibi for failures that have other causes, there is no doubt that such fractious politics does not help. What does one do about this? There is no doubt that greater idealism among political leaders and policymakers can help greatly. India needs a critical mass of political leaders who are prepared to lose the next election. To win the future you must have the courage to lose tomorrow.

While we can wish for such idealism, it will be foolish to rely on it. What we need to do in the meantime is to think of electoral systems that eliminate some of the extreme volatilities of coalition governments.

I have a simple suggestion, which is a modification of the system of run-offs that many nations use, to achieve this. Given that voting in India has increasingly moved to electronic means, this is easy to implement. Let me clarify that I am suggesting this only for the national election and not for state or local body elections.

Ask each voter to rank their top two candidates by putting down the numbers 1 and 2 next to the two names of their choice. After balloting is over, begin by ignoring people's number 2 votes. In other words, do the counting at first the way we currently do. Now fix a cut-off number of members from a single party below which the party is considered too small to be represented in parliament. For the sake of illustration, take this to be 4 per cent. Then all parties that get less than 4 per cent of the seats in parliament on the basis of this first count are treated as disqualified from parliamentary representation. For all ballot papers that gave first preference to a candidate from these disqualified parties, count their second preferences as their true votes (except in cases where the second preference goes to a member of one of the disqualified parties, in which case just ignore such a ballot).

By this simple technique, we will make sure that parliament will consist of fewer and more substantial parties. The agonies of coalition dharma will be reduced vastly. In fact, by making the cut-off higher than 4 per cent it should be possible to virtually ensure that the ruling party has an actual majority in parliament.

I can see that a chorus of objections will be raised about this new system of balloting. But that is simply a reflection of our resistance to anything new. Of course, there is a need to debate the details, and these may be different from the precise formulation given above. However, moving quickly to something like the above system will vastly improve the quality and efficiency of economic policymaking. Moreover, this will also alter the nature of politics. It will ensure that until political parties feel that they have managed to amass support beyond a critical level they will not find it worthwhile to contest elections. The tendency towards political and ideological agglomeration that this will give rise to would also be good for national unity, since small regional parties will be disadvantaged under this system and so will be incentivised to reach out to more people over larger tracts of the nation.

It is time to turn to matters of economic policy.[4] A basic principle that distinguishes sophisticated policy regimes from more feudal ones is based on the recognition of a simple fact, namely, that good economic policy does not consist of phoning and urging captains of industry and members of trade unions to deliver, but on finding the vital levers and knobs of the economy and adjusting them to ensure that it is in the *interests* of industrialists and workers to deliver. This is at the heart of good policy design and most nations that have done well have at some point graduated to this realisation.

A corollary of this is that when inflation occurs you do not say it is caused by traders trying to earn larger profits and urge them to change their behaviour. That may be true, but since traders always try to make more profits, to identify that as a cause and appeal to them, or pass a diktat against this, is as useful as saying that the collapse of the building was caused by gravity and trying to alter that. To be successful, we need to locate the key features of the economy that must have changed and made it possible for or incentivised traders to raise prices in a sustained way and cause inflation.

Stated in such a stark way, this basic principle of economic policy, important though it is, seems to suggest too mechanistic and mean a view of humans and makes people out to be devoid of emotions beyond greed and acquisition. Economics as a profession has rightly been held guilty of such a mechanistic approach. But since I do not want to be held guilty of such a mechanistic approach, let me clarify.

When I say that we must craft policy keeping in mind the interests of individuals, I do not want to make the mistake that textbook economics often make, namely that of treating these interests as entirely centred on

---

4   Some of the technical backdrop for what is argued here occurs in Basu (2012).

the self and inspired by nothing but greed. We must realise that individuals are endowed with varying degrees of altruism, trustworthiness, integrity and regard for other, and also that these qualities can be nurtured or dampened (see Basu 2011a). What is being argued is that whatever these interests are we must realistically take account of them in designing policy.

Take India's current system of food rationing for the poor. The method that is followed is for government to announce a minimum support price (MSP) for some essential foods, like rice and wheat, and have the Food Corporation of India procure food from farmers at the MSP. A part of this is released to 500,000 Public Distribution System (PDS) stores or ration shops scattered all over the nation with the instruction that the PDS stores must sell the grain at special low prices to households that are below the poverty line (BPL) and some other especially vulnerable categories. At this point, we run up against the interest of the PDS store owner. If he can sell some of this subsidised food on the open market and turn away the BPL customers, or sell them food grain that is adulterated with stone shavings, he can make a lot of money. Indeed, evidence suggests that this happens in fairly handsome measure. More than 40 per cent of the food grain meant for the poor does not reach the poor (see Khera 2011). This colossal waste causes our fiscal deficit to rise and, much more importantly, leaves the poor ill served.

The folly of this policy lies in the assumption that those supposed to sell to the poor will carry out their duty, irrespective of their self-interest. I am not assuming that human beings can never be selfless and committed to their work professionally with no regard to self-interest. However, the areas in which we hold back our self-interest and live by other rules or customs differs from one society to another and also over time.[5] It is critical to assess this correctly and to make allowances.

If we are talking about Norway or Japan, it may be fair to assume that a ration shop owner, when told to sell rations to poor households, will do precisely that. But that is not everywhere and always the case. While we must not forget that social norms can be moulded and altered, at any point of time they are shaped by history and environment. As policymakers, we have to be realistic about the way they are and, *keeping that in mind,* design policies that will be incentive compatible.

---

5   Illustrative examples occur in Basu (2011b).

It is important in India to try to nurture and build the kind of social norms that lead to progress and development. But to assume that certain norms are in place when they are not is to design policy interventions that will be defective and will fail to deliver efficiently.

The recognition that social norms and culture play an important role in economic outcomes that goes back to the works of at least Polanyi (1944) and Granovetter (1985) is at times viewed as politically regressive on the presumption that these norms may be hardwired into societies. There is, however, plenty of reason to reject such a presumption. There is enough evidence from around the world that norms are malleable. As the environment changes, norms can mutate and vanish and new norms can emerge.

There are plenty of examples of this but a most striking one that I have discussed elsewhere is to do with punctuality in Japan. Japan is arguably the world's most punctual society — some would argue over-punctual, with individuals incurring excessive costs to avoid the charge of tardiness. It therefore comes as a surprise to learn that this was not the case as recently as 100 years ago. Here is a description of Japan that makes it clear that there is little difference between Japan of a century ago and the most tardy nations of today. I present the quote suppressing the reference to Japan to make it more striking:

> In his published memoir, Kattendyke (a European visiting Japan) cited a series of events to illustrate the frustrating slowness of the nation. For example, the supplies necessary to make repairs, which he had specifically ordered to be delivered at high tide, did not arrive on time; one worker showed up just once and never returned … Kattendyke's frustrations were in fact shared by most of the foreign engineers in the country … They often found themselves vexed by the work habits of the locals, and the main reason for their vexation was the apparent lack of any sense of time. To these foreigners, the locals worked with an apparent indifference to the clock. (Hashimoto 2008)

India's other, and not unrelated, hurdle to more rapid development is its large transactions and bureaucratic costs and the culture of 'permissionism' that pervades our system. In this regard, reforms are needed, small and big. Let me first give an example from the small. Small clutter in the bureaucracy is quite pervasive in India. We need to go through the slew of all our bureaucratic practices and try to weed out all the debris from the old licence control raj days, when procedures were put together for functions or intentions that are no longer — and maybe never were — relevant.[6] Take an example that appears to be unique to India — namely, the stamping of baggage labels after security screening. We Indians take it for granted that, for safety, we need to put our baggage through security screening like everywhere in the world and, unlike anywhere else, have it stamped by a liveried officer, which means 'checked and deemed safe'. We are so used to it that once, when I was boarding in Singapore, I found an Indian man making a big fuss insisting that the security personnel stamp his baggage tag. When I told him that these officers would not understand what he was asking for and that he would be fine without a stamp, he refused to believe me. As I moved on, I heard him asking for the supervisor to whom he would complain.

The question is whether the Indian system, which results in additional officers having to be employed and each passenger taking 5 to 10 seconds more at security, which in the aggregate is a colossal waste of time, serves any purpose. The answer is no, because it is too easy to create stamped tags.

Here is what you need to do. Take a soft bag full of trash paper. After it goes through security and the baggage tag is stamped, remove the stamped tag, throw away the trash paper, fold the soft bag and put it inside your other bag. You have created a stamped tag that you can put on any other bag that you may wish.

Some may object that there is no point in creating spare stamped tags, since anyway it is not possible to carry bombs and weaponry through security and into the terminal. But if that were so, then why do we have the system of stamping the tags in the first place? Conclusion: the practice of stamping baggage tags is a pointless exercise.

This is a minor example, but the reason I use up space here to outline it is because if we do not point these out on grounds of their being minor, our system will persist in being cluttered with the minor rules, which serve no purpose but, together, create substantial obstacles to efficiency and speed.

---

6   Government intervention is often viewed as the more progressive policy, one that radical scholars should support. This is a highly mistaken view since it is permissionism and excessive control that usually results in capture by big businesses and leads to the worst form of a market economy, to wit, crony capitalism (Ahluwalia 2010).

If we begin to move on these, there will be the additional benefit of these being treated as signals that India has woken to the need for greater bureaucratic efficiency. Declaring the people of some pre-specified countries do not need to apply for visas in advance, but can get visas on arrival in any of India's international airports is a case in point. If we make such an announcement, it may seem to have little connection with *economic* reform; yet it can have a large beneficial effect by signalling a changed attitude on the part of government.

Turning to large reforms and those that feed directly into economic functioning, the need is obvious by looking through any recent issue of *Doing Business* produced by the World Bank. In a list measuring 'ease of doing business', such as the time it takes to get permits to start a business, the amount of time it takes to close down a firm that has gone bankrupt and the time taken to enforce a contract when someone tries to renege, India performs very poorly. We need administrative reform to change this. The benefits of doing this right can be greater than virtually any other policy. Once we make it easy for people to go about their economic activities — working, trading, running a business and so on — many of the responsibilities that currently fall on the shoulders of the government will automatically be taken care of. Government can then use its precious resources and time for more critical activities, such as providing basic needs support for the poor, creating public goods and investing in better infrastructure.

India has moved forward on all these fronts, especially since 1991, and it owes a large part of its arrival on the global scene and rapid growth since the mid-1990s to this, but there is still a distance to go in bringing greater professionalism and scientific knowledge into policymaking.

Let me give an example. Air India (AI) as a topic of discussion invariably leads to heat and dust in India. Should AI continue to be owned and managed by the state or should it be privatised? In India, as soon as this question is raised it runs into a storm. The debate takes the form of whether privatisation amounts to selling off family jewellery to private agents or the refusal to privatise is a sign of state capture. The debate quickly reduces to ideology. If you are left wing, you oppose privatisation; if you belong to the right you support it. This is reminiscent of what Geoff Harcourt (1972) had once provocatively pointed out — namely, that if you knew an economist's position on the then current Vietnam War, you could pretty well guess what his or her position would be on several theoretical debates in economics, such as the capital controversy.

But this is not the way it ought to be (and one should hasten to add that there were prominent exceptions among those engaged in the capital controversy). Just as we are not able to tell from a physicist's research on the boson what her ideology is, or be able to tell from her ideology what position she takes on the God particle, we should not be able to correlate an economist's ideology with the economist's research findings. The ultimate decision we take on AI would, of course, depend on one's normative line, but the pure analysis of the consequences of privatising or not privatising AI should have nothing to do with the analyst's ideology.

Once we keep this in mind, we can see more clearly what our current policy is doing. As things stand, AI is run fairly inefficiently. With political leaders and the senior bureaucracy making demands on it, AI has, for a long time, been a loss-making enterprise. As a consequence of this, and also the shallowness of debate on this topic, the only cost of running AI the way we currently do that is being talked about is the burden it places on the exchequer. So much of the debate turns on the question of whether it is right to run a larger fiscal deficit in order to have AI in the state sector. This has obliterated other important and more complicated matters from the debate. One such matter pertains to the effect AI has on the private sector in general.

One consequence of keeping AI viable by subsidising it that often goes unnoticed is the effect on the private airline industry that competes with it. The assurance of state subsidies implies that AI need not do its commercial calculations too carefully. If it does its ticket pricing 'wrong', is over-generous with its upgrades, pays too much to airline catering services or overpays its staff, it can still survive. But this ability to survive means that its competing airlines are forced to offer some of the same benefits to ensure that they find passengers, staff and catering services. Hence, the inefficiency spreads to other airlines, including the private sector. If the subsidies are too high, it becomes impossible for private players to survive, since they do not have access to such state subsidies. They run up losses and may have to eventually close down.

That this is not mere theory and can happen in reality one can see by looking at India's oil marketing companies. For a long time we had a number of state-owned companies operating side-by-side with some private companies, such as Essar and Reliance. This was fine as long as government kept away from the scene. But, over time, the policy that has been followed is to hold down the price of petrol and diesel by fiat (though petrol was eventually freed in June 2010), impose some indirect taxes and — to make sure that the state-owned enterprises do not become unviable by notching up large losses or 'under-recoveries', as they are called — subsidise state-owned enterprises. This, of course, contributed in a big way to increasing the fiscal deficit, but that was not all. This combination of policies made it impossible for the private sector to survive. Indeed, they have virtually all shut down.

This policy of tilting the playing field can do large damage to efficiency. By driving out private competitors and ensuring that state-owned firms are protected by the state's policy of covering their costs whatever they happen to be, you ensure that the costs will be large.

Before moving on, let me clarify that what we need to do in the fuel sector, such as diesel, is decontrol the sector, at least partially. This is not as obvious as it appears at first sight. It has to be carefully designed and executed. Unfortunately, too much of the debate turns on whether or not government should raise the price by decree. It is true that this may be necessary in the short run, especially if we are deferring on decontrol. But what is more important to do is to fix the subsidy on diesel on a per litre basis, for certain pre-specified ranges of world crude prices and exchange rates; and also place some restrictions on how much prices can rise and fall at one go. Moreover, both the taxes and subsidies should be placed on public and private sector firms. This levelling of the playing field will bring new entrants into this sector and make it more efficient. This is not an easy exercise but if it is done properly, the benefits of efficiency to the consumer can be large. It is important to understand that a reform of this kind will not necessarily cause the price of diesel to rise. It will mean that the price will fall and rise gently depending on global indicators, and the burden will be shared between consumers and the state. What is being suggested in terms of brakes on sudden rises in prices is somewhat akin to what most industrialised nations do to prevent ordinary home buyers from being exposed to sudden volatilities in interest rates.

If we are going to reform our administration and structures of governance, we have to get into many of the kinds of details discussed above, but there is also a broad guiding principle of decision-making in a democracy that needs to be kept in mind. In India, there is a propensity to think of democracy as a system in which everybody is involved in every decision. That may indeed be one kind of democracy: I have elsewhere called it an overlapping democracy — one in which decision-making is perforce sluggish. A better democracy is one in which everybody has a domain where he or she has a say in decision-making but it is not that everyone has a say on every decision. I called it a partitioned democracy. This is what we must aspire towards. And there should be much more scope for single-person decisions. Thus, when we form a commission to reform something — our administrative system, for instance — we should increasingly think of a commission in which the ultimate report is the report of one person. Currently, we tend to form all commissions in the form of multiple individuals entrusted to produce a consensus document. Instead, and not everywhere but in many fields, we should have commissions that take the form of one commissioner and n advisers. The commissioner would consult all advisers but the ultimate report would be the report of that one commissioner. This is likely to make these reports more full of content and dynamism than happens under the current system.

This broad principle should carry over to more areas of decision-making in government. We tend to form groups for every decision, giving each member effectively a veto power. This tilts the system towards the status quo and that is what plagues India. If we partition the slew of decisions that government needs to make, giving one person or a small group the charge of decisions in each element of the partition, there will be some mistakes of course. But we will not have a system that is frozen by the fear of making mistakes.

The Road Ahead

The challenges that India encounters today, some of which were discussed above, are, by way of challenges, the best. They arise from India's phenomenal and unexpected success over the past two decades. This has catapulted the Indian economy to a global perch with a suddenness for which few were prepared. There will no doubt be choppy waters that the nation will have to navigate but, at the same time, there is reason to believe that India has chosen an irrevocable path to becoming an industrialised nation.

Most observers, including experts, have a propensity to overreact to the current situation. Two years ago, many were forecasting that India would grow in double digits. With last year's slowdown, the same experts have swung to the gloom scenario. My own belief — one that I have maintained for a while, let me hasten to add — is that it is entirely possible for India to grow at 7 per cent per annum, per capita, over the next two or three decades. This will mean that, notwithstanding the trials of the last year, India can join the cluster of industrialised nations, often demarcated by the crossover line of per capita income of $10,000, by the year 2039. This will be a remarkable achievement, but we have to remember that this must not be treated as an end in itself. We will have to work hard to ensure that this translates into happier and more fulfilling lives, and also that this larger national income is better distributed across the population.

At the dawn of the nation in 1947, the founding fathers of India made a momentous decision — a commitment to democracy. There were very few role models for this — a vast, poor nation, making a commitment to democracy and secularism even before it had shown any stirrings of economic growth was certainly an uncharted course. Yet, it seems today that of the two reforms, those pertaining to economics and those to politics, the latter are the harder. Economic policies can be modified and corrected as one goes along. Delays do slow down development but they are rarely insurmountable. On the other hand, political participation and democracy, once left by the wayside, are very difficult to usher in at a later stage, and can give rise to occasional but much more insurmountable roadblocks. Efforts to alter such a political structure can give rise to struggle and trauma.

Hence, we may conclude that, when two roads diverged on the wooded path of independent India, the nation chose the path less travelled, and luckily so, because that seems to have made all the difference. There will no doubt be many further political reforms that India will have to undertake; there are economic policy reforms that are awaiting implementation. But the most important planks and foundations are in place. The nation did stagger and stutter while they were being put in place and allowed to cement in. But starting approximately two decades ago, India began to move with firm steps and growth picked up with unmistakable firmness.

Poverty, still large, is now beginning to slope off and literacy, which seemed stubbornly low for the first several decades, is suddenly rising. India seems set to take its place in the comity of nations. And when it does, it will be important to bear in mind that industrialisation and wealth are not worth much in themselves if they do not allow us to create a more humane and tolerant society. It must then carry to the world the message of its founding fathers and poets, the message of universal tolerance, peace and sharing.

References

Ahluwalia, M.S. (2010), *India's Prospects in the Post-Crisis World*, 2010 K.R. Narayanan Oration, The Australian National University, Canberra.

Basu, K. (2001), 'On the Goals of Development', in G. Meier and J. Stiglitz (eds), *Frontiers of Development Economics: The Future in Perspective*, World Bank and Oxford University Press, Washington, DC.

Basu, K. (2011a), *Beyond the Invisible Hand: Groundwork for a New Economics*, Princeton University Press and Penguin, doi.org/10.1515/9781400836277

Basu, K. (2011b), *An Economist's Miscellany*, Oxford University Press.

Basu, K. (2012), 'The Rise of the Indian Economy: Fiscal, Monetary and Other Policy Challenges', *Rivista Italiana Degli Economisti*, vol. 17 (Chinese translation in *Comparative Studies*, 2012).

Gokarn, S. (2012), 'An Assessment of Recent Macroeconomic Developments', *Reserve Bank of India Bulletin*, January, vol. 66.

Government of India (2012), *Economic Survey 2010–11*, Ministry of Finance and Oxford University Press, New Delhi.

Granovetter, M. (1985), 'Economic Action and Social Structure: The Problem of Embeddedness', *American Journal of Sociology*, 91(3), doi.org/10.1086/228311

Harcourt, G. (1972), *Some Cambridge Controversies in the Theory of Capital*, Cambridge University Press, Cambridge, doi.org/10.1017/CBO9780511560026

Hashimoto, T. (2008), 'Japanese Clocks and the History of Punctuality in Modern Japan', *East Asian Science, Technology and Society: An International Journal*, 2(1): 123–33, doi.org/10.1215/s12280-008-9031-z

Khera, R. (2011), 'Trends in Diversion of Grain from Public Distribution System', *Economic and Political Weekly*, vol. 46, 21 May.

Polanyi, K. (1944), *The Great Transformation*, Beacon Press, Boston.

Subbarao, D. (2011), *India and the Global Financial Crisis: What Have We Learnt?*, 2011 K.R. Narayanan Oration, The Australian National University, Canberra.

Oration 17:
2015 K.R. Narayanan Oration

Australia and India: Combining Technology and Entrepreneurship to Innovate the Future

Kiran Mazumdar-Shaw

I am indeed honoured to deliver the 17th Dr K.R. Narayanan Oration instituted in memory of the late president of India, a great statesman and a close friend of Australia. At a time when technology is transforming the world we live in, I would like to take this opportunity of sharing my thoughts on how our two countries can collaborate to leverage technology and innovate a better future.

The Technology Revolution

Information technology, communication technology and biotechnology are rapidly and disruptively changing the way we communicate, educate, medicate and eradicate. The internet has created the true generation gap, in which those of us who grew up in a world without computers, mobile phones and wi-fi have to adapt to an unrecognisable world that requires skills that can deal with instant real-time responses — a transparent world where there is little confidentiality — and, above all, develop the ability to leverage technology to innovate continuously to make life simpler and more efficient.

Genomics, similarly, has created a new breed of life scientists and researchers who look at disease in a very different way than their older peers. It is no longer about treating symptoms but about understanding disease at a cellular and genetic level to deliver personalised diagnostics and therapies. It was the unravelling of the human genome in 2000 that made this possible. Technological advancement has brought down the cost of sequencing an entire human genome from $100 million to less than $1,000 within a decade, thus enabling personalised medicine to leapfrog. Multiplexing genomics with molecular diagnostics, imaging and data analytics is now being leveraged at a cellular level wherein cancer cells are being deciphered and translated into tailor-made treatment regimens. Today's medical paradigm is rapidly evolving from a 'one size fits all' to a customised solution of 'the right treatment for the right patient at the right time', with the aim of minimising side effects and maximising positive outcomes. The increasing importance of personalised medicine is evident from the US$215 million Precision Medicine Initiative recently announced by US President Obama.

Health care tomorrow will have no resemblance to what exists today. Imagine a world where every one of us will have a lifelong genome map that will be tracked for mutations that are linked to their disease causing potential. This can enable early diagnosis and early therapeutic intervention, thereby arresting disease progression and enhancing quality of life. Or, for that matter, imagine 3D printing technology that can print bespoke organs or blood vessels or bones and joints. In fact, according to consulting firm Visiongain, the forecast for the 3D printing medical market is estimated to be around $4 billion by 2018.

It is well accepted that advancements in medical science have increased life expectancy in the developed world to over 80 years. There are 60,000 centenarians in the US today and it is estimated that there will be 1 million by 2050! Tomorrow's world will have an ageing population but with a better quality of life where the retirement age will perhaps be 80!

Technology, Innovation and Entrepreneurship

Technology, therefore, can be both daunting and tremendously exciting. To me, perhaps the most transformative power of technology is that of entrepreneurship. Technology is unleashing innovation through entrepreneurial zeal like never before. No longer is value creation linked to scale but to the power of the idea.

In 2014, the global biotech sector raised $40 billion through venture funds, private equity and initial public offerings (IPOs) — the highest ever to date. Add information and communication technology (ICT) and this number zooms to $200 billion. These 'technopreneurs' are all focused on breakthrough ideas and money is chasing every one of them.

Not everyone will succeed, but we are already seeing the crazy valuations being ascribed to young entrepreneurs who are wet behind the ears in terms of business experience but smart as they come in terms of innovative business models. For example, Google, Facebook, Twitter, WhatsApp, Amazon and Uber to name but a few. This has created a 'start-up' revolution the world over, from Boston to Bangalore, from Sydney to Singapore and from Melbourne to Mumbai!

We are today witnessing the birth of the 'ideas economy', in which the value of a company is measured by its 'innovation quotient' rather than traditional metrics such as revenue, profit, physical assets, etc. The potential of the WhatsApp messaging platform to change the way the world communicates led Facebook to pay an 'innovation premium', resulting in a blockbuster deal value of US$19 billion. The power of the idea is being reinforced by the dizzying valuations being commanded by companies like Snapchat (US$20 billion), Uber (US$40 billion) and Xiaomi Corp (US$45 billion)!

The fact that this 'innovation premium' is getting larger over the years is illustrated by a Bloomberg analysis that traces this through the Amazon and Netflix public offerings in 1998 and 2002 at values of just US$450 million and $750 million, respectively, followed by the Google IPO in 2004 at a value of US$23 billion, which in turn quadrupled to the $100 billion IPO that Facebook had in 2012. While all these companies have similar risk–return profiles, the investor appetite for 'new ideas' has emerged only recently.

Let me now focus on medical and life sciences where a technology revolution is already apparent. Cancer is no longer a death sentence but a chronic disease; rare diseases have life-enhancing therapies that can save fragile lives; and miracle therapies can make the blind see, the deaf hear and the paralysed walk. One such medical innovation is an Australian hearing implant, cochlear, to deal with deafness. Another is an Indian innovation for rapid tuberculosis detection. My own company is developing the world's first oral insulin as a tablet.

There is no dearth of innovative ideas in life sciences but, unlike the ICT sector, there does seem to be a dearth of investor appetite to digest the long time lines and complex regulatory pathways that are involved in taking these exciting biomedical ideas to the market. The US is perhaps the only ecosystem that has drawn inspiration from the marvels of biomedical science and created an investment environment that ascribes high value to innovative ideas. This has generated a virtuous and value accretive investment cycle of venture funding, mergers and acquisitions, and public offerings. The US biotech sector, therefore, rightfully dwarfs the rest of the world both in breakthrough products and market capitalisation.

I do believe that Australia and India need to emulate the US model of value creation through backing innovative start-ups if we wish to create an 'ideas economy' that generates perpetual value accretion and thereby economic and employment growth.

Genomics and big data analytics are emerging areas where Indian IT skills provide an advantaged impetus. Combine this with advanced scientific and medical knowledge in Australia and we have a win–win.

Life sciences in general provide this powerful synergy between our two countries, be it within academia or in business. Both nations have a strong tradition of science, medicine and engineering that has enabled Indians and Australians to flourish in academic and industrial research activities the world over. Australia's medical intellect has been widely acclaimed with many Nobel prizes awarded since 1945 when Sir Howard Florey was awarded the Nobel for his work on penicillin. It is noteworthy that 50 per cent of Nobel Prize winners from Australia are from the medical field. This illustrious list includes Frank Burnet, John Eccles, Bernard Katz, Peter Doherty, Robin Warren, Barry Marshall and Elizabeth Blackburn.

India's scientific intellect likewise has been showcased by several Nobel Laureates: Sir C.V. Raman, Professor Har Gobind Khorana, Professor S. Chandrasekhar and Professor Venkatraman Ramakrishnan. However, unless our respective governments recognise the potential of this scientific synergy, it will remain rhetoric. We need foreign policies to reflect on the power of collaborative innovation, especially in a world that is truly boundaryless, interconnected and virtual, thanks to technology.

The Global Employment Challenge

Today, every economy is challenged with employment. India needs to create 10 million jobs per year for the next 10 years to sustain acceptable GDP growth. European countries like Spain, Greece and Italy need to create employment for half its youth who are currently jobless, and even a country like Australia has to deal with 6 per cent unemployment. I do believe that the job market of the future will not be able to rely on the traditional pillars of lifetime employment in large companies and the public sector.

We are likely to see a much more fluid pattern of employment with people moving in and out of a vast number of fast-moving companies that are small, nimble and entrepreneurial. These companies will constantly evolve and reinvent themselves to adapt with the changing pace and face of new technologies. It is instructive to note that 86 per cent of Fortune 500 companies have either disappeared or dropped off the list over the last 50 years and the rate of displacement continues to accelerate as mega corporations like General Motors, Pfizer and Microsoft try to stave off the challenge from the likes of Tesla Motors, Gilead Sciences, Google and others. Creative disruption is radicalising the marketplace where leadership is transient and innovation is king.

An Accidental Entrepreneur

I remember when I embarked on my own employment journey. It started right here in Australia when I graduated as a young brewer from the Ballarat Brewing School in 1975. My aspiration was to pursue a professional career in brewing anywhere in the world. However, I was unprepared for the hostility and gender bias that I faced from the brewing industry, which saw me turn to entrepreneurship quite by accident and become a job creator rather than a job seeker! I therefore call myself an accidental entrepreneur, as I never thought I was capable of starting my own business. This was an inflection point that I can proudly reflect upon and realise that, instead of the one job that I was seeking, I have created 7,000 jobs today, and, if I add the ancillary businesses that I rely on or support, it has had a multiplier effect. This is the power of entrepreneurship that must be unleashed the world over. India and Australia should create a borderless, virtual ecosystem that fosters a start-up culture that can create thousands of technology-led enterprises that can generate millions of jobs.

The Advent of Microcomputers and Genetic Modification

The 1970s was undoubtedly the advent of the technology era. In 1973, biologists Herb Boyer and Stanley Cohen showed the world that it was possible to take a human gene and insert it into a bacterium to mass-produce the protein expressed by the gene. Three years later, Boyer teamed up with a venture capitalist, Bob Swanson, to form the world's first biotech company, Genentech, with the goal of genetically modifying bacteria to produce human insulin. Coincidentally, I chose to adopt the same technology in 2000 to produce recombinant human insulin, not in a bacterium, but in a yeast.

Another breakthrough development in medical technology in the 1970s was the discovery of magnetic resonance imaging (MRI) by Raymond Damadian. This technology allowed doctors to look inside the body without the need for surgery, harmful dyes or X-rays.

The 1970s was also the decade that saw the birth of the 'internet' when Vince Cerf, Yogen Dalal and Carl Sunshine published their historic paper 'Specification of Internet Transmission Control Program'. Another major development in the area of ICT was when Martin Cooper, an engineer at Motorola, invented and demonstrated the first cellular phone in 1973.

The seeds of the electronically connected world that we experience today were also sown in the 1970s. It was the decade that saw the beginning of the journey where microprocessors would make computing faster and more mainstream. The Intel 8080 microprocessor introduced in 1974 sparked off a chain of events that led to the ubiquity of personal computing and inspired Bill Gates and Paul Allen to start Microsoft in 1975, and Steve Jobs and Steve Wozniak to co-found Apple Computers in 1976. The rest as they say is history!

Biotechnology and information technology were in their nascency in the 1970s and the communication technology that we take for granted today was probably still in the realm of science fiction then. In fact, electric typewriters, calculators and the Sony Walkman were probably considered the 'technological marvels' of that time! It is interesting to note that none of them are used today!

The India of the 1970s was primitive and under-resourced. Only the privileged and affluent had landline telephones and television sets with a single black-and-white channel for viewing! Computers and mobile phones were objects of James Bond movies. When I arrived at Tullamarine Airport in 1974, Australia seemed light-years ahead of my home country with telephones everywhere and multi-channel, colour TVs and 24/7 electricity. When I started my biotech company, Biocon, in 1978, I did not have a telephone line or computer; nor, for that matter, did I have reliable electricity.

Fast forward to 2015 and you will see that there is very little to differentiate the youth in India or Australia. The youth of today's globalised world live fast-paced lives, multitask and seek out new avenues for themselves, all of which are enabled by the technology of the day. Smartphones enable them to be omnipresent while the internet provides them access to real-time knowledge, something that was simply not possible in the 1970s.

Technology has played a truly transformative role in India's development. A country that had no phones in the 1970s leapfrogged to mobile phones with over 800 million subscribers today, making it the largest market for mobile phones. Digital technology has also enabled India to develop a mega population database with unique identification numbers that will cover over a billion people. This has been leveraged for creating bank accounts for the masses, enabling direct cash transfers for subsidies and welfare schemes. Another electronic marvel is our voting system, which enabled over 500 million people to cast their votes electronically in the recently conducted general elections. India has embraced technology to address a number of challenges in health, education, agriculture and governance. Today, India is developing a universal health care system based on electronic medical records and e-health centres that rely on modern computer aided diagnostics. Massive open online courses (MOOCs) and computers are enabling e-schools, technical training and higher education.

Agriculture is also a beneficiary of new technology. The early benefits of biotechnology are already being reaped by Indian farmers who are seeing enhanced productivity through the use of genetically modified cotton. Approved in 2002, Bt cotton is the country's only GM crop and covers 95 per cent of India's cotton cultivation of 11.6 million hectares. Apart from this, agricultural biotechnology is leveraging molecular markers in crop breeding for the selective propagation of genes that improve yields and resist disease.

Agri-biotechnology is providing powerful solutions to irrigation and arable land challenges in a country that has only 2.3 per cent of the world's land area but must ensure food security for 17.5 per cent of the world's population.

Biotechnology is also providing ecofriendly solutions and energy options through enzyme technologies and biofuels that will make India an environmentally responsible nation. India's daunting challenges throws up unlimited opportunities to innovate and create business solutions. Therein lies the entrepreneurial potential.

Building a Knowledge Society Together

The building blocks for close cooperation between India and Australia to create a knowledge society are already there. Australia is a destination of choice for Indian students seeking an overseas education and the number of Indian students continues to grow. In 2014, over 36,000 Indian students were enrolled into Australian universities, which is a tad higher than the UK. Moreover, India and Australia have a history of robust, productive and sustained bilateral research collaborations. For example, the Australian Centre for International Agricultural Research collaborates with the Indian Council for Agricultural Research on a range of problems of mutual interest, such as food security and the management of natural resources.

The two countries have also set up the Australia–India Strategic Research Fund (AISRF), which provides a platform for collaborative, cutting-edge research between scientists in India and Australia across a range of agreed priority areas. This platform has helped build linkages between premier research institutions in both countries. It is Australia's largest fund dedicated to bilateral research with any country, and is one of India's largest sources of support for international research. The Australian Government has committed an additional $20 million to AISRF over four years from the current financial year 2015–16.

Last year, India's National Skill Development Corporation and Australia's Department of Industry, signed a memorandum of understanding to strengthen their bilateral relationship in the area of technical vocational education and training. The aim is to develop transnational standards to strengthen skills mobility and facilitate greater access to skilled labour across the region.

Closer cooperation and collaboration between India and Australia can create a knowledge society that unleashes the huge potential of the entrepreneurial energy in both countries, leading to start-ups that think locally but have the potential to make enormous global impact.

Start-ups: Creating Jobs of the Future

Policymakers all over the world are increasingly recognising the job creation potential of start-ups. Germany is looking at a start-up initiative to create more than 100,000 new jobs by 2020. The UK has an Entrepreneurial Action Plan that, over a three-year period, has seen tech start-ups increase from 200 in 2010 to 1,200 in 2013. Israel is running a 'Start-up City Tel Aviv' program to create an early stage innovative ecosystem that can extend to Europe and beyond. India recently announced a US$1.7 billion (Rs: 10,000 crore) fund for start-ups, a US$1.2 billion (Rs: 7,000 crores) budget to fund smart cities, and a US$90 million (Rs: 500 crore) fund for a National Rural Internet and Technology Mission.

India's ICT industry body Nasscom estimates that between 2010 and 2014, US$3 billion has been invested in start-ups. India is now the fourth largest global start-up hub with over 3,000 tech/digital start-ups.

Nasscom further forecasts that, by 2020, an additional 11,500 start-ups will mushroom in India, generating at least 250,000 employment opportunities.

Bangalore is today the start-up capital of India and accounts for nearly 30 per cent of the country's start-ups. Sydney is home to half of Australian start-ups. What these two cities share is a conducive entrepreneurial ecosystem that links research, capital and technology-led ideas to the marketplace. The opportunity lies in bringing these two ecosystems together through policies and mechanisms that unleash the combined strengths of all such ecosystems in both countries.

The IT industry in India, built largely by first-generation entrepreneurs based out of Bangalore, generates annual revenues of over $100 billion and employs some 3.2 million people. It is estimated that there will be 2 million IT workers in Bangalore alone by 2020, outnumbering those in California's Silicon Valley.

Bangalore has also attracted a diverse number of life science start-ups over the years and has grown to be the biotech capital of India. I established my own company Biocon in a small garage in 1978 as the country's first biotech start-up and built it up into Asia's largest biotech enterprise today. I owe my success to Bangalore's scientific ecosystem and India's cost competitiveness, which has been leveraged by others to create a wide and diverse biotech cluster of bio-pharmaceutical, agri-biotech, industrial biotech, bio-energy and bio-informatics companies.

As a first-generation entrepreneur who started my own business in response to my unsuccessful job pursuit, I urge every jobless person to opt for self-employment. If I could build a billion-dollar business on a foundation of innovative ideas and meagre resources, with no business experience but an abundant spirit and youthful confidence, anyone can do so. I have learnt along the way that innovation creates value and differentiation builds competitive advantage. I have also realised that businesses need to evolve dynamically as a way to adapt and leverage new technologies. I started out as a biotech entrepreneur with a mission to 'green the world' through innovative enzyme technologies for a diverse range of industries. Perhaps this was an idea ahead of its time. The '70s and '80s were not about challenges of climate change but of poverty alleviation through industrialisation. Over time, my mission evolved to 'heal the world', driven by a business philosophy to provide globally affordable access to life-saving biotech drugs through economies of scale. I often say, a blockbuster drug is not about realising a billion dollars of sales but about treating a billion patients.

Conclusion

Prime Minister Narendra Modi recently paid a historic visit to Australia breaking a 28-year jinx and reinforcing the importance of building strong bilateral ties between our two countries. Prime Minister Tony Abbott echoed these sentiments and welcomed the ongoing and emerging business partnerships especially in mining and IT. While the focus was on mega projects, the potential to create partnerships in the small and medium-sized enterprise sector through technopreneurs, and the scope of jointly taking innovative ideas to global markets, is compelling. As Mike Cannon Brookes, co-founder of one of Australia's most successful start-ups, Atlassian, said: 'Australia does not offer the scale to support a credible start-up sector that can compete with those in the US, China and India'. In 2014, Indian start-ups attracted $1.8 billion and China $3.5 billion, whereas Australian start-ups received a mere $111 million. This is no indication of the quality of innovation, but rather the ability to scale up. There exists, therefore, a natural fit for partnerships with India that offer both size and scale in markets, manufacturing and services.

As an entrepreneur, I am cognisant of the need to partner and collaborate in order to leverage new technologies that will propel our business growth. Today, we are focused on personalising our products for global markets by adapting to new technological breakthroughs in gene-based diagnostics and smart medical devices that connect us with patients through novel service and delivery models. However, this is not through being vertically integrated, but by partnering with multiple providers of smart and innovative technologies. These companies are precursors of what the future holds — a vast and vibrant marketplace of millions of small, medium and large enterprises symbiotically interconnected to deliver superior and sustainable solutions.

I would like to conclude by saying that the future will belong to those countries and companies that can unleash the power of cross-border collaborations, invest in innovation and embrace entrepreneurship as an economic model of growth.

Oration 18:
2016 K.R. Narayanan Oration

Message from the President
of the Republic of India

I am happy to learn that the Australia South Asia Research Centre (ASARC) at The Australian National University (ANU) is organising the 18th K.R. Narayanan Oration on the theme 'The New Economics of Financial Inclusion in India' by Shri Arun Jaitley, Honourable Union Minister for Finance, Corporate Affairs and Information and Broadcasting, at The Australian National University on 31 March 2016.

While the Indian economy has made considerable progress in accelerating economic growth and poverty reduction, more work remains to be done to involve a larger proportion of the population in the formal financial sector. World Bank data for 2014 show that the proportion of Indians aged 15 and over with bank accounts was lower than that for a number of other countries. The proportion of women and of the relatively poor with bank accounts was even lower.

A rapid increase in financial inclusion would help mobilise savings, create new opportunities for credit off-take and facilitate increasing prosperity for our citizens. The new Jan Dhan Yojana is a significant step in this direction. Further, the use of biometric based Aadhaar Cards for Direct Benefit Transfers to bank accounts is an efficient method of removing intermediaries in the process of administering government subsidies and welfare payments. The fact that most of these operations can be done through technology embedded in mobile phones should further improve the efficiency of the financial sector and lead to a quantum jump in financial inclusion.

The focus on financial inclusion is timely and I wish the event all success.

Pranab Mukherjee
New Delhi
30 March 2016

The New Economics of Financial Inclusion in India

Arun Jaitely

The Chancellor of the University, Vice-Chancellor, High Commissioner, Professor Jha, ladies and gentlemen, many thanks to The Australian National University for inviting me to deliver this year's K.R. Narayanan Oration. K.R. Narayanan was one of the most distinguished diplomats and civil servants that India has produced. He came from a background that reflected the historically disadvantaged groups in India. He grew up in poverty and turned out to be an extremely brilliant diplomat and, eventually, president of India.

On a personal note, I happened to work closely with him when he was president, because I was sworn in as a minister by him for the first time and, as a law minister in the government at that time, I had to deal with him quite regularly. An extremely sharp mind, a strict constitutionalist, someone dedicated to the rules of good governance and good principles — that is the memory of Dr K.R. Narayanan that we all have. I am indeed privileged to join the list of some very eminent people who, in the past, have delivered this annual oration.

When we speak in terms of reforms and growth in India, a lot seems to have happened in the last two and a half decades. The Chancellor was mentioning that, in his various capacities as a former foreign minister and in any other ways, he had travelled extensively in India, and his initial memories seem to be of a ride in an Indian train in 1968, travelling in what was then called a third class compartment. We have come a long way since then.

The Chancellor also mentioned my fondness for cricket and, if I go back to where India was in those decades, I can recall incidents described in the Australian cricketer Steve Waugh's autobiography. Steve Waugh came to India in 1987 to play in the World Cup. From Mumbai, he would regularly telephone his girlfriend. The Indian telephone system at that time was that he had to sit next to the telephone the whole night, because he would be added to what we used to call the 'trunk call' queue. We have come a long way since then as well!

Twenty-one years ago (in 1995), India's telephone density was 0.8 per cent — less than 1 per cent of Indians had a telephone. Today, India has over 1 billion phones. This is only one illustration of how India has progressed from an economy that was essentially one of shortages. To give you another illustration: when I first became a member of parliament, this transformation was still taking place and each one of us used to be given a discretion. This discretion used to be that we could dole out special favours: for example, allocating cooking gas connections and telephone connections to people out of turn. Suddenly, within a year or two, I found that nobody would come to me to ask for this favour, because we were slowly turning from an economy of shortages to one of surpluses.

My then leader, Prime Minister Mr Vajpayee, said that we were only distributing telephones and gas connections. He said that he recollected that, in his earlier days as a member of parliament, he also had a discretion to allocate HMT watches. All members of parliament were allowed two HMT watches every year to allocate to people out of turn. That is the manner in which India's regulated economy worked. But I must say that the direction we followed from 1991 onwards has indeed served us well. It improved upon our growth rates and it brought down poverty levels.

Last week, I had the opportunity to deliver an annual lecture at the National Minorities Commission. I was extremely pleasantly surprised with the research I did for that lecture, which revealed that the maximum drop in poverty rates, even among minority communities, took place post-1991, so, as India grew, the economy improved.

Prior to 1991, we were quite happy and satisfied with an economy with a smaller base, growing at about 2–3 per cent every year. The world would sarcastically refer to this 2–3 per cent growth as the 'Hindu' rate of growth. Such growth was incapable of either significantly depleting poverty levels in India or giving enough resources to the state to improve the lot of the people. After opening out in 1991, successive governments did their little bit and the present government seems to be taking that to its logical conclusion.

The trend growth rate of the Indian economy has increased significantly. However, two to three years back, it was struggling with lower economic growth, unacceptably high inflation, high levels of current account deficit and fiscal deficit, huge piles of stalled infrastructure projects, drying employment opportunities and industrial weakness. Just two and a half years ago economists conducted an important analysis on the BRICS economies. After comparing Brazil, Russia, India, China and South Africa, they observed that there was a possibility of the 'I' in BRICS (i.e. India) being knocked off. However, today, as a result of rapid changes in the global economic order, thankfully this analysis has not come true, and the 'I' seems to stand for a faster growth rate.

Now, a gradual, but far-reaching transformation is taking place and our macroeconomic situation is characterised by strong economic growth, a comfortable price situation, low current account deficit, the highest ever foreign exchange reserve and a contracting fiscal deficit to GDP ratio. Investors have come to view India as a haven of stability and an outpost of opportunity for investments. Multilateral organisations, like the International Monetary Fund and World Bank refer to India as the 'bright spot' in the global economy and project a higher economic growth in 2016 as compared to 2015. Overall, the economy is moving in the right direction and is expected to perform better and gather momentum in the coming years, once the impact of the ongoing economic reforms takes root. India's long-run potential growth rate is still around 8–10 per cent, and achieving this potential would be the best way for India to achieve its varied socioeconomic objectives. High growth is necessary to help the poor to get out of the scourge of poverty, generate employment opportunities for unemployed youth, create more irrigation facilities for farmers and generate more resources for development in a fiscally sustainable manner.

One important aspect of economic debate has been whether reforms have helped economically and socially deprived sections of society. Initially, it was difficult and challenging for governments to conduct market reforms: it was argued that such reforms helped businesses and the private sector to grow, but did not significantly improve peoples' lives. A very large section of India's population live in adverse circumstances (e.g. Scheduled Castes and Scheduled Tribes) and these historically disadvantaged groups lack sources of employment. Many people live below the poverty line — at one stage it was more than 52–60 per cent — and we have some groups of minorities and others who have not prospered economically. Hence, the question: how have the reforms affected them?

Sectorally, if we look at the growth of the Indian economy, our services sector seems to be the best performing. Even with a global slowdown, our services sector grows at about 9–10 per cent per year. Our manufacturing sector can do better, but it is our agriculture sector that is the real challenge. Almost 55 per cent of India's population, even today, is dependent on agriculture, whereas the share of agriculture has shrunk to almost below 15 per cent of India's GDP. This indicates that more than 55 per cent of the population depends on this 15 per cent of national income. Therefore, this community is economically disadvantaged. This is the hard reality to be kept in mind.

What has been the Indian model of dealing with this? In my view, one of the mistakes that was made in the pre-liberalisation era, particularly in the 1960s and 1970s, was that we concentrated on distributive justice (i.e. distribution of the existing resources) and did not concentrate on increasing productivity. Both were necessary and that is why the 1960s and the 1970s, from the point of view of the Indian economy, virtually became a wasted period.

Post-liberalisation, the criticism was that we were growing faster, but this advantage of faster growth was not distributed fairly. Against this background, governments in India converged upon an economic model that entailed opening out, allowing investment and allowing the market to dominate so that our economy could grow faster.

Hence, we must ask: is the pull-up effect or the trickle-down effect — whatever you call it — adequate to take care of those who live below the poverty line in India? Unhesitatingly, the answer is 'no'. The pull-up effect does take place, but is inadequate, whence, with higher growth rates you need higher levels of revenue and resources to be made available for the government to give a boost to the economy and finance large numbers of poverty alleviation schemes.

The Indian model in that sense is now more that of a market economy, but with a social conscience, so that the resources earned by the state can also be used to service the less well-off sections of the population to expedite their exit out of poverty. That is the model, in larger or lesser measure, successive governments in India have been following.

Before I come to the subject of financial inclusion, where do we stand today? In terms of growth rate, it is a challenging situation globally for the whole world. The entire global economy is facing one of its most acute challenges in recent history. I think the new norm itself is unpredictability, not stability.

We are not sure how long this phase is going to last. Oil and commodity prices have hit rock bottom and growth rates across the world have been impacted. Are we in India satisfied with this? Compared to how the rest of the world is doing, I think we are rated as the fastest growing major economy in the world. But, if we assess this by our own standards, we believe we can do better. The financial year in India ends today (31 March), and we hope to finish this financial year at about 7.6 per cent growth rate. Last year, our growth rate was 7.2 per cent. So our basic parameters seem to be doing well. Hopefully, we will be able to maintain or even improve upon this figure, depending on the evolution of certain variables in the next year.

Our current account deficit is well under control. Inflation in India has been well under control for the last 16 consecutive months, and wholesale price index inflation has been negative for some time. Consumer price index inflation has been in the range of about 4–5 per cent at the highest, and interest rates are slowly coming down. Foreign exchange reserves are the highest ever. Until about August last year, the rupee was the only currency, other than the Swiss franc, that was able to maintain its value against the US dollar; however, following the devaluation in China, the rupee was also somewhat adversely affected.

With the basic parameters of the Indian economy doing well, where do we feel we can do better? Four variables are key here. The first variable is global headwinds. Today, the global situation is obstructive to very high rates of growth. For one, our exports are significantly impacted because global trade itself has shrunk; therefore, in terms of value, our exports have shrunk. Even if volumes remain the same, in value terms, our exports have shrunk because of falling commodity prices.

Second, we have had two years of bad monsoons. Fortunately, in Indian history, we have never had three bad monsoon seasons in a row. With relatively good monsoons, we have not had a food crisis recently in India. In fact, our surplus of food impacts on the purchasing power of the rural population, which in turn has a spiralling effect on industry, manufacturing and market demand generally.

Third, of course, is our ability to continue with the reforms process and to add to its base. The fourth point, which is something that has not helped the rest of the world but has helped us, are the low oil and commodity prices and their impact on our import bill. We are net buyers and have, therefore, been able to save a lot of money on account of lower oil prices, and to divert that resource into more useful areas of operation.

How do I see the reforms continuing in India? I think India still has a great appetite for reforms. In India there is a clear realisation that, post the 1990s, the country is a much better place to live and is performing much better than it was prior to 1991. Hence, there is a larger political consensus, both at the centre and with the states, about continuing with reforms. Reforms unleash India's energies and allow the free flow of capital into the country. They remove many forms of restrictions, whence, with the strength of entrepreneurship, the economy itself is able to grow faster.

As a part of the reforms process, we have opened up the economy significantly. Almost all sectors are open to foreign direct investment. In green field investment, we have the largest inflow anywhere in the world. In the last year alone, foreign direct investment has increased by 40 per cent.

In addition to this, formerly we had a bad reputation for not being the best place to conduct business. However, considerable work has now been done in this area, both by the central and the state governments. We have now moved up the global rankings.

We had a fairly aggressive taxation system. Now, we have rationalised our direct tax system and are trying to bring down taxes to a global level. In speaking to my counterparts in Australia, I have discovered that our taxes are more reasonable than the ones you pay here. In indirect tax, of course, you are a decade and a half ahead of us. We are now trying to implement a goods and services tax (GST) and economists still feel that, if we are able to implement it over the next few years, a successful GST is capable of adding to India's growth story.

Our main concentration, in terms of expenditure, is inflow into rural India, since one of the objectives of public finance is to fill up the gaps in private investment wherever you find them and create physical infrastructure. These are two very important areas to which public investment is going. Our infrastructure — almost every part of it, whether it is railways, rural roads, national highways, ports, airports or the power sector — is experiencing huge amounts of activity and growth. These require considerable investment and I quite candidly concede that this magnitude of investment is not available in India. Therefore, we have been reaching out to investors, pension funds and superannuation funds to come and invest in India. By maintaining this reform momentum, we intend to add to India's growth story.

Now, one aspect of financial inclusion relevant to rural areas is to give the benefit of increased growth to sections that have not yet received adequate benefits. What is our long-term planning about rural India? President Narayanan's successor, President Abdul Kalam's favourite subject for discussion used to be that India must end up giving urban-like facilities to rural areas. That may be a great vision, but it is also very challenging.

Let us examine what has recently been happening with regard to inclusive growth in rural areas. We have nearly 700,000 villages in India and, by 2019, we intend each village to be connected by a regular *pucca* (solid/permanent) road. The roads program for villages in India is one of the government's most successful programs. It involves every member of parliament, because every member knows that they have to visit the villages in their constituencies, and that their constituents will demand answers if they do not have access to improved roads. Between central and state governments, we will almost triple the allocation for rural roads this year.

A second point: out of the 700,000 villages, we found that 18,000 of them were not electrified. The Prime Minister has decreed that, in the next 1,000 days, all 18,000 villages have to be individually targeted for electrification. We do not want a single non-electrified village in India. As I speak to you today, last week we had electrified 5,000 out of these 18,000, and the indications are that we may be able to achieve this target ahead of time.

Apart from the electrification of all villages and road access to all villages, the Prime Minister's call for a clean India — the Swachh Bharat Abhiyan campaign — now speaks in terms of a toilet in every home. Last year, we envisaged that every school in every village must have a toilet, so that lakhs and lakhs of toilets had to be constructed. We have completely achieved this target. This is a huge campaign: as well as the government, the World Bank is also partly helping to finance the project and corporate India is putting a lot of CSR (corporate social responsibility) money into the campaign. The goal is to enable every home in every village to have a toilet and, where this is not possible, to make clean collective community toilets available to villagers in rural areas. Housing for all is a very tall order: the provision of regular, *pucca* houses in rural areas is another ongoing program.

The interest component of repayments on loans taken out by farmers for purposes of cultivation is now being subsidised partly by the central government and partly by state governments. Hence, the net interest rates on such loans has been substantially reduced. This is another avenue for helping farmers.

The previous government had started the Rural Employment Guarantee Scheme. I have added to it and amended it, so that it can also result in some asset creation in villages. The amounts now being earmarked for this scheme are much larger. Starting from tomorrow, a campaign is being launched to ensure that the payments that unemployed people get as part of the Rural Employment Guarantee Scheme are directly transferred to people's bank accounts (rather than the monies going from the central government to state governments, from state governments to the district, from the district to the *panchayat* (village council) and then being billed forward before reaching the farmer). We have thus removed a number of intermediaries.

Various avenues of funding for empowering rural India are ongoing. What is it that the financial inclusion campaign specifically envisioned? Two years ago, we realised that only 58 per cent of families in India had bank accounts — 42 per cent were completely outside the banking network. One of the first programs of the government was to make sure that every family is connected to a bank, even if there was no balance to deposit in the bank. The banks hired employees, called business correspondents, who went from house to house and reached each one of the 42 per cent who were outside the banking system. Those who were opening bank accounts were incentivised by telling them that they would get a debit card and a facility for an overdraft if they operated that account.

When we conceptualised the Pradhan Mantri Jan Dhan Yojana (PMJDY), which is our National Mission for Financial Inclusion, we were aware that some attempts had been made in this space in the past. However, our ambition was much larger. For instance, instead of reaching out to geographically larger villages, we targeted every household and provided them with the facility of a bank account. Second, we leveraged technology to our advantage. We opened all bank accounts using a core banking platform, so that all new customers could be provided with the facility of a debit card. This was something that had not been considered before, as it was felt that the poor could not use such cards. Third, we combined all aspects of financial services, like savings, credit, insurance and pensions, with this overall mission. And, finally, we adopted a mission mode with very tough time lines and completed the herculean task of opening 125 million bank accounts in less than 150 days.

For us, these bank accounts were not an end in themselves but the gateway to something bigger. In the past, many international agencies in the financial inclusion space held the view that India had the dubious distinction of having the largest number of zero balance accounts. Indeed, poverty levels are such that almost 73 per cent of these accounts did not have a single rupee in them. In order to transfer money into these accounts, the government introduced a system of direct cash transfers for certain subsidies. These subsidies originate from various government schemes, for example, scholarships, widows pensions, old-age pensions and minorities scholarships. The recipient's cash subsidy is directly transmitted to the account of every beneficiary. These transfers have become operational and, in a period of about two years, today about 75 per cent of these accounts are actually operational. There is money in them, people operate them and use the debit cards given to them. Indeed, this has turned out to be one of the most successful programs.

We have ensured that, out of the 213 million accounts that have been opened so far, less than 28 per cent are dormant. Our new customers have deposited more than Rs 348 billion, approximately US$5 billion. As we talk, there is a mission team back home in India that is monitoring these accounts to ensure that the zero balance accounts decrease to less than 20 per cent.

Financial inclusion is at the core of our development philosophy. We therefore immediately started utilising these new accounts for:

1. providing social security to people
2. providing affordable credit to entrepreneurs
3. plugging the leakage in our subsidy disbursements.

In order to provide social security, we launched three schemes last year. The first provides life cover of Rs 200,000, the second provides accident insurance cover of Rs 200,000 and the third is a pension scheme for people aged between 18 and 40 years. The beauty of these schemes is not only that they are being offered at very nominal premium, but also that they are linked to the bank accounts opened by the people. This linking ensures that the auto-debit takes place from the accounts and the customers only need to be aware that they need to have sufficient balance in their accounts. More than 130 million customers have joined the two insurance schemes so far. We ensured that social security coverage was paid for by the people themselves, by ensuring that the rates were the lowest so far in the industry.

Now, building on this, we have a database of what is called the JAM trinity, whereby 'J' is the Jan Dhan Yojana account (i.e. the bank accounts), 'A' is an Aadhaar card (which I will explain below) and 'M' stands for 1 billion mobile telephone connections.

We created — and now it has legislative support in parliament — an Aadhaar number, which is a unique identity number that every Indian resident has. Already, about 1 billion people have been allotted this: 98 per cent of adults and 67 per cent of children. We are adding about five to seven lakh people per day to this identity scheme. This unique identity has some particular features of the individual and so every individual is now identified by this number.

This enables us to identify those who need support. There are a large number of subsidies in India: petrol is subsidised, diesel is subsidised, cooking gas is subsidised, food for poor people is subsidised, fertiliser for farmers is subsidised. All state governments support these subsidies. Formerly, the challenge was that unquantified amounts of subsides were given to unidentified sections of people.

The problem of leakages in government subsidies had been affecting the nation for some time. To fix this, we started linking accounts opened under the Jan Dhan scheme with the Aadhar card and with mobile numbers. A database of 1.2 billion bank accounts, when linked with 1 billion mobile phone numbers and about a billion Aadhar numbers, would ensure that subsidies only flowed to those who needed them. India's direct benefits transfer schemes have become the largest in the world. So far, our estimates show that about Rs 170 billion in subsidies has been saved in cooking gas alone. Parliament's approval of statutory status for Aadhar will further accelerate Aadhar seeding in bank accounts.

When the scheme started, each one of us, including me, was getting the benefit of, say, a cooking gas subsidy. Cooking gas attracts a subsidy ceiling of about 25 per cent, which is a considerable amount. Any money released from this subsidy can be utilised for helping various people. We have added this as part of the social security campaign. Now, there is no reason why this subsidy should have been made available to people like me, so we started a campaign to remove those who did not deserve the subsidy. This parallel campaign, called 'Give It Up', asked people to voluntarily give up their LPG (liquefied petroleum gas) subsidy. Fortunately for us, oil prices fell, so we were able to link petrol and diesel prices to the market. The cooking gas subsidy now reaches 210 million (21 crore) accounts through the Jan Dhan. The cooking gas subsidy now goes to the account of 140 million people each month, so do the scholarships and the other pensions in various forms, so these people have some operational balances always available to them. All this was accomplished in about four months.

Now that Aadhaar has legislative backing, we intend to use it for the fertiliser subsidy in the first instance and then the food subsidy. We will implement it wherever we deem this possible.

The third thing we did was to use these accounts to offer pensions. Outside the government, India is an unpensioned society. Most Indians do not get a pension and most pension plans have very few subscribers. It is only government or quasi-government employers who get pensions.

There is thus a need to make India into a pension society. Some of my proposals, despite being well-intentioned, failed because people did not realise the consequences of ageing and having nothing to fall back on. Subsequently, we started offering extremely low-cost insurance policies. For instance, we have about 130 million poor people opting for 2 lakh rupee accident insurance. So, if a bread earner dies, his family gets at least some assistance. The total amount of premium that is required to be paid out of these Jan Dhan accounts is 1 rupee per month.

Similarly, we brought in a normal life insurance policy. This also provides a reasonably low-cost pension scheme. These two insurance policies have been runaway successes. The pension scheme is still taking time to register, because people have not realised the benefits of having a pension program for themselves. I think one day, hopefully, following the pattern in Australia, the US and Europe, we could insist on people compulsorily contributing — at least those who can afford it — towards a pension.

In short, bank accounts have been opened, money has been put into these bank accounts, and insurance facilities have been made available. However, what do we do with the large body of people who cannot get a job either in the government or in the private sector? Across the world, the provision of credit to entrepreneurs is the need of the hour. For this purpose, we launched the MUDRA scheme, which provides credit, at bank rates of interest, of up to Rs 1 million to entrepreneurs without any collateral. We encouraged entrepreneurs to set up businesses and small establishments on their own. The banks were naturally worried about the prospect of any such credit turning bad. Hence, we created a credit guarantee mechanism for the banks so that defaults could be taken care of. Our larger view is that the self-employed and small entrepreneur sector in India is the largest employment provider. According to our surveys, there are 57.7 million small business units in the country, which employ 120 million people and are mostly outside the formal banking system. Hence, we want to strengthen this sector. The MUDRA scheme has also been a runaway success. So far, 29.8 million customers have benefited under the scheme with total loans of Rs 1,180 billion. As the financial year expires today, I will have the final figures for this year in the next two days.

Each such borrower is given a credit card and can use ATM machines. They can withdraw money up to their credit limit. Each one of these small entrepreneurs tries to deposit money into their account because these ATMs are open 24 hours a day and they wish to save on interest costs by making deposits by 12.00 pm.

This has become a massive program of financial inclusion: from bank accounts, to state support, to insurance, to pension programs, to making funds available through banking. It is quite heartening to note that, in this sector, like in most micro-finance schemes that the banks arrange themselves or through various micro-finance agencies, bad debt is almost negligible. These are people who want to do business and set up small enterprises.

What are we doing with the savings that we are making out of these subsidy programs? This year, I will announce three schemes. One is entirely state supported. The entire benefit we got from rationalising the cooking gas subsidy is slated to gift 50 million (5 crore) female-headed households with cooking gas connections. Otherwise, these households would use the conventional *chulhas* (earthen or brick stove). Medical studies have shown that, in a single day, a conventional *chulha* can do as much damage to the health of the lady who cooks as smoking 400 cigarettes. We picked up the poorest 5 crore families in India for this scheme. Hence, the savings we have made by keeping wealthy people from receiving subsidies and excluding duplicate connections has gone to the poor.

Second, for the Indian farmer, we have come up with a very low-cost crop insurance scheme. When crops fail, farmers suffer, and some have even be pushed to commit suicide because they are unable to repay the loans taken against the harvest. This new insurance scheme will enable farmers to repay the loans, so that they can get back at least part of their investment, even if there is a crop failure. In this insurance scheme, 25 per cent of the premium is to be paid by the farmer, 25 per cent by the state government and 50 per cent by the central government. Any farmer who wants his crop to be insured can get the benefit of this insurance.

The third initiative financed by the monies saved is a health scheme. This is in two parts. One-third of India's population — the poorest one-third — will get, at state expense, health insurance, which covers hospital charges up to a limit of 1 lakh rupees. Anybody who is a senior citizen in that category will get additional cover of about Rs 30,000. This is an annual insurance policy.

Therefore, we have initiated crop insurance, health insurance, crop insurance subsidised substantially by the state, health insurance subsidised entirely by the state, and a cooking gas facility provided entirely by the state. These are the directions in which we have been taking India's financial inclusion.

The net object of this exercise is that, when we grow faster, the state gets more revenue. However, in addition to the natural advantage of jobs being created and so on, one is able to use this additional resource to provide help in areas that need support.

The last scheme, which we are launching in the coming week, is something called Stand Up India. Stand Up India is addressed to three sections of Indian society: Scheduled Castes, Scheduled Tribes and women. Every bank branch in India, public or private, has been asked to support one entrepreneur from either the Scheduled Castes, Scheduled Tribes or who is a woman.

The banks will lend up to 1 crore (10 million) rupees and create, in the first instance, about 2 lakhs (50,000) new entrepreneurs coming from these sections. There have not been too many entrepreneurs coming up from these groups. This is a scheme we intend to launch as a part of our support to the social sector and as part of this government's financial inclusions schemes.

As can be seen from our journey so far, we have largely adopted a self-funding model for financial inclusion. We have been successful in telling people that certain services need to be paid for and certain subsidies are meant only for the poor and downtrodden and not for the middle class. The deregulation of diesel prices, a new fertiliser policy and the introduction of the PAHAL scheme for the transfer of the cooking gas subsidy have rationalised India's subsidy expenditure. The deployment of the JAM trinity is a hugely innovative intervention to carry this forward and place government finances at prudent levels.

Meanwhile, the government is also bringing about several measures for the promotion of payments through cards and digital means. The goal of the proposed policy changes is to replace the use of cash — either in government transactions or in regular commerce — by providing the necessary incentives to use digital financial transactions over a period of time through policy intervention. These measures will further strengthen our efforts at financial inclusion, as they will help to ensure that each eligible account holder under PMJDY is provided access to digital financial services in addition to the 'RuPay Card'. In this regard, 'PayGov India' will be developed as a 'single unified portal' across central and state governments and their public sector undertakings for collection purposes. Wherever needed, the departments and ministries shall make modifications in the rules and regulations that may have been issued, so that appropriate changes are incorporated to allow payments and receipts by using cards or other digital means. Mobile banking will be promoted to leverage upon the huge infrastructure available at lower cost. This will also bring efficiency in payments systems and ensure that merchants and consumers can leverage their credit histories to access instant, low-cost micro-credit through digital means, and also create necessary linkages between payment transaction histories and credit information. The efficiencies gained, and the reduction in transaction costs, will benefit all, including the poorer sections of society.

The current government's quest to extend financial inclusion to the most deprived sections of society will be made possible by another of its initiatives: Digital India. As stated by Prime Minister Shri Narendra Modi, it is not enough for India to say that it is an ancient civilisation, and a country of 1.25 billion people enjoying demographic dividends. Modern technology should also be blended with these strengths. Our prime minister has reiterated our government's resolve to not allow the digital divide to become a barrier between people. Our vision of e-governance and mobile governance is one in which all important government services, including financial services, are available on mobile instruments. Our prime minister has resolved, and I quote: 'I dream of a digital India where High-speed Digital Highways unite the Nation; 1.2 billion connected Indians drive innovation; technology ensures the citizen-government interface is incorruptible.'

From a commercial viewpoint, banks get 1 per cent commission on the amounts transferred under direct benefits transfers, particularly for those schemes that are rural oriented. This effectively compensates them for the costs they incur in extending the last mile reach of the Bank Mitras, which are our channels of branchless banking in the villages.

The Indian model of financial inclusion has been recognised and appreciated across the world. While others have talked about it, we have demonstrated that there is fortune at the bottom of the pyramid. I would like to conclude by saying that a clear political will combined with effective monitoring structures can accomplish such great financial inclusion milestones as have been achieved in India. Hopefully, in the years to come, as our government earns more resources, additional benefits will continue to accrue to the poorest sections of society. That is all I have to say and thank you very much.

Oration 19:
2017 K.R. Narayanan Oration

Message from the President
of the Republic of India

I am happy to know that the Australia South Asia Research Centre (ASARC) at The Australian National University is organising the 19th K.R. Narayanan Oration on 'India: A Resurgent Maritime Nation, Harnessing the Blue Economy' by Admiral R.K. Dhowan (Retd), currently Chairman, National Maritime Foundation on 25 May 2017.

India is a major maritime nation. The Indian seaboard has been the centre of intense maritime activity over several centuries. India has been cooperating with other maritime nations in the sustainable utilisation of ocean resources and providing security. Recent Indian initiatives in this area include the International Fleet Review in February, 2016 in Visakhapatnam where the Prime Minister outlined India's policy of the development of the Indian Ocean through 'SAGAR', or ocean, which is also an acronym for 'Security and Growth for all in the Region'.

The concept of 'blue economy' is emerging as the new paradigm and aims at sustainable development of the oceans. The importance of this 'blue economy' is underscored by the fact that in 2014 international trade accounted for nearly 50 per cent of India's GDP with 95 per cent of this trade by volume and 72 per cent by value dependent on ocean transport.

I wish the event all success.

Pranab Mukherjee
New Delhi
22 May 2017

India: A Resurgent Maritime Nation, Harnessing the Blue Economy

R.K. Dhowan

The Deputy Vice-Chancellor of The Australian National University, High Commissioner of India, Professor Jha, distinguished guests, ladies and gentlemen. It is indeed a distinct honour and a proud privilege for me to be present here today at The Australian National University to deliver this year's K.R. Narayanan Oration and share my thoughts with such an eminent audience.

President K.R. Narayanan, India's 10th president, was born on 27 October 1920 in the coastal state of Kerala. He was a distinguished diplomat, an erudite scholar and a capable leader with a maritime vision. As president of India, he reviewed the first International Fleet Review off Mumbai in 2001. Nearly 30 navies of the world participated. During his address, he said that a nation's independence and prosperity depended on the security of the seas, and he described the Fleet Review as a magnificent demonstration by navies of the world to build bridges of friendship among nations.

The subject of my talk today is also related to the seas and oceans and I shall specifically talk about India as a resurgent maritime nation, harnessing the blue economy.

The ocean and the seas have always enthused each one of us, as we all are tied and connected to the oceans. The world's history, its geography, its interactions in a globalised world, its development and security, are all intimately and intricately connected to the oceans around us. Our blue planet, the Earth, has a large maritime domain, with over 70 per cent of its surface covered by water, nearly 80 per cent of its population living within 200 nautical miles of the coast and about 90 per cent of its trade transiting by sea.

India is essentially a maritime nation and the Indian seaboard has been the vortex of intense maritime activity over centuries. The Indus Valley civilisation that existed in the western parts of India dates back to 3,300 BC. Even today we have a dry dock at Lothal in Gujarat that dates back to 2,200 BC. It is from these small ports that seafarers sailed to distant ports in Mesopotamia, ancient Egypt and the east coast of Africa. On the east coast of India we had the seafaring kingdoms of the Kalinga, the Cholas, the Pandyas and the Cheras who sailed to distant countries in South-East Asia and established trade and cultural links. Even today, in some South-East Asian countries, we can see glimpses of Indian cultural heritage in language, architecture, customs and traditions.

India lost it supremacy over its surrounding sea areas with the arrival of European sea powers, beginning with the arrival of the Portuguese sailor Vasco da Gama on 20 May 1498 at Calicut. Vasco da Gama was followed by Dutch, British and French seafarers.

Indian shipbuilding is synonymous with India's seafaring tradition. Indian shipbuilding was legendary for its high quality even during the British period. In the 100 years after 1753, the Bombay naval dockyard built more than 115 war vessels and 144 merchant ships, including 84 gunships for the Royal Navy. In fact, HMS *Trincomalee*, the oldest British warship afloat and still in commission in the UK as a museum ship (at Hartlepool), was built in India for the Royal Navy by Wadia shipbuilders of Bombay in 1817. The period from 1900 onwards began India's gradual maritime revival and we see a renewed vigour in this century.

Oceans are central to life on Earth. They are rich in oil and minerals resources, suppliers of oxygen, absorbers of carbon dioxide, a virtual heat sink and rich in biodiversity, and they have emerged as the global economic highways for the transit of trade.

With the depletion of resources on land, humankind has turned towards the oceans. There is a common misperception that oceans have an unending resource base and are an infinite sink. Yet, nothing could be further from the truth. Over the past few decades, we have witnessed pollution of the oceans, contamination of the natural marine habitat and the adverse impacts of climate change on the oceans. Studies have indicated that 80 per cent of pollutants in the seas emanate from land and, if the current rate of pollution continues, in a few decades we will have more plastic in the oceans than fish.

The concept of a 'blue economy' is emerging as a new paradigm that aims at sustainable development of the oceans. Harnessing the oceans based on a blue economy calls for efficient utilisation of marine resources without substantial environmental impact and ensuring sustained growth of the oceans.

Like Australia, India has a unique maritime disposition. India has a natural outflow towards the seas and the country sits astride busy sea lines of communication that transit across the Indian Ocean region. The Indian Ocean is the third-largest water body in the world, spanning an area of approximately 68.5 million sq. km. Rich in natural resources, it is the world's energy hub and global economic highway; the countries on the rim of the Indian Ocean are home to nearly one-third of humanity. Sixty-six per cent of the world's oil, 50 per cent of the world's container traffic and 33 per cent of the world's cargo traffic transit over the waters of the Indian Ocean.

Peninsular India enjoys a central position in the Indian Ocean region, with our island territories of Andaman and Nicobar in the Bay of Bengal and the Lakshadweep Islands in the Arabian Sea as the virtual extended arms of India. India has a coastline of over 7,500 km, more than 1,300 islands and islets, and an exclusive economic zone (EEZ) of over 2 million sq. km. Our waters hold the immense promise of sustainable development for the seas around India, and for the region as a whole. Apart from the length of the coastline, the importance of India's coastal regions is accentuated by the fact that 20 per cent of India's population lives in coastal states, contributing to 60 per cent of India's GDP.

Approximately 95 per cent of India's trade by volume and 72 per cent by value transits through the sea. Therefore, India is heavily dependent on the maritime domain, and foreign trade accounts for nearly 50 per cent of India's GDP (2014). India's vast maritime interests, which are enablers of a blue economy, have a vital relationship with the nation's economic growth. I will now highlight some of the growing maritime sectors in India and the opportunities they present therein.

India has 12 major ports and over 200 minor and intermediate ports. With regard to port infrastructure, there is scope for growth to cater for the growing Indian economy. Cargo traffic in Indian ports is expected to increase from 1,052 million metric tonnes per annum (MMTPA) in 2014–15 to more than 2,500 MMTPA by 2025. To harness India's maritime growth potential, the Government of India has embarked on the ambitious Sagarmala Project, which aims to boost development through the promotion of ports and shipping. The port-led development plan is based on four pillars of port modernisation: connectivity, port-led industrialisation and coastal community development. Under this plan, more than 150 projects have been identified at an estimated infrastructure investment of US$60–70 billion. Due impetus is being given to this initiative to boost green and environmentally friendly infrastructure development. The port development perspective plan envisages setting up shipping hubs on both coasts. Connectivity for coastal shipping, inland waterways, and road and rail networks is also being expanded in a systematic manner.

Currently, 94 per cent of Indian freight is transported by either road or rail with only 6 per cent using the coastal or inland waterways. As is well known, waterborne transportation is safer, cheaper and cleaner compared to other modes of transportation. Efforts are therefore being made to enhance and improve the coastal shipping routes.

India currently has 14,500 km of navigable inland waterways that contributes only 2 per cent towards traffic evacuation at major ports, as against an optimum of 10 per cent in coordination with coastal shipping. The Inland Waterways Authority of India is developing five national waterways totalling more than 4,500 km. The authority has commenced work on the 'Jal Marg Vikas' project on the river Ganga (National Waterway I), to be developed between Allahabad and Haldia by 2020 for commercial navigation. Further, to facilitate this project, Kolkata port has already initiated plans for an investment of more than US$170 million for construction of riverine terminals, jetties and augmentation of navigational infrastructure. The other major national waterways include National Waterway 2 on the Brahmaputra River, National Waterway 3 in the state of Kerala, National Waterway 4 on the east coast in the states of Tamil Nadu and Andhra Pradesh, and National Waterway 5 in the coastal state of Orissa. This highlights the huge investment and growth opportunity being opened up with the planned development of additional inland waterways.

The mercantile marine and shipping industry is also envisaged to grow in the near future. India currently has a merchant fleet of approximately 1,174 ships flying the Indian flag, totalling nearly 22 million gross registered tons. While over 90 per cent of India's trade by volume transits by sea, the share of Indian shipping in the country's foreign external trade has declined from about 30 per cent in the 1980s to approximately 10 per cent today. To enable India's growing foreign trade to be carried on Indian hulls, the Indian Government is providing incentives for registering ships as 'Indian Hull Ships' and initiating measures to increase the tonnage of 'Indian Controlled Shipping' by promoting our shipbuilding industry. The enhanced requirements of crude and LNG carriers are also being taken into account considering that 80 per cent of our oil and 40 per cent of LNG requirements are met by import and this is likely to grow in the future.

India has a vibrant shipbuilding industry with 27 shipyards. The government has initiated several steps to provide support to shipbuilding, as well as ship-repair and ship-recycling, with the aim of enhancing India's global share of shipbuilding by 2020. Incentives for indigenous ship production include tax waivers, induction of new technology, setting up design centres, and a special infrastructure status for the shipbuilding industry. In order to provide a further boost, the government has also permitted 100 per cent foreign direct investment in the shipbuilding sector.

Another aspect I would like to mention is the warship-building industry in India, which is firmly anchored on self-reliance and indigenisation. The Indian Navy set up its naval design directorate in 1964. India built its first indigenous naval warship, a patrol vessel named INS *Ajay*, in 1961 at Garden Reach Shipyard in Kolkata. Over the past 50 years, our naval designers have designed, and our indigenous shipyards have built, numerous ships for the Indian Navy. Today, it is a matter of great pride that all 46 ships and submarines under construction are being built in Indian shipyards. These range from aircraft carrier to frigates, and from destroyers to submarines. It is our endeavour to progressively increase indigenous content so that future warships and submarines are 100 per cent 'Made in India'.

The fishing industry is another sector that provides significant opportunities for growth. India has approximately 250,000 fishing boats, 4 million active fishermen and 14 million people involved in the fishing industry. Annual marine fish landings in India are approximately 9.58 million tons, which accounts for approximately 5.3 per cent of the world's production. The sector contributes around US$5,511 million to India's foreign exchange earnings and has the potential to grow much more.

However, this is only scratching the surface of the vast potential of the fishing industry in India, which is largely coastal in nature, with logistic and maintenance support being provided by local, small-scale enterprises and fishing boats operating in coastal waters. There exists a huge potential for growth in the fishing sector by undertaking deep-sea fishing; increasing the size and numbers of current fishing fleets; and enhancing the support infrastructure for stowage, processing and transporting the catch. This would also provide the opportunity to build large numbers of deep-sea fishing trawlers in our own boat and shipyards.

India's EEZ also provides offshore energy resources that are critical to our economy. This includes offshore petroleum and natural gas exploration areas off the west and east coasts of India. Nearly 50 per cent of our total domestic crude production and 80 per cent of domestic natural gas production comes from offshore areas. India has nearly 6.9 billion metric tonnes of in-place oil reserves and 3.98 billion cubic metres of in-place natural gas reserves. There exists ample scope to ramp-up our production to meet the growing domestic demand by engaging the private sector, offering exploration licences and using advanced technologies for deep-sea drilling.

Island development is another major thrust area for the government. India has over 1,300 islands and islets, including the islands of Andaman and Nicobar in the Bay of Bengal, Lakshadweep Islands in the Arabian Sea and islands off the west and east coast of the country. There is considerable potential to develop these areas for controlled ecotourism. A comprehensive island development plan that takes into account aspects of security, economic sustenance, environmental preservation, and social and cultural sustenance is being implemented by the government.

Marine tourism is another dynamic and fast-growing component of the leisure industry worldwide. India, with its vast and beautiful coastline, island territories and lagoons, is an attractive destination for cruise tourism. The cruise tourism sector is a promising focus area for the tourism industry, and there are plans for the investment of more than $490 million (across nine projects) for promoting cruise shipping.

Another innovative marine tourism initiative by the government is 'lighthouse tourism'. There are nearly 190 lighthouses along the Indian coast and the surrounding areas offer opportunities for the development of hotels, resorts, adventure sports and allied tourism facilities. Marina-based tourism and leisure sailing is another segment that has significant scope for growth in India. India's long coastline and the Lakshadweep, Andaman and Nicobar islands present a scenic and picturesque landscape that is being harnessed for marinas and leisure sailing. These provide attractive avenues for growth, investment and job creation.

Marine-based renewable energy is another up-and-coming maritime sector. India is one of the five largest wind energy markets in the world today. The first demonstration offshore wind power project of about 100 MW capacity is underway along the Gujarat coast. With a vast coastline, India has significant potential to tap offshore wind to meet its growing energy and electricity demands.

Renewable ocean energy is another unharnessed niche sector with immense future scope. This includes ocean thermal, tidal and wave energy in particular. The application of ocean thermal energy can transform the way we provide electricity to our islands and even coastal cities. The Indian Navy has already initiated a unique project for using renewable energy by ocean thermal energy conversion in our islands. I am convinced that ocean energy is the energy source of the future, and hence an excellent investment option.

The growth of India's maritime sector necessitates significant improvement and growth in our nautical training capabilities. There are significant numbers of Indians in the international seafaring community, with approximately 7 per cent of the world's seafarers being Indian. There are nearly 150 approved marine training institutions in India and the number is growing. These act as feeder institutions for the growing demand of human capital for the global shipping industry and makes India an ideal place to groom the seafarers of the future. This calls for investment to set up world-class maritime training institutions in India. While projects worth more than US$180 million are already in the pipeline for the establishment of maritime education, training and skill development, there is scope for further growth and expansion.

Clearly, there are many opportunities for the development of maritime interests for economic growth; however, the challenge lies in harnessing the enablers of a blue economy, in which oceans are seen as the common heritage of mankind and protection of the environment is as important as economic growth to ensure sustainable development.

The seas are no longer a benign medium and globalisation has resulted in the increased vulnerability of the oceans. The threats and challenges in the maritime domain of the Indian Ocean are as wide and varied as they come. Who could have imagined that, in the 21st century, we would once again be grappling with pirates, or that the major threat in the maritime domain would emanate from asymmetric warfare and maritime terrorism. Other challenges include arms trafficking, drug smuggling, human trafficking and poaching. The instabilities and tensions in the Indian Ocean region have the potential to flow into the maritime domain and the situation may best be described as fragile. In addition, nearly 70 per cent of natural disasters emanate in the Indian Ocean region, providing additional challenges. Given the geostrategic importance of the region, and the fact that the Indian Ocean has emerged as a global economic highway, nearly 120 warships from over 20 nations are always present in the Indian Ocean region to safeguard their maritime interests. India has vast maritime interests and the responsibility of protecting these interests falls squarely on the shoulders of men in white uniforms — the Indian Navy and the coastguard. It is their responsibility to ensure that our maritime interests, which have a vital relationship with the nation's economic growth, are allowed to be developed unhindered at all times.

The Indian Navy has emerged as a multidimensional networked force that is ready to take on challenges in the Indian Ocean region. It ensures maritime security for national prosperity under four basic roles: military, constabulary, benign and diplomatic. Under the military role, the Indian Navy is always prepared to deal with any exigency and threat to maritime security and undertakes frequent exercises to enhance its capabilities. Under the constabulary role, it ensures coastal and offshore security in our waters and the EEZ. In addition, ships of the Indian Navy have been deployed in the Gulf of Aden for anti-piracy patrols since 2008 and cooperation between the navies of the world has been effective to combat piracy and bring it under control.

The Indian Navy also carries out surveillance and patrol in the EEZ of our maritime neighbours in coordination with the maritime forces of these countries. Under the benign role, the Indian Navy undertakes maritime and disaster relief operations and provides rapid responses to contingencies. This exemplifies the unique brotherhood of the seas and the ability of navies to facilitate cooperation.

Under the diplomatic role, the Navy has expanded its operational footprint in the Indian Ocean and beyond to engage with other navies of the world including the Royal Australian Navy for interaction and exercises. The aim is to shape a favourable maritime environment and provide avenues of cooperation for mutual benefit. Such engagement with other navies includes capacity building and capability enhancement initiatives and information exchange for comprehensive maritime domain awareness.

In 2008, the Indian Navy launched a unique initiative of the Indian Ocean Naval Symposium (IONS) — a construct to manage the maritime affairs of the countries of the Indian Ocean region. Over the years, the IONS has emerged as an effective organisation with membership of 22 navies and four observers. In my view, IONS has the potential to provide an effective template to promote cooperation in the maritime domain in the Indian Ocean region.

The Indian Ocean Rim Association (IORA) is another organisation that provides avenues for strengthening maritime cooperation between countries of the Indian Ocean region. Incidentally, 20 members of IORA have navies that are members of IONS, and there has been increasing synergy between IORA and IONS for promoting maritime cooperation in recent years. Australia has been the chair for both IORA and IONS and has contributed significantly towards strengthening the maritime cooperation mechanism between member nations.

In our continuing efforts to bring the navies of the world together, the Indian Navy conducted the International Fleet Review at Visakhapatnam on the east coast of India in February 2016. Fifty navies of the world came together and we had nearly 100 ships at the review anchorage. The international fleets were reviewed by Honourable President of India Shri Pranab Mukherjee. The underlying theme of the review was that we may be separated by geography but we are 'united through oceans'.

Each continent was represented, as were navies big and small, and the grand maritime event offered an opportunity for navies to partner together for a secure maritime future.

During the International Fleet Review, Shri Narendra Modi outlined India's vision for the Indian Ocean through 'SAGAR' (meaning ocean), which stands for 'Security And Growth for All in the Region'. India later conducted the Maritime Summit at Mumbai in April 2016, where the Prime Minister articulated his maritime vision for the nation. India's recent initiatives in the maritime domain, including the quest for harnessing the blue economy, are pointers to indicate that India has once again turned towards the sea and is destined to emerge as a resurgent maritime nation.

In conclusion, the seas around us are gaining new-found importance due to their linkages with the blue economy and there is no doubt that the twenty-first century is the century of the seas. The Indian Ocean has emerged as the world's centre of gravity in the maritime domain. Another unique feature of the Indian Ocean is that 80 per cent of oil and trade that emanates in the Indian Ocean is extra-regional in nature. This implies that if there is any impediment to the free flow of oil and trade it would have a detrimental impact not just on the economies of the region, but also on global economies. Therefore, safety, security and stability on the waters of the Indian Ocean is of paramount importance, and it is the collective responsibility of the navies and the coastguards to ensure the security of the global commons. Networking among navies and global maritime partnerships are emerging as the new order in the current century.

The Indian Navy and the Royal Australian Navy have had friendly relations over decades and have pursued many avenues of cooperation ranging from port visits, exercises, maritime domain information exchanges and training of personnel. In the coming years, these avenues of cooperation are likely to grow, further strengthening the bonds of friendship between our navies.

India and Australia are maritime neighbours who have extended their hand across the Indian Ocean for maritime cooperation. I am sure that, in the coming decade, our two great maritime nations will partner together to harness the blue economy, which I would like to term as a 'partnership for prosperity' in the maritime domain. This will open up many areas of cooperation in the maritime sector and will ensure sustainable development of the oceans.

Oration 20:
2018 K.R. Narayanan Oration

Message from the President
of the Republic of India

I am happy to learn that the Australia South Asia Research Centre, at The Australian National University, Canberra, is hosting the 20th K.R. Narayanan Oration on the topic 'Dismantling Inequality through ASSURED Innovation'. The oration is to be delivered by Dr R.A. Mashelkar, FRS, Chairman, National Innovation Foundation of India, on 19 April 2018.

It is imperative for our society to assure inclusive progress so that all sections benefit. For India, the world's fastest growing large economy, inclusive progress remains a cherished commitment. To accelerate this process, the Government of India has taken several policy initiatives — in the areas of tax simplification and investment, governance and regulatory affairs, and citizen empowerment, among others. It is our endeavour that these steps will serve to ensure inclusive growth and reduce inequality.

Technological innovations too have the potential to reduce inequalities. At the very least, they can help bring about equality of access to the essentials of human life and dignity. And both the public and private sectors can promote advances in this direction.

With that optimism, I wish the oration, named in honour of my distinguished predecessor, President Narayanan, every success. I am confident it will contribute to policy debates on developmental challenges.

Ram Nath Kovind
New Delhi
5 March 2018

Dismantling Inequality through ASSURED Innovation

R.A. Mashelkar

Honourable Provost, Deputy Vice-Chancellor, High Commissioner, Professor Jha, ladies and gentlemen. I deeply appreciate the honour done to me by The Australian National University by inviting me to deliver the prestigious K.R. Narayanan Oration.

Kocheril Raman Narayanan was the 10th president of India, and one of our most accomplished civil servants, distinguished diplomats and stellar academicians. I met him for the very first time in 1982. He was visiting my National Chemical Laboratory. I had the unique opportunity to demonstrate my team's latest innovation, a super absorbing polymer — the Jalshakti — that could absorb water, amazingly, over 100 times its own weight. I still remember the probing questions that President Narayanan asked me about the potential use of Jalshakti in agriculture in rain starved areas in India. Later, I had the privilege of interacting with him on issues concerning science and innovation in India on numerous occasions.

President Narayanan and I were born 22 years apart — but his life's story bears a striking resemblance to mine. He was born in a small village in Kerala; I was born in a small village in Goa. He walked 15 km to get to school, much like I walked barefoot to a municipal school. He sometimes stood outside class and eavesdropped on lectures because his family did not have enough money for tuition. Due to extreme poverty, my widowed mother could not afford notebooks or shoes, and I remember many nights on which I studied under street lights. He took his brother's help to copy notebooks and books and return them, and I remember sitting on a footpath, borrowing books from a kind bookstall owner, quickly reading them and returning them.

In fact, we both even share the turning point of our academic lives. Both of us were Tata scholars. We both left India, only to return when we were fairly young with a zeal to do more for our homeland, he at the age of 27, and I at the age of 32.

President Narayanan once said:

> I see and understand both the symbolic as well as the substantive elements of my life. Sometimes I visualise it as a journey of an individual from a remote village on the side-lines of society to the hub of social standing. But at the same time I also realise that *my life encapsulates the ability of the democratic system to accommodate and empower marginalised sections of society.*

You can see how right he was. Despite standing 11th among 135,000 students in Maharashtra at the matriculation exam in 1960, I would have had to leave my studies. It was a Tata scholarship of Rs 60 per month for six years that helped me study. In 1960, when I used to go to Bombay House, Tata headquarters, to collect that Rs 60 a month, if someone would have said that Ratan Tata, the head of the Tata family, and I would be among the seven Indians who, from the time of the establishment of the American Academy of Arts and Sciences in 1870, would be elected as foreign fellows of that academy, or that we both would sign the academy's fellows book, one after the other on the same page, on 15 October 2011, I would not have believed it.

And here is yet another validation of what President Narayanan had said. On 30 March 2000, one of the highest civilian honours in India, Padmabhushan, was bestowed on both me, a Tata scholar, and Ratan Tata, head of the house of Tatas. By whom? President Narayanan, another Tata scholar. This was the best endorsement of President Narayanan's remarks about moving from the 'side-lines of the society to the hub of social standing'.

CSR 1.0: Doing Well and Doing Good

The Tata scholarships that K.R Narayanan and I received were a direct result of the sense of corporate trusteeship that Tatas had always demonstrated. Perhaps it is not widely known that the world's first ever charitable trust was set up by Jamsetji Tata in 1892, a long time before the Andrew Carnegie Trust (1901), Rockefeller Foundation (1913), Ford Foundation (1936) and Lord Lever Hulme Trust (1925).

The establishment of these trusts was driven by the Tatas' belief in giving back to the people that which came from the people. As J.R.D. Tata once said:

> The wealth gathered by Jamsetji Tata and his sons in half a century of industrial pioneering formed but a minute fraction of the amount by which they enriched the nation. The whole of that wealth is held in trust for the people and used exclusively for their benefit. The cycle is thus complete. What came from the people has gone back to the people many times over.

The meaning of such philanthropy has changed over the years. What was once considered corporate trusteeship is now called corporate social responsibility (CSR). The Tatas performed CSR, since they considered it to be their moral responsibility. The Government of India has recently legislated that 2 per cent of the net profits earned by corporations must be spent on CSR. I would call this as CSR 1.0. Here, part of the surplus wealth goes back to the people, either by free will (as in the case of charitable foundations or trusts) or because of the need to comply with government legislation (like India's CSR Act). So I would consider CSR 1.0 as 'doing well and doing good'. This means that after one has done 'well' by amassing wealth, one turns to doing 'good', by setting up charitable trusts or foundations.

What I wish to propose is CSR 2.0 — not replacing CSR 1.0, but complementing it and increasing its impact by touching the lives of millions. I call this as 'doing well *by* doing good'. This means 'doing good' itself becomes 'good business'.

But why should doing good be considered important? The answer is simple — because rising inequality is one of the greatest challenges of our time. Income inequalities, for instance, create access inequalities that lead to social disharmony. However, reducing income inequalities takes generations. Can we do the magic of creating access equality despite income inequality? Yes, we can — through CSR 2.0.

CSR 2.0: Doing Well by Doing Good

How do we achieve CSR 2.0? We have to make a change in the way we do business — a change in which we, the policymakers, rethink the way we do science, etc. I will now talk about the why, what and how of CSR 2.0 through which enterprises can 'do well *by* doing good'.

What Do Indian Businesses Need to Do to Achieve CSR 2.0?

I propose that the private sector can do well by doing good if they adopt an ASSURED innovation strategy. ASSURED stands for affordable, scalable, sustainable, universal, rapid, excellence and distinctive:

- **Affordability** is required to create access for everyone across the economic pyramid, especially the bottom. 'Affordability' obviously depends on the target consumer's position in the economic pyramid, the type of product and its value, as well as the opportunities it may help to create. But, for the 2.6 billion people in the world earning less than US$2 per day, affordable products cannot just be 'low cost' but must be 'ultra-low cost'. Such extreme reduction targets require disruptive and not just incremental innovation.

- **Scalability** is required to make a real impact by reaching out to every individual in the society, not just a privileged few. Depending on the product, the target population may only be a few hundred thousand, or a few million, though, in some cases, it may reach hundreds of millions. We will cite examples of each.

- **Sustainability** is required in many contexts: environmental, economic and societal. In the long-term, ASSURED innovation must promote affordable access by relying on the basic market principles with which the private sector works comfortably, and not on continued government subsidies or procurement support. The crucial importance of this feature is obvious: higher output, better competition (i.e. competition induced by market-oriented players and not intermediated by political actors), lower cost to taxpayers, and, most importantly, the critical market check that ensures inclusive products provide good value to consumers and represent a genuine social undertaking. It must be noted that the principle of long-term sustainable production does not negate, but rather helps to highlight, the critical role of the government in establishing and maintaining a well-functioning innovation ecosystem capable of producing ASSURED innovations at a socially optimal level.

- **Universal** implies user friendliness, so that the innovation can be used irrespective of the skill levels of an individual citizen across the economic pyramid.

- **Rapid** means speedy movement from mind to marketplace. Acceleration in inclusive growth cannot be achieved without speed of action matching the speed of innovative thoughts.

- **Excellence** in technological as well non-technological innovation (such as a business model), product quality and service quality is required, not just for the elite few but for everyone in the society, since the rising aspirations of resource-poor people have to be fulfilled.

- **Distinctive** is required, since one does not want to promote copycat, 'me too' products and services. In fact, we should raise our ambitions and make 'D' stand for 'disruptive' too, which will be truly game changing.

Achieving all the individual elements of ASSURED innovation looks seemingly impossible, but this is not necessarily so. Let us ask some challenging questions:

- Can we make high-speed 4G internet available at 10 cents per GB, and make all voice calls free of cost in a large and diverse country like India?

- Can we make high-quality but simple breast cancer screening available to every woman at the extremely affordable cost of $1 per scan?

- Can we make a portable, high-tech ECG machine that can provide reports immediately at the cost of 8 cents a test?

- Can we make an eye imaging device that is portable, non-invasive and costs 3 times less than conventional devices?

- Can we make a robust test for mosquito-borne dengue that can detect the disease on day one at a cost of $2 per test?

Amazingly, all this has been achieved in India, not only by using technological innovation but also non-technological innovation.

ASSURED Indian Innovation

An exemplar in ASSURED innovation has recently been very successfully demonstrated by India's private sector. One of India's early successes was the mobile revolution. In the two decades from 1995 to 2014, about 910 million mobile phone subscribers were added — the numbers are incredible in themselves, but especially so if you consider that this was 18 times the number of landline connections in 2006, when landline subscriptions peaked at 50 million. The era of 'trunk calls' and ISD and STD booths had come to a definitive end. Thanks to liberalisation, the private sector rose to the occasion and innovation flourished in devices, processes and business models, among others. It represented a joint victory for the public sector, private enterprise and the people.

Despite India's impressive achievements, the benefits of the digital revolution were not shared by all, thus creating the 'digital divide'. In spite of having a phone and a telecom connection, many could not afford to actually make calls. Some of you may have heard of the Indian term *jugaad* — the *Oxford Dictionary* defines it as 'a flexible approach to problem-solving that uses limited resources in an innovative way'. So Indian *jugaad* came to the rescue and people began using 'missed calls' to communicate. Many a parent, spouse and loved one signalled that they had arrived at their destination by giving a missed call to their anxious relatives and friends. Restaurants that catered to students started 'missed call ordering' — the students would place a missed call, and the restaurant would call them back and take their meal orders. In fact, an entire marketing field called 'missed call marketing' was born.

Look around today and you will see that the situation has changed drastically. Competition in the Indian telecom sector reached fever pitch in 2016 with the entry of Reliance Jio Infocomm Ltd, or Jio. Today, millions of Indians enjoy the benefits of free voice calling and extremely affordable (10 cents per GB!) high-speed 4G internet using their Jio connections. Communication behaviours are changing across India as we speak, with the focus shifting from exchanging information to expressing emotion.

One incredible example is that of speech and hearing impaired people using video calls to communicate with each other in sign language. Earlier, they were confined to using SMS and other texting apps. This transformation has happened through myriad technological, product and business model innovations at Jio.

One of the most important innovations at Jio was its configuration: Jio's greenfield LTE network is the first countrywide deployment of VoLTE or voice over LTE in India. Jio has a 4G LTE network with no legacy 3G or 2G services, making it the only network in the world with this configuration. This unique configuration allowed Jio to offer free voice calls to any network across the country — at a time when it accounted for the majority of revenue for other telecom operators. Jio also did away with national 'roaming charges', marking the first time in India's history that the length and breadth of the nation are truly connected.

There are many other product, business model, process and service innovations at Jio that fulfil the elements of ASSURED innovation. Consider this: Jio fast-tracked Aadhaar-based eKYC (know your customer) rollout across thousands of stores. This allowed SIM activation in under 5 minutes! Before Jio, the activation process usually took hours if not days and racked up significant costs for telecom companies. Each one of its over 100,000 telecom towers was pre-fabricated and consumes three times less power than conventional towers. Other equally important infrastructure development included 250,000 route kilometres of fibre optic cables laid, done using high-tech machines that laid the fibre deep underground with minimal surface disturbance just by drilling two holes.

The JioPhone is an Indian innovation — by Indians, for Indians — and is offered effectively free of cost to customers. It is a feature phone that again fulfils all the elements of ASSURED innovation and allows users to benefit from access to the internet. I am convinced that this will fast track access to high-speed internet across the country and empower each Indian to enhance their quality of life.

All these efforts have seen India rise from #155 just one year ago to #1 today in terms of global mobile internet usage. India now has one of the most competitive telecom networks anywhere in the world. More importantly, Jio has moved India from 'missed call' to 'video call' — a shift from *jugaad* to systematic innovation. Jio is a true exemplar in ASSURED innovation.

You will say: this is doing good for the people of India, but is Jio doing well? Is it making a profit? Yes, it is. In the very second quarter of operations, it turned profitable. So this is indeed a case of doing well *by* doing good.

Young Innovators Doing Well by Doing Good

One might say that a company like Reliance Jio has deep pockets so they could do afford to do well by doing good. But what about small businesses? What about start-ups? Yes, they can also aspire to do well *by* doing good, and many of them do.

Let me illustrate this point by talking about some winners of the Anjani Mashelkar Inclusive Innovation Award — an award I instituted in my mother's name for innovations that will do good for the society at large, not just a privileged few.

The awardees are those who believe in not just 'best practices', but 'next practices'. Most importantly, they also represent 'affordable excellence', thereby breaking the myth that 'affordability' and 'excellence' cannot go together. Let me talk about young Indian start-ups with their hearts in the right place and how they are proving that all this is indeed possible!

In 2015, breast cancer replaced cervical cancer as the leading cause of cancer deaths among women in India. In India alone, almost 200 million women aged 35–55 do not undergo the necessary annual breast exams that could potentially save their lives. Worldwide, this number is even higher. Late stage detection is the main reason behind breast cancer deaths. So how can we ensure that women in every corner of India — in fact, the world — undergoes breast cancer screening?

UE LifeSciences led by Mihir Shah has developed a handheld device that is used for early detection of breast tumours. It is simple, accurate and affordable. It is painless because it is non-invasive. Mammography and radiation are eliminated. Screenings are safe, pain free and private. Instead of targeting direct sales, they have deployed an innovative pay-per-use model, which can empower doctors in every corner of the country to start screening women for breast cancer immediately. The device is US FDA cleared and CE marked. It is operable by any community health worker and it only costs an amazing Rs 65 (US$1) per scan!

But UE LifeSciences is not only doing good, it is also doing well. In the last year or so, the device has earned nearly $1 million in revenue and received purchase orders totalling nearly $2 million. The company has also entered into a strategic partnership with GE Healthcare for marketing and distribution of iBreastExam across more than 25 countries in Africa, South Asia and South-East Asia to the benefit of more than 500 million women. Most recently, it was launched in Botswana with a local partner.

This example is not a one-off success story. Here is another: cardiovascular diseases are predicted to be the largest cause of death and disability in India by 2020. Amid the rising incidents of cardiac diseases — even among younger people — there is a pressing need to affordably, speedily and accurately monitor the heart health of Indians. This has been achieved by another awardee, Rahul Rastogi, who created a portable, matchbox-sized, 12-lead electrocardiogram (ECG) machine — the 'Sanket' ECG device. The cost is just Rs 5 (8 cents) per ECG test. His company created this disruptive high-tech innovative solution for personal cardiac care.

Sanket is a credit card–sized heart monitor that acts like a portable ECG machine, making it possible to monitor a person's heart condition as simply as their body temperature. The high-tech 12-lead ECG recorder wirelessly connects to a smartphone, displaying and recording ECG graphs. The ECG report can be shared instantly with a doctor via e-mail, bluetooth or message. The affordable device marks a dramatic shift in the way we approach cardiac care — doing away with expensive ECG machines, distant hospitals or laboratories, and skilled technicians. Sanket has filed multiple patents and is all set to bring about a revolution in cardiac care and disrupt this space.

Most recently, they partnered with Tata Trusts to deploy 45 devices in clinics in Tripura for quick screening and diagnosis of cardiac diseases. In the remote and hilly state of Tripura, regular screening would have been virtually impossible.

And then there is the third Anjani Mashelkar Inclusive Innovation Awardee, 3nethra, an eye screening device. It is so sad that 80 per cent of all blindness is avoidable or curable. India is home to the largest number of vision impaired individuals — but it is not just a numbers problem. The problem of preventable blindness is fraught with challenges — such as the very low number of properly trained ophthalmologists, lack of awareness, unscalable solutions and inadequate reach — that magnify the problem manifoldly. Adding to these challenges are problems of cost and accessibility barriers for diagnostic services.

The eye screening device 3nethra provides a portable and cost-effective solution. The innovation is one-fifth of the cost of a regular ophthalmic screening device and can be operated by a minimally trained operator. It is an intelligent, portable, non-invasive, non-mydriatic (meaning not requiring eye dilation) low-cost device that helps in pre-screening of five major eye diseases — cataract, diabetic retinopathy, glaucoma, defects in the cornea and refractive errors — using its powerful inbuilt auto-detection software. It is a combination of robust hardware with cloud-based computing and sophisticated image analysis solutions. The unique feature of the product is its versatile functionality (detection of five common eye problems in a single screening, automated analysis and report generation) and cloud-based storage of individual data, all rolled into a single, compact machine. Today, they have 1,700 device installations across 26 countries and have touched 2 million lives.

Public Procurement Policy for ASSURED Innovation

I have shared with you a few examples of ASSURED innovations, but India is home to dozens, perhaps hundreds of such innovations, that could have been ASSURED innovations. There are many young Indians championing the cause of development who have been endowed with unique attributes of innovation, compassion and passion.

But it is a sad fact that, in terms of ASSURED innovation, from the supply-side, while they managed the elements of A, U, R, E and D, they missed S and S, meaning they could not achieve 'scale' and 'sustainability'. I can think of two recent examples. One was a near miss. Another was a total miss. Let me talk about the near miss first.

We covered the Anjani Mashelkar Inclusive Innovation Award in three of India's most pressing health concerns — cancer, cardiovascular disease and needless blindness. But there's another health concern that demands our attention: dengue. The award winner last year was Dr Navin Khanna, who presented a possible solution to the challenge of dengue detection. Dengue is a neglected mosquito-borne viral disease that is rapidly spreading globally. Dengue incidence has increased more than 30-fold in the past 50 years. Currently, half of the global population lives under dengue threat.

At the International Centre for Genetic Engineering and Biotechnology in India, Dr Khanna developed an affordable test to help address this problem. His three-in-one 'Dengue Day 1' test can detect dengue fever within minutes on the first day of the fever. It can differentiate between primary and secondary dengue virus infections, which is so vital for clinical management of dengue infected individuals. Interestingly, it can also detect the presence of the virus in a mosquito. The test kit is now a market leader in India, having captured more than 80 per cent market share. Its cost is three to four times less than a conventional test at a little over $2 per test. The test kit is now being exported to other countries too. However, the path to success was not an easy one.

Despite having a high-performing rapid dengue test that could detect both primary and secondary dengue virus infections in a reliable manner, it was still an uphill task to get it accepted by end users. It was 2013, and many cities in India witnessed large numbers of dengue cases. Three companies from the US, Australia and South Korea sold their yearly stock of dengue test kits within a few weeks and no test kit was available for use in the Indian market. When the India-made kit was offered to the Indian market, it was met with great resistance. Most end users were unwilling to try a new kit, preferring to wait for the arrival of new consignments of dengue kits from other countries.

Because of the extensive paperwork required to import these tests, companies from the US and Australia were unable to make the next shipment of dengue kits to India; however, a South Korean company was able to ship a new consignment to India, but this shipment landed in Africa by mistake! So the scenario was bleak in India: no dengue kits were available and suspected dengue cases were increasing and creating mass panic. It was at this stage that end users relented and tried the Indian kit — after which there was no looking back. All stakeholders were delighted with the easily available, high-performing and affordable dengue test kit. When the stocks of imported kits finally showed up in India, there were no takers. In this case, serendipity — and not a system — played the biggest role.

So, the near miss was Navin Khanna's Dengue Day 1 test. The total miss was Simputer. Let me explain. Simputer was designed to be a low-cost and portable alternative to personal computers. The idea was to create shared devices that permit truly simple and natural user interfaces based on sight, touch and audio. Simputer was to read and speak in several Indian languages in its initial release. Simputer prototypes were launched by the Simputer Trust on 25 April 2001.

It was hailed for its 'radical simplicity for universal access'. Before the arrival of the smartphone in 2003, Simputer had anticipated some breakthrough technologies that are now commonplace in mobile devices. One of them was the accelerometer, introduced to the rest of the world for the first time in the iPhone. The other was doodle on mail — the ability to write on a phone — that was later a major feature on Samsung Galaxy phones.

Bruce Sterling, writing in the *New York Times* magazine said:

> The most significant innovation in computer technology in 2001 was not Apple's gleaming titanium PowerBook G4 or Microsoft's Windows XP. It was the Simputer, a net-linked, radically simple portable computer, intended to bring the computer revolution to the third world.

Despite having achieved the elements of A, U, R, E and D in ASSURED, what was missing was S and S, namely, scale and sustainability. This was because of the absence of an innovation-friendly public procurement policy, despite many rural-specific demonstrations.

Innovations are products of creative interaction of supply and demand. Besides supply-side initiatives, we need aggressive demand-side initiatives — and public procurement is an obvious choice. With large procurement budgets, the government can not only be the biggest, but also the most influential and demanding customer of these innovations, making them truly ASSURED.

The government approach could be based on three pillars. First, government could act as the 'first buyer' and an 'early user' for small, innovative firms, and manage the consequent risk, thus providing the initial revenue and customer feedback they need to survive and refine their products and services so that they can later compete effectively in the global marketplace. Interestingly, based on a survey of 1,100 innovative firms in Germany, it was found that public procurement is especially effective for smaller firms in regions under economic stress, a helpful lesson for India.

Second, government could set up regulations that successfully drive innovation, either indirectly through altering market structures and affecting the funds available for investment, or directly through boosting or limiting demand for particular products and services.

Third, government could set standards that create market power by creating demand for innovation. Agreed standards would ensure that the risk taken by both early adopters and innovators is lower, thus increasing investment in innovation. The standards should be set at a demanding level of functionality without specifying which solution must be followed. By not prescribing a specific route, innovation is bound to flourish.

Role of Strong Public Policy

I can also recall a case where the private sector wanted to do public good but, due to a lack of public policy, it did not scale up.

As we all know — and some of us may have experienced — poverty forms a vicious circle. People are poor because they are illiterate. They are illiterate because they are poor. India's National Literacy Mission has been making slow progress to address the challenge of adult literacy in India since 1988 — 'slow progress' because there are still almost 300 million adult illiterates in India.

An Indian company developed a unique technique to address this problem. F.C. Kohli from Tata Consultancy Services came up with an innovative teaching method based on the theory of cognition and laws of perception. The initiative, called computer-based functional literacy or CBFL, could teach an illiterate individual to read a newspaper with only 40 hours of training! They took a systems approach and used multimedia to focus on words rather than the alphabet. Their technique harmonised visual and audio patterns to enable reading, and helped retention of cognised patterns in subconscious memory. The cost worked out to only $2 per person, as opposed to $16 per person using conventional methods.

CBFL did not require any certified professional teachers — only para-teachers called *preraks*, which is Hindi for inspirers. CBFL's dropout rates at 10–12 per cent were much lower than that of conventional initiatives. It allowed for both flexibility in learning and standardisation in teaching. While the method focused on reading, it acted as a trigger for people

411

to learn to write on their own. This experiment was first conducted in Medak village near Hyderabad. Without a trained teacher, the women started reading the newspaper in Telugu in eight to 10 weeks. Thereafter, F.C. Kohli's team carried out more experiments at 80 centres, and with over 1,000 adult participants. The results were spectacular.

If we had wholeheartedly adopted this in India, our entire population could have been made literate in just five to seven years! The potential was massive — there are 800 million illiterates in the world — and this innovation could make them literate by spending less than US$2 billion. However, lack of the right policy environment limited CBFL's scale up. IT ministries or literacy departments did not partner with CBFL. There was no infrastructure support for the network and the mass procurement of IT hardware posed huge logistical problems. Add to that issues related to customs clearances, octroi and other similar tariffs. This is a glaring example of when an innovation could have impacted not just India, but the entire world, but still failed to scale up due to lack of support.

But here is a contrary example of how a hard and strong public policy can work. Just over a year ago, I would have said that we stand on the cusp of a digital revolution. Today, I can say without any ambiguity that we are right in the midst of it. Our nation created history in 2014 when, under the Pradhan Mantri Jan Dhan Yojna, 18,096,130 bank accounts were opened in India in just one week, creating a Guinness World Record. These will provide access to various basic financial services for the excluded: basic savings bank accounts, needs-based credit, remittance facilities, insurances and pensions. JAM — combining J (Pradhan Mantri Jan Dhan Yojna), A (Aaadhar identification and authentication) and M (mobile telecommunications) — created the fastest and largest financial inclusion in the world, with 300 million-plus bank accounts opening up in record time. Before JAM, the disadvantaged sections of Indian society were exploited by money lenders, both in rural and urban area. This bold policy innovation will allow for large-scale, technology-enabled and real-time delivery of welfare services.

Just like India jumped from landline to mobile telephony, JAM will allow us to leapfrog into the next phase of financial inclusion. It will allow millions of people to become a part of the mainstream economy and provide them access equality despite income inequality. JAM has all the seven elements of ASSURED.

It is glaringly obvious that the tide of exponential technology, in which performance is rising exponentially and costs are falling exponentially, will make many things previously considered impossible possible in entirely unbelievable ways, making the goal of achieving ASSURED innovation easier. ASSURED innovation can greatly help any country in achieving multiple objectives. First, social harmony. It will help in creating access equality despite income inequality. Second, affordability. It will lead to scale, thus bringing equity to any population. Third, excellence. On the one hand, excellence will meet the rising aspirations of the local populace for high-quality goods and services. On the other hand, excellence will open up opportunities for competitive exports to global markets.

Indian Business Can Do Well by Doing Good: How?

Many of these game-changing ASSURED innovations have some tenets in common. For instance, converting non-consumers to consumers; rethinking, not just remodelling, offerings; innovating across product, process and business model; and putting 'better' before 'cheaper'. The perspective should shift to seeing suppliers as partners, employees as innovators and customers as people.

On the consumer front, it is important to foster empathy and explore co-creation, and to attack problems that MUST be solved, not just those that CAN be solved. There is much that can be done internally, for example, setting 'stretch goals' that sound impossible, challenging the fundamentals, putting your best minds to work, learning from unrelated domains and interacting with top-notch innovators. Making high technology work for the poor is important, but even more important is believing that they can adapt to it — they always do. The poor are demanding and exacting about what they want from a product or service.

Research, design and development teams must change their mindsets. Besides aiming at technologically sophisticated, performance rich products, they must move towards frugal, functional but high-quality products. Rather than removing features to reduce costs, they must reinvent products from the ground up. Rather than a 'technology push product out' approach, they must move to a 'customer-centric, market-based' approach. Rather than using developed world products to transform the existing markets, they must build new global growth platforms based on emerging market needs. Further, business must try to straddle the entire economic pyramid by not just aiming for premium-priced, high-margin products but also going for affordably priced, high-volume products. Finally, they must move from the current markets' 'old money' mindset, in which they fight for an increased share of a constant-sized pie, to a new markets' 'new money' mindset, which will enable them to take a share of a bigger-sized pie.

But, fundamentally, more than anything else, it requires one to believe in the idea that happiness, health, prosperity and peace are basic human rights; that people, regardless of caste, creed, gender, nationality, etc., are people first; that innovation is not just for those who can afford it, but for those who need it most.

Let me sum this up. ASSURED innovation is the backbone of CSR 2.0. ASSURED innovation is the way by which the private sector can achieve the noble goal of 'doing well by doing good'. ASSURED innovation can be a 'two-word' national innovation policy statement for many countries in the world. ASSURED innovation can dismantle inequalities by creating the magic of access equality, despite income inequality, thereby bringing back social harmony, which is the need of the hour.

Finally, as a proud Indian, I constantly remind myself that India has been a nation that has always been an ambassador of peace and goodwill for the rest of the world. I am confident that India is well placed to become the next global ambassador of ASSURED innovation for our assured future — not for a privileged few, but for all.

Thank you.